The Pretender of Pitcairn Island

Pitcairn, a tiny Pacific island that was refuge to the mutineers of HMAV *Bounty* and home to their descendants, later became the stage on which one imposter played out his influential vision for British control over the nineteenth-century Pacific Ocean. Joshua W. Hill arrived on Pitcairn in 1832 and began his fraudulent half-decade rule that has, until now, been swept aside as an idiosyncratic moment in the larger saga of Fletcher Christian's mutiny against Captain Bligh and the mutineers' unlikely settlement of Pitcairn. Here, Hill is shown instead as someone alert to the full scope and power of the British Empire, to the geopolitics of international imperial competition, to the ins and outs of naval command, to the vicissitudes of court politics, and, as such, to Pitcairn's symbolic power for the British Empire more broadly.

Tillman W. Nechtman is Professor and Chair of the Department of History at Skidmore College. He writes extensively on the British Empire in the eighteenth and nineteenth centuries, and his previous works include *Nabobs: Identity and Empire in Eighteenth-Century Britain* (2010).

D0911973

The Pretender of Pitcairn Island

Joshua W. Hill – The Man Who Would Be King Among the Bounty *Mutineers*

Tillman W. Nechtman

Skidmore College

CAMBRIDGE
UNIVERSITY PRESS

CAMBRIDGE
UNIVERSITY PRESS

University Printing House, Cambridge CB2 8BS, United Kingdom

One Liberty Plaza, 20th Floor, New York, NY 10006, USA

477 Williamstown Road, Port Melbourne, VIC 3207, Australia

314–321, 3rd Floor, Plot 3, Splendor Forum, Jasola District Centre, New Delhi – 110025, India

79 Anson Road, #06–04/06, Singapore 079906

Cambridge University Press is part of the University of Cambridge.

It furthers the University's mission by disseminating knowledge in the pursuit of education, learning, and research at the highest international levels of excellence.

www.cambridge.org
Information on this title: www.cambridge.org/9781108424684
DOI: 10.1017/9781108341318

© Tillman W. Nechtman 2018

First published 2018

Printed in the United Kingdom by TJ International Ltd. Padstow, Cornwall

A catalogue record for this publication is available from the British Library.

Library of Congress Cataloging-in-Publication Data
Names: Nechtman, Tillman W., author.
Title: The pretender of Pitcairn Island : Joshua W. Hill – the man who would be king among the Bounty mutineers / Tillman W. Nechtman.
Other titles: Joshua W. Hill, the man who would be king among the Bounty mutineers
Description: First edition. | Cambridge, United Kingdom ; New York, NY : Cambridge University Press, 2018. | Includes bibliographical references and index.
Identifiers: LCCN 2018015245| ISBN 9781108424684 (hardback) | ISBN 9781108440806 (paperback)
Subjects: LCSH: Hill, Joshua W., 1773– | Pitcairn Island – History. | Pitcairn Island – Politics and government. | Impostors and imposture – Pitcairn Island – Biography. | Bounty Mutiny, 1789. | BISAC: HISTORY / World.
Classification: LCC DU800 .N43 2018 | DDC 996.18–dc23
LC record available at https://lccn.loc.gov/2018015245

ISBN 978-1-108-42468-4 Hardback
ISBN 978-1-108-44080-6 Paperback

This book is dedicated to Laura – as always, and forever

Sailors are the only class of men who now-a-days see anything like stirring adventure; and many things which to fire-side people appear strange and romantic, to them seem as common-place as a jacket at elbows. Yet, notwithstanding the familiarity of sailors with all sorts of curious adventure, the incidents recorded in the following pages have often served, when "spun as a yarn," not only to relieve the weariness of many a night-watch at sea, but to excite the warmest sympathies of the author's shipmates. He has been therefore led to think that his story could scarcely fail to interest those who are less familiar than the sailor with a life of adventure.

Herman Melville, *Typee: A Peep at Polynesian Life* (1846)

Contents

Figures

Acknowledgments

This was supposed to have been a small book. It was *supposed* to have been a chapter in a much different book. Stories, though, sometimes grow. History surprises us!

In writing a book that has unexpectedly come to encompass a global story, I have amassed a world of debts and obligations. Many I will never be able to repay in full.

It was in a casual conversation on the way to the Albany-Rensselaer Train Station that Peter Mancall first hinted to me that what I had here was a book and not a chapter. Thank you, Peter, for helping me to see what I had missed.

In order to chase Joshua Hill around the world, I have had to dig in a globe's worth of archives. The Mitchell Library at the State Library of New South Wales in Sydney is one of the loveliest places a historian could work, and the staff there is astonishing. I thank them all. I have equally profited from time in the exhibits and the archives at the National Maritime Museum of Australia, also in Sydney.

In New Zealand, I thank the staff at Te Puna Mātauranga o Aotearoa (the National Library of New Zealand) in Wellington, where the collections in the Alexander Turnbull Library were of immense value. I also thank the archivists at Te Rua Mahara o te Kāwanatanga (the National Archives of New Zealand). Nobody can or should research in Wellington and skip Te Papa Tongarewa (the National Museum of New Zealand). All of these locations were vital to the work I did for this book. But, I owe a special thank you to the staff at the Museum of Wellington City and Sea. I visited the museum as a matter of pure tourism, but it changed the way I think about storytelling. It is a treasure.

In Paris, I have to thank Hélène Coudray, from the Press Services Office at the Opéra national de Paris for helping me track down ticket receipts from the nineteenth century as well as information about the French dancing dynasty, the Vestris family. I also thank Catherine Heuls of the Opéra de Paris; Romain Feist, curator of La Bibliothèque-Musèe de l'Opéra; and Pierre Vidal, the Opéra's director, for their help in tracking Joshua Hill through France.

In London, as always, I thank those dedicated men and women at the British Library and the National Archives who help researchers daily and without whom researching British imperial history would simply not be possible. This project took me to the Royal Geographic Society, where I found equally helpful archivists and staff. The same can be said of the days I spent working my way through the archives of the London Missionary Society at SOAS, University of London. Readers will note that this book has also profited from a lot of time spent in the National Maritime Museum in Greenwich.

I am particularly indebted to Dorian Leveque of the Asia, Pacific, and Africa Collections at the British Library for helping me track down Joshua Hill's employment records with the East India Company. Liane MacIver of the British Museum was critical to my search for Joshua Hill in the papers and letters of Sir Joseph Banks. Joe Maldonado at the British Library helped me with this same endeavor. Ben White graciously dug through records for me at the Bank of England. Adrian Webb, Guy Hannaford, and Matthew Millard did the same at the United Kingdom Hydrographic Office.

Joshua Hill's claims about his life went in every which direction. At the Lord Mayor of London's office, Bridget Howlett, the senior archivist, helped me follow some of the leads Hill offered in his curriculum vitae. Heather Johnson did the same at the National Museum of the Royal Navy. Sarah Aitken answered questions for me out of the Gloucestershire Archives, and Shona Milton, of the Brighton History Centre, helped me hunt for Joshua Hill among the prince regent's guests at Brighton Pavilion, as did Allison Derrett of the Royal Archives at Windsor Castle. Alison Bennis and Andrew Sergeant at the State Library of New South Wales also deserve my particular thanks, as does Onesimus Ngundu of the Bible Society's Library at Cambridge University.

Richard Baldwin of the Islington and St. Pancras Cemeteries and Crematorium as well as Peter Southwood, the Parish Manager at the Parish of Old St. Pancras in London, were courteous enough to help me try to track down Joshua Hill's tombstone from among those moved to make way for new rail networks in the nineteenth century. Though we did not find the stone itself, I appreciate the help.

In Canada, Nan Robinette guided me through the Archives of Ontario. Mary Munk sorted and sent copies of loyalist remuneration reports from the Library and Archives of Canada. I thank them both for their assistance.

In the United States, I have profited from the help of Henry Z. Jones Jr. at the America Society for Genealogists, Jennifer Lemak and Paul Mercer at the New York State Museum, Frankie King at the Tennessee State Library and Archives, Stephanie Henry at the East Tennessee Historical Society, and Sue Ann Reese and Steve Cotham, who both helped me find my way through the McClung Historical Collection in the Knox County Public Library in Tennessee. Cynthia Van Ness, Director of the Library and Archives at Buffalo and Erie County Historical Society, assisted me in my search for Joshua Hill in western New York State. Peter Wilson Coldham assisted me in my search for genealogical information relative to Joshua Hill's "claimed" family connections to colonial North America. For her assistance in my search for Hill's other North American adventures, I thank Ann Upton, Quaker Bibliographer at Haverford College. Susan Halpert, Reference Librarian at the Houghton Library at Harvard University assisted me with tracking down microfilm copies of Hiram Bingham's papers – copies that, notably, could be delivered to me here in Saratoga Springs via interlibrary loan.

It is a fine and pleasant misery to write a book that requires research out of Hawai'i, particularly if you live in a place with winters like those we have here in Upstate New York. At the Mission Houses Museum in Honolulu, I thank Michael Smola and Carol White for all the assistance they gave me as I made my way through their collections.

Mark Procknik of the New Bedford Whaling Museum helped me secure the lovely artwork that graces the cover of this book.

When you write a book about tiny Pitcairn Island, people always ask you, "Did you go there? Are you planning to?" My answers have to be, no, I did not go there. And, no, I am not planning a trip at present. But, I confess that I would like to go. I still recall my first encounter with Pitcairn, in the fictional accounts authored by Nordhoff and Hall. I still have the book club edition of the books that I found on a shelf in my grandparents' house in McKenzie, Tennessee, when I was a very young boy. I have not been to Pitcairn, but it has been with me for some time. I have met many Pitcairn Islanders, though. Some I met while at a conference at the Pitcairn Islands Study Center at Pacific Union College in Angwin, California. Some I have communicated with via email. To all who live at Pitcairn, I wish you the best, and I send you my thanks.

I did get to visit Norfolk Island as I wrote this book. On Norfolk, my debts are unparalleled. First, I have to thank Ron and Maureen Edwards. Anybody who wants to write a book about Pitcairn would do well to consult with Ron. But, above all, it is for their hospitality that I thank

Ron and Maureen. I could not have been better cared for had my parents themselves hosted me on the island. Thank you both!

Elsewhere on Norfolk, I appreciate the time that Sue Draper at the Norfolk Cyclorama took to help me work with that magnificent historical image. I still enjoy the poster that I got there. It hangs in my office today. Charles Christian-Bailey of the Norfolk Island/Pitcairn Settlers' Village and Judith Davidson of the Research and Genealogy Center at Norfolk helped me sort out some *Bounty*-related genealogy, particularly a couple of tangled knots related to family names. Lisa Richards, Director and Curator of the Norfolk Island Museum, guided me through the collections at her institution, and it was there that I found a great deal of valuable information on the Nobbs family. Katie Walden at Burnt Pines Travel helped me sort out the details of my toing and froing at Norfolk.

I was only at Norfolk Island for a weekend, but some of the conversations I had in that couple of days shaped this book. I would like to thank Arthur Evans and Eddie Hooker in particular. I would be remiss if I did not also acknowledge conversations I had with Erik Craig of St. Barnabas Chapel, Moira Winner of the Bounty Folk Museum, and, in particular, Rick Kleiner. Rick's thoughts on Ned Young and the family dynamics at Pitcairn have been particularly fruitful, as readers will see in the chapters ahead. I thank Rick for a wonderful afternoon at his house and for the substantive conversations we had that day.

At Skidmore, I appreciate the dedicated work that John Cosgrove and Amy Syrell have done for me at Scribner Library. They have made it possible to research the South Pacific while living in Upstate New York. My colleagues in the history department continue to be the best colleagues I could imagine. Jennifer Delton and I had a chat about American rogues and filibusters that helped shape some of my earliest thinking about Joshua Hill. Jordana Dym guided me to titles that helped me sort out the collapse of colonial Spanish America. Eric Morser did much the same with regard to Joshua Hill's claims about his time in colonial and early republican America. Sue Matrazzo, Departmental Assistant in History, deserves particular thanks. I have been Department Chair for most of the time I have been working on this book. Without Sue's expert guidance and, I have to confess, psychological support, I could not have juggled everything. Thank you, Sue. Sincerely.

This book has also profited from the help of students here at Skidmore College. Kelsey Lawler was abroad as a junior in London when she agreed to help me dig around graveyards to try to find Joshua Hill's final resting place. Sarah Elwell wrote a Kuroda Symposium paper under my guidance as I was just starting this book. It was an astonishingly good paper, one so good that I still keep a copy in my office. Sarah, thank you for the conversations we had about that paper. They shaped my own thinking over the years that I have been working on this project. Devin Mellor and Ben Polsky both worked as my administrative assistants as I was writing this book. Devin was the first student I actually took into an archive with me, and he was there the day I first saw a ratty old letter with terrible handwriting on it – from Joshua W. Hill. What a day! Ben worked with me as a peer mentor in my Captain Cook course and offered thoughts and insights about this book, as he got to read large chunks of the manuscript as it was being written. I thank both Devin and Ben. If my two boys grow up to be anything like these two young men, I will have done a good job as a father.

Amalia (Molly) Krause was my assistant as this project entered its final editorial stages. Molly read this manuscript more closely, I think, than even I have done. She has an eagle eye for detail, and someday we will all be reading her book. I predict it will be a very good one, too.

Steve May, author of *The Governor*, a radio play about Joshua Hill's time at Pitcairn was gracious enough to send me a file with the production of his work. Raymond Nobbs, whose biography of his great-great-grandfather George Hunn Nobbs has been a vital source for this book, helpfully guided me to and through his family's papers around the globe and has offered thoughts and reflections on the Nobbs–Hill relationship that have been enormously valuable to my own thinking and arguments here.

The Skidmore history department benefits from the gracious and generous support of Judy and Bill Carrico. Their donations to the department have now helped fund a growing shelf ful of books. This book adds to that growing list. I thank both Bill and Judy for their support, and I look forward to signing their copy of this work soon.

Many academics have helped me over the years it took to research and write this book. I met Gregory Cushman when he visited Skidmore to give a lecture. The reader will see his influence on my thoughts in Chapter 5. Kathleen Wilson offered comments that helped me reframe parts of Chapter 6. I presented portions of this work at a symposium at the University of California, Riverside, in the autumn of 2017. I appreciate all the comments that those in attendance offered that day. Richard Allen has consistently pushed me to make this a bigger project than I first thought it might be. I thank Richard for many, many big and global conversations, and for his friendship over the years. Nadja Durbach read early pieces of this book and offered helpful commentary and guidance. Lisa Cody has been a constant friend and a supportive academic mentor since I first started graduate school. And, finally, I cannot even imagine my academic career were it not for Philippa Levine. My wish for every student I send to graduate school from Skidmore is that they find in their PhD advisor somebody who starts off as a guide and teacher, who becomes a mentor and colleague, and who ends up as a friend. That has been my journey with Philippa, and this book, my teaching, and indeed all I do as an historian is better as a result.

It is impossible to write a book about the HMAV *Bounty* or the *Bounty*–Pitcairn saga without consulting the collections that Herb Ford has amassed at the Pitcairn Islands Study Center, held at Pacific Union College Library in Angwin, California. Herb has been astonishingly helpful to me at nearly every step of this journey. He invited me to speak at a conference on the *Bounty*–Pitcairn Saga at the Study Center. The invitation not only bought me a trip to one of the loveliest campuses in the United States, it also connected me with scholars (from within the academy and without) who have helped make this book better. Herb invited me back to address the administration and faculty at PUC later on, so I actually have to thank him for two trips to that Olympian mountaintop campus. But, I owe him so much more. He is a smart and good and generous man, as all who have met him will attest. One of the greatest pleasures of seeing this book in print will be that I get to give him a copy for the Study Center's library. I hope that the book in some small ways shows Herb how much I appreciate all he has done to make this book a reality.

Global travel to research this book has required global hospitality. I have already thanked Ron and Maureen Edwards for hosting me at Norfolk Island. In London, I continue to cherish my friendship with Justine Taylor and her next-door neighbor Judi Andersen. Judi hosts me in London, and between Judi and Justine, Greenwich has become my home neighborhood when I am in Britain. It may be a bit out of the way if you have to get to Kew to research at the National Archives, but I would not want to be anywhere else. Tuskar Street is home!

In Australia, Abi Taylor hosted me for my time in Sydney. My dear college friend Sandy Grekas now lives in Sydney. She and her husband, Dave Curtis, welcomed me to their home and humored my desires to see some out-of-the-way places related to Captain Cook's landings in Australia. We enjoyed a good picnic or two together, and I snuck in more than a bit of historical tourism. Thank you, Sandy and Dave.

Long trips away from home have meant that I have had to call in reenforcements on the home front. Daniel and Matthew Matrazzo helped with household maintenance while I was traveling. It is because of them that I returned from weeks in the South Pacific to a nicely trimmed lawn instead of an Adirondack forest. Amanda Shults and Denise Migliozzi helped Laura juggle our two sons and their schedules while she was alone as a single parent in my absences.

Those who know me well know that my family has been rocked by a hurricane of epic proportions during the years it took me to write this book. I could not have weathered that tempest – much less finished this book – with out the deepest and most profound set of friendships and family. Catherine Golden, my colleague from Skidmore's English department, has been supportive academically, but she has held me up on some of the worst days of my life. I appreciate her support on both fronts, and I appreciate too that I know that I can call on her and her husband, Michael Marx – also a colleague from Skidmore's English department – at any time. They always have been and always will be there for me.

St. Thomas Aquinas observed that "friendship is the source of the greatest pleasures." Natalie and Flagg Taylor, both colleagues from Skidmore's political science department, are stellar friends – friends in the Aquinian sense. I have, quite literally, had to entrust them with the care of my family at times, and they have never failed me. As colleagues and as friends, these two, and their two lovely children, make my life richer.

John Hayes sold me my house when I first moved to New York. He and his wife, Helen, have become family. They have sat with me at hospitals and taken my kids to school when I could not. I love them both.

In Saratoga Springs, NY, my parish family at the Church of St. Peter has been a safe ship in the tempest of life over the past three years. I thank everyone in that community. I am particularly grateful for the support of Father Thomas Chevalier and Father Dominic Ingemie. I thank them both for their witness. Their faith empowers so many. It has done so for me. Deacon Brian Levine and Deacon Ed Solomon have been mentors and guides on this difficult journey.

In the Diocese of Albany more broadly, I owe my thanks also to Father Marty Fischer, Father Michael Cambi, Father Matt Wetsel, Father Steve Matthews, and Deacon Al Manzella. Each of these men, in his own way, has ministered to me and to my family, and I thank them for that grace.

It may be odd to thank doctors in the acknowledgements of an academic book, but I have spent a lot of time with medical professionals over the past two and a half years. None of those listed below have helped me write this book, but they are all part of an effort to eradicate lung cancer, which is the most common cancer killer in the world. It takes more lives annually than do breast cancer, colorectal cancer, and pancreatic cancer combined! And it is not just a disease for smokers. Some 60 percent of those diagnosed with lung cancer will be people who have never smoked or who have stopped smoking years before they get the disease. Despite these figures, only 6 percent of federal cancer research dollars in the United States goes to lung cancer research. The lopsided statistics are shameful. Despite it all, teams of doctors around the globe are working to fight this plague. They are, in that way, helping me to save my family, and I thank them all for their efforts. In particular and for their direct medical care, I thank Dr. Leena Gandhi, Dr. Yolanda Colson, Dr. Aileen Chen, Allison DiBiaso, Kathleen Boyle, Dr. Alice Shaw, and Dr. Jessica Lin.

This is my second book with Cambridge University Press. I thank Michael Watson for his continued support for me and my work. I must also thank Melissa Shivers, Lisa Carter, and Ian McIver for their help over the course of this book's production. The external readers who read the manuscript of this book offered insights and observations that have made the final version of this work so much richer. Cambridge entrusted the production management of this book to Krishna Prasath Ganesan, with whom it has been a pleasure to work.

And, of course, I owe a particular debt of gratitude to Dawn Wade, whose careful attention to detail helped me weed out many, many errors that I had missed in the manuscript.

Any errors that persist in the book, of course, are of my own doing.

And, family? How would we do any of what we do without our families? My parents, Carl and Sam Nechtman, and my in-laws, Steve and Mary Anne Greco, have carried me and Laura and our sons over many miles in the past couple of years. It is what parents do. I know that. But it is right and good to stop and say thank you. Laura and I love all four of you, and we thank you – from the depths of our hearts – for the help and support you have shown us in this maelstrom.

Thanks too to my brother-in-law Mark, who spent a week in Boston with his sister while she received treatments. I know the time was hard and the trip a sacrifice, but it was comforting to me to know that while I could not be on hand, Laura was in good hands. Thanks to Mark, too, for the many talks he and I have had about this book, and for the time he spent with me in the Bernice Pauahi Bishop Museum in Honolulu. My other brother-in-law Paul subjected himself to more than a few mosquito bites while I scurried my way through a grove of breadfruit trees near Waimānalo on Oʻahu. I thank Miko, whose grove it was, for not upbraiding me when I was spotted among the trees by his neighbors and for giving me two ripe breadfruits to sample, despite my trespassing. I may not have been to Pitcairn, but I have roasted a breadfruit or two in my day. I thank Paul for joining me on that adventure. We now have a tale to tell.

Closest to home, there are my two astonishing sons – Rhys and Fletcher. And yes, dear reader, you read that correctly. We named the boy Fletcher. Even if they have not known they were doing it, these two boys have supported me and their mom more than two young boys ought to have to do. They have reminded us that life is worth fighting for even when the two of us were just flat out tired of the fight. Their smiles and giggles, their simple happiness, and their futures give us hope. But, they are young, and they are boys. And, as such, I confess, they have – from time to time – reminded their dad that a little bit of "mutiny" can be a whole lot of fun.

And, Laura. What to say about a woman who has been my companion and friend and wife for so many years? What to say to a woman whose fight has inspired so many, a woman who has turned terrible news into a cause and who has mobilized so many to march with her. Laura, you are heroic. Physically, mentally, morally, spiritually. You are, simply, heroic.

Every life is a voyage. Every voyage needs a compass. In my life, Laura has been my compass.

Toady, as I sit typing this, Laura and I are celebrating our eighteenth wedding anniversary. With that – and so much more – in mind, I dedicate this book to her.

Abbreviations

ABCFM	American Board of Commissioners for Foreign Missions
BM	British Museum, London
CMS	Anglican Church Missionary Society
GMS	Glasgow Missionary Society
LMS	London Missionary Society
ML	Mitchell Library, Sydney
NMM	National Maritime Museum, Greenwich
NPG	National Portrait Gallery, London
PMB	Pacific Manuscripts Bureau
RA	Royal Archives, Windsor Castle
RGS	Royal Geographic Society, London
RHO	Royal Hydrographic Office
SLNSW	State Library of New South Wales, Sydney
SMS	Scottish Missionary Society
SOAS	School of Oriental and African Studies, University of London
SPCK	Society for Promoting Christian Knowledge
SPG	Society for the Propagation of the Gospel
Te Puna	Te Puna Mātauranga o Aotearoa, National Library of New Zealand, Wellington
TNA	The National Archives, Kew
UKHO	United Kingdom Hydrographic Office, Taunton
WMMS	Wesleyan Methodist Missionary Society

Prologue: Telling Tales of the South Pacific

> I wish I could tell you about the South Pacific. The way it actually was. The endless ocean. The infinite specks of coral we called islands. Coconut palms nodding gracefully towards the ocean. Reefs upon which waves broke into spray, and inner lagoons, lovely beyond description. I wish I could tell you about the sweating jungle, the full moon rising behind the volcanoes, and the waiting. The waiting. The timeless, repetitive waiting.
>
> James A. Michener, *Tales of the South Pacific* (1947)[1]

On October 28, 1832, after sailing for how many days history will likely never know, an enigmatic man, then aged fifty-nine, landed at Pitcairn Island. It was a Sunday. Joshua W. Hill had sailed from Tahiti, more than 1,300 nautical miles to the northeast of the tiny Pacific island best known as the home of the descendants of the mutineers from His Majesty's Armed Vessel (HMAV) *Bounty* and its ill-fated breadfruit mission under Captain William Bligh in 1789.[2] Hardly a major tourist destination, Pitcairn was and remains an inhospitable rock formed from an upwelling of magma deep beneath the waters of the Pacific Ocean. Less than two-square miles in area, Pitcairn Island has no natural landing for visiting boats; its sloping hills drop off into the ocean as dangerous cliffs against which the turbid waters of the Pacific beat a ferocious music.[3] The only small beach at the island is located at a bay so elongated and flattened that it hardly merits the geographical label of "bay." Known as Bounty Bay – for it was there that that infamous vessel made its last anchorage in 1790 – the inlet is sealed in by coral and rocks so high and so sharp that only expert longboat men are able to "surf" in from the open ocean on the crests of incoming waves (Figure 1).[4] The climb from the beach to the island's only settlement, Adamstown, is as steep and

[1] James A. Michener, *Tales of the South Pacific* (New York: Fawcett, 1973), 9.

[2] For more on the *Bounty* saga, see Caroline Alexander, *The Bounty: The True Story of the Mutiny on the Bounty* (New York: Viking, 2003).

[3] Captain Henry William Bruce (R.N.), *Extract from a Letter to Lady Troubridge* (Valparaíso, Chilé: January 17, 1838), NMM TRO 119/9. See also Trevor Lummis, *Life and Death in Eden: Pitcairn Island and the Bounty Mutineers* (London: Phoenix, 1999), 76.

[4] See Maurice Allward, *Pitcairn Island: Refuge of the Bounty Mutineers* (Stroud, Gloucestershire: Tempus Publishing Limited, 2000), 77.

Figure 1   Frederick William Beechey, *Landing in Bounty Bay, Pitcairn Island, December 1825*. Te Puna A-118–009. Published by permission of the Alexander Turnbull Library, Willington, New Zealand.

unwelcoming as is the island more generally. The Pitcairnese people call the corniche one must climb to reach Adamstown "the Hill of Difficulty."

Joshua Hill's voyage from Tahiti to Pitcairn is cloaked in uncertainty. Petitions written years later by the Pitcairn islanders indicate that Hill arrived on a small Tahitian vessel, the *Pomare*, captained by Thomas Ebril.[5] The official island register, known since its inception as "The Bounty Register," records that no such ship landed at the island in 1832, though it does record the arrival on October 28 of the *Maria*, under the command of Thomas Ebril.[6] Ebril, for his part, was one of a new wave of European settlers to the Pacific in the first three decades of the nineteenth century, men like Samuel Pinder Henry, George Bicknell, and Jacques-Antoine Moerenhout. These men were merchants, sailing between Tahiti, Valparaíso, and other ports of the

---

[5] The Humble Petition of the Principal Native Inhabitants of Pitcairn's Island to His Excellency James Townshend, Commander in Chief of His Britannic Majesty's Naval Forces upon the west coast of South America (June 19, 1834), in Walter Brodie, *Pitcairn's Island and the Islanders, in 1850* (Uckfield, East Sussex: Rediscovery Books, 2006), 205.

[6] The Pitcairn Island Register, 1790–1854, NMM Rec/61.

Pacific basin and trading in commodities such as coconuts, coconut oil, arrowroot, sugar, and sandalwood. Henry, Bicknell, and Ebril had been employed by Pomare II of Tahiti to transport sugar back and forth between that island and Port Jackson, better known today as Sydney Harbor, though, after the Tahitian monarch's death, Ebril engaged almost exclusively in private trade in the South Pacific.[7] The *Maria*, if the Bounty Register is accurate, was one of only five ships to reach Pitcairn in 1832.[8] It is peculiar, though, as we shall see, far from uncommon, that there should be no sense of certainty about an event as rare or as noteworthy as the arrival of a ship off the shores of Pitcairn Island.[9]

There is no record of Hill's actual landing in Bounty Bay either. It is likely that a crew from among the island's adult men sailed out to the *Pomare* or the *Maria*, collected Mr. Hill from Captain Ebril's care, and transported him to the beachhead. Seated on the front of a longboat, Hill would have felt the ocean breezes whistle across his balding scalp as a swell lifted the craft over the coral and boulders of the bay and onto the rocky beach. It is not likely that many, if any, of the island's seventy-eight inhabitants would have met Hill at the water's edge. His first encounter with the majority of the islanders, therefore, came after he had mounted the steep hill and rounded the path into Adamstown, a small collection of rough buildings (Figure 2).

If we do not know what Hill made of his landing at Pitcairn, we do know what he made of Adamstown. Having touched at Pitcairn in 1833, only a few months after Hill's arrival, Captain Charles Freemantle of HMS *Challenger* recorded that Hill "found the island in the greatest state of irregularity." Most of the islanders were intoxicated from overindulgence in spirits distilled from the root of the ti plant. This group included one Englishman by the name of George Hunn Nobbs, who was the island's pastor.[10] By all accounts, Hill was horrified by the state

---

[7] George Pritchard, Letter to Lord Palmerston (Tahiti: December 24, 1839), TNA FO 58/15; and Foreign Office, Letter to George Pritchard (London: June 27, 1840), TNA FO 58/16. See, J. W. Davidson and Deryck Scarr, *Pacific Island Portraits* (Canberra: Australian National University Press, 1970), 79–81. See also, Dorothy Shineberg, *They Came for Sandalwood: A Study of the Sandalwood Trade in the South-West Pacific, 1830–1865* (New York: Melbourne University Press, 1967), 17 and 28; and Colin Newbury, *Tahiti Nui: Change and Survival in French Polynesia, 1767–1945* (Honolulu: The University of Hawai'i Press, 1980), 78.

[8] Pitcairn Island Register, 1790–1854, NMM Rec/61.

[9] Richard Charlton, Letter to Lord Palmerston (Tahiti: September 8, 1834), TNA FO 58/8.

[10] Captain Charles Freemantle (R.N.), Despatch of the HMS *Challenger* (May 30, 1833), reprinted in *The Sydney Morning Herald* (October 2, 1834), and Captain F.W. Beechey

Figure 2 George Frederick Dashwood, *View in Pitcairn's Island, Janry. 1833*, in Sketchbooks, 1830–1835. SLNSW PXA 1679, 58b. Published by permission of the State Library of New South Wales, Mitchell Library, Sydney.

of things on the small island, but what happened next remains something of a mystery.

If we believe Hill and his partisans, he convinced the Pitcairners that they were in need of reform, volunteering his services as an agent of change. Captain Freemantle was, initially, concerned that Hill was little more than an "adventurer" but was quickly impressed by a mountain of papers and a lengthy curriculum vitae that Hill presented as his bona fides.[11] These documents suggested that Hill had lived a peripatetic sixty or so years before he ventured to Pitcairn in the 1830s. By his own

(R.N.), *Narrative of a Voyage to the Pacific and Bering's Strait to Co-Operate with the Polar Expeditions*, two vols. (London: Henry Colburn and Richard Bentley, 1831), i, 92.

[11] Freemantle, *Despatch* (May 30, 1833).

admission, he had "in the course of a long life passed among the various foreign dependencies of Great Britain, visited many of the islands in the Pacific Ocean."[12] His travels had brought him into contact and communication with the rich and the famous. He knew William Wilberforce as well as Captain F. W. Beechey, whose 1825 voyage on the *Blossom* had famously stopped at Pitcairn.[13] He had, he boasted, "visited the four quadrants of the globe," and he had done so in style. He had lived and dined in palaces (and with no less than the likes of Madame Bonaparte and Lady Hamilton, mistress to the great Lord Nelson), he was friends with George IV and William IV, he had been a guest at meetings of the Royal Society and was an associate of its president, Sir Joseph Banks (whose idea it had been to send Captain Bligh on his breadfruit mission).[14] He had published in some of the leading newspapers of the day and visited some of the greatest tourist destinations in South Asia and North America. He had sampled some of the finest wines at the tables of royal hosts across Europe, though he also boasted (perhaps hypocritically) of his nephalism as a member of various temperance societies. He attended Napoleon's coronation.

These were, at least, some of his claims.[15] The island's residents told another story.

George Hunn Nobbs, the island's erstwhile preacher, later noted that the newly arrived Englishman announced that he had been sent from London to "adjust the internal affairs of the island." Hill claimed to have "British ships of war on the coast ... under his direction," a threat the islanders seem to have taken seriously.[16] There were, though, no boats. There were no orders. Though, as we shall see, Hill had tried to convince the British government and the London Missionary Society (LMS) to take up the issue of Pitcairn Island, neither had done so. He seems, therefore, to have arrived on the island of his own accord. He was but

---

[12] Joshua Hill, *The Humble Memorial of Joshua Hill* (London, May 27, 1841), 1.

[13] Ibid., 1.

[14] Glyndwr Williams, *Naturalists at Sea: From Dampier to Darwin* (New Haven: Yale University Press, 2013), 135. See also, Harry Liebersohn, *The Travelers' World: Europe to the Pacific* (Cambridge, MA: Harvard University Press, 2006), 98 and 232. See also, Anne Salmond, *Bligh: William Bligh in the South Seas* (Los Angeles: University of California Press, 2011), 108; Jill H. Casid, *Sowing Empire: Landscape and Colonization* (Minneapolis: University of Minnesota Press, 2005), 23–24; and Stuart McCook, "'Squares of Tropic Summer': The Wardian Case, Victorian Horticulture, and the Logistics of Global Plant Transfers, 1770–1910," in Patrick Manning and Daniel Rood, eds., *Global Scientific Practice in the Age of Revolutions, 1750–1850* (Pittsburgh, PA: University of Pittsburgh Press, 2016), 202.

[15] Joshua Hill, Letter (June 1834). Quoted in Brodie, *Pitcairn's Island and the Islanders*, 211–215.

[16] George Hunn Nobbs, The Humble Petition of George Hunn Nobbs, late Teacher at Pitcairn's Island, quoted in Brodie, *Pitcairn's Island and the Islanders*, 181.

one man, and yet, from 1832 until his removal from the island late in 1837, Joshua Hill ruled at Pitcairn as the island's high priest, its president, and its schoolteacher. He managed, in short, to dislodge Pitcairn from any authorized form of British colonial control without ever firing a single shot. As veritable dictator over the Pitcairners, he would attempt to reform their system of land ownership, he would institute a temperance society, he would break up stills and found schools. He established new religious policies, and he sought to reform the manners of a community of people whose moral fate, he believed, was on the brink.

But, who was Joshua Hill? Where exactly had he come from? Why did he decide that Pitcairn, of all places, ought to be the ultimate target of his "philanthropic tour among the islands of the Pacific"?[17] Few historians who have looked at the history of Pitcairn Island have ventured to ask any of these, admittedly basic, questions about this pavonine tin god. Instead of researching Hill's time at Pitcairn as a matter of biography, scholars have written only pathography. Most have assumed he was a madman. He has been labeled "psychopathic," a "stalker," and a "confidence artist *par excellence*."[18] Accordingly, most have written this short period of Pitcairnese history off as something of a lark, though the acclaimed Pacific historian H. E. Maude went further when he labeled Hill as a "somewhat sinister figure."[19] Most, it is certainly true, have been far more interested in Pitcairn as the ultimate home to the mutineers from the *Bounty* than they have as a part of the broader history of Britain's global nineteenth-century empire, but the general tendency to be done with the Icarian story of Mr. Hill's fraudulent rule at Pitcairn in a few quick lines or a short paragraph is, to say the least, surprising.[20] Nearly all of the historians who have written about Hill's sojourn at Pitcairn have assumed that all of his claims were lies, and they have concluded, as

---

[17] Joshua Hill. Letter to Lord Palmerston (Tahiti: January 13, 1832), TNA FO 58/14.

[18] See Sven Wahlroos, *Mutiny and Romance in the South Seas: A Companion to the Bounty Adventure* (Topsfield, MA: Salem House Publishers, 1989), 293; and Roberk Kirk, *Pitcairn Island, the Bounty Mutineers, and Their Descendants* (Jefferson, NC: McFarland & Co., 2008), 82.

[19] H. E. Maude, "The Migration of the Pitcairn Islanders to the Motherland in 1831," in *The Journal of the Polynesian Society* 48:2 (June 1959), 122. See also, Lady Diana Belcher, *The Mutineers of the Bounty and Their Descendants in Pitcairn and Norfolk Islands* (London: John Murray, 1870), 206; David Silverman, *Pitcairn Island* (New York: The World Publishing Company, 1967), 78, 118, and 177; Robert Kirk, *Pitcairn Island*, 82–83; Susanne Chauvel Carlsson, *Pitcairn Island: At the Edge of Time* (Rockhampton, Queensland: Central Queensland University Press, 2000), 39–40; Raymond Nobbs, *George Hunn Nobbs, 1799–1884: Chaplain on Pitcairn and Norfolk Island* (Norfolk Island: The Pitcairn Descendants Society, 1984), 32; and Lummis, *Life and Death in Eden*, 215.

[20] Kirk, *Pitcairn Island*, chapter 12.

a result, that it is nearly impossible to know much about this Pacific mountebank.

I want to start from a different premise. We know so little of this man, but his story begs us to dig deeper. Writing in 1885, J. J. Spruson, the assistant registrar of copyright at Sydney, may have offered what has to date been the most generous assessment of Joshua Hill's time at Pitcairn. "From 1832 to 1838," he wrote, "there resided on Pitcairn a Mr. Joshua Hill, who arrived from Otaheite." Spruson confessed that previous books had described Hill "as a person who imposed on the people with extravagant accounts of himself and his importance and his influence and who exercised a tyranny over them." But he cautioned that

this view of the case should be regarded with great caution till more is known about it, for subsequent investigation favours the belief that Mr. Hill was a good man, who arrived at the island just in time to save the inhabitants from the curse of drink, into which they had fallen, and who, after gaining the confidence of most of the better disposed of the people, caused them to adopt such firm measures as were necessary for the removal of this curse.

In the course of this work, Hill naturally made some enemies, which suggested, to Spruson at least, that Hill's biography was "a remarkable instance of persecution for righteousness' sake."[21]

Without making judgments on righteousness, let us imagine that there is more to this story than one impostor, three score gullible Pacific islanders, and a half decade of British colonial neglect on London's part. Let us assume that Joshua Hill was connected to bigger colonial concerns, that he did have global connections, and that his arrival at Pitcairn was part of a larger, if still idiosyncratic, sense of how to reform and refortify British imperialism around the globe. Let us assume he had a purpose in going to Pitcairn that was more than an attempt to euchre a bunch of islanders. Let us imagine that Hill's life was, to quote Sena Jeter Naslund's beautiful turn of phrase, "pleated," that there was "more gathered up and stored behind than one can see."[22] Let us assume, in short, that Joshua Hill had a reason to go to Pitcairn. After all, in 1832, as today, one did not end up on that small little rock of an island by accident. Let us assume, therefore, that Hill's arrival off Bounty Bay in either the *Pomare* or the *Maria* on October 28, 1832, was intentional. That, I want to suggest, may be a tale worth the telling.

[21] J. J. Spruson, *Norfolk Island: Outline of Its History, from 1788–1884* (Sydney: Thomas Richards, 1885), 27.
[22] Sena Jeter Naslund, *Ahab's Wife, or, The Star-Gazer* (New York: Harper Perennial, 1999), 288.

In the early nineteenth century, it would have been difficult indeed to have been unaware of Pitcairn Island. As one journalist observed in *Chamber's Edinburgh Journal* in 1850, "there are few unacquainted with that romance of naval history, the 'Mutiny on the *Bounty*'."[23] The romantic story of swashbuckling mutineers still captivates audiences to this day (helped, no doubt, by Hollywood adaptations staring the likes of Errol Flynn, Clark Gable, Marlon Brando, and a young Mel Gibson), but its power to seduce was even more palpable to contemporaries.[24] From the first hint that a mutiny had occurred on board the *Bounty*, everyone wanted to know the same thing.[25] Where was the ship? Where were the mutineers? Where was the cabal's leader, Fletcher Christian? Bligh and his bosses at the Admiralty, of course, wanted to know so that justice could be done. There were courts martial to be held. Captain Edward Edwards of HMS *Pandora* was ordered out in search of the mutineers in November 1790.[26] The families of the mutineers wanted to know what had happened in order to (possibly) find and clear their loved ones and simply as a matter of familial concern. For the broader public, this was a mystery story of epic proportions.[27]

Sales of Captain Bligh's account of the mutiny were brisk. Brisker still were sales of a pamphlet refuting Bligh's claims by Edward Christian, Fletcher's older brother who, admittedly, was not on board the *Bounty* to know what had transpired during the mutiny.[28] Christian had the backing of his family, including Edward Law, his prominent first cousin. Law, who was a well-respected attorney by profession, was the defense council in the impeachment trial against Warren Hastings, the former governor general of India.[29] The published battle between Bligh and Christian

[23] "Pitcairn Islanders in 1849," in *Chamber's Edinburgh Journal* (1850), in Pitcairn Extracts, SLNSW F999.7/9, 10.

[24] Stephen A. Royle, *A Geography of Islands: Small Island Insularity* (New York: Routledge, 2001), 15. See also, Michael Sturma, *South Sea Maidens: Western Fantasy and Sexual Politics in the South Pacific* (Westpoint, CT: Greenwood Press, 2002), 42–47.

[25] William Bligh, Letter to Elizabeth (Betsy) Bligh (Coupang: August 19, 1789), SLNSW ML Safe 1/45. See also, Salmond, *Bligh*, 228.

[26] Edward Edwards, Captain, and George Hamilton, Surgeon, *Voyage of the HMS* Pandora (London: Francis Edwards, 1915. Kindle Edition).

[27] Bengt Danielsson, *What Happened on the Bounty*, Ala Tapsell, trans. (London: George Allen & Unwin, 1963), 205.

[28] William Bligh and Edward Christian, *The* Bounty *Mutiny* (New York: Penguin Books, 2001). See also, Gavin Kennedy, *Bligh* (London: Duckworth & Co. 1978), 93–98. See also, Glynn Christian, *Fragile Paradise: The Discovery of Fletcher Christian*, Bounty Mutineer (Boston: Little, Brown, and Company, 1982), 34; Lummis, *Life and Death in Eden*, 12; Donald A. Maxton, *The Mutiny on HMS* Bounty: *A Guide to Nonfiction, Poetry, Films, Articles, and Music* (Jefferson, NC: McFarland & Company, Inc., 2008), 17; and Salmond, *Bligh*, 436–441.

[29] Kennedy, *Bligh*, 229.

made the case a cause célèbre in the last years of the eighteenth century, made more exciting because it offered Europeans a South Sea adventure in what was one of the coldest winters in Europe in living memory.[30] As the lagoon in Venice froze over, the *Bounty*'s tropical saga had to seem even more tempting. Furthermore, the mutinous history of the *Bounty* resonated against the larger story of the French Revolution, still in its earliest days. Before the Terror made the events in France seem too dangerous, stories that pitted individual liberty against a stronger central authority had real purchase.[31]

So well-known was the story of the *Bounty*'s lost crew members that when Mayhew Folger, an American whaling captain, sailed upon an uncharted island in 1808, he knew from the very first syllables of English off the lips of the natives who sailed out to greet him that he had found the final landing place of Bligh's rebellious crew and that infamous ship, the *Bounty*. This island, one might argue, was populated by history's ghosts.

To tell the history of Pitcairn Island has always been to tell *the* tale, if not also to tell outright tales. It has been a story, a myth, and a legend all at once, but the compounded nature of the island's history has not made for an easy narrative.[32] To quote W. B. Yeats, "mirror on mirror mirrored is all the show."[33] This complex narrative tale-ish-ness (if I may be forgiven the neologism) is hardly unique to Pitcairn. As David Chappell has observed, "seamen have a language of their own; a dictionary peculiar to themselves."[34] Consider, furthermore, how deeply embedded islands and maritime voyaging are rooted in the vocabulary of storytelling. When a story is difficult to believe, it is "hard to fathom." The narrator is thought to have "gone overboard" or "off the deep end." To interrupt the narration is to "barge" in, and any dispute emerging about a story's

---

[30] See, Joseph Coleman, Affidavit (July 31, 1794), SLNSW DL MSQ 163. See also, Thomas Boyles Murray, *Pitcairn: the Islands, the People, and the Pastor* (London: The Society for Promoting Christian Knowledge, 1860), 61, and Peter Heywood and Nessy Heywood, *Innocent on the* Bounty: *The Court-Martial and Pardon of Midshipman Peter Heywood, in Letters*, Donald A. Maxton and Rolf E. Du Rietz, eds. (Jefferson, NC: McFarland and Company, Inc. 20143), particularly 3–7.

[31] Sturma, *South Sea Maidens*, 35. See also, John Barrow, *A Description of Pitcairn's Islands and Its Inhabitants* (New York: Harper and Brothers, 1845), 72. See also, Salmond, *Bligh*, 21.

[32] Alan Moorehead, *The Fatal Impact: An Account of the Invasion of the South Pacific, 1767–1840* (New York: Harper & Row Publishers, 1966), 76.

[33] W. B. Yeats, "The Statues," in Richard J. Finneran, ed., *The Poems* (New York: Macmillan Publishing Company, 1983), 337.

[34] David A. Chappell, *Double Ghosts: Oceanian Voyagers on Euro-American Ships* (London: A.E. Sharpe, 1997), 62.

veracity could put two parties "at loggerheads." Those observing the feud could be said to be caught "between the devil and the deep blue sea."[35]

More specifically, novelists, poets, journalists, essayists, and other writers have long found the Pacific to be a particularly fruitful geography in which to set their tales, though, not surprisingly, it has always been difficult to delimit the Pacific Ocean within a singular, coherent narrative. The author and anthropologist Epeli Hau'ofa, whose biography was itself an example of the Pacific region's complex narrative flow (he was descended from Tongan missionaries but was, at the time of his death, a citizen of Fiji), wrote in his *Tales of the Tikongs*, a fictional account of Pacific Islanders and their reaction to Western infiltration, that truth in the Pacific "comes in portions, some large, some small, but never whole." Anybody "who believes that truth, like beauty, is straight and narrow," he continued, "should not visit our country or they will be led up the garden path or sold down the river (so to speak, since we have no rivers). Truth is flexible and can be bent this way so and that way so; it can be stood on its head, be hidden in a box, and be sat upon."[36] The Pacific, it would seem, creates storytellers.

No wonder, then, that Pacific islands have featured so prominently in the writing of some of literary history's best authors as well as many of its lesser lights: Herman Melville, Jack London, Somerset Maugham, James Michener, Robert Louis Stevenson, Lord Byron, Mark Twain, Robert Michael Ballantyne, Edgar Allan Poe, William Golding, William Cullen Bryant, Richard Henry Dana, James Norman Hall, and Charles Nordhoff, to name but a few.[37] Islands, Jill Franks has argued, "fulfill

---

[35] This interesting set of maritime-related vocabulary was brought pointedly to mind in an exhibit I toured on June 1, 2014, at the Museum of Wellington City and Sea in Wellington, New Zealand.

[36] Epeli Hau'ofa, *Tales of the Tikongs* (Honolulu: University of Hawai'i Press, 1983), 7–8.

[37] See, Herman Melville, *Typee: A Peep at Polynesian Life* (New York: Penguin, 1996); Herman Melville, *Omoo: A Narrative of Adventures in the South Seas* (New York: Penguin, 2007); and of course, Herman Melville, *Moby-Dick, or, The Whale* (Los Angeles: The Arion Press, 1979). By way of example, see also Jack London, *South Sea Tales* (New York: Modern Library, 2002); W. Somerset Maugham, *The Moon and Sixpence* (New York: Vintage Books, 2000); Michener, *Tales of the South Pacific*; Robert Louis Stevenson, *Treasure Island* (New York: Barnes and Noble Classics, 2005) and Robert Louis Stevenson, *In the South Seas* (New York: Scribner's Sons, 1905); Edgar Allan Poe, *The Narrative of Arthur Gordon Pym of Nantucket* (Buffalo, NY: Broadview Press, 2010); William Golding, *To the Ends of the Earth: A Sea Trilogy* (New York: Farrar, Straus, and Giroux, 2006); and Richard Henry Dana, *Two Years before the Mast and Other Voyages* (New York: The Library of America, 2005). Small though it may be, the history of Pitcairn Island has interested more than a few writers. The most famous here, of course, would be Charles Nordhoff and James Norman Hall, *The* Bounty *Trilogy* (New York: Little, Brown, and Company, 1964). See also, James Norman Hall and Charles Norhoff, *Faery Lands of the South Seas* (Garden City, NY: Garden City Publishing Co., 1921). In other works, Hall wrote specifically of Joshua Hill, labeling

a specific need in the human psyche," something she refers to as "imaginable space." As Franks puts it, "islands suggest themselves as both controllable and paradisical."[38] The eminent biographer of Captain James Cook, J. C. Beaglehole wrote that eighteenth-century sailors were justifiably "imparadised" by the "green of spontaneous growth, the smell of earth and blossom" that defined the South Pacific.[39] According to Robert Louis Stevenson, it was no less captivating to the nineteenth-century eye. In a letter to Sidney Colvin dated from Honolulu in 1889, Stevenson wrote that "the Pacific is a strange place; the nineteenth century only exists there in spots: all around, it is a no man's land of the ages, a stirabout of epochs and races, barbarisms and civilisations, virtues and crimes."[40]

But, to suggest that the Pacific is a geographic space in which the imagination can run wild is not to cede Pacific history as an act of mere wool-gathering. Rather, it is worth contemplating a history of the Pacific Ocean that embraces both historical *and* fictive accounts as integral parts of a singular narrative.[41] As the geographer O. K. H. Spate has argued, "wild romancings" about the Pacific operate as

him as "the Mussolini of Pitcairn." See, James Norman Hall, *The Tales of a Shipwreck* (New York: Houghton Mifflin Company, 1934), 89. Mark Twain may be the only author to focus a piece of fiction on Joshua Hill's dictatorship at Pitcairn; see Mark Twain, "The Great Revolution in Pitcairn (1879)," in Mark Twain, *Collected Tales, Sketches, Speeches, & Essays, 1852–1890* (New York: The Library of America, 1992), 710–721. See also, Alan Frost, "New Geographical Perspectives and the Emergence of the Romantic Imagination," in Robin Fisher and Hugh Johnston, eds., *Captain James Cook and His Times* (Seattle: University of Washington Press, 1979), 10–11; and Ian M. Ball, *Pitcairn: Children of Mutiny* (Boston: Little Brown and Company, 1973), 112. George Gordon, Lord Byron, "The Island, or Christian and his Comrades," in *The Poetical Works, in Six Volumes* (London: John Murray, 1879), 345–392; Mary Russell Mitford, *Christina, the Maid of the South Seas: A Poem in Four Cantos* (London: A.J. Valpy, 1811); and William Cullen Bryant, "A Song of Pitcairn's Island (1825)," in Henry Wadsworth Longfellow, ed., *Poems of Places: An Anthology in Thirty-One Volumes – Oceania (Vol. XXXI)* (Boston: J.R. Osgood and Company, 1876–79), 65–66.

[38] Jill Franks, *Islands and the Modernists: The Allure of Isolation in Art, Literature, and Science* (Jefferson, NC: McFarland & Company, Inc., 2006), 1.

[39] J. C. Beaglehole, *The Life of Captain James Cook* (Stanford: Stanford University Press, 1974), 173. See also, David Howarth, *Tahiti: A Paradise Lost* (New York: The Viking Press, 1983), 64; and Ian Cameron, *Lost Paradise: The Exploration of the Pacific* (Topsfield, MA: Salem House Publishers, 1987), 10. See also, Rainers F. Buschmann, Edward R. Slack, Jr., and James B. Tueller. *Navigating the Spanish Lake: The Pacific in the Iberian World, 1521–1898* (Honolulu: University of Hawai'i Press, 2014), 30.

[40] Robert Louis Stevenson, *Letters and Miscellanies of Robert Louis Stevenson – Letters to His Family and Friends*, 27 vols., Sidney Colvin, ed. (New York: Charles Scribner's Sons, 1901), xxiv, 189.

[41] Jodie Matthews and Daniel Travers, "Introduction," in Jodie Matthews and Daniel Travers, eds., *Islands and Britishness: A Global Perspective* (Newcastle upon Tyne: Cambridge Scholars Publishing, 2012), 2.

part of the critical thinking of the [eighteenth] century which in so many fields – science, economics, industry, politics – laid the foundations of our modern world ... Not only what happened in the Pacific but also what was thought or dreamt about the Pacific must be counted into its history.[42]

As the story of Joshua Hill's confused landing at Pitcairn in 1832 suggests, history – at least as we often understand that word in the West – seems to offer no real anchor with which to stabilize the tales we can tell about the Pacific Ocean. It merits remembering that, until 1759, it was impossible for sailors to calculate longitude at sea accurately. Charts, therefore, were hardly reliable; sailors never had any real sense of where they were. As Simon Winchester has observed, in the Pacific one has to travel westward to get to the East – at least as perceived by European geographic standards.[43] Even something as basic as one's location was only a matter of conjecture on board a ship afloat on the Pacific's wide waters.[44]

The Pacific, then, was a source of uneasiness for late eighteenth- and early nineteenth-century sailors. As Peter Kreeft has written, "the sea never forgives. It is the world's largest graveyard."[45] For Herman Melville, whose earliest novels were only thinly veiled bits of autobiography from his own years at sea as a whaler in the Pacific, there was little romantic about sailing the South Seas. "Forever advancing," he wrote in *Omoo*, "we seemed always in the same place, and every day was the former lived over again. We saw no ships, expected to see none."[46] Mark Twain, with his customary wit, turned ennui to humor, noting in particular the way time shifted on a nautical voyage. "It is odd," he wrote, "these sudden jumps from season to season," noting that a trip from the United States to Fiji had also been a shift from mid-summer to mid-winter (though a warm winter, given Fiji's climate).[47]

---

[42] O. K. H. Spate, *Paradise Found and Lost* (Minneapolis: University of Minnesota Press, 1988), 85.

[43] Simon Winchester, *Pacific: Silicon Chips and Surfboards, Coral Reefs and Atom Bombs, Brutal Dictatorships, Fading Empires, and the Coming Collision of the World's Superpowers* (New York: Harper Collins Publishers, 2015. Kindle Edition), location 6502. See also, David Igler, "On Coral Reefs, Volcanoes, Gods, and Patriotic Geography; or, James Dwight Dana Assembles the Pacific Basin," in *Pacific Historical Review* 79:1 (2010), 23–49.

[44] Margaret Cohn, *The Novel and the Sea* (Princeton: Princeton University Press, 2010), 4. See also, Steven Roger Fischer, *A History of the Pacific Islands* (New York: Palgrave, 2002), 84. See also, Michael S. Reidy, *Tides of History: Ocean Science and Her Majesty's Navy* (Chicago: University of Chicago Press, 2008), 1.

[45] Peter Kreeft, *The Sea Within: Waves and the Meanings of All Things* (South Bend, IN: St. Augustine's Press, 2006), 81.

[46] Melville, *Omoo*, 39.

[47] Quoted in Joyce E. Chaplin, *Round About the Earth: Circumnavigation from Magellan to Orbit* (New York: Simon and Schuster, 2012), 261–262.

Adrift (a more palatable way of saying "lost") between both continents and seasons, sailors' bodies were subject to the ravages of scurvy until that disease came to be better understood in the last years of the eighteenth century. Even then, scurvy persisted as a dreaded naval disease into the twentieth century. Between 1500 and 1800, estimates suggest that as many as two million deaths at sea may have been caused by the simple lack of a vitamin in the European naval diet, making scurvy "the premier occupational disease of the great maritime era."[48]

Those beset with the illness felt lethargy overtake their bodies and depression darken their minds. Their wounds ceased healing properly, and the regenerative scar tissue over their old wounds or broken bones melted away. Their joints grew swollen and painful as connective tissues broke down, and their teeth dropped out of their enflamed gums.[49]

As Jonathan Lamb has written, "those in the last stages of decay were regarded as living dead, rotting before they were in the grave."[50] Uncertain where he was on an ocean chart, a sailor sick with scurvy could sincerely believe that his body was dissolving around him.[51] Lord Byron may, in his poetic way, have found in the ocean "a pleasing fear," but for early nineteenth-century sailors, "the uncertainties that troubled the stability of the European self were intensified in the South Pacific."[52]

And, of course, there was the simple matter that European sailors in the Pacific were still unfamiliar with all of the ocean's countless islands. As Lamb has observed, "the terra incognita, the unmapped space of the world and mind, is a habitat of monsters that are the vehicles of an extravagant self-assertion whose only narrative form is romance."[53] The Pacific is, as Donald Freeman has said, "a water hemisphere."[54] It is the largest single geographic feature that planet Earth can boast, simply offering more room for monsters, more room for romance.[55]

---

[48] Jonathan Lamb, *Scurvy: The Disease of Discovery* (Princeton, NJ: Princeton University Press, 2017. Kindle Edition), 6.

[49] Ibid., 64.   [50] Ibid., 43.

[51] Jonathan Lamb, *Preserving the Self in the South Seas, 1680–1840* (Chicago: University of Chicago Press, 2001), 114–117. See also, Geoffrey Blainey, *Sea of Dangers: Captain Cook and his Rivals in the South Pacific* (Chicago: Ivan R. Dee, 2009), 58; Howarth, *Tahiti*, 42; and James Watt, "Medical Aspects and Consequences of Cook's Voyages," in Robin Fisher and Hugh Johnson, eds., *Captain James Cook and His Times* (Seattle: University of Washington Press, 1979), 129–157.

[52] Lord Byron quoted in Kreeft, *The Sea Within*, 16. See also, Lamb, *Preserving the Self*, 5.

[53] Lamb, *Preserving the Self*, 41.

[54] Donald B. Freeman, *The Pacific* (New York: Routledge, 2010), 9.

[55] Tom Kennedy, *An Ocean of Islands: A Pacific Memoir* (Ngakuta Bay, New Zealand: Nandina Press, 2004), 9. See also, Spate, *Paradise Found and Lost*, 31; Ernest S. Dodge, *Islanders and Empires: Western Impact on the Pacific and East Asia* (Minneapolis: University of Minnesota Press, 1976), 7; and John Bach, *The Australia*

That the Pacific is large is obvious.[56] But, to fully comprehend just how large it is can be challenging. As Charles Darwin, whose voyage on the *Beagle* more or less overlapped with Joshua Hill's Pacific years, noted in 1835,

it is necessary to sail over this great ocean to comprehend its immensity ... Accustomed to look at maps drawn on a smaller scale, where dots, shading and names are crowded together, we do not rightly judge how infinitely small the proportion of dry land is to the water of this vast expanse.[57]

The Pacific is home to more than 20,000 islands, roughly 80 percent of all the islands on the planet.[58] Assuming that Europeans charted the islands they found accurately, which is not a safe assumption before proper longitudinal measurements, there was also the question of naming islands.[59] Every captain who dropped anchor at an island was eager to impose a name upon it. The Cornish navigator Captain Samuel Wallis, for instance, labeled Tahiti "King George III's Island" in honor of his sovereign when he landed there in 1767. Less than one year later, the Frenchman Louis Antoine de Bougainville referred to it as La Nouvelle Cythère.[60] Even with a chart to find islands in the Pacific, you could be excused for not knowing what the island was called when you got there![61]

Beyond these uncertainties, there is a history to be told of the Pacific prior to European contact. Indeed, the Pacific has the potential to insult the very notion of European history, for, as Matt Matsuda has observed, the Pacific occupies a third of the surface of the planet, and yet it touches on "no part of Europe at all."[62] As O. H. K. Spate wrote, the Pacific does not technically exist in Western history until Magellan's voyage of

Station: A History of the Royal Navy in the South West Pacific, 1821–1913 (Kensington, NSW: The New South Wales University Press, 1986), 7–10.

[56] William L. Thomas, Jr. "The Variety of Physical Environments among Pacific Islands," in F. R. Fosberg, ed., *Man's Place in the Island Ecosystem: A Symposium* (Honolulu: Bishop Museum Press, 1965), 7.

[57] Quoted in Howarth, *Tahiti*, 42. See also, Christina Thompson, *Come on Shore and We Will Kill and Eat You All: A New Zealand Story* (New York: Bloomsbury, 2008), 173.

[58] Fischer, *A History of the Pacific Islands*, xvi.

[59] See Philip Edwards, *The Story of the Voyage: Sea-Narratives in Eighteenth-Century England* (New York: Cambridge University Press, 1994), 99; and Blainey, *Sea of Dangers*, 139.

[60] Edwards, *The Story of the Voyage*, 99.

[61] Paul Carter, *The Road to Botany Bay: An Exploration of Landscape and History* (Minneapolis: University of Minnesota Press, 1987. Kindle Edition), chapter 1.

[62] Matt K. Matsuda, *Empire of Love: Histories of France and the Pacific* (New York: Oxford University Press, 2005), 4. See also Robert Borofsky, "An Invitation," in Robert Borofsky, ed., *Remembrance of Pacific Pasts: An Invitation to Remake History* (Honolulu: University of Hawai'i Press, 2000), 25.

1520–1521.[63] There is, though, a history to be told of the Pacific before Magellan, and that is a long history – longer, in fact, than the history most historians tell about the period since contact.[64] "The Pacific, as a named, comprehensive entity," Matt Matsuda has argued, "is historically European."[65] And yet, Epeli Hauʻofa has provocatively suggested that Pacific history poses serious epistemological challenges to Western modes of historical narration. "If we look at the myths, legends, and oral traditions, indeed the cosmologies of the people of Oceania," Hauʻofa has written, "we find a long history of imaging space, time, and human history – a vision of the Pacific not so much as an ocean as an oceanic continent."[66] This can be a difficult concept for those of us – I could almost say all of us when speaking of the twenty-first century – who have been educated in the West's post-Enlightenment tradition.

By the late eighteenth century, the Atlantic could be spoken of as an "Atlantic World." Colonial settlements, trading patterns, the institutional horrors of the slave trade, and other trans-Atlantic movements had mapped a network of connectivities across the ocean. And yet, the water was still only *just* a way to connect continents; it was not a space unto itself.[67] In Oceania, Huaʻofa has argued, pre-contact narratives wrote the ocean differently. "There is a world of difference," he cautioned,

between viewing the Pacific as "islands in a far sea" and as "a sea of islands." The first emphasizes dry surfaces in a vast ocean far from the centres of power. Focusing in this way stresses the smallness and remoteness of the islands.

---

[63] O. H. K. Spate, *The Spanish Lake* (Canberra: The Australian National University Press, 2004), 1. See also, Alfred W. Crosby, *Ecological Imperialism: The Biological Expansion of Europe, 900–1900* (New York: Cambridge University Press, 1986), 123.

[64] O. H. K. Spate, *Monopolists and Freebooters* (Minneapolis: University of Minnesota Press, 1983), vii; Jerry H. Bentley, "Sea and Ocean Basins as Frameworks of Historical Analysis," in *Geographical Review* 89:2 (April, 1999), 219; I. F. Helu, "South Pacific Mythology," in Alex Calder, Jonathan Lamb, and Bridget Orr, eds., *Voyages and Beaches: Pacific Encounters, 1769–1840* (Honolulu: University of Hawaiʻi Press, 1999), 49; and Robert W. Kirk. *History of the South Pacific since 1513: Chronicle of Australia, New Zealand, New Guinea, Polynesia, Melanesia, and Robinson Crusoe Island* (Denver, CO: Outskirts Press, Inc., 2011. Kindle Edition), location 105.

[65] Matt K. Matsuda, *Pacific Worlds: A History of Seas, Peoples, and Cultures* (New York: Cambridge University Press, 2012), 3.

[66] Epeli Hauʻofa, *We Are the Ocean* (Honolulu: University of Hawaiʻi Press, 2008), 31. See also, Vilsoni Hereniko, "Indigenous Knowledge and Academic Imperialism," in Robert Borofsky, ed., *Remembrance of Pacific Pasts: An Invitation to Remake History* (Honolulu: University of Hawaiʻi Press, 2000), 84.

[67] Donald Denoon, "Human Settlement," in Donald Denoon, ed., *The Cambridge History of the Pacific Islanders* (New York: Cambridge University Press, 1997), 75. See also, John Mack, *The Sea: A Cultural History* (London: Reaktion Books, 2011), 16.

The second is a more holistic perspective in which things are seen in the totality of their relationships.[68]

The Western attempt to narrate the Pacific – to chart it, to name it, to claim it – resonated not at all with this indigenous conceptualization of a sea of islands.[69] The inhabitants of Oceania had been using the ocean to connect their societies for centuries by the time Europeans began to edge their way into the Pacific. Historians, ethnographers, anthropologists, and sociologists have long bickered over how the islands of the Pacific came to be settled, but most scholars now agree that early Pacific settlement was hardly a higgledy-piggledy process. Captain Cook was impressed, and he marveled that a people – seemingly so primitive in so many ways – could have built a pan-oceanic community like the one he found in his three voyages over the Earth's largest ocean.[70]

Settlement of this sort was a massive social undertaking, one that speaks to highly organized and technologically sophisticated societies.[71] Indeed, the establishment of societies across the islands of the Pacific Ocean may well constitute one of the greatest feats of human voyaging ever accomplished. What South Pacific Islanders achieved in the centuries before European contact is better likened to the work of modern space agencies like NASA than it is to the voyaging and exploring done by Europeans in the Pacific from the eighteenth century onwards.[72] But, like contemporary space travel, it was also an undertaking that was not without its perils. We have no way of knowing how many Polynesian, Micronesian, and Melanesian scouts were swallowed by the water that so defined their world. And indeed, over time, the difficulties of ocean mobility did mean that settlers from one island, island group, or region in the Pacific developed new cultures, new religions, new societies, and new languages in their new homes. Without forgetting that they were part

---

[68] Hau'ofa, *We Are the Ocean*, 31. See also, Denoon, "Human Settlement," in Denoon, ed., *The Cambridge History of Pacific Islanders*, 75.

[69] Greg Dening, "Encompassing the Sea of Islands," in *Common-place: A Common Place, an Uncommon Voice* 5:2 (January 2005): www.common-place-archives.org/vol-05/no-02/. See also, Rod Edmond, *Representing the South Pacific: Colonial Discourse from Cook to Gauguin* (New York: Cambridge University Press, 2005), 1–6.

[70] Brian Durrans, "Ancient Pacific Voyaging: Cooks' Views and the Development of Interpretation," in *Captain Cook and the South Pacific (The British Museum Yearbook 3)* (London: British Museum Publications, 1979), 145. See also, Spate, *Paradise Found and Lost*, 12; and Andrew Lewis, *We, the Navigators: The Ancient Art of Landfinding in the Pacific* (Honolulu: University of Hawai'i Press, 1994), 3, 11, and 53.

[71] Peter H. Buck, *Vikings of the Pacific* (Chicago: University of Chicago Press, 1938). See also, Nicholas Thomas, *Islanders: The Pacific in the Age of Empire* (New Haven: Yale University Press, 2010), 7–12. See also, Spate, *The Spanish Lake*, 3.

[72] See Cohn, *The Novel and the Sea*, 51. See also, Scott, *When the Waves Ruled Britannia*, 194.

of a network of people inhabiting the Pacific continent, Pacific Islanders slowly diverged and diversified into the myriad communities, ethnicities, and societies we know today.

This narrative is historical, but it is fabricated without the written archives that are required to buttress histories in the Western tradition.[73] Western intervention in the Pacific brought with it new ways of knowing, and in the terms of Western epistemologies, Polynesian history of the time before contact has a conjectural and unreal quality to it. To be certain, the history is real, but, as Jonathan Scott has argued, "experiences of travel, and of distance, within Polynesian migrations across the Pacific, and during European circum-navigations, were not the same."[74] Hua'ofa is helpful here again, inasmuch as he argued that Western ways of knowing "bounded" the ocean and created isolated islands, discrete communities of people, and singular narratives from what was "a once boundless world."[75] We see this shift in the archival records left by Europeans in the Pacific. Captains' logs, some hundreds of pages long and spanning periods of years, are filled with page after page of terse records of wind speeds, latitudes, and (eventually) longitudes, and maybe an occasional observation about birds or fish. Only when the ship hove to at a new island do these records become effusive. Here, they pour out detailed descriptions of the landscape, the people, the flora, and the fauna. There are pictures, sketches, and watercolors, as well as charts. A visit to a small Pacific rock that lasted two or three days might fill six or seven pages in such a log. The two-month voyaging between that island and the next might require but a few lines.[76] The imbalance says everything. The Pacific, as ocean, became a void when the Europeans entered. It was, for them, something merely to be crossed; the real value, particularly in the game of Euro imperialism, was to be found on the thousands of tiny islands that peppered the aquatic continent.

And so, the story that I am telling here is but a very small part of a much larger history. Everything gets dwarfed in the Pacific. In that larger story, the Pacific itself is remade; an ocean continent becomes a mere ocean. But, that history is a story of process. The Pacific did not just become an ocean on the day Captain Cook hove ashore at Tahiti on

---

[73] H. E. Maude, "History – Past, Present, and Future," in *The Journal of Pacific History* 6 (1971), 11–12.
[74] Scott, *When the Waves Ruled* Britannia, 15.   [75] Hua'ofa, *We Are the Ocean*, 34.
[76] Bernard Smith, *European Vision and the South Pacific, 1768–1850* (New York: Oxford University press, 1960), 8. See also, Mack, *The Sea*, 165; Beth Fowkes Tobin, *Colonizing Nature: The Tropics in British Arts and Letters, 1760–1820* (Philadelphia: University of Pennsylvania Press, 2005), 155; and Carter, *The Road to Botany Bay*, chapter 3.

his first voyage. It took years for the change to come to full fruition. It was a process wrought by explorers and imperialists, scientists and missionaries, beachcombers and whalers, adventurers, private sailors, traders, sealers, pearlers, and, yes, Pacific Islanders too.[77] The process of becoming, though, opened a vast temporal chasm, a space in which echoes bounce back and forth. Those echoes are an important part of any tale about the Pacific.

Indeed, one might argue that a linear narrative hardly seems appropriate for telling the tale of Joshua Hill's years at Pitcairn Island. True, Hill – our erstwhile adventurer, missionary, scoundrel, and dictator – was a European. And as a European, he has a simple, chronological biography. He was born ... He lived ... He did this and that ... And, finally, he died ... But we cannot tell his story that way. He comes into view at a specific moment in Pacific history, his actions at those moments amplify our capacity to know him, and then he vanishes. Knowing much more about Joshua Hill is frustratingly difficult, and one of the primary arguments this book will make will be that much of the unknowability of Hill's story hinges on his having merged his life with this significantly transitional moment in Pacific history. At times, then, Joshua Hill lands firmly on the printed pages of archival material, while at others, he melts into oral history and tradition. At still other times, we find him only in legend and in lies. His is, then, a story told only in echoes.

---

[77] Thomas, *Islanders*, 48.

1   The Masquerade

His cheek was fair, his chin downy, his hair flaxen, his hat a white fur one, with a long fleecy nap. He had neither trunk, nor valise, carpet-bag, nor parcel. No porter followed him. He was unaccompanied by friends. From the shrugged shoulders, titters, whispers, wonderings of the crowd, it was plain that he was, in the extremest sense of the word, a stranger.

Herman Melville, *The Confidence-Man: His Masquerade* (1857)[1]

February 6, 1808. Eighteen years had passed since Fletcher Christian had captained the *Bounty* into Bounty Bay at Pitcairn Island. At about half past one o'clock in the afternoon, a ship rose up above the horizon and into view off the coast. It was a sealing ship, the *Topaz*. It had sailed from Boston. The canton of the flag that fluttered over the vessel's deck was a blue rectangle with fifteen white stars. Its field was comprised of fifteen stripes of alternating red and white, one star *and* one stripe for each of the fifteen states that made up the very young United States of America. As Captain Mayhew Folger and his crew sailed about the South Pacific in search of seals, it is hard to imagine that talk did not, from time to time, turn to the *Bounty*. That great naval mystery was, after all, still unsolved. Had Christian survived in the South Seas? Some rumors had it that he had returned to London and lived out his days in hiding.[2] But that was unlikely. Had he settled somewhere? To find the *Bounty*, its wreck, or its crew or their remains would have been akin to finding Amelia Earhart today.[3] There is no way that the crew, if not Folger himself, did not think – even if only for a fleeting moment – about what it would be like

---

[1] Herman Melville, *The Confidence-Man: His Masquerade* (New York: W.W. Norton & Company, 2006), 9.

[2] See *Letters from Mr. Fletcher Christian, Containing a Narrative of the Transactions on Board His Majesty's Ship* Bounty, *before and after the Mutiny, with His Subsequent Voyages and Travels in South America* (London: H.D. Symonds, 1796). See also, Kennedy, *Bligh*, 260–65; Ball, *Pitcairn*, 112, and Val McDermid, *The Grave Tattoo* (New York: St. Martin's Paperbacks, 2006).

[3] John Dunmore, *Where Fate Beckons: The Life of Jean-François de La Pérouse* (Wallombi, NSW: Exisle Publishing, 2015. Kindle Edition), Part Seven.

to find Fletcher Christian or to remove the question mark that punctuated the end of his story in British maritime history.

The crew of the *Bounty* might well have recognized the flag flying on the *Topaz*. In 1777, the Second Continental Congress had created a flag that made use of red and white stripes alongside a blue canton with white stars. Indeed, having sailed for Tahiti in December 1787, the *Bounty* crew were in Britain when news arrived that the former colonists in North America had formally adopted a new constitution and established themselves as a new nation just three months earlier. But when Folger's ship sailed upon Pitcairn that February afternoon, only one of the remaining inhabitants on the island had been on board the *Bounty* back in 1787 to hear that news.

Folger was puzzled by the island he had found. He and his crew were in need of water, and, using old charts, he decided to try his fortunes at a small island first recorded by Captain Philip Carteret of the *Swallow*, which was the companion ship to Captain Samuel Wallis' *Dolphin* on its 1766 voyage into the Pacific. Separated at the Straits of Magellan from Wallis, who would go on to encounter Tahiti, Carteret and his crew had sighted Pitcairn Island (named for the crewman who first spotted it)[4] and the Carteret Islands, among other small and (ultimately) inconsequential islands, rocks, and atolls.[5] But, Carteret sailed before longitude could be plotted accurately, and so he mischarted Pitcairn. As was still the norm in 1808 for those seeking to make land at any specific island, Folger had sailed to the latitude where he expected to find Pitcairn, made certain he was well to one side (in his case to the east) of where he thought the island to be, and then sailed on that latitude due west, knowing he would eventually hit his target.[6] But to hit land so soon? Was this Pitcairn? Had he found a new island?

Close inspection of the island from the ship's deck indicated that it was a solid match for the island that Carteret had identified from on board the *Swallow*. Clearly (Folger might have felt, fortunately, given his need for fresh water), the longitude on Carteret's chart was incorrect.[7] If the American captain had not discovered a new island and with it some small ray of nautical glory, at least he could be remembered as the one who fixed the naval errors recorded by earlier, perhaps even greater,

---

[4] Rosalind Amelia Young, *Mutiny of the* Bounty *and Story of Pitcairn Islands, 1790–1894* (Honolulu: University Press of the Pacific, 2003), 22. See also, Murray, *Pitcairn*, 106; and Kirk, *History of the South Pacific*, location 580–584.

[5] Spate, *Paradise Found and Lost*, 95. See also, Edwards, *The Story of the Voyage*, 97; and Frank Sherry, *Pacific Passions: The European Struggle for Power in the Great Ocean in the Age of Exploration* (New York: William Morrow and Company, 1994), 306.

[6] Howarth, *Tahiti*, 43.

[7] Dea Birkett, *Serpent in Paradise* (New York: Doubleday, 1997), 12.

Figure 3 William Smyth, *Pitcairns Island*, in Sketchbook of Places Visited during the Voyage of the HMS *Blossom*, 1825–1826. SLNSW PXB 55. Published by permission of the State Library of New South Wales, Mitchell Library, Sydney.

sailors than himself.[8] He was, after all, the first Westerner to have sailed into view of the island in at least forty years. Or that is what he thought.

If he was happy to be able to fix Carteret's chart, Folger must have been even more excited when he sighted smoke drifting over the island. Carteret had been clear; Pitcairn was uninhabited.[9] Here again, he had been wrong. Pitcairn was clearly home to people, but were they native inhabitants that Carteret had missed? Or, had some band of shipwrecked sailors settled here more recently? The mood on the deck of the *Topaz* was electric. What was to have been a landing for water was shaping up to be the most titillating part of the ship's Pacific sealing voyage. And then, a canoe set sail from the edge of the island, the ship as its target. Three young men paddled.

And then the three men spoke.

"Who are you?" One question; three words that spoke volumes. The men were tall, strong, and muscular. They were dark-skinned, they had broad noses, and Folger knew they were Polynesian – but he also knew they were not wholly so. Folger inquired about the island's name. It was Pitcairn. Where were these men from? They were English, the three men replied before inquiring about the *Topaz*'s origins. When told that the *Topaz* was American, the young men seemed puzzled. America? Was that in Ireland? Folger's mind had to have been aflutter at this point. Who were these boys? Had he begun to suspect that he had sailed himself into history by landing for water on this small Pacific rock? And then, one of the young men introduced himself. He was, he said, Thursday October Christian.

[8] Salmond, *Bligh*, 343–344.
[9] H. E. Maude, "The History of Pitcairn," in Alan S. C. Ross and A. W. Moverley, *The Pitcairnese Language* (New York: Oxford University Press, 1964), 46.

Christian. That name. Folger knew it; knew it only too well. Later, he would recollect the emotions he felt as he heard Christian's name. "The whole story immediately burst upon my mind," he remembered, "and produced a shock of mingled feelings, surprise, wonder, and pleasure, not to be described."[10] He had found *them*. There was no need to specify who "them" was.[11]

Off the shores of Pitcairn, Thursday October introduced Folger and his crew to Charles, his brother, and their companion James Young, obviously the son of Edward Young, a midshipman on the *Bounty*. Folger would have known of these men's fathers instantly. There had only been nine *Bounty* crew on the ship when Christian sailed away from Tahiti for the last time. Along with Christian, they were Jack Williams, Isaac Martin, John Mills, William Brown, Alexander Smith, Edward Young, William McCoy, and Matthew Quintal. Folger knew them, or, at least, he knew their names. And now, he was talking to the sons of two of them. Mayhew Folger was about to hear the final chapter of a naval story that had been nearly two decades in the making.

Were their fathers still living? No, the young men replied. Only Aleck. Familiar with the *Bounty*, its men, and their fate, Folger could safely assume that Aleck could only have been Alexander Smith.

When Aleck Smith shook Mayhew Folger's hand, he was forty-one years old. He was the only living European male at Pitcairn, the leader of a community that consisted of eight or nine Tahitian women and their children. It was a small community, whose ending could have been far less happy than it appeared to Folger and his crew. Certainly, the story that Smith told of the years between 1790 and 1800 was difficult to hear. After leaving Tahiti, Christian and his men settled at Pitcairn in 1790. On January 23, 1790, Matthew Quintal seems to have set fire to the *Bounty* as soon as it was stripped of most of its useful supplies so that passing ships would not see its masts and grow suspicious about the island.[12] By most accounts, he seems to have taken this rash step unilaterally. A horribly violent drama played out from there – one filled with sexual assault, physical violence, murder, plotting, servitude, alcoholism, suicide, and chaos. Indeed, by 1793, a clannish feud had claimed the lives

---

[10] Danielsson, *What Happened on the* Bounty, 206–207.

[11] Robert Nicolson, *The Pitcairners* (Honolulu: University of Hawaiʻi Press, 1997), 4.

[12] See Frederick Debell Bennett, *Narrative of a Whaling Voyage Round the Globe* (London: Richard Bentley, 1840), Volume I, 46. Today January 23, called "*Bounty* Day," is Pitcairn's "national" holiday. See " Pitcairn Island," in Brij V. Lal and Kate Fortune, eds., *The Pacific Islands: An Encyclopedia* (Honolulu: University of Hawaiʻi Press, 2000), 602. See also W. K. Hancock, *Politics in Pitcairn and Other Essays* (London: MacMillan and Co., 1947), 1; and "An Account of the *Bounty*," in Nobbs Papers, SLNSW ML A 2881, 103.

of almost every male settler, British and Polynesian, on the island. Born in mutiny, Pitcairn had been forged in blood.[13]

Smith was reluctant to talk to Folger about the events surrounding the mutiny on the *Bounty*. As with his decision to wait on the island and send young Thursday October Christian and his companions out to the *Topaz*, most of Smith's actions during Folger's visit suggest that he was deeply alert to the peril he faced. Now that Pitcairn was discovered as the home to the *Bounty* mutineers, there was no reason to believe that Britain would not reach out its long legal arms to bring him home and to bring him to justice. As an American, Folger did not worry himself with Smith's past. "Whatever may have been the Errors or Crimes of Smith the Mutineer in times back," he recorded, "he is at present in my opinion a worthy man and may be useful to Navigators who traverse this immense ocean."[14] As he prepared to sail from Pitcairn, only ten hours after setting foot on the island, Folger received a gift from Smith – the Kendall chronometer with which Bligh (and then Christian) had measured the longitudinal lines that helped them chart and manage the Pacific's vast surfaces. That chronometer, better known as the K2, is now on display at the National Maritime Museum in Greenwich.[15]

It took six years after the rediscovery of Pitcairn for British vessels to land on the island. In 1814, Captain Sir Thomas Staines of HMS *Briton*, accompanied by Captain Pipon of HMS *Tagus*, reported an arrival off the coast of Pitcairn that was not unlike the one Folger had received in 1808. The two captains had not been searching for Pitcairn, the *Bounty*, or her mutinous crew. Indeed, neither Pipon nor Staines had yet heard about Folger's Pacific discovery, as that news had hardly reached the Admiralty when word that Staines and Pipon had encountered the descendants of the *Bounty* arrived.[16] They were in the Pacific searching for the American frigate the USS *Essex*, which had decimated British whaling fleets in the Pacific during the heyday of the War of 1812. The two British ships had orders to find the *Essex* and to deal a heavy blow to the growing might of America's blue-water force.[17] Neither captain could have expected that their mission would include an encounter with the mythic story of the HMAV *Bounty*.

---

[13] See Lummis, *Life and Death in Eden*, 14.   [14] Wahlroos, *Mutiny and Romance*, 276.
[15] Barrow, *A Description of Pitcairn's Island*, 245–46; and Allward, *Pitcairn Island*, 49.
[16] "Descendants of the *Bounty's* Crew, on Pitcairn's Island," in *The Calcutta Journal, or, Political, Commercial, and Literary Gazette* (July 13, 1819).
[17] Irvin Anthony, ed. *The Saga of the* Bounty: *Its Strange History as Related by the Participants Themselves* (New York: G.P. Putnam's Sons, 1935), 354. See also, Herman Melville, *Billy Budd and Other Stories* (New York: Bantham Books, 2006. Kindle Edition); and George C. Daughan, *The Shining Sea: David Porter and the Epic Voyage of the USS Essex During the War of 1812* (New York: Basic Books, 2013. Kindle Edition).

And yet, as they sailed past Pitcairn Island, Staines and Pipon's experience was not unlike Folger's. Another group of young men sailed out to meet them. Introductions passed between them, and the young men announced that their community was led by its sole surviving adult male, Mr. Adams. Mr. Adams? Yes. Mr. John Adams. But, there was no John Adams on the *Bounty*. Where was Smith, and who was this man whose name failed to match the mythical naval lore of Bligh, Christian, and the *Bounty*? Who was this man, seemingly the leader of a band of people whose history was rooted in rebellion from British central authority and whose name echoed another, more famous, critic of British power? The story had become more complicated. When the young men asked Staines and Pipon if they and their crew would come ashore, they must have laughed, at least inwardly. There was no chance that they would skip a meeting with this man who shared his name with an American president and was, if mysteriously, now the leader of Fletcher Christian's small colony at Pitcairn.[18]

The fabrication was rather clear here. Aleck Smith had been cagey with Captain Folger, the first Westerner he had encountered since his arrival at Pitcairn. But Folger sailed under an American flag. Smith would have recognized that the Union Jacks unfurled atop the masts of the *Tagus* and *Briton* were much more dangerous to him than the stars and stripes above the *Topaz*.[19] Had these men come to collect him, to see him tried, to convict him, to hang him? And, with those questions looming over his head (or around his neck), Aleck Smith changed his real name (whatever it was) to Adams. Captain Folger had been clear. Smith demonstrated an almost passionate love of England. When he heard of the great victories of British heroes like Howe, St. Vincent, Duncan, and Nelson, he "rose from his seat, took off his hat, sw[u]ng it three times round his head with three cheers, threw it on the ground sailor like, and cried out 'Old-England forever!'"[20]

But mutiny was still mutiny, and Smith's patriotism was hardly enough to save him if these British ships had come to see justice done. The only way to survive, it must have seemed, was to cease being Alexander Smith of the *Bounty*, and so John Adams was born. Perhaps, the name was

[18] Danielsson, *What Happened on the* Bounty, 206–207. See also, Richard Hough, *Captain Bligh and Mr. Christian: The Men and the Mutiny* (New York: E.P. Dutton & Co., 1973), 270–271; Wahlroos, *Mutiny and Romance*, 274–278. See also, J. Shillibeer, *A Narrative of the Briton's Voyage to Pitcairn's Island* (Taunton: J.W. Marriott, 1817), 81.

[19] Harry L. Shapiro, *The Pitcairn Islanders (Formerly the Heritage of the Bounty)* (New York: Clarion Books, 1962), 67.

[20] Quoted in Amasa Delano, *A Narrative of Voyages and Travels in the Northern and Southern Hemispheres: Together with a Voyage of Survey and Discovery in the Pacific Ocean and Oriental Islands* (Boston: E.G. House, 1817), 142.

a direct reference to that more famous John Adams from Braintree, Massachusetts. Perhaps, it was a tongue-in-cheek jab at the British captains, as if to say "at the hand of one John Adams, you lost North America, and at the hand of this John Adams, you lost the *Bounty*." Some have suggested that John Adams, who eventually re-identified himself as Alexander Smith of the *Bounty*'s crew manifest, may actually have been the mutineer's name, though, like so many other of the details of this story, that cannot be verified.[21]

Interestingly, the narrative history of Pitcairn that Adams gave to Staines and Pipon did not match the one Smith had told to Folger.[22] By 1814, Christian, Staines recorded in his letters to London, had been "the leader and sole cause of the mutiny." Adams seems to have declared "his abhorrence of the crime," noting that he had been sick in his hammock at the time it began.[23] Both Pipon and Staines knew that this particular claim was not true.[24] Still, as they assessed Adams, they found him to be

a venerable old man . . . whose exemplary conduct and fatherly care of the whole of the little colony could not but command admiration. The pious manner in which all those born on the island have been reared, the correct sense of religion which has been instilled into their young minds by this old man, has given him the pre-eminence over the whole of them, to whom they look up as the father of the whole family.[25]

---

[21] Delano, *A Narrative of Voyages and Travels*, 143. The confusion caused by Adams'/Smith's name is wide-ranging and includes those who feel his name was originally Smith, those who feel it was Adams, and those who are not sure. For those who argue for Smith, see J. A. Moerenhout, *Travels to the Islands of the Pacific Ocean*, Arthur R. Borden Jr., trans. (New York: University Press of America, 1993), 431; Barrow, *A Description of Pitcairn's Island*, 259; Samuel Topliff, "Pitcairn's Island," in *New-England Galaxy* (Friday, January 12, 1821); Kennedy, *Bligh*, 250; and Deryck Scarr, *A History of the Pacific Islands: Passages through Tropical Time* (Richmond, Surrey: Curzon Press, 2001), 67. Those who argue for Adams, include the *Dictionary of National Biography*. See, J. K. L., "John Adams," in *The Dictionary of National Biography – Volume I* (London: Oxford University Press, 1921–1922), 98–99. See also, Maude, "The History of Pitcairn," 50; Christian, *Fragile Paradise*, 195; Barrow, *A Description of Pitcairn's Island*, 259; Silverman, *Pitcairn Island*, 36; Wahlroos, *Mutiny and Romance*, 387; Nicolson, *The Pitcairners*, 65; Bennett, *Narrative of a Whaling Voyage*, 48–49; and Glynn Christian, *Mrs. Christian: Bounty Mutineer* (Long Riders' Guild Press, 2011), 3. For those on the fence, see Hall, *The Tales of a Shipwreck*, 30; Birkett, *Serpent in Paradise*, 227; and Robert Macklin, *Dark Paradise: Norfolk Island – Isolation, Savagery, Mystery, and Murder* (Sydney: Hachette, 2013), 111.

[22] Maxton, *The Mutiny on HMS* Bounty, 25.

[23] Alexander Smith, *The Life of Alexander Smith, Captain of the Island if Pitcairn; One of the Mutineers on Board His Majesty's Ship Bounty; Commanded by Lieut. Wm. Bligh – Written by Himself* (Boston: Sylverster T. Goss, 1819. Kindle Edition), location 964.

[24] "Descendants of the *Bounty*'s Crew," in *The Calcutta Journal* (July 13, 1819). Also quoted in Barrow, *A Description of Pitcairn's Island*, 247–48.

[25] Ibid.

Clearly, Staines knew that Adams/Smith was lying to him – about his name, if not about much more – and, yet, he seems to have suspended his capacity for disbelief just long enough to admire this "quondam mutineer," this man whose past crimes had the capacity to shake the foundations of naval authority – the very authority Staines relied upon to hold his crew together.[26]

John Adams/Alexander Smith did not die until March 5, 1829. Longevity, therefore, meant that Adams/Smith lived long enough to welcome Captain Frederick William Beechey to Pitcairn during his celebrated Pacific voyage aboard HMS *Blossom* in 1825. The narrative Beechey heard from the now nearly sixty-year-old mutineer was different yet again from the ones heard by Staines, Pipon, and Folger.[27] Perhaps the mutineer's memory had slipped with time. Or perhaps he continued to use his place in history as the sole surviving mutineer – as we shall see, few ever asked the surviving Tahitian women their stories – to improve on the story in ways advantageous to himself as he had done in the past, expurgating bits here and adding others there.[28] Being the only one alive to tell the tale meant that there was nobody there to catch you telling tales.[29]

What remained constant from Staines' 1814 report on was the notion that Pitcairn and its community had become a tranquil place, that it had extirpated the violence and crime that so marked its early years and had become a Pacific paradise. Of particular note was the religiosity of the islanders. John Orlebar, sailing as a midshipman aboard HMS *Seringapatam* under Captain William Waldegrave from 1829 to 1832, had a chance to observe the people of Pitcairn in 1830.

It was delightful to meet every-where with the clear brow and smiling countenance of health and content; their happiness centered in the bosom of their families, and all the capabilities of living comfortably within their

[26] Rosalind A. Young, "Pitcairn Islanders, 1859–1880," in *Scribner's Monthly* 22 (May 1881), 55. See also, Kennedy, *Bligh*, 250. Barrow, *A Description of Pitcairn's Island*, 64. See also Hancock, *Politics in Pitcairn*, 2.

[27] See John Adams, Manuscript Narrative of the mutiny on the *Bounty* Given by John Adams to Captain Beechey in December 1825. SLNSW ZA1804, Microfilm Reel CY 3991, frames 41–50. See also, Barrow, *A Description of Pitcairn's Island*, 260; Birkett, *Serpent in Paradise*, 230; and Shapiro, *The Pitcairn Islanders*, 52.

[28] Barrow, *A Description of Pitcairn's Island*, 266. See also, N. W. Fiske, *Story of Aleck: Pitcairn's Island: Being a True Account of a Very Singular and Interesting Colony* (Amherst, MA: J.S. and C. Adams, 1829), 24, and N. W. Fiske, *Aleck; The Last of the Mutineers; or The History of Pitcairn's Island* (Amherst, MA: J.S. and C. Adams, 1845).

[29] Gananath Obeyesekere, *Cannibal Talk: The Man-Eating Myth and Human Sacrifice in the South Seas* (Los Angeles: University of California Press, 2005), 4. See also, "Pitcairn's Island," in *The Mirror* (1831), in Pitcairn Extracts, SLNSW F999.7/9, 376; Lummis, *Life and Death in Eden*, 14; Macklin, *Dark Paradise*, 115; and George Peard, *To the Pacific and Arctic with Beechey: The Journal of Lieutenant George Peard of HMS Blossom, 1825–1828*. Barry M. Gough, ed. (New York: Cambridge University Press, 1973), 34.

reach; – hallowed by religion, their lives must be one continued stream of uninterrupted pleasures.[30]

It was a magnificent image. A South Pacific Eden grown up from mutinous violence and the island's bloodstained soil. All built by one man – a good man, an honorable liar, a decent mutineer. All predicated on the word of a man in masquerade who had everything to lose and nothing to gain from full narrative discloser. All built upon the yarns of a man who was obviously making things up, and, fabulously, everyone seems to have believed him.

Lies, of course, were nothing new in the Pacific. Many South Pacific cultures have long accepted multiple versions of truth, even if those versions were mutually contradictory. In this sense, the South Pacific may well have been postmodern before it was modern.[31] Jonathan Lamb has reiterated this point about the Pacific after European contact. "The interaction of romance and new worlds," he suggests, "imparts to the narrators of the one and the discoverers of the other a wild but indisputable place in history." At that intersection, "it becomes very hard to tell imaginary and real voyages apart."[32]

Lies, then, must be understood as part of the history of European voyaging in the Pacific. Captain Cook certainly told them. For instance, while on his first voyage to the Pacific (1768–1771), Cook entered his sons' names on the crew manifest of his ship, *Endeavour*.[33] Deep in the southern hemisphere as he was, there was no official eye to spot that young James and Nathaniel Cook were not actually on board. Cook's sons received no pay as a result of their father's deceptions. What they did accrue, though, was seniority in the Royal Navy. Cook's sleight-of-hand, then, was an effort to advance his boys' careers with an "imaginary voyage" through the South Seas. His actions were "illegal and out of character but not unique in the navy of his day."[34]

Captain William Bligh was no more honest than Cook.[35] Indeed, he was quite clear with his crew that they were not to tell the Tahitians that Cook was, to borrow an expression from the Pitcairnese vernacular,

---

[30] J. Orlebar, Lieutenant R.N., *A Midshipman's Journal on Board HMS Seringapatam, during the Year 1830; Containing Observations of the Tonga Islands and Other Islands in the South Sea* (San Diego, CA: Tofua Press, 1976), 20.

[31] Malama Meleisea, "The Postmodern Legacy of a Premodern Warrior Goddess in Modern Samoa," in Alex Calder, Jonathan Lamb, and Bridget Orr, eds., *Voyages and Beaches: Pacific Encounters, 1769–1840* (Honolulu: University of Hawai'i Press, 1999), 49.

[32] Lamb, *Preserving the Self*, 41–46.

[33] Trevor Lummis, *Pacific Paradises: The Discovery of Tahiti and Hawai'i* (Stroud, Gloucestershire: Sutton Publishing, 2005), 34.

[34] Blainey, *Sea of Dangers*, 274.   [35] See Christian, *Mrs. Christian*, 80.

"dead as a hatchet" when they arrived on the island to collect breadfruit plants in October 1788.[36] Moreover, Bligh seems to have told the Tahitians that he was Cook's son in an attempt to merit a larger share of the islander's good favor, for Bligh was deeply alert to the high esteem that the Tahitians had for "Tute," as they called Captain Cook.[37] He had witnessed Cook's fame in Tahiti firsthand during the 1776–1779 voyage of the *Resolution*, aboard which Bligh served as the sailing master.

The *Resolution*'s stay at Tahiti in 1777 had marked the eleventh time Europeans had come to the island. The *Bounty*'s sojourn would be the thirteenth. The twelfth European vessel to land at Tahiti was the *Lady Penrhyn*, a transport under the command of Captain William C. Sever.[38] Sever landed at Tahiti only a few months before Bligh did, and he told the islanders the gruesome history of Cook's final Pacific voyage. His story included Cook's brutal death at the hands of natives of the Hawai'ian Islands at Kealakekua Bay on Valentine's Day 1779.[39] The islanders, thus, knew that Bligh was telling tales when he delivered greetings on behalf of Captain Cook.[40]

Like Bligh before him, Fletcher Christian wanted to blur the truth about what happened between his first visit to Tahiti and his oddly sudden return. Not wanting to let the Tahitian chiefs in on what had happened on board the *Bounty*, Christian had his mutinous crew rehearse a lie to explain why the *Bounty* would be returning to Matavai Bay. The ship had, the yarn ran, stopped for water at a nearby island. There, they had met up with Captain Cook – who was supposedly still alive, according to the European lie Bligh had concocted and which the Tahitians knew to be false. Bligh and Cook had gone on together to

---

[36] Birkett, *Serpent in Paradise*, 176. See also, Wahlroos, *Mutiny and Romance*, 128; Vanessa Smith, *Intimate Strangers: Friendship, Exchange, and Pacific Encounters* (New York: Cambridge University Press, 2010), 240; Edmond, *Representing the South Pacific*, 66; John Toohey, *Captain Bligh's Portable Nightmare: From the Bounty to Safety – 4,162 Miles across the Pacific in a Rowing Boat* (New York: Harper Collins Publishers, 1998), 17 and 44; and Kennedy, *Bligh*, 182.

[37] Thomas, *Islanders*, 126. See also, Kennedy, *Bligh*, 60.

[38] Lynne Withey, *Voyages of Discovery: Captain Cook and the Exploration of the Pacific* (New York: William Morrow and Company, Inc., 1987), 430.

[39] See, Richard Hough, *The Last Voyage of Captain James Cook* (New York: William Morrow and Company, 1979), 221–233. The most (in)famous work on Cook's death has featured in the anthropological feud between Marshall Sahlins and Gananath Obeyesekere. See Marshall Sahlins, *Islands of History* (Chicago: University of Chicago Press, 1985); Gananath Obeyesekere, *The Apotheosis of Captain Cook: European Mythmaking in the Pacific* (Princeton: Princeton University Press, 1992); Marshall Sahlins, *How "Natives" Think: About Captain Cook, For Example* (Chicago: University of Chicago Press, 1995); and Obeyesekere, *Cannibal Talk*.

[40] See Edmond, *Representing the South Pacific*, 66. See also, Wahlroos, *Mutiny and Romance*, 128.

establish a settlement somewhere, and Christian was now on a mission to gather more supplies for that project from Britain's good friends at Tahiti.[41]

And it merits noting that Pacific Islanders were known to tell falsehoods in their encounters with Europeans as well. When Captain Bligh sailed to the Society Island of Huahine in April 1789 to inquire about Mai, the Tahitian voyager who had sailed to Britain with Cook in 1775 as a navigator and interpreter on his second Pacific voyage and then returned to the Pacific with Cook on his third voyage, no two people told Bligh the same story. It was clear from the material evidence – Mai's house had been demolished and his horse, a gift from Cook, roamed free on the island – that Mai had died. But had he been killed? Contracted a disease? Or just died? Every time Bligh asked, he received a different answer.[42]

When, late in 1832, Joshua Hill arrived at Pitcairn, ready to lie to the island's small community about both his mission and his credentials, he was partaking in a long history of telling tales in the Pacific, and he did not seem to let one moment pass before he began. Almost immediately upon arriving, he inquired of the Pitcairners as to whether or not a British man-of-war had passed by the island in recent months. No, they answered. Then, one soon would, Hill explained. The HMS *Dublin*, under Captain Lord George Townshend, was scheduled to arrive at Pitcairn at any moment. Hill was, he claimed, "intimately acquainted" with Lord Townshend. According to some accounts, he insisted that he himself was a nobleman – Lord Hill.[43] He had been sent from London to "adjust the internal affairs of the island." He would not remain long. He would be leaving on the *Dublin*, as he was to travel to the Marquesas Islands in a diplomatic capacity.[44] When the *Dublin* arrived, Hill argued, everyone would have proof of his claims.[45]

[41] Captain J. Pipon, *An Interesting Account of the Mutineers of HM Ship* Bounty *Under Command of Captain Bligh*, SLNSW DLMSQ 341. See also, Kennedy, *Bligh*, 139–142, Diana Souhami, *Coconut Chaos: Pitcairn, Mutiny, and a Seduction at Sea* (London: Phoenix Press, 2008), 68; and "Pitcairn's Island," in *The Dublin Literary Journal and Select Family Visitor* 28:3 (July 1, 1845), 443. See also Salmond, *Bligh*, 261.

[42] Danielsson, *What Happened on the* Bounty, 77–78; and Thomas Blake Clark, *Omai: First Polynesian Ambassador to England* (San Francisco: The Colt Press, 1941), 87. See also, Barrow, *A Description of Pitcairn's Island*, 51.

[43] Kirk, *Pitcairn Island*, 82.

[44] John Evans, "The Humble Petition of John Evans, Two Years Resident on Pitcairn's Island," quoted in Brodie, *Pitcairn's Island and the Islanders*, 190–191.

[45] John Buffett, "Twenty Years Residence on Pitcairn's Island," in *The Friend* 4:7 (April 1, 1846), part V. Hill's claim to have been authorized to govern at Pitcairn by London is repeated in many sources. See also, Young, *Mutiny of the* Bounty, 77; Brodie, *Pitcairn's Island*, 76–77; Nobbs, "The Humble Petition," in Brodie, *Pitcairn's Island and the Islanders*, 181–182.

According to Pitcairn islander John Buffett, who admittedly was Hill's enemy by the time he recorded his account of Hill's arrival at Pitcairn, the islanders knew at once that this tall Englishman, dapper and adventurous as he may have been at nearly sixty years of age, was telling them stories. "In looking over the Navy-List," Buffett recorded, "I found that Lord James, and not George Townshend, commanded the *Dublin*, and I supposed he could not be so well acquainted as he had said."[46] Writing, as he was, some thirteen years after the fact, it hardly did Buffett any good to admit that he knew Hill was lying from the start. If that had been the case, why had he not stopped the impostor right away? Why had he allowed Hill to continue in his lie? How had Hill come to have the influence over the island that he would come to have from 1832 until his removal in 1837? As Buffett recalled, the discrepancies in Hill's story about the *Dublin* made him and the rest of the islanders doubt "the truth of his mission," and still, everybody seems to have gone along with the newly arrived Hill's show as he regaled the Pitcairnese men and women with news that he intended "to be a little king among them."[47] As had been the case during the meeting between John Adams and Captains Staines and Pipon, everyone seems to have known Hill was not telling the truth, and nobody seems to have cared.

Indeed, Hill seems to have consolidated power at Pitcairn in fairly short order. When Captain Charles H. Freemantle of HMS *Challenger* landed at Pitcairn early in 1833, he found that Hill had fully established himself among the islanders "as a kind of pastor and monitor." Hill was, Freemantle recorded, "officiating as a schoolmaster and had quite suc-ceeded in supplanting the Englishman who had acted previously in that station."[48] As had the islanders more broadly, Freemantle seems to have been taken in by Hill's yarns even though he knew Hill's authority at Pitcairn was not based on any official government order from London. George Nobbs, one of three English residents at Pitcairn at the time of Hill's arrival and the man Hill had replaced as pastor and schoolmaster, noted that Freemantle informed the islanders in no uncertain terms that "Mr. Hill was not acting under the authority of the British Government."[49] Still, Freemantle did nothing to unseat Hill from his South Pacific perch. "It appeared to me," Freemantle noted, "so extra-ordinary a circumstance – a gentleman of Mr. Hill's age and apparent respectability, coming from England for the express purpose of residing

---

[46] Buffett, *Twenty Years Residence*, Part V.   [47] Ibid.

[48] Captain Charles H. Freemantle, Letter to Captain the Hon. George Elliott, Secretary, &c. &c., &c., Admiralty (May 30, 1833), quoted in Brodie, *Pitcairn's Island and the Islanders*, 161.

[49] Nobbs, "The Humble Petition," quoted in Brodie, *Pitcairn's Island and the Islanders*, 182.

upon Pitcairn's Island." Indeed, before he left the island, Freemantle was so convinced by Hill's intentions and so taken by his reformist agenda for the island that he gave Hill "all the assistance in my power to support him in his situation."[50]

Freemantle, who would go on to serve as the private secretary to the secretary of war during the Peel administration, was not alone in supporting Hill.[51] Indeed, several of the same islanders who were dubious of Hill's claims seem to have welcomed him to the island. John Evans later wrote that he "cheerfully contributed to his support."[52] George Nobbs lent him a room in his house.[53] Edward Quintal, a direct descendant of the *Bounty* mutineers, seems to have written to George Pritchard, who was then serving as the unofficial British Consul at Tahiti, on several occasions to praise Hill. "Our good friend, Capt. Hill, has been, and is doing all in his power for our general welfare, and I am sure that his plans are well calculated to insure both our present and future happiness," he wrote on one occasion.[54] On yet another, he went so far as to suggest that "Capt. Hill has all along acted like a father to us all, and we really owe him more than we shall ever be able to discharge."[55] For a group of islanders who knew their new guest was lying to them, the Pitcairners did more than a little to make Joshua Hill feel welcome in the first months after his arrival among them. But why?

When Hill told the Pitcairners that he had British warships at his disposal, that he was a titled man, and that he had been sent to help them quickly reform their internal administration before moving on to serve as a diplomat in the Marquesas, he also shared with them a rather extensive collection of letters and papers that outlined his biography. He shared this same collection of materials with Captain Freemantle, who was so impressed by Hill's credentials that he praised Hill in a short note he attached to the documents when he returned them to their owner in January 1833.

My dear Sir, -
    I have the pleasure to return the papers you were good enough to allow me to have to copy . . . I shall always be glad to hear of the welfare of the inhabitants of

---

[50] Freemantle, Letter to Captain the Hon. George Elliott (May 30, 1833), quoted in Brodie, *Pitcairn's Island and the Islanders*, 161.

[51] Jane Samson, *Imperial Benevolence: Making British Authority in the Pacific Islands* (Honolulu: University of Hawai'i Press, 1998), 31.

[52] Evans, "The Humble Petition," quoted in Brodie, *Pitcairn's Island and the Islanders*, 191.

[53] Nobbs, "The Humble Petition," quoted in Brodie, *Pitcairn's Island and the Islanders*, 182.

[54] Edward Quintal, Letter to the Rev. George Pritchard (April 6, 1833), quoted in Brodie, *Pitcairn's Island and the Islanders*, 195.

[55] Quintal, Letter to the Rev. George Pritchard (March 8, 1833), quoted in Brodie, *Pitcairn's Island and the Islanders*, 196.

Pitcairn's Island, and I most sincerely trust that they will continue to go on and prosper, be happy, and contented. I shall exert myself on my arrival in England in furthering your views with respect to a clergyman being sent to them, which, I think, may be accomplished.[56]

What were the claims that Hill made that so impressed not only the Pitcairn islanders but also Captain Freemantle? What was it about his curriculum vitae that was so impressive that people submitted to Hill's authority even though they knew he was not telling them the whole truth about either himself or his mission in the Pacific? How did all of these people get taken in so fully and so quickly by a confidence man whose masquerade was exposed from the very outset?

It is not possible to recapture the exact autobiography that Hill narrated to the Pitcairners in October 1832. Fortunately though, several pieces of Hill's writing survive that do much the same work. Two, in particular, are of great value. The first is a letter Hill seems to have written at Pitcairn in June 1834.[57] The second is a memorial Hill sent to the Lords Commissioners of the Royal Admiralty in 1841 seeking remuneration for his services to the British Empire broadly and to Pitcairn Island more specifically.[58] From these two documents, one is able to sketch a rough outline of Hill's life – at least his life as he wanted us to know it, for there is a decided purposefulness to both accounts. In an extraordinary act of paralipsis, for instance, Hill opens his 1834 letter deferentially with a reference to Proverbs 27:2 and the cautionary claim that "pedantry and egotism become no one" before begging forgiveness for elaborating his credentials, a list that begins *"in limine"* with the observation that he had maintained his status as "an English gentleman" throughout a life that had included visits to "the four quadrants of the globe."[59]

Hill's 1834 letter then enters into a litany of claims:

I have lived a considerable while in a palace, and had my dinner parties with a princess on my right, and a General's lady upon my left. I have had a French cook, a box at the Opera. I have drove my dress carriage (thought the neatest then in Paris, where I spent five or six years; as well I have known Calcutta), and the handsomest lady (said), Madame R——, to grace my carriage. I have drove a curricle with my two outriders, and two saddle-horses, besides a travelling-carriage. A valet, coachman, footman, groom, and, upon extraordinary occasions, my *maître d'hôtel*. I have (at her request) visited Madame Bonaparte, at the

---

[56] Captain C. H. Freemantle, R.N., Letter to Joshua Hill (January 12, 1833), quoted in Brodie, *Pitcairn's Island and the Islanders*, 196–197.

[57] Joshua Hill, Letter from Pitcairn Island (June 1834), quoted in Brodie, *Pitcairn's Island and the Islanders*, 211–15.

[58] Joshua Hill, *The Humble Memorial*.

[59] Quoted in Brodie, *Pitcairn's Island and the Islanders*, 211.

Tuileries, St. Cloud, and Malmaison. I might thus mention many others of note abroad. I have frequently dined with that remarkable woman, Madame Carburas, afterwards the Princess de C——. I have had the honour of being in company, *i.e.* at the same parties, with both his late Majesty George IV. then Prince Regent, and his present Majesty William IV. then H.R.H. Duke of Clarence, as well with their royal brothers.[60]

The letter goes on from there – pages of boasting that never quite capture the tone of one who was looking to avoid "pedantry and egotism." It is this swaggering sense of braggadocio (also demonstrated in Hill's 1841 memorial to the Admiralty) that has allowed many historians to dismiss him as a delusional egomaniac, the kind of man who might be inclined to sail more than 10,000 miles around the globe in order to fraudulently govern a small island of sixty or so people. Similarly, it is the vagueness of so many of Hill's claims that begs questions.

I have entertained Governors, Generals, Captains (R.N.), ... I received the dress sword, and nautical instruments, &c. of a noble lord (at his death), a Vice-Admiral of the Red, ... I have visited the Falls of Niagara and Montmorency, the natural bridge in Virginia, the great Reciprocating Fountain in East Tennessee, the great Temple of Elephanta at Bombay. I have dined with a prince, as well as a princess; and with a count, a baron, an ambassador, a minister (ordinary and extraordinary), and have travelled with one for some weeks ...[61]

It is claims of this sort that have driven others to dismiss his autobiography as little more than nugatory prattle from an obvious tongue-pad. After all, Hill's most substantive claim – from an historical perspective – was that he had been sent from London to administer at Pitcairn, and that claim is patently untrue. But, if we can learn one thing from the yarns, lies, and half-truths of men like Alexander Smith/John Adams, James Cook, William Bligh, and Fletcher Christian, it is that one lie need not undermine an entire narrative, and the same holds for Joshua Hill's biography.

There is truth to Kirsten McKenzie's argument that an impostor's lies are historically significant because they "lay bare the assumptions of his own society ... Impostors and confidence men and women are likely to flourish," McKenzie concludes, "at precisely those moments when social hierarchies are most fluid."[62] Empire certainly provided this sort of social fluidity, but before we lump Hill into the historiographic bin with other frauds and charlatans, it behooves us to ask whether or not there was more to his story. It simply does not follow that Hill did not visit the natural bridge of Virginia, the Reciprocating Fountain in Tennessee, or Niagara

---

[60] Quoted in Ibid., 211–212.   [61] Quoted in Ibid., 212–213.
[62] Kirsten McKenzie, *A Swindler's Progress: Nobles and Convicts in the Age of Liberty* (Cambridge, MA: Harvard University Press, 2010), 295.

Falls just because he lied about having been sent to Pitcairn by and with a mission on behalf of the British Crown.

Tracing out a biography from Hill's 1834 letter and his 1841 memorial is not easy work. Neither source is chronological. Neither is terribly narrative. The 1834 letter, for instance, references only three specific dates, though readers are able to ascertain the rough dates for about a dozen or so other events based on the information Hill provides. The Admiralty memorial, on the other hand, is a rich petition, complete with supporting evidence to verify the claims that Hill is making for back wages from a government that is in arrears on its payments to him, at least in his own mind. Focused on Hill's time at Pitcairn, though, the memorial pays little attention to chronology, tending instead to highlight instances where Hill might make some claim against the public coffers.

Taken apart individually and reassembled as a single, chronological narrative absent any claims that cannot be roughly dated, Hill's autobiography reads as an impressive tale of a global nineteenth-century life. Joshua W. Hill was born on April 15, 1773, in colonial North America. He was the product of "a patriotic and wealthy family of high standing." His father, "an English country gentleman, of the 'old school,' was an opulent planter" who remained loyal to the British crown in the tumultuous events surrounding the American Revolution, even "taking active measures on the side of his sovereign."[63]

An assortment of Hill's less concrete claims about North American travel might well be plausible, if he was, in fact, born in colonial North America. The Great Stone Bridge of Virginia was a popular natural attraction in the late colonial period.[64] The same could be said of the Reciprocating Fountain of eastern Tennessee. Now known as the Ebbing and Flowing Spring, the Reciprocating Fountain is located in Hawkins County, Tennessee, not far from the town of Rogersville. It has the distinction of being one of only two springs in the world to follow a predictable tidal pattern.[65] It, like the mighty falls at Montmorency in Quebec or Niagara in New York state, was a hydraulic wonder in the late eighteenth century, featured in textbooks on the science of hydraulics, and any traveler with what Hill himself called "a natural turn of mind to scientific pursuits" would

---

[63] Hill, *The Humble Memorial*, 10.

[64] Melville, *Moby-Dick*, 550. See also, John E. Crowley, *Imperial Landscapes: Britain's Global Visual Culture, 1745–1820* (New Haven: Yale University Press, 2011), 140, 147, 157–58.

[65] Henry R. Price, *Hawkins County Tennessee: A Pictorial History* (Virginia Beach, VA: Donning Company Publishers, 1996), 57; and Randy Ball and Rodney Ferrell, *Rogersville: Then & Now* (Charleston, SC: Arcadia Press, 2009).

have endeavored to visit all three.[66] If Hill indeed traveled to western New York to see Niagara Falls, he would almost certainly have traveled through Albany, and he might well have encountered the Seneca orator and chief Sagoyewatha, better known as Red Jacket, as he claims to have done in his 1834 letter.[67]

Between the 1770s and 1793, there is a wide gap of uncertainty that runs through Hill's autobiography. The story picks back up in the 1790s, however, when he claims to have been "entirely" responsible for the capture of the French privateer, the *Général Dumourier*. According to Hill's narrative, it was he who warned Captain Graves of the *Neptune* on which he was sailing that they ought to alert the English ships in the Bay of Biscay – the HMS *Egmont*, the *Edgar*, the *Ganges*, and the *Phaeton* – of the presence of the *Dumourier* and its Spanish prize, the *St. Jago*. For *his* services, Graves would later be promoted to a position in the Royal Navy. Hill was left empty-handed.[68]

On May 1, 1794, Hill claims to have sailed for the East Indies and China under Lord Howe as part of "the largest fleet, possibly, that ever was."[69] But by March 1801, he was on the other side of the globe, commanding (at the request of Captain Graves) the prize ship *Patapscos* as part of the flotilla under Sir John Duckworth in the Caribbean.[70] Within three years, he was back in Europe, this time in Paris, where he seems to have been on hand for Napoleon's coronation on December 2, 1804.[71]

In his 1834 letter, Hill makes several claims about his subsequent years in Paris. It was in this period, he claims, that he was admitted to sittings of learned societies like *L'Académie française*.[72] He claims also to have become close enough to the Bonapartes – Josephine, at least – to have been invited to their private residences at St. Cloud, Malmaison, and the Tuileries.[73] More revealing, he claims to have been present at the only performance where all three generations of the famous French dancing dynasty, the Vestrises, performed together.[74]

Hill seems to have returned to London by 1807, as Sir Joseph Banks invited him to attend meetings of the Royal Society in

---

[66] Hill, *The Humble Memorial*, 10. See also, James Ferguson and David Brewster, *Lectures on Select Subjects in Mechanics, Hydrostatics, Hydraulics, Pneumatics, Optics, Geography, Astronomy, and Dialling – In Two Volumes* (Edinburgh: Stirling & Slade and Bell & Bradfute, 1823), i, 92.

[67] Brodie, *Pitcairn's Island and the Islanders*, 213. See also, John Niles Hubbard, *An Account of Sa-go-ye-wat-ha, or, Red Jacket, and His People, 1750–1830* (Albany, NY: Joel Munsell's Sons, 1886).

[68] Brodie, *Pitcairn's Island and the Islanders*, 15.   [69] Ibid., 212.

[70] Hill, *The Humble Memorial*, 15.

[71] Brodie, *Pitcairn's Island and the Islanders*, 211 and 214.   [72] Ibid., 212.   [73] Ibid., 211.

[74] Ibid., 214.

that year.[75] At least, that is what Hill claims. In 1809, an unspecified company of London merchants, aware of Hill's previous naval prowess, asked him to command a twenty-four-gun ship on their behalf, and by 1810, he seems to have grown so prominent in London's high society as to have been invited to the opulent (and sometimes bawdy) table of the newly named prince regent, later George IV.[76] Moving in such rarified circles seems to have done wonders for Hill's self-esteem, as he claims to have written an essay – published in the *London Morning Post* on March 7, 1811 – that advised the government on matters of global naval strategy.

But, if Joshua Hill was anything, it was mobile. To remain in London for too long – despite London's comforts and the charming company of its glitterati – was not Hill's style. Thus, by 1813, he was in South America, where he spent time fighting on behalf of those struggling to free them-selves from Spanish colonial control and working for his own government and its efforts to secure British interests amidst the chaos wrought by the end of Spanish imperialism in the region.[77] In 1813, Robert Ponsoby Staples, the first British consul appointed to any of the new South American republics, asked Hill to loan his small boat to Captain William Bowles, who had just arrived in Buenos Aires to help secure British interests against the American frigate the USS *Essex*.[78] As with his previous services to the empire, Hill was never remunerated for his assistance or for the loan of his property.

Like so many others, Hill seems to have turned his attention to Pitcairn Island in the wake of Captain Beechey's celebrated Pacific voyage in 1825. Beechey and his crew published various accounts of the voyage that popularized not only South Pacific voyaging but also many of the specific islands located inside Britain's growing sphere of influence in the region. Pitcairn, with its romantic origins, its swashbuckling history, its clear links to British colonial control, and its moral of redemptive

---

[75] For more on Banks, see Patrick O'Brian, *Joseph Banks: A Life* (Chicago: University of Chicago Press, 1987).

[76] Brodie, *Pitcairn's Island and the Islanders*, 211.

[77] Christon I. Archer, ed., *The Wars of Independence in Spanish America* (Wilmington, Delaware: Scholarly Resources, 2000), 187. See also, Matthew Brown, *Adventuring through Spanish Colonies: Simón Bolívar, Foreign Mercenaries, and the Birth of New Nations* (Liverpool: Liverpool University Press, 2006); Jaime E. Rodriguez O. *The Independence of Spanish America* (New York: Cambridge University Press, 1998); and Matthew Brown, "Gregor MacGregor: Clansman, Conquistador, and Coloniser on the Fringes of the British Empire," in David Lambert and Alan Lester, eds. *Colonial Lives across the British Empire: Imperial Careering in the Long Nineteenth Century* (New York: Cambridge University Press, 2006), 32–57.

[78] See *The London Gazette* (March 19, 1811). For Hill's claims, see Hill, *The Humble Memorial*, 17.

Christianity, was particularly appealing. In the years after Beechey's return, Hill seems to have written not only to the famed captain but also to celebrated evangelical leaders like William Wilberforce about the Pitcairnese people, and he seems also to have collected a substantial library of books on Pacific topics, with the goal not only to offer informed opinions on how to regulate the island but also to supply him with the tools to do that regulating should his government call upon him to take up the task.[79]

A resident of Liverpool in these years, Hill was in touch with other evangelical groups, the London Missionary Society (LMS) chief among them, about Pitcairn, and he also wrote to high-ranking government officials. None seem to have taken up his call to arms on behalf of the Pitcairnese people. The leading religious figures in Liverpool, on the other had, were enthusiastic about his mission, or so he claimed. "Eminent, as well as other Divines" from Liverpool encouraged him to answer the call he was hearing on behalf of the small community on that tiny island. Indeed, when he left Liverpool early in 1831, Hill claims to have been supported by a "public requisition" taken up among the broader Liverpudlian community on behalf of his "religious tour of the islands."[80]

Joshua Hill's voyage to Pitcairn was, he claimed, richly eventful. His time in the Hawai'ian Islands coincided with the arrival of Catholic missionaries who were pressing in on the evangelical turf of the American Board of Commissioners for Foreign Missions (ABCFM). Hill claimed to have intervened with Hiram Bingham, the intellectual leader of the American missionaries, to find a solution to the tense religious standoff before quickly moving on for Tahiti, where he believed the Pitcairn islanders were living at that time.

Hill was surprised to find that the Pitcairners were not at Tahiti. Having been removed from their native island in 1830, the people of Pitcairn had been settled at Tahiti through the collaborative efforts of the British government and the Tahitian queen, Pomare IV. Tahiti, it was thought, was a more bountiful place for the half-English and half-Tahitian Pitcairners than their small and isolated island with its limited resources. But, Tahiti had proven insalubrious to the islanders, and they quickly arranged to have themselves restored to Pitcairn.

Tahiti, like Hawai'i, had its own problems when Joshua Hill arrived. George Pritchard, the leading British missionary from the LMS was away from the island, and Queen Pomare's government was imperiled both by external pressures from passing commercial vessels and by internal

---

[79] Hill, *The Humble Memorial*, 1 and 12.   [80] Ibid., 1–2.

factions. If we believe Hill's autobiographical sketch, it was he who helped Pomare restore Tahitian respect for British authority, and it was he who employed that authority to help secure her status as the singular leader of Tahiti. Indeed, so smitten by Hill's gravitas was Queen Pomare that she asked Britain to appoint a permanent consul to Tahiti and further requested that Hill be tapped to fill the new post.[81]

That Hill knew to search out the Pitcairners not at Pitcairn but at Tahiti suggests just how closely he was following their story in the years leading up to his grand Pacific adventure. To have been so deeply connected to these people must have compounded the concern Hill felt when he first arrived at Pitcairn in October 1832 to find the island in a state of disarray so soon after the return from Tahiti.[82] Hill would later claim to have written to many in London, particularly the Secretary of State for the Colonies, the Earl of Rippon, to detail the terrible conditions at Pitcairn, and he felt that the praise he received from Captain Freemantle of the *Challenger* served to confirm any plans he had to reform and remake the society among the descendants of the *Bounty*.[83] Hill's confidence that London backed him was further verified, he felt, by an 1834 letter he received from Edward Stanley, Rippon's successor as the secretary of state for the colonies.[84]

Hill's work at Pitcairn cost him. Later in his life, he would claim that the last letter he received from his wife, whom he seems to have left behind in Liverpool, arrived at Pitcairn in February 1834.[85] His work at Pitcairn, meanwhile, was not universally supported by the islanders, and he found he had to expel three Englishmen living on the island, causing division and discord among the Pitcairners.[86] The tension ate at his health, and by 1835, Hill, already an old man to be doing the work he was doing, showed the early signs of a diabetic ailment.[87]

According to the memorial that Hill wrote to the British government in 1841, he was offered – most kindly, he added – a voyage home by Captain Bruce of HMS *Imogene* in 1837. Nowhere does Hill mention that part of Bruce's orders had been to sort out what was going on at Pitcairn and, if necessary, to remove Hill from power and from the island. But, as we shall see, even members of Bruce's crew were unsure as to who was the source of the quarrels at Pitcairn, Hill or his detractors.[88] Bruce and his crew seem to have left Hill at Valparaíso, and Hill does little to fill the narrative gap in his life between 1838 and 1841. By 1841, though, he was back in

[81] Ibid., 18–19   [82] Ibid., 2.   [83] Ibid., 4–6.   [84] Ibid., 6–7.   [85] Ibid., 12.
[86] Ibid., 6.
[87] Ibid., 11. See also, Robert Tattersall, *Diabetes: The Biography* (New York: Oxford University Press, 2009).
[88] Hill, *The Humble Memorial*, 11.

London, living at Tavistock Place in Russell Square, after having first visited Liverpool.[89] His health seems to have kept him in Liverpool longer than he would have liked, as did the search for his wife. The last word Hill seems ever to have had of her was that she had left him for a life on the European continent, a loss that cut him more deeply than any other he endured for Pitcairn and its residents.[90]

In London, Hill hoped to win some recognition – if not remuneration – for his work on behalf of the British Empire. He went to the Treasury to inquire whether the Viscount Melbourne would hear his case. His Lordship's secretary, C. W. Howard, referred Hill to the Colonial Department, from whence he was passed on again, this time to the Admiralty. At the Admiralty, Hill met with Sir John Barrow, that institution's Second Secretary. If Hill's claims about his own life are true, then he and Barrow moved in similar circles and had similar interests. Barrow was a protégé of none other than Sir Joseph Banks.[91] Having begun his career as an interpreter on Lord Macartney's mission to China, Barrow had proven his worth as both a manager and an administrator. The connections he made on that embassy later helped him secure the posting as Second Secretary to the Admiralty, a job that carried with it more power and prestige (to say nothing of pay) than the title itself might imply.[92] Barrow would, with only very limited interruption, serve at the Admiralty for nearly forty-one years. He would rise in social prominence, be elected as a fellow of the Royal Society, and come to be known as an influential force in British overseas ventures and naval planning.[93]

Like Hill, Barrow was also captivated by the *Bounty* saga, and in the late 1820s, he spent the better part of four years researching and writing a book about the *Bounty* and its mission as well as about the mutiny and the legal history that came from that episode.[94] His book appeared in 1831 and was an immediate success. A year later, Barrow published a second volume that focused its attention on Pitcairn and the settlement there. More than one hundred years later, both books were still in print.[95] In response to Hill's request for back pay for the services he rendered at Pitcairn, Barrow asked Hill for documents to support his claim against the

[89] Ibid., 13 and 23.   [90] Ibid., 12–13.   [91] Liebersohn, *The Travlers' World*, 111.
[92] Fergus Fleming, *Barrow's Boys* (New York: Atlantic Monthly Press, 1998), 2–6.
[93] Libersohn, *The Travelers' World*, 112; and Fleming, *Barrow's Boys*, 9.
[94] See Shapiro, *The Pitcairn Islanders*, 27. See also, I. S. MacLaren, "John Barrow's Darling Project," in Frédéric Regard, ed., *Arctic Exploration in the Nineteenth Century: Discovering the Northwest Passage* (Brookfield, VT: Pickering and Chatto, 2013), 19.
[95] Fleming, *Barrow's Boys*, 175. See also, John Barrow, *Mutiny!: The Real History of the HMS Bounty* (New York: Cooper Square Press, 2003); and John Barrow, *A Description of Pitcairn's Island*.

government's coffers, and it is that collection of documentation that constitutes the memorial from which we have so much of Hill's story.[96]

As for the question of payment, the British government never paid Joshua Hill for his services as the "governor" of Pitcairn Island.[97]

Here, then, we have an outline of the biography of Joshua W. Hill, the fraudulent colonial administrator of Pitcairn Island from 1832 to 1838. This is the autobiography that Hill told to the Pitcairners and to those willing (or forced) to listen in the years after his time in the Pacific. It is an impressive narrative, a story with a global sweep, with imperial implications and consequences, and with enough gravitas and heft that the people of Pitcairn might just have believed that this man was the sort of man that London would send to govern them – if, that is, London had been looking for somebody to govern at Pitcairn and if the story was true. But was it?

If even part of Joshua W. Hill's autobiography is true, then it is possible that he is not the complete losel that he has been made out to be, the "Mussolini of Pitcairn" as both Robert Kirk and James Norman Hall have called him.[98] If Hill's story – other than the Pitcairn fib – is verifiable, then historians have burked a rich Pacific history for no reason at all, failing to follow an imperial dragoman who might have a great deal to tell us about the way the British Empire engaged with the South Pacific in the first half of the nineteenth century. And, as should be clear, a great deal of what Hill had to say about his own life was so detailed that to unmask it as truth or fiction is not a terribly difficult proposition. Coming to know the biography of Joshua W. Hill is to remove the mask from a narrative that was, in fact, never really masked at all.

What is required to know Joshua Hill is a good bit of *sitzfleisch*, for to interrogate his biography does require, first, that the biography be assembled in some sort of chronological order, as we have done here, from the several places where Hill narrated his history in scattered and random ways. Second, it requires the patience to troll through the assembled narrative for the odd biographical detail that has some hook that can be snagged upon for historical verifiability. That is no easy task given that Hill's story stretches from North America to Britain, from Britain to South America, from South America to South Asia, from South Asia to the South Pacific, and from the South Pacific back to Europe. This is a dendroid story, one that reaches out widely in every direction. Furthermore, a great deal of what Hill had to say about himself

---

[96] Hill, *The Humble Memorial*, 13–14.   [97] Ibid., 20.

[98] See Kirk, *Pitcairn Island*, chapter twelve; and Robert Kirk, *Paradise Past: The Transformation of the South Pacific, 1520–1920* (Jefferson, NC: McFarland & Co., 2012), 63. See also Hall, *The Tale of a Shipwreck*, 89.

was susurrous, rich in historical whispers – vague details that will likely never be confirmed one way or the other. Was his dress carriage considered the finest in Paris? Did he inherit the dress sword and nautical instruments of a Vice-Admiral of the Red?[99] We may never know.

At the same time, there is here a great deal that can be fact-checked against the historical record, details that beg us to engage in a global manhunt for this imperial impostor. Joshua Hill, for instance, was very specific about the date of his birth, and he offered similarly tempting details about the location. Writing in his 1841 memorial to the Government, Joshua Hill claimed to have been born on April 15, 1773.[100] If Hill is honest here, then his earliest days were passed in colonial North America, where his father, whose given name is never mentioned, was "an English country gentleman, of the 'old school,'" and a "strict loyalist" who went so far as to take up arms on behalf of the British crown at the beginning of revolutionary hostilities. As a consequence, the elder Hill lost all of his American holdings to the rebel cause, and he was forced to return to Britain, as was the case with so many colonial American loyalists. The younger Hill – our Joshua – seems to have followed his father later.[101]

Crown loyalists have received renewed attention thanks to Maya Jasanoff's *Liberty's Exiles*, a book written with the help of the records left behind by the British government's efforts to remunerate loyalists for the losses they suffered in the service of the crown.[102] Reviewing the lists of names included in those records, one finds many a *Hill*.[103] Very few of them are men of any real property, and none of them match the descriptions Hill offered of his own father in the 1841 memorial, not the sizeable landholdings nor the timeline of the elder Hill's departure from North America. None, that is except one – a Delaware man by the very tantalizing name of *Joshua* Hill.[104]

[99] Quoted in Brodie, *Pitcairn's Island and the Islanders*, 212–213.
[100] Hill, *The Humble Memorial*, 12.   [101] Ibid., 10.
[102] Maya Jasanoff, *Liberty's Exiles: American Loyalists in the Revolutionary World* (New York: Knopf, 2011).
[103] Peter Wilson Coldham, *American Migrations, 1765–1799: The Lives, Times, and Families of Colonial Americans Who Remained Loyal to the British Crown before, during, and after the Revolutionary War, as Related in Their Own Words and Through Their Correspondence* (Baltimore: Genealogical Publishing Co., 2000), 77, 156, 254, 464 (for Joshua Hill of Delaware) 499, 569, and 698. See also, Lorenzo Sabine, *The American Loyalists; or, Biographical Sketches of Adherents to the British Crown in the War of the Revolution; Alphabetically Arranged; with a Preliminary Historical Essay* (Boston: Little and Brown, 1847), 361–62; or Lorenzo Sabine, *Biographical Sketches of Loyalists of the American Revolution, with an Historical Essay* (Boston: Little Brown, 1865), 535–36.
[104] The records for this Joshua Hill indicate that he was a property owner with an estate, called Springfield, of more than 400 acres. His buildings and improvements on the estate brought its estimated value to near £900. Hill's other properties brought his

If Joshua Hill of Delaware was, in fact, our Joshua Hill's father, he was not originally a crown loyalist. Indeed, Mr. Hill from Delaware served in the colonial (later state) legislature and was loyal to the Continental Congress until 1778. In that year, he spoke out, rather ill-advisedly, about the Congress in critical terms, whereupon a small, armed band was sent to arrest him for his disloyal and intemperate remarks. In the kerfuffle that followed, two of the soldiers sent against him were killed. Now having taken up arms against the American cause, Hill fled to the British side, eventually leaving the rebellious colonies for Canada from whence he then traveled back to Britain.[105]

None of the documents related to Delaware's Joshua Hill specifically mention a son named Joshua (though they do mention several sons).[106] Admittedly, there is much here that is historically fissiparous. The details of Mr. Hill from Delaware match up with those offered by our Joshua Hill, but only enough to be tempting. Any sense of historical certainty we might be tempted to grasp at crumbles like ash in our hands. And yet, the details *are* very tantalizing, and not just in relationship to the claims about his birth and parentage. Let us look, for example, to Hill's claim to have published an essay in the *London Morning Post* on British naval power. Hill made this claim in a letter to the government in London dated from Pitcairn in June 1834, and he was very specific about the date of his essay – March 7, 1811.[107]

A quick survey of the microfilm reel archives of the *Morning Post* verifies that there was a rather lengthy editorial essay on British naval affairs published on March 7, 1811.[108] Unsurprisingly, given the editorial customs of the period, there was no byline on the essay, and so we cannot know for certain whether this piece was written by Hill or not. Of course, Hill made his claim about this essay in the 1830s, leaving us to wonder. How was the claim so accurate? Had he appreciated the essay when he

---

financial losses over the course of the Revolution to a total of more than £2,000. In addition, Hill seems to have been a slave owner with as many as seven female slaves and nine male slaves. Together, the value of his slaves constituted another £930. See, "Joshua Hill of Delaware and Shelburne, Nova Scotia," in *Loyalists Claims for Losses* (MG14), National Library of Canada, A012, v. 58, reel B-1168; and "Joshua Hill of Delaware and Shelburne, Nova Scotia," *Loyalist Claims for Losses* (MG14), National Library of Canada, A013, v. 96, reel B-2200.

[105] See "Joshua Hill of Delaware and Shelburne, Nova Scotia," A013, v. 93, reel B-2200. See also, "Joshua Hill of Delaware and Shelburne, Nova Scotia," in *Loyalist Claims for Losses* (MG14), National Library of Canada, A012, v. 95, reel B-1176; and "Joshua Hill of Delaware and Shelburne, Nova Scotia," in *Loyalist Claims for Losses* (MG14), National Library of Canada, A012, v. 41, reel B-1164.

[106] "Joshua Hill of Delaware and Shelburne, Nova Scotia," A012, v. 41, reel B-1164.

[107] Cited in Brodie, *Pitcairn's Island and the Islanders*, 214.

[108] "On Naval Power: Its Use, Fluctuations, and Present State," in *The Morning Post* (London, March 7, 1811).

first read it several *decades* before and remembered its publication details on the off chance he decided to use it in an elaborate autobiographical hoax later on? Had he searched through all the bumf of some newspaper archive just to dredge up concrete details that would sustain his life's story? Or is it possible that the simplest explanation – that Hill actually wrote this essay – is the best one here?

The long list of Joshua Hill's claims – to say nothing of the tone in which he made them – leave us no choice but to conclude that this man was an absolute flannelmouth. Words came easily to him; pride he had in abundance. But, to be a proud smooth-talker is not ipso facto to be dishonest, and there is much in the 1811 essay on naval power that resonates with Hill's later actions in the Pacific, making this piece a potentially valuable manifesto of Hill's broader sense of how Britain's imperial power ought to function across the planet's oceans.

"A Prince employing his navy with spirit and courage," the 1811 essay opens, "is Arbiter and Lord of the World." Whereas "Arms upon land threaten and strike in one part only," sea power can be unleashed everywhere.[109] In what follows, the author of this piece connects naval strength to trade, which is presented as being "extremely serviceable to any nation, let the form of its Government be what it will, because it introduces industry and arts, by which the manners of a people are entirely altered."[110] This essay was a call for what Michael Reidy has dubbed "liquid imperialism" and for global mastery.[111] Maritime trading powers, though, had waxed and waned over time. The article traced out a narrative history from the Phoenicians to the eighteenth century to demonstrate the cyclical progression that had witnessed the rise and eventual decline of maritime leaders since the time of Nebuchadnezzar.

At the dawn of the nineteenth century, Great Britain was, the article posited, "most completely the mistress of the seas," but that status was precarious, particularly in the Pacific. To be sure, Britain was a latecomer to the Pacific, an ocean that had long been considered "the Spanish lake."[112] British interest in the Pacific mushroomed in the wake of Admiral George Anson's Pacific voyages and, particularly, after the publication of his *Voyage Round the World* in 1748. With a subscription rate of more than 1,800 for the first edition, four published editions in 1748 alone, and rapid translations into Dutch, French, German, and Italian, Anson's book suggested significant public interest in the Pacific; and subsequent voyages by John Byron (1764) and Samuel Wallis (1766)

---

[109] Ibid.   [110] Ibid.   [111] Reidy, *Tides of History*, 294.
[112] Fischer, *A History of the Pacific Islands*, 88–92.

soon followed.[113] Captain Cook's subsequent voyages changed Britain's influence in the Pacific even further.

In London, though, official British policy remained, as Steven Fischer has said, "seemingly forever dedicated to the principle of insular indifference."[114] As I. C. Campbell has argued, there was no real "scramble for the Pacific."[115] As we shall explore more fully hereafter, official British policy towards the Pacific was, at best, thin in the late eighteenth and early nineteenth centuries. The Pacific was held at arm's length, and, while many of the islands in the Pacific were "*de facto* colonial" possessions, "the British seem to have been reluctant to take any official responsibility for areas like Polynesia." Instead, the British government – not unlike that of the United States – allowed missionaries to act as surrogate agents on behalf of the broader imperial state.[116] As we will see, missionaries forged their own theological networks that operated somewhere between church, the domestic state, and the indigenous governments of the Pacific Islands. In some instances, notably in Hawai'i and Tahiti, the missionaries were crucial to the formation of the viable, modern, and centralized political communities we know today.

But to leave British imperial policy in the hands of independent missionary societies was hardly sufficient to the author of the essay in *The Morning Post*, whether it was Joshua Hill or otherwise. Naval power was crucial to the success of states, and to Britain in particular. Competition for naval supremacy was one of the sure truths of geopolitics. It had to be guarded, as "commerce and power are always in a state of fluctuation." It was imperative for maritime leaders like Britain "to always be jealous of every power that appears formidable at sea." It was never enough to count on the relative weakness of other powers; naval supremacy had to be worked at conscientiously and constantly.[117]

The central policy arguments of the 1811 essay in *The Morning Post* sit easily alongside the actions we know Joshua Hill took vis-à-vis the British colonial outpost at Pitcairn Island; they foreshadow the work we know Hill would try to do years later. They are the sorts of arguments that would have demanded that London take stock of its Pitcairnese subjects, their moral fate, their strategic mid-Pacific location, and their potential to be a colonial, commercial, and evangelical resource for the Pacific basin

---

[113] Crowley, *Imperial Landscapes*, 79. See also, Withey, *Voyages of Discovery*, 18–19.

[114] Fischer, *A History of the Pacific Islands*, 167.

[115] I. C. Campbell, *A History of the Pacific Islands* (Los Angeles: University of California Press, 1989), 145–47.

[116] Anna Johnston, "Antipodean Heathens: The London Missionary Society in Polynesia and Australia, 1800–50," in Lynetter Russell, ed., *Colonial Frontiers: Indigenous Encounters in Settler Societies* (Manchester: Manchester University Press, 2001), 69.

[117] "On Naval Power."

more broadly. And, as we shall see, these were exactly the arguments Joshua Hill did make to influential policymakers in London and beyond before his missionary voyage to the South Seas. If the essay was not the product of Hill's hand, it is easy to see why it caught his eye in 1811, enough even that he would recall it still in the 1830s.

Joshua Hill made other claims too. He sailed, so he said, from Portsmouth as part of one of the largest fleets ever bound for India and China on May 1, 1794.[118] Investigations in the East India Company's archives in London indicate that a J. Hill was part of the crew on board the Company's Indiaman *Bridgewater* on that date.[119] To be certain, the surname Hill is a common one (frustratingly so, given its centrality in this archival scavenger hunt), and the first initial J. here does not delimit our search much further. But, the pattern is becoming telling. A Joshua Hill among the list of colonial American loyalists whose story matches the one our Joshua Hill tells of his family, an article published on just the right topic in just the right paper on just the right day, and now a matching name on board a crew manifest that fits the story too. Either Joshua W. Hill was history's most fortunate fanfaron, or he was more honest about his autobiography than historians have previously allowed.

Hill made many claims regarding his familiarity with late eighteenth-century Britain's rich and famous, and he does seem to have communicated with some very prominent people – not always without incident. Indeed, a letter Hill wrote to the Duke of Wellington in August 1846 indicates that his Pitcairn sojourn may not have been Hill's only dalliance with truth and imposture. In his letter, Hill narrated for the recently retired Wellington a melodramatic scandal concocted by Sophia Elizabeth Guelph Sims, the wife of an Islington baker. In her version of things, Sims was the daughter of none other than George IV and his illicit "wife," the Catholic Maria Fitzherbert. She had, she alleged, been raised by one Captain William Hill, who had ties to various servants at the Court, and his wife, Mary White. Hill, Sims claimed, had received some £2,000 to defray the costs of maintaining the child for the court. Furthermore, Sims had recently indicated that Joshua Hill was the very same Captain William Hill from her story, though, she explained, he had changed his name to hide the deceit.[120]

Sims' claims, Hill argued to Wellington, could not be true, as official records demonstrated that he – Joshua Hill – had operated under that

[118] Brodie, *Pitcairn's Island and the Islanders*, 211.

[119] Anthony Farrington, *A Biographical Index of East India Company Maritime Service Officers, 1600–1834* (London: British Museum, 1999), 377.

[120] Joshua Hill, Letter to the Duke of Wellington (London: August 15, 1846), TNA HO 44/39.

name as far back as 1793–1795, specifically in the service of the East India Company on board the *Bridgewater* under Commodore William Parker. "I hereby solemnly affirm, as upon oath, before the ever-blessed God of Truth," Hill concluded, "that I am not the Captain William Hill in question, nor have I ever borne that name; – that I have never received any money for the maintenance of any child whatsoever . . . So help me God!"[121] Wellington's response to Hill's exaggerated defense was to be almost comically nonplussed. The duke sent his compliments to the captain but affirmed that he really had no knowledge whatsoever of this Mrs. Sims or her claims. In addition, Wellington seriously doubted – indeed was "quite convinced" – that George IV and Mrs. Fitzherbert never had any children as a result of their publically acknowledged "connexion."[122]

The paper trail left by Hill's correspondence with Wellington regarding the patrimony of Sophia Sims is of value at two levels here. First, it lends credence to Hill's claim that he corresponded with prominent members of the British squirearchy. Written long after Hill's time at Pitcairn – indeed, five years after Hill's memorial to the Admiralty in search of payment for his fraudulent rule at the island – Hill's letter to Wellington demonstrates that this man was just the sort of gadfly who might put pen and ink to paper to draw to himself the attention of Britain's high and mighty. It helps us to believe that Hill may well have been in communication with some of the prominent figures – Wilberforce, Beechey, etc. – he claimed to know.

At the same time, the letter suggests that our Hill moved through society like a slippery fish. Of course, it is possible that Hill was unfairly the target of Mrs. Sims' scandalous accusations, and it is equally possible that he sat down to write the Duke of Wellington to clear his name of her aspersions. But, Joshua Hill had, by 1846, been publicly exposed as the confidence man of Pitcairn Island, and we will never know for certain that his letter to Wellington was not an eloquent bit of flannel designed to clear Hill of another earlier fraud. Even as we are forced to trust Hill and his autobiographical claims in order to excavate his biography from the historical archive, we do well to recall that this man was, at least partially, a scamp who was not above four-flushing his way out of a tight corner when he was trapped in a masquerade.

Of course, Joshua Hill did more than make claims to have corresponded with Britain's elite. He told the people of Pitcairn that he was a close associate to some of Britain's most influential people, and he was very precise about whom those people were. In 1834, for instance, Hill

---

[121] Ibid.   [122] Ibid.

made it quite clear that he knew Joseph Banks, the long-time president of the Royal Society and the man whose breadfruit scheme can plausibly be credited with starting this whole story.[123] Not only had Hill breakfasted with Banks, but Banks granted Hill admission to meetings of the Royal Society and sent him overseas with letters of invitation to similar learned societies. On July 19, 1802, Dr. Sir Charles Blagden, the long-serving secretary to the Royal Society, sent a letter to his good friend Joseph Banks informing Banks that he had, per Banks' instructions, introduced one J. Hill at the *Institut de France*.[124] Not only does Blagden's letter confirm that Hill did sit in on meetings of international learned societies and that he knew Joseph Banks, at least enough to merit a letter of introduction from the great naturalist, it also opens up other interesting possibilities.

In the days after Bladgen introduced Hill at the *Institut*, he wrote to Banks of his visits to Josephine Bonaparte at the *Château de Malmaison*. It is not impossible to imagine that Hill's high-placed contacts among the expatriate British community in Paris might have won him an invitation to similarly rarefied circles among the French elite. Blagden did end his letter to Banks with the observation that he "hoped to see more of" Hill.[125] So, what was Hill's life like in Paris? Did he have a French cook? A box at the Parisian opera? We may never know, but Hill's claims here seem less arrogant, less bombastic, and less crazy once we begin to unpack some of the more concrete claims he made for himself. Indeed, if Hill spent five or six years in Paris, as he claims to have done, it is possible that he was in Paris at the time of Napoleon's coronation on December 2, 1804. He might also have been on hand for the only dance performance to feature all three generations of the Vestris family, perhaps the most influential French ballet dynasty of all time.

Gaéton Vestris (1729–1808), his son August (1760–1842), and August's son Armand (1788–1825) were gods of the Parisian dance stage in the late eighteenth century. According to the *Revue De Paris*, the three dancers only ever danced one professional performance together. That

---

[123] Tatiana Holway, *The Flower of Empire: An Amazonian Water Lily, the Quest to Make It Bloom, and the World It Created* (New York: Oxford University Press, 2013. Kindle Edition), 75–78.

[124] Dr. Sir Charles Blagden, Letter to Sir Joseph Banks (Paris, July 19, 1802), BL MS ADD 33272. See also, Sir Joseph Banks, *The Banks Letters: A Collection of the Manuscript Correspondence of Sir Joseph Banks, Preserved in the British Museum, the British Museum (Natural History), and Other Collections in Great Britain*, Warren R. Dawson, ed. (London: British Museum, 1958), 89. See also, John Gascoigne, *Joseph Banks and the English Enlightenment: Useful Knowledge and Polite Culture* (New York: Cambridge University Press, 1994), 21.

[125] Blagden, Letter to Sir Joseph Banks (July 19, 1802). See also Banks, *The Banks Letters*, 89.

performance, of *Caravane*, took place in the 1799–1800 season. It was young Armand's debut. He was just eleven years old. His grandfather, Gaéton, at the age of seventy, came out of retirement for the performance, which was hailed as a triumph for the three men individually and for the family as a group.[126] Was Hill at that one amazing and historic dance performance? We simply cannot know. We know he *wanted* to be there. We know he *felt* that being there would say something about his biography and make him seem more important. We know that he *was* in Paris, for all that that is worth. And Hill's having added this bit of detail to his story makes it *seem* that much more likely to be true. But in Hill's case, it is the *seeming* to be true that is the rub.

Not dissimilarly, we know for relative certain that Hill attempted to visit the prince regent, the future George IV, at least once at Brighton Pavilion. The guest lists at the prince regent's seaside playground for the weekend of November 23, 1817 include a Captain J. Hill.[127] Only a few days removed from the funeral of the prince regent's daughter, Charlotte Augusta, who had died in childbirth, the weekend of November 23, 1817, includes a surfeit of visitors to Brighton, presumably people wanting to pay their respects to the bereaved prince regent on the loss of his beloved daughter and heir. Hill's name does not appear on a dinner list, so it seems certain he did not eat with the Prince or his brother, the future George IV, nor did he drink from their father's wine collections as he claims to have done. At least, he did not do so that weekend. But, Hill does seem to have been willing to force himself into the penumbra of the rich and the famous, as he did on this sad weekend for the royal family.

The most recent biographical details that Hill had to offer the Pitcairners when he arrived on their island in 1832 were about his voyage from Liverpool, and a great deal of what he said of that voyage was fully true. Hill suggested that he had landed in Hawai'i to find King Kamehameha III (born as Kauikeaouli) engaged in a battle to keep Catholic missionaries from France from landing on his shores and evangelizing among his people. Already closely tied to the Protestant missionary establishment of the ABCFM out of Massachusetts, the Kamehameha dynasty in Honolulu was reluctant to take in more missionary outfits, and Kamehameha III was feeling pressure from his Protestant advisors to stand firm in his resistance.[128] For their part, the

---

[126] *Revue de Paris* (Paris: 1837), 158.
[127] Royal Guest Logs, Brighton Pavilion. The Royal Archives, Windsor Castle. RA MRH/MRHF/GUEST/BRIGHTON.
[128] P. Christiaan Klieger, *Kamehameha III: He Mo'olelo no ka Mō'ī Lokomaika'I – King of the Hawai'ian Islands, 1824–1854* (San Francisco, CA: Green Arrow Press, 2015), 147–148.

Catholic missionaries were rather firm about their goals, Catholic evangelical work in the Pacific having only just been authorized by Pope Leo
XII in 1825.[129]

Feeling the pressure from outside groups, King Kamehameha was
eager to limit his exposure to Euro-American forces in these years, and
he was deeply suspicious of the French priest, Father Alexis Bachelot,
whom Pope Leo had tapped as the first Prefect Apostolic of the Sandwich
Islands, and his confriars from the Congregation of the Sacred Heart of
Jesus and Mary.[130] Religious differences had, after all, torn apart the
political alliance between Queen Regent Ka'ahumanu, the influential
widow of King Kamehameha I, and Boki, the royal governor of O'ahu,
after Boki's conversion to Catholicism in the early 1820s.[131] Indeed,
Ka'ahumanu registered Boki's conversion as a direct challenge to her
authority and her control over the boy king Kamehameha III.[132]

Indeed, nobody would have faulted Kamehameha had he grown tired
of outsiders altogether.[133] Episodes of violence between missionaries and
whalers in the Pacific had grown more frequent, and they were disturbing
the balance of power in the sea-surrounded kingdom.[134] Perhaps the
most infamous of these conflicts was the turmoil caused by Captain
Buckley of the London whale ship *Daniel* that landed at Lahaina in
Hawai'i in October 1825.[135] Taking umbrage at new ordinances that
prohibited Hawai'ian women from going on board visiting ships,

[129] "Alexis John Augustine Bachelot, Prefect Apostolic of the Sandwich Islands," in Charles
G. Herbermann, Edward A. Pace, Condé B. Pallen, Thomas J. Shahan, John J. Wynne,
et al., eds., *The Catholic Encyclopedia: An International Work of Reference on the
Constitution, Doctrine, Discipline, and History of the Catholic Church*. 15 vols.
(New York: The Universal Knowledge Foundation, 1907–1912), xvi (1914), 6. See
also "The Sandwich Islands," in Herberman, *The Catholic Encyclopedia*, xiii (1912), 438.
See also, Dodge, *Islanders and Empires*, 168–169.

[130] See, Ralph M. Wiltgen, *The Founding of the Roman Catholic Church in Oceania,
1825–1850* (Norwalk, CT: Australian National University Press, 1981), 11. See also,
Douglas L. Oliver, *The Pacific Islands* (Honolulu: University of Hawai'i Press, 1989),
56–57; Newbury, *Tahiti Nui*, 92; and Jocelyn Linnekin, "New Political Orders," in
Donald Denoon, ed., *The Cambridge History of the Pacific Islanders* (New York:
Cambridge University Press, 1997), 191; Campbell, *A History of the Pacific Islands*, 149.

[131] Gavin Daws, "The High Chief Boki," in *The Journal of the Polynesian Society* 75:1
(1966), 65–83.

[132] Linnekin, "New Political Orders," in Denoon, ed., *The Cambridge History of the Pacific
Islanders*, 201. See also, Fischer, *A History of the Pacific Islands*, 99; Chappell, *Double
Ghosts*, 141–142; Edward D. Beechert, *Honolulu: Crossroads of the Pacific* (Columbia:
The University of South Carolina Press, 1991), 38; and Shineberg, *They Came for
Sandalwood*, 16.

[133] Fischer, *A History of the Pacific Islands*, 138.

[134] Nancy Shoemaker, ed. *Living with Whales: Documents and Oral Histories of Native New
England Whaling History* (Boston: University of Massachusetts Press, 2014), 65.

[135] London Missionary Society, South Seas – Incoming Correspondence, SOAS CMW/
LMS 6, Folder 8/Jacket A. See also, Dodge, *Islanders and Empires*, 82–83.

Captain Buckley and his crew harassed Reverend William Richards for the better part of a week, insisting that it was missionary interference that had cost the sailors their traditional right of access to Hawai'ian women. On the fourth day of the standoff, Buckley and his crew stormed Richards' property, raging outside the missionary's house with knives and pistols and threatening to murder the meddlesome American. Later whale ships made similar charges against Richards, and one crew went so far as to pull his house down.[136] It was exactly these sorts of outside conflicts that Kamehameha hoped to curtail by better controlling who landed and stayed on the beaches of his kingdom.

The Americans from the ABCFM, under the leadership of Hiram Bingham, were equally worried and for many of the same reasons. Catholic missionaries (and French ones at that) threatened new pressures on the Hawai'ian monarchy and jeopardized the ABCFM's status as an unofficial advisory body to Kamehameha's government. Bingham's letters to his superiors at the ABCFM's headquarters during this period indicate that he was deeply engaged in helping the Hawai'ian government in its negotiations with the Catholics, even advising Ka'ahumanu as to how to approach the French priests in the autumn of 1831.[137]

According to Bingham's records, a Captain J. W. Hill (here the middle initial helps us identify our Hill with more certainty) was newly arrived at Honolulu in the summer months of 1831. He was, Bingham wrote, "an interesting stranger," who willingly took a seat alongside the ABCFM missionaries in worship. "Here you would have seen," Bingham recorded, "Christian brethren at the table of our common Lord from England, Scotland, the United States of America & from the Society Islands, and from the ... churches at Kauai, Honolulu, Lahaina, Kailua, ... & Hilo all bowing at the same altar."[138]

The confluence of politics, religion, and international imperial competition at Bingham's altar is a telling example of the international and cultural influences that were sweeping the Pacific in these years, and Bingham places Joshua Hill right at the center of all of this history, much as Hill did himself in his autobiographical boasting. Indeed, Bingham was unequivocal about Hill's role in calming the tensions that Bachelot and his companions had caused. The Hawai'ian aristocracy was

---

[136] Dodge, *Islanders and Empires*, 82. See also, Rev. Levi Chamberlain. Letter to William Ellis (Honolulu: November 3, 1825), TNA FO 58/14; and SOAS CWM/LMS Box 6.

[137] Hiram Bingham, *Selected Writings of Hiram Bingham, 1814–1869: Missioanry to the Hawai'ian Islands – To Raise the Lord's Banner*, Clar Miller, ed. (Lewiston, NY: The Edwin Mellen Press, 1988), 341.

[138] American Board of Commissioners for Foreign Missions, Papers, Harvard University, Houghton Library, Unit 6, ABC 19.1, Reel 796.

greatly agitated by the presence of the Catholic party. Ka'ahumanu was so adamant that Bachelot should be sent away that she arranged to have one of her own boats readied for his transport. The British consul, Richard Charlton, intervened. It was, he noted, "kapu" for the queen regent to involve herself in this matter and wholly objectionable that she should banish the Catholic priests.[139]

Bingham and his American missionary associates were not at all happy that French Catholics had impinged on their evangelical turf. They were equally unhappy that the British consul had taken sides with the Catholic party. But, it was Ka'ahumanu who expressed the most rage at the situation. According to Bingham, she excoriated Charlton. "I thought you came here to help us," she told the British representative, "and you told me you would yourself . . . Now you shake your head."[140] Abandoned by official British policymakers, Ka'ahumanu found succor in the visiting Captain Hill. It was Hill, Bingham argued, who strengthened the chiefs positions vis-à-vis the Catholic missionaries, and it was Hill's assertion "not only that they had a right to send the Catholics away, but that they ought to go, and if they would not go by being ordered away, [that] they ought to be compelled to go" that eventually convinced the French priests to leave the Hawai'ian Islands.[141]

Indeed, Hill's argument seems to have centered on the very pragmatic notion that the Pacific was rich in islands where no evangelical work had been done and where the Catholics could spread the word of God without causing international discord. "The Romish and Protestant religions" would never "coalesce," Bingham later wrote, but it was Hill's sense that Bachelot ought not "kick against the goad."[142] There was work to be done elsewhere, and the Catholic priests could serve God more efficiently if they went and sought out that other work in other places. Bachelot and his companions were not fully convinced by Hill's arguments on the subject, but they did not put up any substantial fight when they were packed on board the *Waverly* and effectively deported from Hawai'i on January 29, 1832. Positioned between the American Protestants and the French Catholics, this British interloper seems to have been exactly the sort of mediator that was required.

John Buffett of Pitcairn later recollected that American missionaries from Hawai'i had told him that Hill had wanted to stay on in the Sandwich Islands. He seems to have applied to the governor of Maui

---

[139] Bingham, *Selected Writings*, 341–2. See also, W. P. Morrell, *Britain in the Pacific Islands* (New York: Oxford University Press, 1960), 41.

[140] Bingham, *Selected Writings*, 342.   [141] Ibid., 348.

[142] Hiram Bingham, *A Residence of Twenty-One Years in the Sandwich Islands* (New York: Praeger Publishers, 1969), 415.

for a tract of land to call his own on that island only to be turned down.[143] Bingham recorded much the same thing, noting that Hill told Ka'ahumanu that he hoped someday to return to Hawai'i. "I want you to let me have a little spot of ground, and build a small house and live here," he is said to have told the queen regent. "I shall not assent," Ka'ahumanu is said to have replied, for, as Bingham noted "she did not think it safe to pledge him a residence without knowing the capacity in which he should come."[144]

If Buffett and Bingham are correct here, Hill's desire to live out his days in Hawai'i is an interesting turn in his Pacific history for two reasons. First, the story – at least in Bingham's telling – leads us to believe that Ka'ahumanu was far more sophisticated in how she approached and managed this stranger than would be the gullible Pitcairners a few years later. Where they took in a man they had just met and established him as their head of state, Ka'ahumanu held Hill at arm's length. Perhaps even more interesting is Hill's sedentary impulse, his willingness to settle down at Hawai'i, for everything else about his voyage seems pointed towards Pitcairn and his zealous sense of what needed to be done on that island and with its residents. What does seem clear, though, is that Hill relished the influence he had in Hawai'i. As we will see, Hill had tried to influence policymaking about Pitcairn (and the Pacific more broadly) from Liverpool in the years before he began his oceanic travels. Those efforts had come to nothing, so to be heard – indeed, heeded – in Honolulu must have been a heady experience for this cockalorum and his overinflated sense of self-worth.

That Hill felt very comfortable at Hawai'i and was emboldened by his time there comes through in letters he subsequently sent back to London, most from Tahiti after his arrival there in 1831. Between November 1831 and May 1832, Hill wrote no fewer than a half dozen letters from Tahiti – most addressed to Lord Palmerston as the Secretary of State for Foreign Affairs, while others were addressed to the Admiralty. In these letters, Hill offered his bold design for British imperial power in the Pacific. Hill had, he noted, been at sea since June. He had visited South America as well as the Sandwich Islands, and he was now in the Society group. These were valuable islands, and, he noted, "if my humble opinion goes for anything," they would only become more significant as Russia, America, and Britain came to compete for territorial mastery in the Pacific. With that future in mind, Hill articulated some of the major perils facing the region and the British Empire more broadly. Whalers, as we have seen,

---

[143] Buffett, *Twenty Years Residence.*
[144] Bingham, *A Residency of Twenty-One Years*, 420–421.

could be quarrelsome to Pacific Islanders, and Hill was of the opinion that "good laws" were needed in the region, as well as the institutional power to enforce such laws against the invading strength of "between two and three hundred licentious foreigners."[145]

As Hill understood the geopolitical realities, there was no mistaking the fact that the Americans and Russians were "wide awake" to both the Sandwich and Society Island groups.[146] As Douglas Oliver has noted, "the vigorous young United States was pushing its frontiers westward in pursuit of its 'Manifest Destiny' to establish republicanism from the Atlantic to the Pacific and share in the opulent trade of the Far East."[147] Russian fur traders were active in the seal-rich waters of the North Pacific, and the Russian government had sent presents to Kamehameha in Honolulu to secure a modicum of his political favor. And why not? The very idea of the Pacific as a frontier was a potent one.[148] Hill noted that "there is nothing to be compared to [the Hawai'ian Islands] elsewhere." His only wonder was that "they should be so imperfectly appreciated at home."[149] So bold, in fact, was Mr. Hill that he advised the secretary of state for foreign affairs that a British "ship of war perhaps ought to transit these islands more frequently." Hill "humbly conceived" that one ship every three to six months ought to do the trick.[150]

Despite Hill's obvious regard for the evangelical work Bingham was doing in the Hawai'ian Islands, he was worried that the British government was simply ceding the ground there. "In the first place," he wrote in December 1831, "the Sandwich Islands were regularly ceded to Grt. Britain through the late Capt. Vancouver, by their former King & Thus we have actually engaged at least to protect them & hence also they have the British Union Jack together with their eight stripes (the number of Islands) in their flag."[151] To allow the islands to slip into American hands or, worse still, into the chaotic sexual mores of passing sailors was to abandon a relationship that dated back almost forty years.[152]

---

[145] Joshua Hill, Letter to Lord Palmerston (Tahiti: November 20, 1831), TNA FO 58/14. 571. See also, Fischer, *A History of the Pacific Islands*, 101.

[146] John Gascoigne, *Encountering the Pacific in the Age of the Enlightenment* (New York: Cambridge University Press, 2014), 480–481.

[147] Oliver, *The Pacific Islands*, 48.

[148] Bill Schwartz, *Memories of Empire: The White Man's World* (New York: Oxford University Press, 2011), 111.

[149] Hill, Letter to Lord Palmerston (November 20, 1831).   [150] Ibid.

[151] Emphasis in the original. Joshua Hill, Letter to Lord Palmerston (Tahiti: December 12, 1831), TNA FO 58/14.

[152] Hill, Letter to Lord Palmerston (January 13, 1832), TNA FO 58/14.

Denied a permanent home at Maui and yet undeterred, Hill continued on. After all, he had set out to live among and govern the Pitcairnese people in the confined camp created for them at Tahiti, and so, he set sail again. Tahiti, though, brought its own disappointments, as the Pitcairners had already sailed back to Pitcairn by the time Hill arrived at Papeete. The island kingdom of the Pomares was in no small amount of chaos in the late 1820s and early 1830s. That the indigenous political elite on many of the Pacific's islands were "low bred" almost went without saying in Hill's mind, but the Euro-American influence surely ought to be one that improved rather than further denigrated the existing order of things. If Bingham and the American missionaries from the ABCFM had tenuous control in Honolulu, Tahiti was being thinly held together by the Reverend George Pritchard of the LMS. Pritchard, whose missionary responsibilities often required that he sail to other parts of the Pacific to coordinate the LMS's regional efforts, was incapable of being the strong advisor that Queen Pomare IV needed.[153] Pomare, who had succeeded her brother to the Tahitian throne in 1827, was still a teenager, then aged just eighteen or nineteen, when Hill arrived in 1832. As only the fourth monarch in Tahiti's Pomare dynasty, the young queen saw her legitimacy questioned not only by internal political rivals but also by Euro-American crews who passed her island kingdom in hope of experiencing some of the Polynesian magic that had so enchanted the Pacific's Virgilian wanderers since the days of Wallis, Cook, and Bougainville.[154]

These crews, though, brought with them all sorts of complications. Early in 1832, for instance, Captain Miner of the whaling vessel *Venilia* stopped at Tahiti specifically to turn out thirteen members of his crew. The crewmembers in question, it would seem, had refused an order to search for wood on shore on the grounds that the orders had been unnecessarily given on a Sunday and that the ship's regular Sunday provisions had not been distributed as was proper.[155] When instructed that Tahitian law forbade such steps, Captain Miner paid no heed to the assembled chiefs. Subsequent testimony demonstrated that Captain Miner was known to draw his pistol on insolent crewmembers, to swat at his men with his sword, and to buffet them with his fists.[156]

---

[153] Fischer, *A History of the Pacific Islands*, 131.

[154] Ibid., 96. For more on Queen Pomare, see George Pritchard, *Queen Pomare and Her Country* (London: Elliot Stock, 1878).

[155] Queen Pomare IV of Tahiti, Dispatch Sent Via Capt. Robert Fitzroy (Tahiti: December 19, 1832), TNA FO 58/14.

[156] Ibid.

According to documents addressed to the Foreign Office from Queen Pomare herself, it was Joshua Hill who helped assuage some of the tensions involved in this standoff. Through the entire episode, the missionary Pritchard, despite his long years of work at Tahiti, seems to have taken a secondary role in this affair, stepping aside while Hill negotiated between Pomare's court and the sailors from the *Venilia*.[157] Whereas the American missionaries at Hawai'i had gone some way towards ending the chaos in the Sandwich Islands, Tahiti had become, Hill wrote to London, "'the Wapping' of the Pacific."[158] As Hill suggested, "I regret to say that little or no influence is any more possessed by" the LMS at Tahiti, "notwithstanding all that may be said in Austin Friars to the contrary."[159]

Pomare's councilors recorded that Hill advised Captain Miner that "it is not at all agreeable to the Laws of Britain that you should discharge or in any manner turn away your men in a foreign land."[160] Hill suggested that Miner draft a complaint against his mutinous crewmen in order that they might then be interrogated by Pomare's authorities. Were they found guilty, Hill noted, the queen's government could hold them over until they could be properly dealt with by the Royal Navy. Captain Miner refused, leaving his crewmen, Hill, and Pomare in a pinch.

Queen Pomare, in particular, felt the impotence of her British advisor. "We entreat you the British Government," she asked,

> to help us in our troubles, punish this Captain, Captain Miner, and command the owners of the ship to pay us three hundred and ninety dollars for thirteen of their men having been left on our land, and also to send the wages for a native man who was employed to feed the whole ships [sic] company with bread fruit while at anchor here.[161]

Pomare seems to have hoped that the British would comply with her request. She had been a good friend to the British, even accepting the relocated Pitcairners two years earlier.

> We have agreed to the wish of the British Government in receiving the Pitcairn's People, and in giving them land. We wish to live in peace and behave well to the British Flag, which we consider our real friend and special protection.[162]

---

[157] Ibid.
[158] Joshua Hill, Letter to Lord Palmerston (Tahiti: April 5, 1832), TNA FO 58/14.
[159] Emphasis in the original. Hill, Letter to Palmerston (April 5, 1832), TNA FO 58/14.
[160] Queen Pomare IV, Dispatch, TNA FO 58/14.
[161] Queen Pomare IV of Tahiti, Letter to King William IV of Great Britain (Tahiti: January 7, 1832), TNA FO 58/14.
[162] Ibid.

The time had come, though, for London to reciprocate, perhaps even by sending someone to act "as a representative of the King of Britain," perhaps even a man like Captain Hill, "that he may assist us."[163]

H. E. Maude, for one, has been sharply critical of Hill's time in Hawai'i and Tahiti, suggesting that Hill "posed as a person of influence" and "duped" leading Pacific Islanders like Queen Pomare.[164] The queen's own words, though, suggest that there was no real posing or duping involved here. Hill really did have influence; he did serve the queen's interests, and he did offer potential value to her and her control at Tahiti. George Pritchard may actually have had an official imprimatur from the LMS to be at Tahiti, but the man who would eventually be tapped as Britain's consul to Tahiti when that post was created in 1837, was the queen's second choice in 1832.[165]

When Joshua Hill claimed to have been engaged in Euro-American diplomatic affairs in the South Pacific, he was, therefore, telling the truth. Indeed, in as much as he wrote about his plans for the islands of the Pacific (including Pitcairn) to Lord Palmerston and others in high offices, there ought to have been no surprise when Hill seized control of the tiny population at Adamstown in October 1832. Many of his letters from Tahiti, in fact, had indicated that he still had Pitcairn in his mind's eye as he dealt with issues for Queen Pomare. That Hill had received no word back about his actions left him, he concluded, with little else but to hope that "the little I have contributed" (to say nothing of what he had "in contemplation for the Pitcairn's people (where I am abt. going),") would "meet with the perfect approbation of His Majesty's Government."[166]

A good deal of Hill's grandiloquent backstory was, in fact, true. He may not have been a boon companion to princes and kings, but he moved in rarefied circles. He may not have breakfasted with Joseph Banks, but he could count on Banks for a letter of recommendation. He had sailed around the globe with the East India Company. And, he did know influential men like George Pritchard and Hiram Bingham. He advised monarchs and, so he imagined, advanced the interests of the British government in the Pacific.

Joshua W. Hill was not, in short, a simple charlatan. As Lewis Hyde expressed it so well in his analysis of the cultural place and meaning of "tricksters" in literature, history, myth, and culture, the story Hill told was "not exactly true, but it isn't exactly false, either."[167] We cannot

---

[163] Ibid.   [164] Maude, "The History of Pitcairn Island," 70.

[165] Queen Pomare, Letter to King William IV, TNA FO 58.14.

[166] Joshua Hill, Letter to Lord Palmerston (Tahiti: January 12, 1832), TNA FO 58/14.

[167] Lewis Hyde, *Trickers Makes This World: Mischief, Myth, and Art* (New York: Farrar, Straus, and Giroux, 2010. Kindle Edition), 3.

dismiss him, as he might have been called in colloquial Hawai'ian, as merely *pupule*. He was not an imaginant madman. There is more to his story than has met the eye. But, if there is more here than meets the eye, then an entirely new set of questions open up vis-à-vis our enigmatic Mr. Hill. Why, for instance? Why did a man who really had such connections decide that Pitcairn Island ought to be the ultimate target of his "philanthropic tour among the Islands in the Pacific?"[168] Why was Hill so bold about narrating his life's story, particularly given that he was prepared to lie to his target audience at Pitcairn? What did it matter that a British adventurer in Honolulu or Matavai Bay should have been well-connected in London, Boston, or Paris? What did it matter that he had moved among the world's glitterati, that he had rubbed elbows with the rich and noses with the famous? The answer, at a basic level, surely hinges on hubris. Hill was nothing if not self-confident, and his biography was admittedly impressive by almost any standard. He sat at the edge of historical greatness, always just out of the central frame of action enough to miss being recorded in a larger historical narrative. Among the small Euro-American communities of the nineteenth-century Pacific, Hill could almost certainly have counted on his life's story to impress.

Hill's autobiography, therefore, opens up several avenues of historical inquiry. The first is a conversation about historical research and trustworthiness. There is, as I have indicated, no shortage of Pacific histories in which the truth stretched further than it perhaps ought to have done. The narrative of Euro-American imperialism and the sheer scope of the Pacific itself make simple questions about biography very slippery. An Alexander Smith becomes a John Adams. Mutineers become, in practice *and* in name, founding fathers. Perhaps, personal identities were more fluid in the Pacific, and Hill's narrative web of fact and fiction speaks to that movement, for Joshua W. Hill used his Pacific voyage to shape his curriculum vitae in ways that made him the colonial administrator that he imagined he could be and to place him in contexts from which he could administer British imperial policy as he had previously argued that that policy should be administered.

There is still much we do not know about Joshua Hill's biography, and we will have to return later to some of the questions raised by what we do not and cannot know of Captain Joshua Hill. But, Hill's biography also begs questions about Pitcairn Island itself, for Hill targeted that island. He did not land there accidentally. Even as Queen Pomare was offering his name to be the British consul at Tahiti, Hill wrote to the British

<hr />

[168] Hill, Letter to Lord Palmerston (January 13, 1832), TNA FO 58/14, 181.

government that he very much wished to "leave here to visit Pitcairn's Island & to become acquainted respecting their unfortunate state, so soon as I can possibly obtain a conveyance."[169]

Joshua Hill was a British filibuster, a man not unlike those mid-nineteenth-century Americans who traveled into the revolutionary turmoil of Latin America to topple regimes for their own political goals, financial ends, or personal adventure. Now better known as a procedural stalling tactic in the US Senate, the term filibuster in its quasi-colonial sense originated from a Dutch word that meant "freebooter."[170] William Walker was, as Robert E. May has noted, "the most famous filibuster ... the so-called 'gray-eyed man of destiny'," who not only conquered but also ruled Nicaragua in 1856–1857.[171] But, as May has also noted, the nineteenth-century history of American filibustering includes emancipated slaves, railway industrialists, prominent authors, famous politicians, and government spies alongside some of the most famous military men of the Civil War period.[172]

These men, like Hill, were liars, rogues, criminals, and scoundrels. But, also like Hill, they aimed for their targets with care, attention, and planning. They had reasons to do what they did. What was Hill's motive? When he could have become an advisor at Hawai'i or Tahiti, when he had influence among London's political elite and the world's evangelical communities, when he had enough money and the physical stamina to sail around the globe without any institutional support, why did he pick Pitcairn? Here, we can profit from Albert L. Hurtado's study of John Sutter. More famous for his association with the California Gold Rush of the late 1840s, the German-born Swiss native was, in Hurtado's assessment, a filibuster in his own right, "a shadowy transnational" figure, a revolutionary, and an agent provocateur.[173] "Sutter's significance," Hurtado has argued, "extends beyond the boundaries of California and the United States. He is a transnational figure in a transnational world."[174]

---

[169] Hill, Letter to Lord Palmerston (January 13, 1832), TNA FO 58/14, 176.
[170] Robert Houston, "Forward," in William Walker, *The War in Nicaragua* (Tucson: The University of Arizona Press, 1985), 6.
[171] Robert E. May, *Manifest Destiny's Underworld: Filibustering in Antebellum America* (Chapel Hill: University of North Carolina Press, 2002), xii. See also, Noel B. Gerson, *Sad Swashbuckler: The Life of William Walker* (New York: Thomas Nelson, Inc., 1976).
[172] May, *Manifest Destiny's Underworld*, xii.
[173] Albert L. Hurtado, "Frontiers, Filibusters, and Pioneers: The Transnational World of John Sutter," in *Pacific Historical Review* 77:1 (February 2008), 23.
[174] Ibid., 21.

Like John Sutter, Joshua Hill lived a transnational life. Born (most likely) in North America, he traveled to the four quadrants of the globe. He worked for multinational corporations. And, when he entered the Pacific, he was entering a space that was profoundly international. Indeed, given the relative newness of the Kamehameha and Pomare dynasties in Hawai'i and Tahiti respectively, the Pacific was, as David Igler has suggested, arguably *inter*national before it was national.[175] Sailors, whalers, pearlers, and merchants from Britain, France, the United States, and Russia plied the Pacific's waters in these years, even as the national governments in London; Paris; Washington, DC; and St. Petersburg all eyed the region with imperial agendas.

This boisterous community was met by missionaries of many different creeds and professions, men like Bingham and Pritchard who protested the "pernicious influence" that the "pleasure-seeking rabble" had on the Pacific islands and the Pacific Islanders. Often, missionaries found themselves standing up against sailors and merchants from their own homelands, lest those sailors further convert the islands of Oceania into transoceanic "grogshops and brothels."[176] This was a tangled world in which indigenous Pacific island elites and Euro-Americans, whether as merchants or missionaries, forged complex and triangulated alliances in the early nineteenth century – alliances that cut across traditional national or imperial boundaries. When we place Joshua Hill into this world, then, we see that his international and/or global biography would have served him well. Hill had credentials that gave him clout in the Pacific, and he seems also to have had a vision of the Pacific that placed Pitcairn Island squarely in a central position, and it is that vision that merits our attention in the coming chapters.

Our ability to engage with Hill's vision of the Pacific and his strategic understanding of Pitcairn Island hinges, though, on our willingness to look beyond the masquerade he perpetrated. Or, better said, it hinges on our ability to appreciate that there was no masquerade in the first place. True, when he landed at Pitcairn Island on October 28, 1832, Joshua W. Hill was a stranger "in the extremest sense of the word," but he never intended to be a stranger for long.[177] As he had done at

[175] David Igler, "Diseased Gods: Global Exchanges in the Eastern Pacific Basin, 1770–1850," in *American Historical Review* 109 (2004): 693–719. See also, Stuart Banner, *Possessing the Pacific: Land, Settlers, and Indigenous People from Australia to Alaska* (Cambridge: Harvard University Press, 2007), 1.

[176] Arrell Morgan Gibson, *Yankees in Paradise: The Pacific Basin Frontier* (Albuquerque: University of New Mexico Press, 1993), 144.

[177] Herman Melville, *The Confidence-Man*, 9.

Hawai'i and at Tahiti previously, Hill identified himself quickly and effusively, and even if he played free and loose with some of the details of his life's story, much of what he said about himself, about his connections, about his sense of the world and his place in it was true.

2   The Chosen People

> It is as if we find ourselves at the beginning of time. Man and Woman in a natural state ... Born under a beautiful sky, nourished on the fruits of the earth which is fertile without tillage, ruled by patriarchs rather than kings, knowing no other god but love. There is no equivalent paradise in Christendom.
>
> Richard Bean, *Pitcairn* (2014)[1]

High above Pitcairn Island, in the side of a rock face called the Goat House, there is a simple cave known, for as long as anyone can remember, as "Christian's Cave."[2] Nobody has ever had to specify which member of the Christian family is the cave's namesake. In the *sturm und drang* that is the *Bounty* saga, the protagonist is always Fletcher.

Upon first glancing at a map of the island, there is nothing terribly striking about the name "Christian's Cave," for many places at Pitcairn are named for the island's residents or for events that have marked the island's history since the arrival of the *Bounty* in 1790. A quick tour around the island's steeply sloping perimeter cliffs gives us such locations as Robert Fall, Freddie Fall, Where Dick Fall, Tom Off, McCoys Drop, Johnny Fall, Martin Larsoo Fall, Nellie Fall, Break Im Hip, and Oh Dear – names that do little to mask the harsh realities, the dangers, or the risks of a life spent isolated on a South Pacific island.[3] On the island's northwestern corner, just to the west of the settlement at Adamstown (named, obviously, for John Adams, whose name may, as we have seen, actually have been Smith), the Goat House rock looms nearly 1,000 feet above the mazarine waters of the Pacific Ocean. Fletcher Christian's cave is located on the rock's northern face, giving it a spectacular vista over Adamstown and down the island towards Bounty Bay.

---

[1] Richard Bean, *Pitcairn* (London: Oberon Books, Ltd., 2014), 25.
[2] See Birkett, *Serpent in Paradise*, 211.
[3] Ben Fogle, *The Teatime Islands: Journeys to Britain's Faraway Outposts* (London: Michael Joseph, 2003), 204.

In the final three years of his life, from 1790 to 1793, Fletcher Christian climbed the steep rock often to take refuge in the cave. Captain Bligh once noted that Christian was "subject to violent perspirations," particularly across his palms, so much so "that he soils anything he handles."[4] His sweaty palms may well have indicated a naturally nervous disposition, but Christian's behavior at Pitcairn was different. As his companions from the *Bounty* cleared and tilled land, fished, or explored their new island home, Fletcher Christian grew saturnine, positively Ophelian.[5] He alone seems to have needed the long, pensive periods he passed in his stony hideaway.

By nearly all accounts, in these last years of his life, Christian lived alongside demons, haunted by his actions, his fate, and the uncertainty that surrounded his future. Others among the *Bounty*'s crew certainly seemed to be settling down into easy patterns at Pitcairn Island, but not the community's leader. He alone was a crapehanger. "To Christian, his fate must have been awful to contemplate."[6] When he turned picaroon, he had thrown so much away. His promising naval career was gone. Captain Bligh's patronage and support were too.[7] There was little chance that he would ever again see his family, and the Christians were known to be a close-knit clan and well-connected to boot. Pitcairn ought to have been everything Christian could have wanted in a refuge from the law. Already an isolated island as a result of its position in the mid-Pacific Ocean, it had, fortunately for Christian, been incorrectly charted by Captain Carteret.[8] Its steep cliffs were inhospitable barriers to any sensible sea captain who might pass by. It had no autochthonous population with whom to trade and no significant resources to tempt outsiders. Nobody would have had a reason to come to Pitcairn, even if anybody knew where to find it in the first place.

Pitcairn was bespoke for a man on the run and in need of a hideaway. Here was a man who had committed mutiny at sea and lived to tell the tale. He had not been – and would never be – captured, shackled, or tried. As the years slipped away, he might well have been justified in believing that he would never be called upon to pay the price for his nautical crimes against his captain, his king, and his country.[9] Still, Fletcher Christian felt haunted as he secreted himself inside his cave. This island offered shelter, safety, and seclusion. Could it, though, offer redemption?

---

[4] William Bligh, Papers, SLNSW ML MSS Safe 1/43.
[5] Pipon, SLNSW DLMSQ 341. See also, Kennedy, *Bligh*, 98; and Lummis, *Life and Death in Eden*, 86.
[6] Shapiro, *The Pitcairn Islanders*, 17.   [7] See Pipon, SLNSW DLMSQ 341.   [8] Ibid.
[9] Patrick Brantlinger, *Rule of Darkness: British Literature and Imperialism, 1830–1914* (Ithaca, NY: Cornell University Press, 1988), 110 and 121.

For Fletcher Christian, the answer was obviously no. Despite the many myth-like imaginings that chart him a fairytale voyage home and a hidden life in Britain, it seems most likely that Christian was killed in the communal violence that scarred Pitcairn in 1793 and that took the lives of so many of the male inhabitants – white and black – who had arrived on the island with the *Bounty*.[10] John Adams' accounts of Christian's final days, not surprisingly, were only ever vague and contradictory.[11] Today, despite Pitcairn's small size, we do not even know where to find Fletcher Christian's final burial place on the island. He has become in death, what he feared he was in life – lost.

There may have been no room for redemption in Christian's final years, but redemption has been a recurring and prominent theme in the history of Pitcairn Island more broadly. It runs through the reflections that Captains Staines and Pipon of, respectively, the HMS *Briton* and *Tagus* offered when the two British sailors landed on the island early in the morning of September 18, 1814. Staines and Pipon were, we have seen, the first British naval officers to land at Pitcairn since the nine remaining members of the *Bounty*'s mutinous crew in 1790. The people of Pitcairn, watching the two ships sailing sharkishly from the horizon and noting that they flew British flags, could not have known at the time that neither Staines nor Pipon had any knowledge of the settlement there on the island.[12] And so, the mood on the island was fraught.[13] Had these ships come to arrest Aleck, the small community's patriarch? Out of just such concern, as we have noted, the islanders seem to have concocted a biographical disguise to bumfuzzle their guests and to hide Alexander Smith behind the name John Adams.

Still, this was the second time that outsiders had visited Pitcairn since its settlement at the end of the *Bounty*'s epic voyage. The first visit had gone well. With the proper caution, this one might too, and so the Pitcairnese people hailed the arrival of the *Briton* and the *Tagus* with no small amount of fanfare, at least by island standards. Roasted yams, coconuts, fruits, and fresh eggs all appeared on the table. "Old Adams,"

---

[10] Thomas Boyles Murray, *Pitcairn: The Islands, the People, and the Pastor* (London: The Society for Promoting Christian Knowledge, 1860), 113; Wahlroos, *Mutiny and Romance*, 246; and Maxton, *The Mutiny on HMS* Bounty, 33. See also, the collection of newspaper clippings associated with Newspaper Extracts, SLNSW DL MSQ 342.

[11] See, Kennedy, *Bligh*, 253.

[12] Sir Joseph Banks, Letter to an Unknown Correspondent (February 25, 1810), in Sir Joseph Banks, *The Indian and Pacific Correspondence of Sir Joseph Banks, 1768–1820*. Neil Chambers, ed. (Brookfield, VT: Pickering & Chatto, 2013), vii, 476. See also Topliff, "Pitcairn's Island;" and Barrow, *A Description of Pitcairn's*, 246.

[13] See Rosalind Young, Letters to Captain and Mrs. Gibbons (Pitcairn Island: 1882–1891), SLNSW PMB 225, 3–5.

Pipon later recorded, "would have immediately dressed a Hog, but this we declined, time not admitting of our long stay with them."[14] What moved Pipon more than the generosity of the islanders or the delight he took in the simple yet savory meal placed before him at Pitcairn was the islander's decent and honest sense of religion. "They invariably say grace before & after meal & frequently repeat their prayers" *during* the course of eating.[15]

Assisted, no doubt, by newspaper accounts that connected Adams' redemptive work to the heroic *Bounty* narrative, Pipon's image of the islanders as a pious people would become central to the image of Pitcairn that Joshua Hill carried with him on his Pacific voyage, and it would endure even after Hill was removed in 1837.[16] In March 1850, Walter Brodie found himself blown up off Pitcairn's coast by a storm. Together with four other crew from the *Noble*, Brodie would spend some twenty days at Pitcairn before he found passage off the island aboard a passing schooner, the *Colonist*. Of course, Brodie knew of Pitcairn before his accidental landing there, but the stories did not do it justice. It was, he later recorded, "the most moral and religious island in the world." Its inhabitants, furthermore, were "amongst the most kind-hearted, hospitable, and generous islanders ever met with."[17]

History owes Brodie a debt, as it is in his memoir that many of the critical documents about Joshua Hill's time at Pitcairn have been preserved across the years. Brodie's observations about the islanders, though, are hardly unique. Everybody seems to have found Pitcairn to be a religious paradise – the "realization of Arcadia."[18] In 1853, the Reverend W. H. Holman wrote to Admiral Fairfax Moresby, noting that he had "no hesitation in saying that the Pitcairn Islanders are the best, the most simple, moral and naturally kind hearted people I have ever met with or heard of." They had "very deep and sincere religious feelings and nearly all are constant and regular in their attendance at Church."

---

[14] Pipon, SLNSW DL MSQ 341, 4. See also, Andrew Lewis, "Pitcairn's Tortured Past: A Legal History," in Dawn Oliver, ed., *Justice, Legality, and the Rule of Law: Lessons from the Pitcairn Prosecutions* (New York: Oxford University Press, 2009), 39–61; *48*.

[15] Pipon, SLNSW DL MSQ 341, 7. See also, Peard, *To the Pacific*, 76–77. See also, Silverman, *Pitcairn Island*, 145; Moerenhout, *Travels to the Islands of the South Pacific*, 30; and "Descendants of the *Bounty*'s Crew, on Pitcairn's Island," in *The Calcutta Journal, or, Political Commercial and Literary Gazette*, July 20, 1819; Orlebar, *A Midshipman's Journal*, 19; and Lieutenant Edward Belcher, Private Journal and Remarks (December 4, 1825), Te Puna, Turnbull Collection, MS Copy Micro 12; "Pitcairn's Island," extracted from *The Mirror* (1831), in Pitcairn Extracts, SLNSW F999.7/9, 376; and Nicolson, *The Pitcairners*, 71.

[16] "Pitcairn's Island," in *The Sailor's Magazine and Naval Journal* 7:81 (May 1835), 258.

[17] Brodie, *Pitcairn's Island and the Islanders*, 13.

[18] Lummis, *Life and Death in Eden*, 184.

John Adams' pupils, in particular, merited Holman's attention, for their "sincere piety." Indeed, Holman was pleased by the reverential ways that many on the island hailed "the traditional virtue" of their patriarch and cherished "the good seed" he had sown.[19]

This image of Pitcairn was ideal for Christian catechetical purposes, coupling, as it did, moral virtue to a dazzlingly romantic tale. Take the subtitle of N. W. Fiske's *Aleck, and the Mutineers of the* Bounty, for instance: *Thrilling Incidents of Life on the Ocean. Being the History of Pitcairn's Island and a Remarkable Illustration of the Influence of the* Bible.[20] Thrilling adventures on the ocean and *biblical* morality. All found on such a small island! No wonder, then, that children's books were filled with tales of Bligh, the *Bounty*, Christian, John Adams, and Pitcairn Island.[21]

In 1841, Samuel Griswold Goodrich noted that visiting sailors were always "delighted" by what they found at Pitcairn. Writing as "Peter Parlay," Goodrich penned *Tales about the Islands in the Pacific*, a children's book that featured a number of South Pacific islands. The work singled the Pitcairners out as being "happy and virtuous," and it repeated Pipon's observation that they never failed to give "thanks to Heaven," both in the morning and before any meal.[22] Other adventure stories intended for a young audience, works like Robert Michael Ballantyne's *The Lonely Island; or, The Refuge of the Mutineers*, picked up on the same theme. Conjuring an agricultural metaphor that he might have borrowed directly from Holman's letter to Morseby, Ballantyne noted that Adams had sown good seed at Pitcairn, seed that continued "to grow and spread and flourish, bringing forth fruit to the glory of God" as late as the final decades of the nineteenth century. "Thus," Ballantyne concluded, was God able to cause "light to spring out of darkness, good to arise from evil; and the Lonely Island, once an almost unknown rock in

---

[19] Rev. W. H. Holman, Letter to Admiral Fairfax Moresby (June 4, 1853), SLNSW CY 352. For a similar report, see, "Pitcairn's Island," in *The Sailor's Magazine and Naval Journal* 7:81 (May 1835), 260. See also "Pitcairn's Island," extracted from *The Mirror* (1831), in Pitcairn Extracts, SLNSW F999.7/9, 375.

[20] N. W. Fiske, *Aleck, and the Mutineers of the* Bounty; *or, Thrilling Incidents of Life on the Ocean. Being a Remarkable Illustration of the Influence of the Bible* (Boston: John P. Jewett and Company, 1855).

[21] Maria Hack, "The Adventures of Captain Bligh, Part I," in Maria Hack, *Adventures by Land and Sea* (New York: George Routledge and Sons, 1877), 113–166; Maria Hack, "The Adventures of Captain Bligh, Part II," in Maria Hack, *Adventures by Land and Sea* (New York: George Routledge and Sons, 1877), 167–185; and Maria Hack, "Pitcairn's Island," in Maria Hack, *In Land Ice and Deserts* (New York: George Routledge and Sons, 1877), 154–172.

[22] Peter Parley (Samuel Griswold Goodrich), *Peter Parley's Tales about the Islands in the Pacific* (Philadelphia: Thomas, Cowperthwait, and Co., 1841), 73.

the Pacific Ocean, was made a center of blessed Christian influence soon after the time when it became – the refuge of the mutineers."[23]

Redemption indeed!

And, it merits repeating, all of these stories of redemption centered on the probity of John Adams, a known mutineer and, very likely, a liar too. Lieutenant John Orlebar of HMS *Seringapatam* described Adams as "a holy character."[24] Orlebar landed at Pitcairn in 1830, just after Adams' death and was, therefore, witness to the continued esteem that the islanders held for their mutinous patriarch. Adams' grave, Orlebar noted, served as something of a shrine to the Pitcairners and as a reminder that, though his early years had been "sullied by the daring act of mutiny," Adams' "latter days were so usefully, so meritoriously employed" that his life inverted Mark Antony's observation that "The evil that men do, lives after them, / The good is oft interred with their bones."[25]

That Britons like Staines, Pipon, or Orlebar, could overlook such obvious defects in Adams/Smith's character is startling. Not one of these men was a dotterel; they all ought to have seen through the lies. Piety, peacefulness, and faith, though, these became the leitmotifs of Pitcairn's story in the nineteenth century. As David Silverman has observed, Pitcairn's "attraction has been principally that of a superlative yarn or of a dramatic instance of human regeneration through religious devotion." The island's ruthless history has sometimes "been forgotten, for the purpose of arriving at a neat conclusion." The impulse has been to suppress "any oral tradition which may have existed ... in deference to the prevailing picture of an island Eden."[26]

It was in just such a climate that Commodore Francis Mason of HMS *Blonde* wrote a letter from Valparaíso in August 1836 in which he praised John Adams as a noble founding figure for the Pitcairn people. Writing to George Hunn Nobbs, then near the end of his struggle for power with Joshua Hill, Mason suggested that the Pitcairners would have to work to "shew themselves worthy of John Adams."[27] It might have been thought odd that British naval captains and commodores should find in the last surviving mutineer of HMAV *Bounty* a moral exemplar, but in his final years at Pitcairn, Adams/Smith had, Mason felt, hewn closely to "the

---

[23] Robert Michael Ballantyne, *The Lonely Island; or, The Refuge of the Mutineers* (London: James Nisbet and Company, 1880), 413. See also, Sturma, *South Sea Maidens*, 105.
[24] Orlebar, *A Midshipman's Journal*, 16.   [25] Ibid., 22.
[26] Silverman, *Pitcairn Island*, xiii–xxiii.
[27] Commodore Francis Mason, Letter to George Hunn Nobbs (Valparaíso: August 17, 1836), SLNSW ML A 2881.

word of Truth" and proven himself a disciple "of our Blessed Redeemer and sensible of the Mercies [he had] received."[28]

As proof that they were fulfilling their destiny, then, the Pitcairners prayed, and, in addition to prayers before, after, and (sometimes) during mealtimes, the Pitcairners kept the Sabbath as a day of rest.[29] Captain Folger of the *Topaz*, having miscalculated his own calendar during the course of his circumnavigation of the globe, had thrown the islanders' dates off so that they celebrated Sundays on Saturdays, but their commitment to religious observance was, to Pipon's mind, commendable.[30] Armed only with the *Bounty*'s *Bible* and *Prayer Book*, Adams had raised a virtuous flock.[31] Even the children on the island knew the Lord's Prayer and the Creed as set out in the Anglican *Book of Common Prayer*. The observation of Sunday as a day of holy rest was widely noted by those who visited Pitcairn. "If Sunday is still anywhere on the earth a day of true devotion, consecrated completely to the service and the adoration of the Supreme Being, it is certainly so," one guest wrote, "among these so profoundly and so sincerely religious people."[32]

Some suggested that the Pitcairners were almost preternaturally religious. Captain Beechey observed that, during his time at Pitcairn, the islanders never once made a joke or any other sort of "levity" that would cause offense in others. Irony, he reported, "was always considered a falsehood," and the islanders "could not see the propriety of uttering what was not strictly true, for any purpose."[33] Consequently, the islanders took things like the swearing of an oath very seriously. For instance, George Adams, John Adams' son, had long been smitten with Polly Young, but Ms. Young had not reciprocated Adams' passion. Indeed, so averse to a connection was Polly Young that, as a younger woman, she swore she "never would have him as long as she lived." Some years later, Polly Young's feelings changed, but she was no longer sure that she was at liberty to accept George Adams' advances towards her. When Captain F. W. Beechey landed at Pitcairn in the *Blossom* in 1825, the islanders felt

---

[28] Ibid.   [29] Barrow, *A Description of Pitcairn's*, 274–275.

[30] Pipon, SLNSW DLMSQ 341. See also, Bennett, *Narrative of a Whaling Voyage*, i, 39; and Anonymous, *Pitcairn's Island: Being a True Account of a Very Singular and Interesting Colony* (Amherst, MA: J.S. and C. Adams, 1829), 32. See also, "Pitcairn's Island," in *Daily Southern Cross* 6:336 (September 17, 1850), 4.

[31] Society for Promoting Christian Knowledge, Society Work in Pitcairn, 1853, SLNSW MfM M 2091–2111, 52.

[32] Moerenhout, *Travels to the Islands*, 37.

[33] Quoted in "Pitcairn's Island," in *The Mirror* (1831), in Pitcairn Extracts, SLNSW F999.7/9, 378. See also, John Barrow, et al., "Accounts of the Pitcairn Islanders," in *The Journal of the Royal Geographical Society of London* 3 (1833), 158.

compelled to take the matter to him and his crew for moral adjudication.[34]

Religion, thus, governed the daily life of the island and the islanders; faith at Pitcairn was deeply felt and publicly practiced.[35] "They frequently call upon our blessed Saviour," Pipon noted, "saying 'I will rise & go to my Father & will say unto him, Father, I have sinned against Heaven & before thee, & am no more worthy to be called thy son'."[36] This prayerful lamentation, Pipon assumed, had to have been taught to them by Fletcher Christian himself before his murder, as an act of contrition for "the shameful part he had acted both against God & his Country."[37] The prayer, Pipon suggested, was Christian's piacular cry for some small, personal portion of salvation.[38] If Pipon is correct in assuming Christian to have been the prayer's author, perhaps we might imagine that he wrote it while sitting in his small, private cathedra high atop the Goat House.

Captain Pipon's final assessment of these islanders is an important one. "It was truly pleasing," he wrote, "to see that these poor people are so well disposed as to listen attentively to moral instruction & to believe in the divine attributes of God."[39] By any measure, the history that the islanders told Pipon and Staines – or Mayhew Folger, for that matter – was not a happy one. And yet, religion seems to have erased so many crimes, even in "Old Adams," a known mutineer. "There is no debauchery here," Pipon reported, "no immoral conduct ... there is not one instance of any young woman having proved unchaste. The men appear equally moral & well behaved & upon every information there has not appeared any inclination to seduction on the part of the young men." The island was a harmonious place, "no quarrels ever answer except it be occasionally a few words which may pass." This was an island paradise filled, Pipon was happy to record, with a community that was "perfectly honest."[40]

Perfectly?

Pipon's assessment stuck. In 1817, correspondents from the London Missionary Society wrote that Pitcairn offered "an Elysian Picture" of "happy innocence and ignorance of evil." It was a world that lacked the "difficulties and dangers" that complicated missionary life in India and

---

[34] Belcher, Private Journal and Remarks (December 4, 1825).

[35] Ibid. See also, Bruce, Extract from to Lady Troubridge (January 17, 1838), NMM TRO 119/9.

[36] Pipon, SLNSW DLMSQ 341, 7.   [37] Ibid.

[38] See Shapiro, The Pitcairn Islanders, 150.   [39] Pipon, SLNSW DLMSQ 341, 7.

[40] Ibid., 5. Emphasis in the original. See also "A Virtuous Colony – Pitcairn," in Once a Week (July 29, 1865), 147–149, in Pitcairn Extracts, SLNSW F999.7/9.

Africa. The climate was comfortable; there were no idols to knock down.[41] Even twentieth-century historians have echoed this account of the Pitcairners, describing them as "a quiet, inoffensive people, much given to psalm signing and not at all to brawling; there was not a criminal amongst them."[42] Andrew Lewis has gone so far as to describe Pitcairn in the time of Adams as a "Biblical monarchy."[43] As W. K. Hancock assesses things, "John Adams solved every problem of society and government by a complete fusion of morals and politics, of Church and State."[44] James Wolfe, who visited Pitcairn as part of Captain Beechey's 1825–1828 Pacific voyage on the HMS *Blossom*, suggested much the same thing when he identified Adams as "the king of the community" and the rest of the island's population as "his grateful little flock."[45] Still, it wants remembering that there were many an Ananias (and even, perhaps, one or two Sapphiras) on this honest little island. John Adams could not even keep his own name straight, after all.

To be sure, very few ships landed at Pitcairn Island between Captain Folger's 1808 "discovery" and Joshua Hill's landing in 1832. Compared with ports like Honolulu on O'ahu in the Hawai'ian (Sandwich) Islands or Matavai Bay in Tahiti, Bounty Bay was isolated and quiet. It did not take more than a few ships a year, though, to distribute the elaborate narrative about the island and its famous community, this story of a veritable paradise. And, much of that story hinged on the tales told by Aleck Smith and/or John Adams, whose religious fervor, some accounts claimed, had been inspired by a brimstone-filled warning from the Archangel Gabriel himself.[46]

Frederick Debell Bennett, on board the London-based whale ship *Tuscan*, landed at Pitcairn in March 1833, only a few months after the arrival of our Mr. Hill. He was determined to find the redeemed island that he had heard about in legend. He was not disappointed. The natives were, he wrote, "early and well instructed in the pure doctrine of the Christian religion." He could only hope that

---

[41] Mathias Woodmason, Letter to Rev. Josiah Pratt (Dublin: June 21, 1817), in London Missionary Society. Home Incoming Correspondence, SOAS CWM/LMS – Home Incoming Correspondence, Box 3.

[42] Merval Hoare, *Norfolk Island: An Outline of Its History, 1774–1968* (St. Lucia, Queensland: University of Queensland Press, 1969), 70.

[43] Lewis, "Pitcairn's Tortured Past," in Oliver, ed., *Justice, Legality, and the Rule of Law*, 48–51. See also, Anonymous, *L'ils de Pitcairn* (c. 1830), SLNSW ML B803.

[44] Hancock, *Politics in Pitcairn*, 6.

[45] James Wolfe, *Journal of a Voyage in HMS* Blossom, *1825–28*. SLNSW PMB 538.

[46] "Pitcairn's Island," in *The New Zealander* 6:467 (October 5, 1850), 2. See also "A Virtuous Colony," in *Once a Week* (July 29, 1865), in Pitcairn Extracts, SLNSW F999.7/9, 149.

no fanaticism may ever intrude upon their present simple and sensible worship of the Creator, nor the intemperate zeal of enthusiasts give them a bane in exchange for that religion "whose function is to heal and to restore, to soothe and cleanse, not madden and pollute."[47]

There was here, to be sure, a celebration of the Pacific as an exotic paradise, what Melville famously called a "labial melody."[48] There was no sin in Melville's *Typee*. It was a world in which "the penalty of the Fall presse[d] very lightly."[49] As such, and as Patty O'Brien has argued, it is almost possible to tell the entire history of the Pacific – at least as the West has viewed it – on the eroticized bodies of Pacific women.[50] There is also more than a hint of the myth of the noble savage written into these accounts of Pitcairn Island, though Pitcairners complicate that trope. Few (if any) of those who commented on Pitcairn in the early part of the nineteenth century cared one jot or tittle about the Tahitian women who were the island's founding mothers.[51] This was the story of John Adams, the redemptive work he seems to have done in the years after 1800, and the half-English/half-Tahitian offspring of the mutineers who looked to Adams as their patriarch. These were not "savages" in any traditional sense, but neither were they fully British. Indeed, insofar as they *were* British, they were heirs to criminal acts – mutiny, murder, kidnapping. Nowhere in these outside observances of the island, though, do we find the kind of reproof we might expect against a community comprised of the mixed-race descendants of mutineers.[52] In a way that is peculiarly Pitcairnese, then, it was the confluence of the nobility of Tahitian savagery, the exoticism of the South Seas, and the reforming influences of Western Christianity that lifted the descendants of the mutiny from their fathers' criminal pasts, transforming an island that might otherwise have been seen as the last refuge of English scoundrels into its own semi-utopian space – the home of a singular people, the Pitcairners.[53]

---

[47] Bennett, *Narrative of a Whaling Voyage*, i, 38–39.   [48] Melville, *Typee*, 227.
[49] Ibid., 195.
[50] Patty O'Brien, *The Pacific Muse: Exotic Feminity and the Colonial Pacific* (Seattle: University of Washington Press, 2006), 50. See also, Michael Shelden, Melville in Love: The Secret Life of Herman Melville and the Muse of Moby-Dick (New York: Harper Collins, 2016. Kindle Edition), location 488; and Paul Theoux, *The Happy Isles of Oceania: Paddling the Pacific* (New York: Houghton Mifflin Company, 2006), 360.
[51] Robert Landon, "'Dusky Damsels': Pitcairn Island's Neglected Matriarchs of the '*Bounty*' Saga," in *The Journal of Pacific History* 35:1 (June, 2000), 29–47.
[52] Adrian Young, Mutiny's Bounty: Pitcairn Islanders and the Making of a Natural Laboratory on the Edge of Britain's Pacific Empire (Princeton: A Dissertation Presented to the Faculty of Princeton University in Candidacy for the Degree of Doctor of Philosophy, 2016), 75.
[53] Gascoigne, *Encountering the Pacific*, 61.

Central to Pitcairn's miraculous history was its isolation. "From its distance from any other of the islands in Polynesia," Captain Beechey recorded, "Pitcairn's Island is perhaps the most isolated place in the world. To this may be ascribed the gratifying tenacity with which the people preserve their simple virtues and modesty." This modesty, though, was a balancing act. It could be broken. "May the day be far distant," Beechey continued, "when the vices of other nations find their way among" the people of Pitcairn.[54] Frederick Bennett was similarly worried that the Pitcairners' idyllic purity would be lost as they became more and more familiar with the outside world, but by the late 1820s, it was increasingly hard for Pitcairn to ignore that world.[55] Not only were more ships arriving than ever before, though the numbers were still small, Europeans had begun settling at the island. Three Englishmen – George Hunn Nobbs, John Evans, and John Buffett – would, in particular, become central to the story of Joshua Hill's time at Pitcairn.

Though Joshua Hill does not seem to have been aware that the three Englishmen had settled at Pitcairn prior to his own landing, he was aware that the Pitcairners had been relocated to Tahiti in 1830, and he was deeply troubled by the moral implications that exposure to the more cosmopolitan world at Tahiti might have for the simple, decent Pitcairnese people. A smellfungus by nature, Hill was always clear that the removal to Tahiti was a flawed policy on London's part.[56] Many years after the removal, Captain William Driver reflected that the islanders themselves had been worried about London's logic. Driver, the captain of the Salem whale ship *Charles Doggett*, was the man who, for a fee of $500, had carried the Pitcairners home from Tahiti in 1831. Writing from his retirement in Nashville, Tennessee, to his nephew, Driver remembered that the islanders had been despised by the Tahitians. The modest Pitcairners, Driver reflected, had refused to partake in Tahitian dances and celebrations – events that frequently involved nudity, thus putting themselves at odds with the culture of their host island. They assumed an air of superiority, he recalled, and they were hated for it. "Sad little flock," he concluded.[57]

John Orlebar had felt the same way after his visit in 1830. External influences could only harm the innocent world John Adams had nurtured

---

[54] Quoted in "Pitcairn Islanders in 1849," in *Chamber's Edinburgh Journal* (1850), 12, in Pitcairn Extracts, SLNSW F999.7/9.

[55] See Moerenhout, *Travels to the Islands*, 439.

[56] Hill, Letter to Palmerston (April 5, 1832), TNA FO 58/14.

[57] Charles Driver, Letter to His Nephew (Nashville, TN: March 24, 1877), in Whaling Log Books, SLNSW PMB 780. See also William Driver, Logbook and Memoir, SLNSW PMB 39.

at Pitcairn, overwhelming the islanders' purity with "deceitful pleasures" and "the discontent we ourselves feel." These influences "will soon be spread amongst them," Orlebar noted (again picking up on an agricultural metaphor), like a "noxious weed." Once introduced to the island, that weed would certainly "over-run and choak all the useful plants in their mental garden."[58]

The persistence of agricultural metaphors with regard to the moral utopia that was Pitcairn Island was not, we must imagine, accidental. The clear reference to gardens and purity was always intended to remind outsiders that Pitcairn had inverted Biblical chronology. Born in sin, the island had been re-made as a new Eden, just as Alexander Smith had been reborn – if not quite a new Adam then certainly a new man, as "Adams."[59]

We know that Joshua Hill had picked up on this persistent image of Pitcairn as a moral utopia, for he worried about the fate of the islanders in letters he wrote both to evangelical organizations and to the government through the 1820s. In the spring of 1829, for instance, Hill posted a letter to George Hodson, the assistant secretary of the London Missionary Society, in which he seems to have *repeated* an offer from an earlier letter to the society, a letter that is now missing. In both correspondences, Hill seems to have feared the impending death of John Adams, who, by Hill's calculations, had to be nearly seventy-five years old. Others shared Hill's concern. One children's history of Pitcairn dreaded the chaos that might come after Adams' death, observing that "there is reason to fear that there may be on his death a dispute, who shall be first in rank and power, or what shall be the form of their government."[60] What would become of the elysian island and its people upon the death of their mutineer-turned-solon? Moreover, Hill worried, what did Britain stand to lose if it did not seize the potential of this moral paradise? "It is to be feared," Hill argued, that the time was coming near when it would no longer be possible to tap into Pitcairn's moral strength, when the British Empire would no longer be able "to use [Pitcairn] to that advantage, I have so long anticipated, as a school, in furtherance of Native Missionaries, & that too of our own missionaries already ... stationed in the Southern hemisphere of the Pacific Ocean."[61]

As we have seen, the lascivious urges and alcoholic overindulgences of Euro-American whaling fleets made for all sorts of trouble in the

---

[58] Orlebar, *A Midshipman's Journal*, 21.   [59] Kennedy, *Bligh*, 247.
[60] Fiske, *Story of Aleck*, 52.
[61] Emphasis in the original. Captain J. W. Hill, Letter to Mr. George Hodson (Liverpool: May 2, 1829), SOAS CWM/LMS Home Office Extra Box 2. Folder 3/Jacket C.

nineteenth-century Pacific. Tony Ballantyne has observed that historical memory, literature, and the popular imagination remember both Pacific whalers and Pacific sealers "as free-spirited, unrestrained working-class adventurers."[62] Recent scholarship, typically in the Marxist tradition, has reimagined Pacific whalers and sealers through a different lens, one that decentralizes Victorian sensibilities about nineteenth-century respectability. Where the Victorians "saw profligacy as a marker of moral weakness," twentieth- and twenty-first-century reappraisals of whalers and sealers have

framed [them] as antiheroes: men who rejected conventions of restraint, respectability, and religiosity for the egalitarian conventions of a rough and ready mateship grounded in grueling labour and an energetic culture of song, drink, and manly liberty.

Indeed, seen in this light, whalers and sealers become exemplars of a protean postmodernity through "their willingness to cross cultural boundaries and establish interracial relationships."[63] But sealers and whalers left a paltry record compared to the accounts that emerged at the hand of Pacific missionaries, and so the primary sources of information about the Pacific region in nineteenth-century Europe came from those who looked askew at this laboring maritime community.[64] The result was a distinctly negative portrait, one in which European sailors were more a moral vice than an example of virtue.[65]

Not unlike the missionaries, Frederick Bennett's concern was that the behavior of the bibulous and oversexed whalers was not only bad for their own moral future, it had degenerative consequences for Pacific Islanders too.[66] A surgeon by profession, Bennett argued that the indiscriminate consumption of alcohol and lax sexuality had "degraded" the Tahitians near Papeete, leaving them in a "slovenly, haggard, and diseased" state far distant from the idyllic descriptions offered by Captain Wallis upon his initial landing at the island.[67] Descriptions like Bennett's were damaging, in no small part, because Tahiti stood in for the Pacific more broadly in

---

[62] Tony Ballantyne, *Webs of Empire: Locating New Zealand's Colonial Past* (Toronto: University of British Columbia Press, 2012), 126.

[63] Ibid., 126–127. See also, Peter Linebaugh and Marcus Rediker, *The Many-Headed Hydra: Sailors, Slaves, Commoners, and the Hidden History of the Revolutionary Atlantic* (Boston: Beacon, 2000).

[64] Ballantyne, *Webs of Empire*, 129.

[65] M. Woolridge, Letter to an Unidentified Recipient (June 18, 1849), Te Puna, MS-Papers-1009–2/51.

[66] Tom Hiney, *On the Missionary Trail: A Journey Through Polynesia, Asia, and Africa with the London Missionary Society* (New York: Grove Press, 2000), 119.

[67] Moorehead, *The Fatal Impact*, 89.

these years; it acted as a metonym for every Pacific island.[68] And Bennett was not alone in judging Tahiti harshly. Joshua Hill, as we have seen, felt that Tahiti was the South Sea's grogshop, "the Wapping of the Pacific."[69] To have moved the Pitcairners there in 1830 was a crime, if not a moral sin. The relocation had, to quote Susanne Chauvel Carlsson, "robbed the little community of some of its innocence and undermined its stability."[70] Both the virtue and the potential of this small island and its small population, Hill suggested to the London Missionary Society, "have hitherto [been] looked upon with rather too much luke warmness, if I may be permitted thus to speak."[71] Hill's suggestion that the LMS and others had overlooked the Pitcairners may, though, have overstated the difference between his position and theirs for dramatic effect. In point of fact, many agreed with his arguments about the ill effects of Tahiti on the Pitcairners, and it was missionary subscriptions that, by and large, helped to fund the costs of the islanders' return to Bounty Bay.[72]

Furthermore, problematic sailors seemed to come from nearly every Western nation.[73] As we have seen, Joshua Hill's (probable) editorial essay in *The Morning* Post from 1811 had argued that a strong naval power had to be "jealous" of its strength relative to competitors.[74] That the encroachments against British power in the Pacific were morally as well as strategically dangerous only served to make matters worse, suggesting that Hill's earlier reflections, which were simply geostrategic in nature, only grew more enflamed when coupled to the evangelical passions he came to display by the 1820s.

Writing to George Canning in London from the Hawai'ian Islands in October 1826, Richard Charlton, then the British consul at the Society, Sandwich, and Friendly Islands, agreed with many of Hill's concerns. Indeed, Charlton noted that English whalers were, sadly, not immune from the bad behavior that marked sailors from other nations. All of these men, he wrote, "occasion a great deal of trouble," and the sexual freedoms on Pacific islands did little to promote the rule of law on board passing ships. Indeed, Pacific women and indigenous tavern

---

[68] Gavin Daws, *A Dream of Islands: Voyages of Self-Discovery in the South Seas* (New York: W.W. Norton and Company, 1980), 4.

[69] Hill, Letter to Lord Palmerston (April 5, 1832), TNA FO 58/14.

[70] Carlsson, *Pitcairn Island*, 39.

[71] Hill, Letter to Mr. George Hodson (May 2, 1829), SOAS CWM/LMS, Home Office Extra Box 2, Folder 3/Jacket C.

[72] Maud, "The History of Pitcairn Island," 69. See also, Driver, Logbook and Memoir, SLNSW PMB 39; Driver, Letter to His Nephew (March 24, 1877), SLNSW PMB 780; and Lewis, "Pitcairn's Tortured Past," in Oliver, ed., *Justice, Legality, and the Rule of Law*, 52.

[73] Dodge, *Islanders and Empires*, 69.   [74] "On Naval Power."

keepers, Charlton thought, were often "the inducements for men to desert."[75] In Tahiti, some of the earliest law codes targeting licentious Europeans predate the arrival of the missionary William Ellis and his printing press in 1817.[76] Chiefs at the Hawai'ian Islands had worked since the 1820s to keep these tosspots off their islands, and they had leaned on European missionaries to help them in the task.[77] In March 1822, the Kamehameha monarchy promulgated "Some Laws for the Port of Honoruru, O'ahu," the first printed law code in Hawai'ian history. The code itself was vague, though, and it lacked the enforcement mechanisms required to hold bacchant sailors at bay. Some of the visiting Europeans went so far as to question whether the local chiefs had the authority to issue laws regarding European behavior, and riots erupted on the islands between 1825 and 1827, as more and more Western sailors pressed for access to spirits and sex.[78]

In Hawai'i, as elsewhere in the Pacific, missionary establishments were crucial to the kind of work the Kamehamehas were doing to assert their sovereignty. Captain John (Mad Jack) Percival of the US naval schooner *Dolphin* felt compelled to stand up to the missionaries on behalf of his crew of Lovelaces. So convinced was Percival that it was the missionaries at Hawai'i who were to blame for the 1822 law code that he threatened to "beat the head" of Hiram Bingham if the prohibition on sexual trafficking was not rescinded.[79] Unlike Tahiti or Hawai'i, where missionaries had strong footholds, Pitcairn wanted a missionary presence in the 1820s and 1830s. The only redemptive force it had was the indigenous faith sown by Adams between 1800 and his death in 1829. In his letters to the London Missionary Society of the late 1820s, Joshua Hill made it quite certain that he felt Pitcairn needed the direct protection of a missionary society.[80]

Hill was not alone in supporting missionary activity in the Pacific. Charles Darwin defended missionary work in the region. His first published work was, in fact, a defense of the London Missionary Society.[81] Sailors, Darwin had to confess, could not stand missionaries or their

---

[75] Richard Charlton, Letter to George Canning (October 4, 1826), TNA FO 58/4. See also, Memorandum (January 1, 1837), TNA FO 58/15; and John Bidwell, Letter to George Pritchard (London: February 14, 1837), TNA FO 58/15.

[76] Thomas, *Islanders*, 104.

[77] Caroline Ralston, *Grass Huts and Warehouses: Pacific Beach Communities of the Nineteenth Century* (St. Lucia, Queensland: University of Queensland Press, 2014. Kindle Edition), location 532.

[78] Beechert, *Honolulu*, 48–50. See also, Campbell, *A History of the Pacific Islands*, 78.

[79] Beechert, *Honolulu*, 49–50. See also James L. Haley, *Captive Paradise: A History of Hawai'i* (New York: St. Martin's Press, 2014. Kindle Edition), location 1851 of 7968.

[80] Hill, Letter to Mr. G. Hodson (May 2, 1829), SOAS CWM/LMS Home Office, Extra Box 2, Folder 3/Jacket C.

[81] Liebersohn, *The Travelers' World*, 273–275.

meddlesome morality. But, any sailor who found himself shipwrecked on a South Pacific island would, he noted, "certainly pray that the islanders had already received missionaries."[82] Not everyone, though, was as certain that missionaries were called for among the islands of the Pacific. Robert Louis Stevenson was deeply suspicious of missionary activity in the Pacific when he arrived in the region in the 1880s.[83] More suspicious still was Herman Melville who famously lamented that South Pacific Islanders were "ill-fated people" in his first novel, *Typee*. "I shudder when I think of the change a few years will produce in their paradisiacal abode," he wrote, particularly citing the arrival of Christianity as a blight. "Heaven help the 'Isles of the Sea!' – The sympathy which Christendom feels for them has, alas! in too many instances proved their bane."[84]

If Pitcairn wanted for missionary fortifications, it did not lack prejudicial outside influences. Of course, the entire removal to Tahiti in 1830 had exposed the Pitcairners to the broader world there, and it was not surprising to those, like Hill, who were concerned about the fate of the islanders that nearly two dozen of the eighty-seven who had been evacuated from Pitcairn died during their brief sojourn at Tahiti.[85] More locally, though, Pitcairn had its own distinctive problem with outsiders, a problem that dated back to the arrival in 1823 of a whaling ship known as *Cyrus*.

Nearly every image of Pitcairn's idyllic purity hinged on John Adams and his tiny flock, that insolated community, but from 1823 onwards, Pitcairn was not only home to Adams' Pitcairnese people.[86] It had, rather, played host to a growing number of English residents. By the time Mr. Joshua W. Hill landed at Pitcairn on October 28, 1832, three Englishmen – John Buffett, John Evans, and George Hunn Nobbs – were living full-time on the island.

Though Buffett, Evans, and Nobbs – like Hill himself – were all Englishmen living at Pitcairn, Joshua Hill's most persistent description of the three men was to call them "foreigners" or, worse still, "lousy foreigners."[87] That he too was an Englishman at Pitcairn and so no more an "insider" at the island than this triumvirate he so reprehended, Hill seemed not to notice. But, who were Buffett, Evans, and Nobbs?

---

[82] Quoted in Hiney, *On the Missionary Trail*, 74.   [83] Daws, *A Dream of Islands*, 193.
[84] Melville, *Typee*, 195. See also, Liebersohn, *The Travlers' World*, 295.
[85] See, Driver, Logbook and Memoir, SLNSW PMB 39, and Spruson, *Norfolk Island*, 26.
[86] John Buffett, Diary Kept on Norfolk Island and Pitcairn Island, 1856–1892. SLNSW ML PMB 123.
[87] Quoted in Brodie, *Pitcairn's Island and the Islanders*, 183. See also, Alan S. C. Ross and A. W. Moverley, *The Pitcairnese Language* (New York: Oxford University Press, 1964), 71.

What shaded backstory brought them to tiny Pitcairn Island – an island that seems to have invited mysterious visitors?

History gives us more information on John Buffett and George Hunn Nobbs than it does John Evans.[88] In an 1845 publication entitled *Twenty Years Residence on Pitcairn's Island*, John Buffett narrated his own life's journey. To be quite certain, we have to take care with this document. As with the pieces of biography that Joshua Hill has left us, Buffett's story merits a great deal of detective work and a suspicious reader. Like Hill's, Buffett's account of his past is replete with heroic encounters, dramatic moments, and romantic yarns. A real-life Robinson Crusoe, Buffett claims to have had the bad luck to have been shipwrecked not once but twice in the years between 1815 and 1820.

Despite his earlier misfortunes at sea, Buffett again took ocean passage – this time on an American ship destined for Canton – in 1821. A typhoon crippled the vessel near Manila, where Buffett booked passage on another ship, this time to Chilé, though Buffett disembarked on the coast of California from whence he joined the whale ship *Cyrus* out of London under the command of Mr. John Hall. By October 1823, the *Cyrus'* hull was filled to near bursting by its haul of whale oil, and so the vessel pulled in for one last stop at O'ahu before charting a course homewards to London. Along that passage, Hall stopped at Pitcairn, and the island seems to have captured Buffett's imagination from the outset. "The inhabitants being in want of some person to teach them to read and write," Buffett records, "the Captain asked me if I should like to remain there. I told him I should, and was discharged and went on shore."[89]

Whether we believe the fables that Buffett spun about his earlier life seems immaterial here. What is interesting is the parallel between Hill's life and Buffett's, and between their arrivals at Pitcairn. As will be the case with George Hunn Nobbs, both Hill and Buffett arrived at the famous little island with the intention of being teachers and community leaders. Both told elaborate stories about their past that, true or not, served to enhance their power, prowess, and prestige in the community at Adamstown. True, Buffett made no claim to have governmental permission to rule at Pitcairn, a lie that is unique to Hill's story, but the pretense to influence and the willingness to abrogate control on both men's part suggest that Joshua W. Hill may not be the only Hogen-Mogen ever to climb the Hill of Difficulty upwards from Bounty Bay.

---

[88] Maxton, *The Mutiny on HMS* Bounty, 40.

[89] Buffett, *Twenty Years Residence*. See also, Lewis, "Pitcairn's Tortured Past," in Oliver, ed., *Justice, Legality, and the Rule of Law*, 51. For another rendering of Buffett's story, see Murray, *Pitcairn*, 201–202.

John Evans' arrival at Pitcairn is somewhat less clear than either Hill's or Buffett's. In his account of the arrival of George Hunn Nobbs at Pitcairn in 1828, Buffett makes a quick reference to Evans as "an Englishman who came in the ship with me and was married to A.'s (John Adams') daughter."[90] Surely this is a rather quick and unrevealing bit of information about the second of the only two immigrants to Pitcairn Island since 1790! Rosalind Amelia Young sheds, perhaps, a bit more light onto Evans' arrival on the island. Evans, she records, was a "great chum of" Buffett's from the *Cyrus*, who, "for love of Buffett," stowed "himself away in some hollow tree" on the island, thereby self-marooning himself at Pitcairn.[91] Young was born into the fourth post-*Bounty* generation, a direct descendant of Fletcher Christian. Her narrative accounts of life both at Pitcairn and Norfolk Islands constitute some of the most important historical material we have relative to this history.

Lady Diana Belcher, *née* Jolliffe, offers a bit more backstory on Evans' life in her book *The Mutineers of the Bounty and their Descendants in Pitcairn and Norfolk Islands*. Belcher, the wife of Admiral Edward Belcher, was the stepdaughter of Peter Heywood, one of the *Bounty* men who remained at Tahiti when Fletcher Christian sailed away for the last time and were, subsequently, found and imprisoned by Captain Edwards on board the *Pandora*. In her telling, Evans was the son of a coach-maker from Long Acre and "a worthy and an educated man." But, her account of Evans' arrival hardly matches the stories told by Buffett and Young, as she states quite clearly that Evans arrived at Pitcairn several years after Buffett aboard another, unnamed vessel.[92] Lady Belcher's account differs not only from Young's but also from that of her husband, who observed that Pitcairnese legend recorded that Evans had hidden in the bushes to avoid being taken back on board the *Cyrus*. He would have been found, though, had it not been for a storm that made it impossible to search the island for the missing sailor.[93] Even listening to those whose firsthand and family connections suggest that they ought to offer us insight into this history, we find that we know everything about Pitcairn even as we know nothing about it at all.

George Hunn Nobbs is recorded as one of the great heroes in the epic story of the Pitcairn islanders, first at Pitcairn and, later, at Norfolk Island. Because he rose to prominence at Pitcairn – indeed, his status as the

---

[90] Buffett, *Twenty Years Residence*.
[91] Young, Letters to Captain and Mrs. Gibbons, SLNSW PMB 225, 5.
[92] Belcher, *The Mutineers of the* Bounty, 182–183.
[93] Lieutenant Edward Belcher, Private Journal and Remarks from the HMS *Blossom* on Discovery during the year 1826. Te Puna, Turnbull Collection, MS Copy Micro 12 and MSX-8774.

pastor, teacher, and leader at Pitcairn eventually won him an audience with Queen Victoria and Prince Albert – and led the tiny community's removal to and successful plantation at Norfolk Island in 1856, Nobbs is often lionized. In 1850, the *Daily Southern Cross* proclaimed that George Nobbs' landing at Pitcairn was "one of the lucky chances in the history of Pitcairn Island."[94] Historian Harry Shapiro has agreed, calling Nobbs' arrival "a momentous event in the colony's history."[95] An entry on his life appears in both the Australian and British *Dictionary of National Biography*.[96] Nobbs' pre-Pitcairn story, though, is as much a biographical farrago as is Joshua Hill's.

By all accounts, Nobbs landed at Pitcairn on October 28, 1828 – four years to the day before Hill's arrival there, a coincidence of mythological (if otherwise unimportant) proportions. Interestingly, John Buffett's account of the arrival does not even spell out Nobbs' full name. More significant to Buffett, then functioning as an assistant to the aging John Adams, was the arrival of Captain Noah Bunker. Bunker and Nobbs seem to have been the only two aboard the twenty-ton sloop that carried them to Pitcairn in 1828. Bunker was sick when they arrived, and Nobbs was employed as the ship's mate.[97] But, who were these two men? How had they managed this vessel all on their own and over such a great distance? Whose boat was it? Where had they come from? Why?

Within weeks of landing at Pitcairn, whatever ailed Bunker grew worse. According to Buffett, Bunker managed to creep away from the islanders who were tending to him one night. In a fit of either despair or pain – we know not which – he walked to one of the island's many cliffs and jumped – not once, but twice. Initially, it seems, Bunker had hoped to dash his head against a rock protruding from the ledge from which he had plunged. Missing the rock, Bunker landed halfway down the cliff on a lower ledge. He then sprattled his way to the hill's edge and tossed himself the rest of the way down the cliff, some 100 feet in all. Through all of this, all Bunker managed was a broken arm and a broken leg. It took the islanders some hours to find him, and when they did, he was Byronic, imploring his hosts either to kill him or to carry him to another cliff so that he could toss himself into the sea. Instead, the Pitcairners carried the shattered visitor to a nearby house and attempted to set his broken bones. Bunker was supplied with laudanum obtained from a passing whaling vessel to ease his pains, but after convincing a young boy who had been placed in his room as an attendant to leave the bottle near his bedside,

---

94 "Pitcairn's Island," in *Daily Southern Cross* (September 17, 1850), 4.
95 Shapiro, *The Pitcairn Islanders*, 72.   96 Nobbs, *George Hunn Nobbs*, 1.
97 Buffett, *Twenty Years Residence*. See also, Pitcairn Registrar, SLNSW DLMSQ7, CY 294; and Silverman, *Pitcairn Island*, 113–116.

Bunker drank the entire flask of the opioid and finished his suicidal mission.[98]

The tale of Noah Bunker's brief history at Pitcairn Island is easily one of the most mysterious and inexplicable episodes in Pitcairnese history, and as we have seen, the mysterious and inexplicable seem to constellate at Pitcairn Island. There is no historical record to track and, thus, no way to know more about Captain Bunker. Had he and Nobbs come by their sloop honestly, as part of a sealing voyage gone wrong, as he claimed? Or had they stolen the vessel?[99] What made them decide upon Pitcairn once they had the vessel?[100] His is a small part in this drama; he has only a few lines to speak. George Nobbs did not help matters, either, when he seized many of Bunker's papers after the latter's death and burned them.[101] But, as the adage would have it, even the smallest role in a drama has its importance, and Noah Bunker's Cimmerian part is noteworthy, for it casts a long shadow over the narrative of one of our other major players, the Reverend George Hunn Nobbs.

According to Thomas Murray, George Hunn Nobbs was born in Ireland in 1799. Murray's biographical sketch suggests that Nobbs went to sea as a youngster, joining the crew of HMS *Roebuck* in 1811. Nobbs' first trip to the South Pacific, according to Murray, came at the age of fourteen on board the *Indefatigable*. Having served in the navy for five years, Nobbs came into possession of a small craft of his own at the age of seventeen. He seems to have sailed this craft to South America, where he served as something of a naval mercenary in the confused conflicts that marked the collapse of Spain's empire.[102] If Murray's biography is to be believed, Nobbs had circumnavigated the globe four times by the time he landed at Pitcairn in 1828. He would have been twenty-nine years old at the time.[103]

Thomas Boyles Murray was an Anglican cleric and an active member of the Society for Promoting Christian Knowledge. In nineteenth-century Britain, the society was deeply interested in the story of Christian redemption that seemed to wash up at Pitcairn's shores as readily as did the waters of the Pacific. In time, Murray would become one of George Nobb's most ardent supporters as well as his close friend. The connection raises serious questions about the objectivity of the biography that Murray weaves in his 1860 work *Pitcairn: The Island, the People, and the Pastor*. Indeed, the entire impulse of the work is to frame Nobbs as a second founding father to the Pitcairn people, a second

[98] Buffett, *Twenty Years Residence*. See also, Nicholson, *The Pitcairners*, 101–104.
[99] Macklin, *Dark Paradise*, 215.   [100] Nobbs, *George Hunn Nobbs*, 11.   [101] Ibid., 12.
[102] Brown, *Adventuring through Spanish Colonies*.   [103] Murray, *Pitcairn*, 170–176.

Adams, almost as if Nobbs' time at Pitcairn functioned as the island's New Testament to the Old Testament legends that surrounded John Adams.[104]

Raymond Nobbs' more contemporary biography lacks the hagiographic thrust of Murray's book, but it is hardly a disinterested account, as the book's subject is the book's author's great-great-grandfather. Still, neither Murray nor Nobbs can dispel the obscurity of George Nobbs' background. Raymond Nobbs records that his ancestor told the Pitcairners stories about his illegitimate parentage. He was, he claimed, the unacknowledged son of Francis Rawdon Hastings, the first Marquis of Hastings and second Earl of Moira.[105] In a letter to Lord Edward Russell, written from Pitcairn, Nobbs himself outlined this background. His mother, Jemima Ffrench, was the daughter of an Irish Baronet who had become tangled in the Irish Rebellion and left Ireland for France. On her deathbed, Ffrench confessed to her son that he was the offspring of a liaison she had had with Francis Rawdon. She had never accepted anything from her lover for the support of young George Hunn. Ffrench was adamant that her son should never seek help from his father's family; indeed, she was even more certain that only in seeking a life outside of Britain could George find a life free from the taint of his birth.

Towards the end of her life, Ffrench became smitten with the stories that her son told her of Pitcairn, and, he claimed, her last words to him before her death in 1822 were "Go to Pitcairn's Island, my Son, dwell there and the blessing of God rest upon you."[106] Here, as elsewhere in our narrative, there is an obviously affected sense of the dramatic. Ffrench's deathbed instructions to her son are as onerously predictive as the prophecy given to Laius by the Oracle at Delphi. It would be hard to make a story like this one up, though it is easy enough to believe that this is exactly what George Hunn Nobbs did. Whether the story is true or not, though, is not important. What matters here is that Nobbs honored his mother's "request," departing England in 1826 and arriving at Pitcairn two years later.

Was George Hunn Nobbs really descended from nobility on both his mother and his father's sides? John Orlebar of the HMS *Seringapatam* suggested that "there was a mystery that hung over [Nobbs'] appearance and character, which I think would hardly bear scrutinizing."[107] To ask these sorts of questions, of course, smacks of salacious gossip, and it would be were it not that so much of this history more generally hinges

---

[104] Shapiro, *The Pitcairn Islanders*, 27. See also, Maxton, *The Mutiny on HMS* Bounty, 38.
[105] Nobbs, *George Hunn Nobbs*, 7.   [106] Nobbs Papers, SLNSW ML A 2881, 139–140.
[107] Orelbar, A Midshipman's Journal, 20.

upon who is telling the truth and who is weaving a yarn. Like Joshua Hill, Nobbs arrived at Pitcairn with a story that spoke to his credentials, his ability to connect the island and the islanders to networks of power back in London. He rose to prominence in no small measure because of these claims; indeed, as we will see, he supplanted Buffett as the island's likely heir to John Adams, just as Hill would push Nobbs from power upon his arrival in 1832.[108] Hill, though, has gone down in history as a footnote to the Pitcairn story – a crank, a scapegrace, a bankster, and a fraud. Nobbs' reputation has faired much better. But if his story was fabricated too . . . ?

We will probably never know the true story of Nobbs' parentage or background. Like Hill's, Nobbs' is "an Alexander Dumas tale," and also like Hill's, it is a story marked by "several apparent irregularities."[109] It is a suggestive enough list of similarities that Raymond Nobbs is forced to ask whether his great-great grandfather suffered "from the same pretentiousness that characterized his later opponent."[110] It is a list of similarities that begs us to pay more attention both to Nobbs' background and, more significantly here, to Hill's Pitcairnese purposes than we have done thus far. It is a list that suggests that there is more to the story than has previously met the eye.

If the theatrical tale of Joshua Hill's time in the South Seas needed a deus ex machina, Jacque Antoine Moerenhout is it. Born in 1796, Moerenhout was a French national from birth because he was native to a *département* in Belgium that had been annexed one year earlier in 1795. Moerenhout served in the French army in the final months of Napoleon's regime, but he also seems to have fought in South America on behalf of the various independence movements there, movements that, as we have seen, also attracted British wanderers in these years. In South America, Moerenhout found subsequent (and safer) work as the secretary to the French consul at Valparaíso before wandering off yet again, this time to build up trading connections for himself throughout the islands of the Pacific. As a merchant, Moerenhout traveled the South Seas widely, developing a reputation in the region as an adventurer.[111] His connections among the people of the Pacific were widely recognized as valuable, and, oddly enough, Moerenhout was tapped by the United States to serve as its consul to Tahiti in 1835. As we will see, Moerenhout's pro-Catholic positions at Tahiti strained his relationship with British missionaries at the islands and put him at cross-purposes with America's Protestant

---

[108] Nobbs, *George Hunn Nobbs*, 7.   [109] Ibid., 8.   [110] Ibid., 9.
[111] Edward Dodd, *The Rape of Tahiti* (New York: Dodd, Mead, and Company, 1983), 93–94.

missionary establishment. Washington removed Moerenhout as the American consul less than a year after making the appointment.[112]

Because his favorable views of Catholic missionary work in the Pacific sat better in Paris than they did in either London or Washington, DC, Moerenhout's status continued to carry weight with French leaders. As did Joshua Hill vis-à-vis British power in the Pacific, Moerenhout argued that France needed to be more assertive about claiming territories in the world's largest ocean. In 1842, it would be Moerenhout who pushed Admiral Dupeit-Thouars to move on the French annexation of Tahiti, a decision that saw Moerenhout returned as consul to the island, this time answering to Paris instead of DC.[113]

Later in his life, J. A. Moerenhout would be promoted first to the French consular office at Monterrey in California, then still Mexican territory, and subsequently to San Francisco in the years surrounding the great Californian Gold Rush. For this old Pacific adventurer, the flutter that surrounded the lucrative discoveries made under and around rickety sawmills like that owned by John Sutter was the last chapter in a long life that often reads like pulp-adventure fiction more than historical biography. Though Moerenhout's memoirs were not widely read in nineteenth-century Britain (they were not translated into English until well after their initial publication), we do know that they were popular in France. One of Moerenhout's greatest admirers was the artist Paul Gauguin.[114] The artists' friends lent Gauguin copies of Moerenhout's 1837 work, *Voyage aux îles du Grand Océan*, and the book captivated the painter with its sense of adventure and romanticism, inspiring his departure from Europe for a life spent apricating on the sunny shores of the South Pacific.

Paris transferred Moerenhout one last time, in this instance back south to its new consular office in Los Angeles. Moerenhout would retire from that office in 1879. He died and was buried there in the summer of 1879 at the age of eighty-three. Other than as a footnote in Gauguin's biography, Moerenhout has been lost to history. In our adventure, though, *Voyage aux îles du Grand Océan* happens to be one of the best sources of information we have about Pitcairn in the epoch of Joshua Hill.

---

[112] William Richards, Letter to Rev. W. Ellis (Northampton: October 5, 1837), in SOAS CWM/LMS Incoming Correspondence – South Seas – 11A, Folder 3/Jacket A; and William Ellis, Letter to Lord Palmerston (November 24, 1837), TNA FO 58/15. See also, Ralston, *Grass Huts and Warehouses*, location 1921.

[113] Campbell, *A History of the Pacific Islands*, 85; Newbury, *Tahiti Nui*, 78; and Morrell, *Britain in the Pacific Islands*, Chapter Four.

[114] Silverman, *Pitcairn Island*, xxi.

Like others who arrived at Pitcairn in the 1820s and 1830s, Moerenhout entangled himself in the myth-making that was central to the island in these years. He was always "most anxious" to visit Pitcairn. The islanders practiced "Christian virtues" with such devotion that one would be hard-pressed to find a more pious community "in any other point of the globe."[115] Pitcairn, once again, was a singular place. "Nowhere have I ever seen the like. I thought I was dreaming," Moerenhout recorded.[116]

In our story, though, Moerenhout acts the part of Virgil or Beatrice in Dante's *Divine Comedy*. He is our observer and guide to this history. We see a great deal more as a result of the impressions he left. We see more because he shows us the way through. For his part, Moerenhout first arrived at Pitcairn in 1829, only a few months after Noah Bunker and George Hunn Nobbs landed at the island, and the addition to the population had disturbed the place. On the surface, Pitcairn was still a paradise. Pitcairn was a place of "extreme beauty." The men were strong, the women lissome. The young were, Moerenhout wrote, extremely striking, "not a single one of [them] had the least deformity."[117] Of Nobbs and Bunker, though, Moerenhout was unequivocal. "There is something mysterious in these two strangers, and I feel indeed that their visit may be fatal to the good inhabitants of Pitcairn."[118]

Seemingly something of a Paul Pry, Moerenhout asked of Nobbs and Bunker all the same questions that we have asked. Indeed, like us, he was astonished at the naïf-like simplicity of the islanders, at these people who treated "strangers whom they had never seen before with this ease, this affability which was even rather familiar."[119] Nobbs refused to offer any answer as to why he had come to Pitcairn, a question Moerenhout put to him on a number of occasions.[120]

During his first encounter with Nobbs, Moerenhout made his opinions crystal clear. "I didn't have too good an opinion of him and his sick comrade."[121] To be certain, the small communal nature of existence at Pitcairn made it impossible for the outsiders to avoid one another. Nobbs and Moerenhout dined together, and the Frenchman was able to watch as Nobbs, from early on, joined the Pitcairners in their religious practices. At the table, Nobbs took it upon himself to say grace before the meal, though, Moerenhout observed

with closed eyes and a lamentable tone in which I believe without slander there was some little affection and pharaseeism. The good people of Pitcairn thought him a saint; may heaven bring it about that they are not much in error![122]

[115] Moerenhout, *Travels to the Islands*, 16.   [116] Ibid., 30.   [117] Ibid., 20.   [118] Ibid.
[119] Ibid., 23.   [120] Ibid., 24 and 29.   [121] Ibid., 29.   [122] Ibid., 28.

The two men conversed, as well, sometimes on the esteemed nature of the Pitcairnese people. "Isn't it true, sir," Nobbs once inquired of Moerenhout, "that people, if they knew these worthy people of Pitcairn, would want to share their happiness?" Sensing that Nobbs' line of questioning ran towards the permanent settlement of outsiders at Pitcairn, Moerenhout responded carefully, even curtly.[123] The same question would arise between the two men when Moerenhout returned to Pitcairn some months later, after the death of John Adams and the suicide of Noah Bunker. Bunker's death was unremarkable; Adams' was "an irreparable loss for this virtuous people who, from this time," Moerenhout predicted, "will be laid open like a flock without its shepherd to the rage of devouring wolves."[124]

For the first time, we see talk of fissures in Adams' island kingdom. Nobbs, Moerenhout reports, had stepped in to preach and say prayers for the island's congregation in Adams' place. Buffett, meanwhile, staking a claim against his longer residence on the island, set himself up for the same purposes in another of the island's houses. A crisis of leadership had begun at Adamstown, and though the conflict was as of yet only a *sitzkrieg*, more open hostilities were soon to follow. The situation was critical, and the problem was obvious. Outsiders. Foreigners. Pitcairn could not accommodate the worldly pressures placed upon it by the arrival of these men. When faced with this challenge, when asked whether he might consider giving up the island and returning to the outside world, Nobbs refused to play the spaniel. He had, he insisted, "come expressly to live with these people, he would only leave when he was compelled by force."[125]

Thus began a new chapter in Pitcairn's history. The insistent rhythm was still there. This was a perfect, island paradise. But, now, the question was whether or not the perfection could be maintained. Would the presence of a new, non-Pitcairnese generation of leadership change the place? Could Nobbs, Moerenhout wondered, "who was not lacking in talent and who even appeared to have a very gentle character, be at all sincere?"[126] As Jacques Antoine Moerenhout viewed the landscape of things in early 1830, the only possible path forward – or at least the only good path forward – was to have European missionary societies take a more active role in preserving the sanctity of this place. Pitcairn needed "some capable pastor," and "a spiritual guide." If cultivated, these islanders had a divine mission. They were the Pacific's chosen people, taken

---

[123] Ibid., 29.   [124] Ibid., 38.   [125] Ibid. See also Robert Macklin, *Dark Paradise*, 154.
[126] Moerenhout, *Travels to the Islands*, 38.

almost directly from St. Peter's first epistle to the early Christian churches in Asia Minor. "You are," Peter had written,

a chosen race, a royal priesthood, a consecrate nation, a people set apart to sing the praises of God who called you out of the darkness into his wonderful light. Once you were not a people at all and now you are the People of God; once you were outside the mercy and now you have been given mercy.[127]

This was a people who could spread their grace and become Pacific missionaries to their Polynesian cousins. They already spoke South Pacific languages, or at least pidgin versions of them, in addition to English.

As Paul Batterby has observed, the Pacific had once been dominated by the exotic myth of *Terra Australis*. By the nineteenth century, though, that myth had been replaced with a real southern continent, a massive island in a sea of islands. In Britain's colonial Pacific, the new colonies emerging at Australia were the "moral frontier and defensive barrier" in that ocean.[128] We might argue, here, that Pitcairn served a very similar function, if on an infinitely smaller geographic scale. What it wanted in size, though, Pitcairn made up for in import, for here was an island that suggested a story of moral reform, religious redemption, and evangelical colonialism. All that was required was that the delicate balance at Pitcairn be preserved against outside forces. Left alone, though, the Eden at Pitcairn would be overrun with foreign weeds. Properly cultivated, the island's spiritual future was fructuous.[129]

Moerenhout's vision for Pitcairn's future was not unique. John Buffett shared the same set of worries in a letter dated from 1824. "By desire of John Adams, and the other inhabitants of this place," he wrote to Hiram Bingham, Pitcairn was in "great need of a minister of the gospel . . . We are now here as sheep without a shepherd."[130] Buffett admitted that he lacked both the merit and the abilities to be all that the Pitcairners needed. The small community's religious efforts were buttressed by the frequent arrival of books and other devotional items from visiting ships, but the growing population (fifty-nine lived on the island as Buffett wrote to Bingham) meant that the community's religious institutions were, at

---

[127] *The Jerusalem Bible* (New York: Doubleday, 2000), 1 Peter 2:9–10.

[128] Paul Batterby, *To the Islands: White Australians and the Malay Archipelago since 1788* (New York: Lexington Books, 2010), 203. See also, Kathleen Wilson, *The Island Race: Englishness, Empire, and Gender in the Eighteenth Century* (New York: Routledge, 2003), 17.

[129] Moerenhout, *Travels to the Islands*, 41.

[130] Letter from John Buffett to Hiram Bingham from Pitcairn Island, dated July 10, 1824. Quoted in Fiske, *Story of Aleck*. ML MSS 7067, CY 4170 (frames 40–73), 45.

best, "imperfect endeavors."[131] We know, for instance, that the Society for Promoting Christian Knowledge responded to a suggestion from Captain Staines and sent the islanders "a small stock of religious books" via Captain John Henderson of HMS *Hercules* as early as 1819.[132] Indeed, there is some indication that Joshua Hill might himself have been charged with delivering books and other stores to the Pitcairners during his voyage out in the 1830s.[133]

Others, then, shared Joshua Hill's opinion that Pitcairn needed a missionary pastor. His thinking was in line with that of Moerenhout, Buffett, and even John Adams himself. The singular difference in Hill's story is that, when others – like the British government or the London Missionary Society – shilly-shallied about the island, he took it upon himself to do the work he called for. Singlehandedly? Yes. Without authorization? Certainly. But, it now seems clear, not with the same level of madness that we might have imagined when we first began our consideration of a man who has previously only ever been called an "impostor."

In his call for a pastor at Pitcairn, John Buffett wrote to Hiram Bingham. Bingham, as we have seen, was an American missionary working for the ABCFM in Hawai'i. That Buffett, on Adams' behalf, would reach out to Hiram Bingham offers us a vital bit of insight into the nature of the historical context in which Joshua Hill was operating in the mid-nineteenth-century Pacific. Why, we might ask, did the Pitcairners, who by all accounts were "British" if they were bound to any national identity at all, seek help from American missionaries at Hawai'i rather than from the British missionaries of the LMS out of Tahiti, which was much closer to the isolated community at Adamstown?

The missionary impulse was, of course, an old one in European history. Europe's global expansion was fueled by a sense that the West had much to offer to the rest of the globe, particularly with regard to religion. Richard Hayluyt summarized this much when he argued that "nothing more glorious ... can be handed down to the future than to tame the

---

[131] John Buffett, Letter to Hiram Bingham (Pitcairn Island: July 10, 1824), quoted in Fiske, *Story of Aleck*. ML MSS 7067, CY 4170, 45. See also, Letter from G. H. Nobbs to Rev. W. T. Bullock, dated from Pitcairns Islands, October 9, 1834, Te Puna MS-Papers-1009–2/51; London Missionary Society, South Seas Incoming Correspondence, SOAS CWM/LMS Box 8, Folder 2/Jacket A; "Descendants of the *Bounty*'s Crew, on Pitcairn's Island," in *The Calcutta Journal* (July 20, 1819); Topliff, "Pitcairn's Island," in *New-England Galaxy* (Friday, January 12, 1821); Murray, *Pitcairn*, 122; and Shapiro, *The Pitcairn Islanders*, 104.

[132] Nobbs, *George Hunn Nobbs*, 18.

[133] R. W. Hay, Letter to Charles Wood, Esq. (London, July 22, 1835), Te Puna. MS-Papers-1009–2/51.

barbarian, to bring back the savage ... to the fellowship of civil existence."[134] Buffett's outreach to Bingham, though, suggests the powerful ways that the missionary impulse and, indeed, the history of the nineteenth-century Pacific more broadly emerged as an international story even before there was a national story to tell in the South Seas. Like the young founders of the ABCFM, the founders of the LMS found inspiration in the notion that they had it in their power to "save the world."[135]

Salvation at the global level necessitates universal goals and international cooperation. In the nineteenth-century Pacific, where no national or imperial interest yet reigned supreme, missionary activity functioned, therefore, as transnational or international history *before* it functioned as a national narrative as our logical chronologies might lead us to expect. Of course, global missions have to start somewhere. So, where to begin? As early as the 1790s, the South Seas offered an obvious and promising field. As we will see in Chapter 6, the earliest accounts of the Pacific as a luxuriant world populated by beautiful and scantily clad women titillated the Western imagination. Harry Liebersohn has observed that "when the official account of Cook's first voyage was published and reports circulated about the travelers' Tahitian experiences, evangelicals were appalled by the descriptions of Polynesian mores; [John] Wesley himself refused to credit the stories of people openly copulating in broad daylight."[136]

That the South Pacific seemed a sensual place to late eighteenth-century Britons was obvious. Even the dour Captain Bligh, so punctiliously faithful to his wife, Betsy, commented that the women of Tahiti were "handsome in their manners and conversation possessed of great sensitivity and have sufficient delicacy to make them admired and beloved."[137] Most, though, "admired" Tahiti and its people – the women in particular – in a more sensuous fashion. Like the more sybarite Lord Byron, they found the Pacific filled with "sunny" islands populated by "summer years and summer women." This was a field "o'er which promiscuous Plenty pour'd."[138] As Sujit Sivasundaram has observed, evangelicals in the Pacific found a world in which nature had been

[134] Quoted in Patrick Brantlinger, *Taming the Cannibals: Race and the Victorians* (Ithaca, NY: Cornell University Press, 2011), 1.

[135] Daws, *A Dream of Islands*, 23.

[136] Liebersohn, *The Travelers' World*, 232. See also, Dodge, *Islanders and Empires*, 52; and K. R. Howe, *Where the Waves Fall: A New South Seas Islands History from First Settlement to Colonial Rule* (Honolulu: University of Hawai'i Press, 1984), 112.

[137] William Bligh, Log and Proceedings of the *Bounty*, Volume 2. SLNSW ML Safe 1/47, 65.

[138] Byron, "The Island," iii, 350. See also, Hiney, *On the Missionary Trail*, 70.

bountiful. And, yet, the natives of that world "could not respect the body as the site of the soul," for "they had chosen to worship the created without recognizing the Creator."[139] For the Western world's more stolid missionaries, who knew nothing of twenty-first-century cultural relativism, the Pacific's sexual license required attention, not as a matter of national or imperial concern but rather as part of a universal and votary crusade to transform the Gehenna that was the Pacific into a moral, Christian paradise.[140]

As Ernest Dodge has observed, early eighteenth-century European spirituality – "both established and noncomformist" – had settled into "a form of dull respectability."[141] By the last half of the century, though, evangelical currents were charged, fueled perhaps by the kind of graphic reports that had come back from Pacific voyages. Born was the age of the missionary. New societies and organizations abounded in the Atlantic world in the last years of the eighteenth century. The Baptists formed a society in 1792.[142] The LMS opened its doors in 1795 as a nondenominational organization, though it would eventually come to be dominated by Congregationalists.[143] The Anglican Church Missionary Society (CMS), and the Wesleyan Methodist Missionary Society (WMMS) followed in short order, joining older groups like the Society for Promoting Christian Knowledge (SPCK, established in 1698), and the Society for the Propagation of the Gospel (SPG, established in 1701). In Scotland, the Glasgow Missionary Society (GMS) emerged in 1796, the same year that witnessed the establishment of the

---

[139] Sujit Sivasundaram, *Nature and the Godly Empire: Science and Evangelical Mission in the Pacific, 1795–1850* (New York: Cambridge University Press, 2005), 6.

[140] Paul T. Burlin, *Imperial Maine and Hawai'i: Interpretative Essays in the History of Nineteenth-Century American Expansion* (New York: Lexington Books, 2008), 262. See also, Daws, *A Dream of Isands*, 24. See also, Patrick Brantlinger, *Dark Vanishings: Discourse on the Extinction of Primitive Races, 1800–1930* (Ithaca, NY: Cornell University Press, 2003), 145; Rod Edmond, "Missionaries on Tahiti, 1797–1840," in Alex Calder, Jonathan Lamb, and Bridget Orr, eds., *Voyages and Beaches: Pacific Encounters, 1769–1840* (Honolulu: University of Hawai'i Press, 1999), 226; Richard D. Fulton and Peter H. Hoffenberg, "Introduction," in Richard D. Fulton and Peter H. Hoffenberg, eds., *Oceania and the Victorian Imagination: Where All Things Are Possible* (Burlington, VT: Ashgate, 2013), 6; Salmond, *Bligh*, 396; and Howe, *Where the Waves Fall*, 112.

[141] Dodge, *Islanders and Empires*, 87.   [142] Ibid., 87.

[143] See Brian Stanley, *The Bible and the Flag: Protestant Missions and British Imperialism in the Nineteenth and Twentieth Centuries* (Leicester: Inter-Varsity Press, 1990), 56; Johnston, "Antipodean Heathens," 68; Andrew Porter, "An Overview," in Norman Etherington, ed., *Missions and Empire – Oxford History of the British Empire, Companion Series* (New York: Oxford University Press, 2005), in Norman Etherington, ed., *Missions and Empire – Oxford History of the British Empire, Companion Series* (New York: Oxford University Press, 2005), 46; Sivasundaram, *Nature and the Godly Empire*, 24–25; and Sturma, *South Sea Maidens*, 3.

Scottish Missionary Society (SMS).[144] As Jane Samson has noted, each of these groups held firmly to their "own jealously guarded territory," but, as Buffett's letter to Bingham suggests, this territorialism transcended national or imperial boundaries.[145]

When the LMS officially inaugurated its crusade, therefore, in September 1795, "its leaders recognized an expedition to Tahiti, which offered an irresistible mixture of material comfort and a people in need of moral uplift."[146] The Society's first missionary ship, the *Duff*, set sail for Tahiti on August 4, 1797, ushering in a wave of European missionary activity in the Pacific that would fundamentally define the ocean's nineteenth-century historical experience.[147] Interestingly, the missionary movement into the Pacific was itself assisted by the mutiny aboard the HMAV *Bounty* that started us on our journey here. When the missionaries on board the *Duff* sailed, they were armed with a vocabulary of the Tahitian language that had been compiled by James Morrison, one of the three *Bounty* sailors to have survived both Captain Edwards' harsh punishments aboard the *Pandora* and the subsequent courts martial back in England.[148]

The global Christian mission in the Pacific made for an overlapping patchwork of endeavors. In the Southern Pacific, British and, to a lesser degree, French missionaries dominated the scene. The LMS attempted missions in Tahiti, the Marquesas, and Tonga, though only the Tahitian mission lasted for any length of time.[149] American missionaries "chose the North Pacific as their pulpit," focusing on the Hawai'ian (Sandwich) Islands.[150] In Australia and New Zealand, Anglicanism and Methodism would secure the strongest footholds, lending the Pacific an air of religious diversity, particularly if we add in the indigenous religious practices and customs of the basin's earliest inhabitants.[151]

---

[144] See Esther Breitenbach, "Religious Literature and Discourse of Empire: The Scottish Presbyterian Foreign Mission Movement," in Hillary M. Carey, ed., *Empires of Religion* (New York: Cambridge University Press, 2008), 84–86; Vanessa Smith, *Literary Culture and the Pacific: Nineteenth-Century Textual Encounters* (New York: Cambridge University Press, 1998), 56–57; Stanley, *The Bible and the Flag*, 56–65; and Anna Johnston, *Missionary Writing and Empire, 1800–1860* (New York: Cambridge University Press, 2003), 15.

[145] Samson, *Imperial Benevolence*, 9; and Hilary M. Carey, *God's Empire: Religion and Colonialism in the British World, c. 1801–1908* (New York: Cambridge University Press, 2011), 54. See also, *Society for Promoting Christian Knowledge*, SLNSW Mfm M 2091–2111.

[146] Liebersohn, *The Travelers' World*, 232. See also, Johnston, *Missionary Writing and Empire*, 118–120.

[147] Thomas, *Islanders*, 31–36; and Smith, *European Vision*, 107–109.

[148] See Liebersohn, *The Travelers' World*, 235; Edmond, *Representing the South Pacific*, 98; and Chappel, *Double Ghosts*, 12.

[149] Fischer, *A History of the Pacific Islands*, 103–106.   [150] Ibid., 105.

[151] Gibson, *Yankees in Paradise*, 266.

To suggest that missionaries operated outside of all national or imperial parameters would, though, be to mischaracterize the story here. Indeed, the question of whether missions advanced the cause of national imperialisms in the Pacific – indeed around the globe – is foundational to the historical study of evangelicalism itself.[152] The plot to this story is intricately and finely braided. That there was a link between missionaries and national and imperial projects is evident, though the connection was always channeled through the missionaries' evangelical work. If "the beachcomber was metropolitan representative to the Pacific by proxy," as Vanessa Smith has written, then, "the missionary was representative by project."[153]

For LMS missionaries to have leapt directly into Tahitian politics as agents of empire would have been a challenge. Tahitian politics had long confused European visitors. Europeans tended "to ascribe rank in terms of territoriality" that did not necessarily match with the political realities on the ground in foreign lands and new places like Tahiti.[154] Uncertainty about the divided nature of chiefly power over the island coupled with misunderstandings about the relationships between the island's two, unequally sized halves generated a host of European misperceptions about who was in charge and over what terrain at Tahiti.[155] For the LMS missionaries working there, the key to successfully evangelizing the island was to link up with and to convert the most powerful political players. But, who were those players? Where to begin?

By the time the *Duff* arrived at Tahiti in 1797, the island was only newly unified under Pomare I, whom the British had formerly known as Tu, the *arii nui* or paramount chief of the region of Tahiti surrounding Matavai Bay. As Tu, Pomare I had been an ally to Captain Cook, but he had cleverly manipulated the changing political landscape caused by the arrival of Europeans from across the seas. If we accept the account of the *Bounty*'s James Morrison, Tu profitably attached himself to the *Bounty* men who had decided to make Tahiti their home. Between the *Bounty*'s departure in 1789 and the arrival of the *Pandora* in 1791, Tu drew on the skills of his *Bounty* men to advance his claims to supremacy

---

[152] See Stanley, *The Bible and the Flag*, 11, 30–33, and 48–49; Hilary M. Carey, "Introduction," in Carey, ed., *Empire of Religion*, 1–2; Norman Etherington, "Introduction," in Norman Etherington, ed., *Missions and Empire – Oxford History of the British Empire, Companion Series* (New York: Oxford University Press, 2005), 1–3 and 15–17; Johnston, "Antipodean Heathens," 77; and Sivasundaram, *Nature and the Godly Empire*, 15.

[153] Smith, *Literary Culture and the Pacific*, 53.   [154] Newbury, *Tahiti Nui*, 17.

[155] Thomas, *Islanders*, 45.

over the entire of Tahiti.[156] Several of the *Bounty* men at Tahiti were even drawn into Tahitian politics in chiefly capacities.[157] As King of Tahiti, though, Tu's affinity for the English did not include the LMS missionaries. Only in 1803, upon the accession of Pomare II did the English missionaries find a sympathetic audience in the Society Islands.[158]

As Rod Edmond has observed, the missionaries tried to partner with the Pomare monarchy from the start, and Pomare II's conversion "made the LMS a kind of established church."[159] Missionary agents of the LMS were not above presenting "themselves as representatives of the British crown" when it suited their purposes, an elision of religious mission and political power that frequently caused tensions between the missionaries on the ground and the organizational leadership in Britain, an intertwined feature of missionary work that we will take up in the next chapter.[160] Writing about the Reverend George Pritchard, who was an archetype of the missionary-cum-colonist, one LMS colleague grumbled, "Never was I so ashamed to see a poor missionary in the tinsel of gold bouncing about and swaggering with a long sword by his side."[161]

Men like George Pritchard may not have governed over a "Protestant theocracy," as some have argued, but they did wield political power well beyond what they could have imagined in the earliest days of the LMS's mission at Tahiti.[162] They functioned as government ministers, valued counselors to the Pomare monarchs.[163] Just as naval commanders could command deference because they seemed to carry the full authority of their European monarchs with them on board their ships, missionaries represented the pinnacle of European religious authority at their island stations.[164] As local chiefs consolidated their own power over islands and archipelagos in the Pacific, they leaned on Europeans like Pritchard at Tahiti to shore up their claims to sovereignty as much as they did to passing sea captains, transient beachcombers, and maritime merchants.

---

[156] Dodd, *The Rape of Tahiti*, 67. See also, Howe, *Where the Waves Fall*, 127–131; H. E. Maude, "Beachcombers and Castaways," in *The Journal of the Polynesian Society* 73:3 (September 1964), 271; and Gascoigne, *Encountering the Pacific*, 333–335.

[157] Howe, *Where the Waves Fall*, 132.

[158] See Dodge, *Islanders and Empires*, 90; and Hiney, *On the Missionary Trail*, 130.

[159] Edmond, *Representing the South Pacific*, 100; and Daws, *A Dream of Islands*, 24.

[160] Sivasundaram, *Nature and the Godly Empire*, 32; and Edmond, *Representing the South Pacific*, 102.

[161] Quoted in Sivasundaram, *Nature and the Godly Empire*, 32.

[162] Rod Edmond, "The Pacific: Tahiti – Queen of the South Sea Isles," in Peter Hulme and Tim Young, eds., *The Cambridge Companion to Travel Writing* (New York: Cambridge University Press, 2002), 139.

[163] Ward, *British Policy in the South Pacific*, 92.   [164] Ibid., 72.

Hence, Bronwen Douglas has argued, "missionisation preceded coloni-alism" in a logical sequence.[165]

As we have seen, Queen Pomare IV asked London to appoint Joshua Hill as consul to Tahiti. When Hill departed for Pitcairn, she turned her request to her second choice, George Pritchard, and it was Pritchard who was tapped to be the first British consul to Tahiti in 1837. For his part, George Pritchard deserves to be recorded in history alongside better known men like Sir John Bates Thurston, who served as premier of the Kingdom of Viti and (later) as the colonial governor of Fiji, and James Busby, a Scot best known for his career as the founding figure of colonial New Zealand's legal regime.[166] Until he was compelled to flee Tahiti after France's annexation of the kingdom in 1843, Pritchard functioned as much in a diplomatic as a consular role, advising Queen Pomare on how to deal with interloping foreigners and other foreign powers as often as he managed the affairs of Britons at Tahiti.[167]

Missionary supremacy on Pacific islands was, however, never immedi-ate. As we have noted, LMS missionaries found very little traction for their agenda under Pomare I. Indeed, Pomare II's willingness to work with English missionaries was highly contingent upon the internal politics of Tahiti itself. From the moment that he came to his father's throne in 1803, Pomare II set out to consolidate power over both halves of the island kingdom. Within five years, though, his efforts had generated such internal hostility that Pomare found himself exiled to nearby Eimeo (later Mo'orea), and it was only there that the would-be Tahitian monarch saw the true value of an Anglo-missionary alliance.[168] So suspicious was Pomare's sudden – seemingly strategic – interest in Christianity that the LMS missionaries, at first, refused him baptism.[169]

Pomare returned to Tahiti in triumph in 1812, bringing a new age of Christian politics with him.[170] With the LMS's Henry Nott at his side as his brass hat, Pomare changed the face of Tahitian culture, even if he himself was somewhat lax about matters of morality. It is worth looking at some of the changes that happened at Tahiti in these years, for, we will

---

[165] Bronwen Douglas, "Religion," in David Armitage and Alison Bashford, eds., *Pacific Histories: Ocean, Land, People* (New York: Palgrave, 2014), 201.

[166] See Deryck Scarr, *Viceroy of the Pacific: The Majesty of Colour – A Life of Sir John Bates Thurston* (Canberra: The Australian National University, 1980). See also, James Busby, *Our Colonial Empire and The Case of New Zealand* (London: Williams and Norgate, 1866).

[167] Ward, *British Policy in the South Pacific*, 73.

[168] See Campbell, *A History of the Pacific Islands*, 75.

[169] Fischer, *A History of the Pacific Islands*, 130; Andrew Porter, "An Overview," in Etherington, ed., *Missions and Empire*, 89; and Thomas, *Islanders*, 102–103.

[170] Thomas, *Islanders*, 102.

find, they look a great deal like some of the policies that Joshua Hill would come to implement at Pitcairn during his time there. Like Hill's policies, the Christian-inspired morality enforced under Pomare II was straitlaced, if not outright draconian.

The LMS acted as "morality police" as they "scoured Tahiti's communities in search of 'sin'."[171] Any form of saturnalia – dancing, for instance – was banned. Indigenous musical traditions were set aside for Christian hymns, and traditional Tahitian dress fell to the wayside, replaced by more "modest" – read European – dress codes. Citing the admonition against printing marks upon the body from Leviticus 19:28, LMS missionaries at Tahiti similarly targeted the Polynesian practice of tattooing as a sign of Tahitian paganism that had to be stopped.[172] Even wearing flowers in one's hair was frowned upon.[173] And above all, missionaries targeted alcohol. Too often was drunkenness, particularly as a result of quaffing from the distilled spirits of the ti-root, associated with immorality.[174] Temperance was now to be the norm at Tahiti; personal ascesis was the goal in this new and astringent age.

For those who held a new evangelical image of the Pacific most dear, tiny Pitcairn Island was a keystone in the new edifice they hoped to build. The notion that Pitcairn had missionary potential dated, arguably, to 1800. After years of turmoil and bloodshed among the island's initial *Bounty* settlers, Ned Young and Alexander Smith (aka John Adams) settled into a peaceful existence with the remaining Tahitian women and the young children born at Pitcairn since 1790. By 1800, though, Young knew he was dying, plagued as he was by a respiratory disease. From his deathbed, Young settled on the idea of teaching the illiterate Smith to read. The two men used the only texts that had been saved from the *Bounty*, a Bible and a Book of Common Prayer. Smith learned to read from those two books, and, if we believe the subsequent accounts, he absorbed their Christian messages. Ned Young died on December 25, 1800. He was the first male resident of the island to die from natural causes since the *Bounty* had landed at Pitcairn a decade before. In death, Young gave the small island a Christmas present – its first shepherd, Alexander Smith.[175]

---

[171] Fischer, *A History of the Pacific Islands*, 130–131.
[172] Anne D'Alleva, "Christian Skins: *Tatau* and the Evengelization of the Society Islands and Samoa," in Nicholas Thomas, Anna Cole, and Brownwen Douglas, eds., *Tatoo: Bodies, Art, and Exchanges in the Pacific and Europe* (London: Reaktion Books, 2005, Kindle Edition), locations 1556–1900 or 5676.
[173] Fischer, *A History of the Pacific Islands*, 130.
[174] See Samson, *Imperial Benevolence*, 26.   [175] Birkett, *Serpent in Paradise*, 228–229.

As we have seen, the narrative of Pitcairn under Smith/Adams was the story of an island with remarkable redemptive powers. The Pitcairners were everywhere favored as an honest, pious, and serene community. The image was, to borrow Anne D'Alleva's evocative phrase, of an island populated by "Polynesian Israelites."[176] But, even the Israelites – that chosen people – needed a Moses. Captain Staines' initial reports on the island offered his opinion "that it [Pitcairn] is well worth the attention of our laudable religious societies, particularly that for propagating the Christian Religion, the whole of the inhabitants speaking the Oteaheitian tongue as well as English."[177]

Captain Pipon agreed. "I must beg leave," Pipon wrote to the Admiralty in December 1817, "to impress the necessity of selecting a person" to function as a missionary at Pitcairn. Indeed, Pipon continued, this request came from the lips of John Adams himself, an aging man with personal fears about the future of his moral utopia.[178] Mathias Woodmason agreed. Writing from Dublin to the evangelical Josiah Pratt in 1817, Woodmason argued that Pitcairn not only needed a pastor, it needed a man with specific qualifications. "This labourer in the Lord's vineyard," Woodmason suggested, "should be a married man, with some slight knowledge of the use of common medicines and if possible of Gardening & his helpmate one who would as earnestly as himself endeavor to be useful."[179]

To George Burder, editor of *Evangelical Magazine*, Pitcairn Island was populated by "promising inhabitants ... who seem to possess a peculiar claim to our attention."[180] The island needed a pastor. John Wood, a correspondent of Burder's, was pleased that the LMS would consider finding such a person for the Pitcairnese people. He hoped "some prudent, wise, and pious man will be found to show unto them the way of life."[181] Nine months later, though, Burder's correspondence indicates that the Society was still in need of a suitable candidate for the job. Several people had been offered the position; all had refused. "I am not

[176] D'Alleva, "Christian Skins," in Thomas, Cole, and Douglas, eds., *Tatoo*, location 1896.
[177] *The Calcutta Journal*, July 13 and 20, 1819. Also quoted in Barrow, *A Description of Pitcairn's Island*, 247–248.
[178] Captain J. Pipon, Letter to John Dyer (Jersey: December 20, 1817), in SOAS CWM/LMS – Home Incoming Correspondence, Box 3.
[179] Woodmason, Letter to Rev. Josiah Pratt (Dublin: June 21, 1817).
[180] George Burder, Letter to the Directors of the London Missionary Society (Undated), SOAS CWM/LMS Home Incoming Correspondence Box 3.
[181] Jn. Wood, Letter to George Burder (October 23, 1818), SOAS CWM/LMS – Home Incoming Correspondence, Box 3.

acquainted with any one who is suitable *and* willing to go."[182] Unable to find a suitable missionary for Pitcairn, London's missionary communities instead began what would become a standing practice. They collected Bibles, prayer books, spelling books, and other materials for the educational and religious instruction of the Pitcairn people, and they forwarded them out into the Pacific.[183] If Pitcairn was a sanctified island in moral peril, these shipments would become the island's evangelical lifeline – at least until Joshua Hill took matters into his own hands.

---

[182] J. A. James, Letter to George Burder (July 11, 1818), SOAS CWM/LMS – Home Incoming Correspondence, Box 3.
[183] Maud, "The History of Pitcairn Island," 62–63.

3 Kingdoms of God

> Better to sleep with a sober cannibal than a drunken Christian.
>
> Herman Melville, *Moby-Dick* (1851)[1]

On February 2, 1838, Captain H. W. Bruce of the HMS *Imogene* wrote from Valparaíso to inform his superiors at the Admiralty that he had formally completed his journey across the Pacific Ocean as well as all the tasks he was to have performed on that voyage. Bruce's "final Object," of course, had been to visit Pitcairn Island, where he had been "welcomed by all its Inhabitants with the greatest Enthusiasm." The Pitcairners, Bruce found, were "guileless," though they were in danger from the bad examples set by "the Debaucheries of three runaway English men who had domesticated themselves living there." But for these three men, "I believe that Vice would be altogether unknown," Bruce concluded.[2]

Bruce's observations about the peccadillos of the three "runaway" Englishmen are noteworthy, for we know that there was a fourth Englishman living at Pitcairn at that time. That fourth man was Joshua Hill, and it was Hill whom Bruce had orders to remove from Pitcairn, for, by 1837, everyone in London knew that Joshua Hill was at Pitcairn, that he had claimed to have authority to govern the small community, that he was a fraud, and that his reign over the island would only ever end if the Royal Navy saw to his formal removal. For his part, Captain Bruce conceded that "Mr. Hill's absence will I think be of benefit to the Community." Hill had not "gone judiciously to work" at Pitcairn, but, after having sailed across half of the Pacific Ocean with Hill as a passenger on his ship, Captain Bruce was convinced that Hill's "object was to do good." He could not say the same for George Hunn Nobbs, John Evans, or John Buffett.[3]

---

[1] Herman Melville, *Moby-Dick*, 26.
[2] Captain Henry W. Bruce, Letter (Valparaíso: February 2, 1838), TNA FO 16/34.
[3] Ibid.

Removing Hill, though, was not Bruce's only assignment as he crossed the Pacific in 1837. At Tahiti, he was ordered to inform the LMS missionary George Pritchard that he had been tapped by Lord Palmerston to be the first British consul at Papeete. Bruce's 1838 letter from Valparaíso confirmed that Pritchard had received his commission. Moreover, it confirmed that the new consul had, upon assuming the mantle of his new assignment, put down his claims as a missionary. That London had required Pritchard to give up his formal ties to the LMS in order to become consul was, to both Bruce and many of Pritchard's congregants at Tahiti, "a Matter of Regret." But, Bruce concluded, Lord Palmerston had argued that the two postings were "incompatible," and Bruce was inclined to agree. A man, after all, could not serve two masters.[4] That much, at least, was Gospel truth.

George Pritchard was an angular man. Each of the contemporary images we have of him depict an arrow-sharp nose underlined by a precisely linear mouth. Pritchard's cuspidated hairline divided his forehead like an isosceles triangle. His posture was rigid, if not outright martial. Pritchard had gray-blue eyes and coarse, wavy, thick hair, which he wore combed forward over both his ears, giving him an almost lupine appearance (Figure 4).

When he arrived at Tahiti in 1824 as an LMS missionary, George Pritchard was only twenty-eight years old. Tahiti would be Pritchard's primary residence for the next two decades. He would serve the LMS for thirteen of those twenty years. By the time he was named British consul at Tahiti in 1837, Pritchard had long been more than merely a missionary. He had come to be a trusted and influential advisor to the Pomare dynasty and to Queen Pomare IV in particular.

When he arrived at Tahiti as an LMS missionary in 1824, George Pritchard encountered a scene that was in dire need of a strong-willed leading actor. He was ready to play the part. His evangelical zeal for missionary work seems never to have been far removed from his sense of propriety and authority. When he makes his appearance in Herman Melville's first novel, *Typee* (1846), George Pritchard is described as "the famous missionary consul."[5]

Pritchard quickly rose to prominence within the European community at Tahiti, particularly among those predisposed to the missionary's cause. His was the first signature on a communal letter addressed to William Ellis in November 1827 in which the "British residents on Tahiti" sought London's help in removing "certain dangerous persons"

---

[4] Ibid.   [5] Melville, *Typee*, 18.

Figure 4 Charles Baugniet, *Lithograph Portrait of George Pritchard* (London: Day and Haghe, 1845). NPG D40760. Published by permission of the National Portrait Gallery, London.

from the island.[6] It would have done these men no good to write to the British government for help. In response to Pomare III's request for

[6] British Residents at Tahiti, Letter to William Ellis (Tahiti: November 19, 1827), TNA FO 58/14.

assistance in 1825, the Foreign Office simply replied that "the customs of Europe" forbade any direct assistance, offering instead "all such Protection as His Majesty can grant to a friendly Power at so remote a distance."[7]

Despite the strong and increasing demand for British intervention in the Pacific – the sort of intervention we know Joshua Hill favored – by both British residents of the region and Pacific Islanders themselves, the British government continued to favor a more passive approach with regard to the South Seas.[8] We know, too, that Queen Pomare and her chiefs hoped, as early as 1832, that London would appoint an official consular officer at Tahiti, dividing the combined consular position that then existed over the Society, Sandwich, and Friendly Islands – a vast territory, to be certain.[9] It would be Washington's appointment of J. A. Moerenhout as the American consul at Tahiti coupled with growing concerns about French activity – French Catholic missionary activity in particular – that would move London to make a decision on Pritchard's promotion in 1837. As we have seen, Moerenhout, a Catholic, was an advocate for Catholic missionaries in the Pacific. Not only would this position come to annoy Washington and cost Moerenhout his job (at least with the American government), it would also put him at odds with Pritchard. The two men would stand as foils at Tahiti until Pritchard was forced from the island after the French annexed it in 1843.[10]

Moerenhout was not alone in expressing suspicion about Pritchard or missionary work among the Protestants more generally.[11] It may be unfair, though, to suggest that Pritchard's missionary zeal was less than genuine. Perhaps instead, we might assume that he arrived at Tahiti at a moment when the island needed political stability and leadership, when it could ill-afford the social upheaval that might have come from a more overt religious revival or conversion. And to his credit, Pritchard did get about the business of promoting the Gospel at Tahiti, once he had helped establish some level of civil control on the island. By the end of 1825, he was pleased to report that he had overseen the construction of a new chapel, and despite having only been in the South Pacific for just over a year, he announced he was ready to begin preaching his sermons in Tahitian.[12] To further the education of the indigenous Tahitians, he

---

[7] George Canning, Letter to King Pomare III (Foreign Office: March 2, 1827), SOAS CWM/LMS – South Seas – Incoming Correspondence, Folder 1/Jacket A.

[8] Ward, *British Policy in the South Pacific*, 57.   [9] Ibid., 91–94.

[10] Dodd, *The Rape of Tahiti*, 75. See also Scarr, *A History of the Pacific Islands*, 88.

[11] Melville, *Moby-Dick*, 26. See also, Gascoigne, *Encountering the Pacific*, 203–205.

[12] George Pritchard, Letter to Missionary House (Tahiti: January 9, 1826), SOAS CWM/ LMS 5B – South Seas Incoming Correspondence, Folder 5/Jacket A.

began work on a new dictionary that translated words from English to Tahitian rather than vice versa as every previous dictionary had.[13] Together with his more upright colleagues, he reprimanded and then suspended one LMS missionary who was a known drunk.[14] Letters to LMS headquarters tell of Pritchard's very real concern about the extension of "Satan's Kingdom" at Tahiti, and he lamented that the directors at Mission House would not believe some of the reports he had to communicate to them.[15]

By 1838, visiting British captains could report that Pritchard deserved the promotion to consul, an office he had (in effect) held for some time and which he had, they argued, done well. Commander Elliot of HMS *Fly* reported that Pritchard had "acquitted himself well."[16] Captain Bruce of HMS *Imogene* similarly approved of Pritchard. Carrying the orders that promoted Pritchard to the office of consul at Tahiti, Bruce noted that Tahiti had grown to be a stable place under Pritchard's eye and the guiding hand of its queen, Pomare IV, who was, in the captain's mind, "a sincere and active Christian."[17]

When he came to power at Pitcairn, Joshua Hill enforced many of the same policies there that George Pritchard demanded under the Pomare monarchy at Tahiti. And "demand" is the right verb here, for both Hill and LMS missionaries were not averse to taking minatory steps to enforce their new codes.

As Glynn Barratt has recognized, the missionaries at Tahiti had been doing a lot more than evangelical work. They had helped draft law codes; they had imposed taxes. Henry Nott was the tutor to the Pomare family, and his hand is all over the Tahitian constitution drafted in 1824.[18] The questions Moerenhout raised about Pritchard should not, then, be taken as merely geostrategic. Rather, they were quite legitimate. What exactly was the relationship between evangelism and politics in the South Pacific? Did the two overlap? Ought they? Was coercive force an appropriate means to bring about a moral end?

[13] George Pritchard, Letter to Missionary House (Tahiti: October 19, 1826), SOAS CWM/ LMS 5B – South Seas Incoming Correspondence, Folder 7/Jacket B.
[14] C. Wilson, G. Pritchard, and D. Darlin, Letter to Mission House (Tahiti: November 20, 1826), SOAS CWM/LMS 5B – South Seas Incoming Correspondence, Folder 7/ Jacket C.
[15] Pritchard, Letter to Missionary House (October 19, 1826).
[16] Ward, *British Policy in the South Pacific*, 96.
[17] Captain Henry Bruce, Letter to Lady Troubridge (Valparaíso: January 2, 1838), NMM TRO/119/4, 5.
[18] Jocelyn Linnekin, "New Political Orders," in Denoon, ed., *The Cambridge History of the Pacific Islanders*, 210. See also, D'Alleva, "Christian Skins," in Thomas, Cole, and Douglas, eds., *Tatoo*, location 1656 of 5676.

Douglas Oliver was right to observe that the influence that LMS missionaries had at Tahiti was not in itself novel. Spanish Catholic missionaries, who will come to play a part in our story soon enough, had long been temporally as well as spiritually powerful.[19] The distinction here is that the activity of the LMS and, as we will see, the ABCFM linked itself to emergent kingdoms – protean nations – in places like Tahiti and Hawai'i. Men like Hiram Bingham in Hawai'i and George Pritchard at Tahiti functioned as much like prime ministers in very weak constitutional monarchies as they did missionary delegates at a sovereign, foreign court. Arguably, they exploited the weaknesses of their respective monarchies to find toeholds for their own political power. At Tahiti, for instance, there seems to have been little effort to prevent Pomare II from indulging in alcohol even after the missionaries banned inebriating spirits. Pomare II was not above bending the new religious codes himself, and alcohol seems to have been his weakness. A shicker by nature, the monarch died in 1821 at the age of forty, done in by a lifelong abuse of alcohol. His son and heir, Pomare III, was still an infant, and the boy-king died before his seventh birthday, passing the throne to his sister, Aimatta, who would reign as Pomare IV, the last fully independent Tahitian monarch.[20]

It was during the reign of Pomare IV that George Pritchard came to have such a powerful influence at Tahiti.[21] Visitors to the islands in these years suggested that the islands existed in a state of "Calvinist despotism," but the missionaries were hardly eager to wield such obvious power. As such, they attempted to devolve sovereignty back to the Pomare monarchs, who were either unwilling or unable to control the social, political, and cultural fallout of the kingdom's recent conversion.[22] "The resulting misgovernment, erratic law enforcement and increasing discontent of both Tahitians and the small (but growing) number of European residents, made reform necessary to avoid a crisis."[23] Even the boy-king Pomare III and his advisors felt the gravity of the situation. In 1823, advisors to the infant king wrote to George IV in London asking the British monarch for assistance and protection against the turmoil that visitors from without and dissidents from within presented to his sovereignty.[24]

---

[19] Oliver, *The Pacific Islands*, 54–55.
[20] Samson, *Imperial Benevolence*, 64. See also, Howe, *Where the Waves Fall*, 151; and Scarr, *A History of the Pacific Islands*, 87.
[21] Newbury, *Tahiti Nui*, 51.
[22] Missionaries at Tahiti, Letter to the LMS Secretary in London (Tahiti: December 15, 1826), TNA FO 58/14.
[23] Campbell, *A History of the Pacific Islands*,   [24] Dodd, *The Rape of Tahiti*, 72.

After Pomare III's death from dysentery, the situation deteriorated quickly. Henry Nott had recently returned to England, leaving something of a power vacuum in Tahiti, and those of the missionary establishment who remained feared for their safety.[25] In a letter to George Canning at the Foreign Office announcing the death of the young monarch, William Ellis suggested that the island was

in a constant state of ferment. I am necessitated to be constantly armed to protect my person from acts of violence and if a vessel of war does not speedily arrive to assist and support me I shall be compelled to quit my station as I am in constant danger of being murdered.[26]

Pomare III died in 1827. Three years later, Joshua Hill stopped at Tahiti on his way to Pitcairn, visiting when Pritchard was away on a missionary visit to the Marquesas.[27] He seems to have found an island that was still unsettled. What we know of Hill's time at Tahiti comes to us largely from Moerenhout, who records that Hill was forceful about the need for further evangelical reform in the Society Islands.

Though Pritchard was away when Hill landed, Hill took up residence at his house. If we believe Moerenhout, Hill even billed the cost of his laundry to Pritchard's accounts. Say what we will about him, Joshua Hill seems to have had a flair for hauteur. Even Moerenhout, whose egotism was famous across the Pacific, took umbrage that Hill should criticize "the manners and habits of those even who were feeding him," but both the Tahitians and the missionaries seem to have believed that Hill was a man of some importance with official work to do across the Pacific.[28]

Moerenhout writes that Hill demonstrated "a dangerous fanaticism, and an implacable hatred for whoever dared to contradict or oppose his plans with the least objection in the world," and that description fits with the image we will get of Hill from his Pitcairnese detractors. If he was anything, Joshua W. Hill was an immovable ideologue and a standpat. LMS missionaries did, though, agree with the concern that Hill registered about the state of things on the island. George Pritchard was not happy about the state of Tahiti or the LMS mission there in the early 1830s, which may explain why he seems to have welcomed Joshua Hill to the

---

[25] George Pritchard, Letter to the LMS (September 26, 1825), SOAS CWM/LMS South Seas Box 5A, Folder 2/Jacket B.

[26] William Ellis, Letter to George Canning (Tahiti: February 28, 1827). TNA FO 58/14. See also, Letter from William Ellis, Letter to George Canning (Tahiti: March 29, 1827), TNA FO 58/14.

[27] George Pritchard, Letter to Rev. W. Orme (Tahiti: December 26, 1828), SOAS CWM/LMS 6 – South Seas – Incoming Correspondence, Folder 7/Jacket B.

[28] Moerenhout, *Voyages*, 445. See also, Kirk, *Pitcairn Island*, 82.

Society Islands upon his return from the Marquesas. He even helped introduce Hill to Queen Pomare.[29]

Recall, Pritchard's first encounter with Hill was as an uninvited house-guest. Pomare was the queen of Tahiti! These were smart people Hill had encountered; it seems a substantive historical mistake to simply put aside Hill's time at Tahiti – or elsewhere in the Pacific – as an episode of lunacy on the part of some shifty South Seas huckster. That Pritchard and Pomare both seem to have responded positively to Hill suggests that he spoke to some of the most pressing concerns facing Tahiti at the time. He was, in short, alert to the broad international issues that defined the South Pacific as a region, and his participation in those social, cultural, religious, and political matters was – if aggressive – not completely the outpouring of a deranged mind.

The same, too, can be said of Hill's contributions at the Sandwich Islands, where he landed on his way to Tahiti. It is important that we remember that John Buffett and John Adams did not reach out to the LMS, to George Pritchard, or to the other missionaries at Tahiti when they began a quest to find a pastor for Pitcairn. In the late 1820s, Tahiti's missionary establishment was not doing well enough to have been of much assistance to tiny Pitcairn. So, the Pitcairners reached past Tahiti and the London-based LMS to the American missionaries of the ABCFM at Hawai'i. The first Christian missionary organization out of the United States, the ABCFM was the brainchild of five students at Williams College in 1806.[30] Driven by the devotional fervor of the Second Great Awakening, ABCFM missionaries looked at the world as their missionary battlefield. The leader of the first group of ABCFM missionaries to work from Hawai'i was Hiram Bingham, whose time in the Pacific spanned from 1820 to 1840.

At Hawai'i, the situation Bingham encountered was much the same as that his LMS counterparts found at Tahiti. From the 1790s, "a skilled, energetic, ruler had arisen."[31] Kamehameha I linked himself directly to the European sea captains who were increasingly sailing into the harbors of his island homeland. His fondness for Britain, in particular, had been demonstrated when he asked George Vancouver for London's assurance that Britain would safeguard the Kamehameha claim to power at Hawai'i against other foreign powers.[32] It was to secure a similar promise of protection that Kamehameha I's heir, Liholiho (Kamehameha II), and his queen Kamāmalu, sailed for London in 1824, a diplomatic mission

---

[29] Hill, *The Humble Memorial*, 18–19.   [30] Dodge, *Islanders and Empires*, 118–119.
[31] Lierbersohn, *The Travelers' World*, 41.
[32] Chappell, *Double Ghosts*, 128. See also Dodge, *Islanders and Empires*, 111.

that cost the royals their lives when they both contracted and died from the measles while in London.[33]

Like their LMS counterparts, ABCFM missionaries arrived at Hawai'i with "an imperial faith or an imperialism of the spirit."[34] The line between evangelical and political pursuits is hard to disentangle in this history. As we have seen time and time again, Euro-American sailors were constantly encroaching on the sovereignty of Pacific islands and their leaders. Crews landed looking for alcohol and sex, and sea captains marooned disobedient seamen. The result, for the islands, was social chaos. There was a pressing need for new laws and new enforcement mechanisms. At Hawai'i, Kauikeaouli turned to Lord George Byron, who had captained the HMS *Blonde* on its voyage to return the bodies of King Kamehameha II and Queen Kamāmalu. Byron had only just succeeded his more famous cousin to the family title when he was tapped for the mission to Hawai'i, but as an official emissary from the crown on a particularly fraught diplomatic mission, his credentials superseded those of many of the other Royal Navy captains who had sailed into Honolulu's port in recent memory. So, the new king – now Kamehameha III – turned to Byron for thoughts on how both to secure his dynasty's political primacy at Hawai'i and to ensure that passing ships respected his sovereign authority across the archipelago.

Byron's suggestions included political goals, new initiatives like trial by jury and a system of customs duties and port taxes. But, he also confirmed the value of preexisting efforts to stamp out adultery and drunkenness on the islands. Byron's instructions from London had been explicit. He was to return the bodies of the deceased monarchs to their people, to express London's deep sorrow at the Hawai'ian Islanders' loss, and to stay as clear of Hawai'ian politics as possible. That his policy outline for securing Kamehameha III's power at Honolulu included major aspects of the missionary agenda, therefore, opened a clear path for Bingham and his allies to influence the young new king and his advisors.[35]

Hiram Bingham arrived at Hawai'i in 1820 on board the *Thaddeuss*, just as the Kamehameha monarchy was coping with the stress of succession caused by the death of King Kamehameha I in 1819. Liholiho – now Kamehameha II – was the eldest son of the great dynastic founder and his preeminent wife Keōpuolani. It was not Keōpuolani, though, but Kamehameha's favorite wife Ka'ahumanu who would most shape Liholiho's reign. Even as she greeted the new monarch at his capital, Ka'ahumanu – dressed in her deceased husband's *'ahu 'ula*, or cloak of

[33] Chappell, *Double Ghosts*, 128. Dodge, *Islanders and Empires*, 122–123.
[34] Burlin, *Imperial Maine and Hawai'i*, 13.   [35] Beechert, *Honolulu*, 40.

state – announced that she and Liholiho would reign side by side over his father's island kingdom. Almost immediately, the two began restructuring religious and political life at Hawai'i. Largely at Ka'ahumanu's urging, Hawai'i's system of religious *tapu* fell, and the pace of religio-political change would only accelerate after Liholiho's death in 1824, as Ka'ahumanu's influence was stronger still over the fallen king's twelve-year-old brother and heir, Kauikeaouli, now Kamehameha III.[36]

As Mark Twain would note, American missionaries arrived to find that "the burned idols were still smoking. They found the nation without a religion, and they repaired the defect."[37] Yankee evangelization, therefore, found particularly fertile soil in the mid-Pacific, and ABCFM missionaries soon expanded the field of their work to the Marshall Islands and beyond.[38] True, Kamehameha II had been indifferent, if not openly ill disposed, to the American missionaries. The young king, though, was persuaded of the need to reform his kingdom, a task that was perhaps beyond his political talents.[39] The king's stepmother, Ka'ahumanu, therefore, was not only the real power behind the throne but also a dynamic ally for the missionaries, and her efforts to overthrow taboos and to burn the island's indigenous gods resonated with the ABCFM's agenda for the archipelago. Bingham was convinced of the need for "profound social change" at Hawai'i, where the native culture was, to his mind, "irredeemably depraved." Marking herself as an astute and majestic political leader, Ka'ahumanu linked her own power to that of the arriving missionaries. As regent in two successive reigns, Ka'ahumanu assured not only the fall of an older political and religious order but also the ascendancy of a new one at Hawai'i.[40]

Singularly the most powerful Hawai'ian of her day, Ka'ahumanu, therefore, forged the link between Hawai'i and the West through the institutional structures of the ABCFM and its evangelical agents.[41] "By the time of Ka'ahumanu's death in 1832, the missionaries regarded her as a genuine Christian, a true friend of the mission, and a powerful ally."[42] If anybody challenged the dowager queen's authority, it was a young chief

[36] Campbell, *A History of the Pacific Islands*, 77–78. See also, Gibson, *Yankees in Paradise*, 270–275.

[37] Mark Twain, *Following the Equator and Anti-Imperialist Essays* (New York: Oxford University Press, 1996), 53–54. See also Dodge, *Islanders and Empire*, 120.

[38] Oliver, *The Pacific Islands*, 55.   [39] Twain, *Following the Equator*, 51.

[40] Jocelyn Linnekin, "New Politics Orders," in Denoon, ed., *The Cambridge History of the Pacific Islanders*, 194.

[41] Jonathan Kay Kamakawiwo'ole Osorio, *Dismembering Lāhui: A History of the Hawai'ian Nation to 1887* (Honolulu: University of Hawai'i Press, 2002), 11. See also, Jennifer Thigpen, *Island Queens and Mission Wives: How Gender and Empire Remade Hawai'i's Pacific World* (Chapel Hill, NC: The University of North Carolia Press, 2014), 96–97.

[42] Thigpen, *Island Queens and Mission Wives*, 97.

by the name of Boki, the governor of Oʻahu. Boki had received his title from Kamehameha I, and he continued to serve as a trusted advisor in the reign of Kamehameha II. As Kaʻahumanu welcomed the second of the ABCFM's missionary expeditions to Hawaiʻi, Boki was in final preparations to sail with Liholiho and his wife on their fateful journey to London.[43] After measles tore through the Hawaiʻian delegation in London, Boki was left as the highest-ranking Hawaiʻian in Britain, and he quickly emerged as the mourner-in-chief on board the *Blonde* as it carried the deceased Hawaiʻian monarchs home.

Back in Hawaiʻi, Boki was suspicious of the ABCFM's sway and of Kaʻahumanu's power. He had not stood in the way of the reforms implemented under Kamehameha II, and, indeed, he had championed the removal of the *tapus*. But, by the time of his return from London, Boki was convinced that the long-term autonomy of the monarchy depended upon its independence from the Protestant missionaries. No doubt, Boki had been influenced by his close relationship with Lord Byron. Byron was deeply suspicious of the American missionaries, Hiram Bingham in particular.[44] It was Lord Byron, for instance, who forbad Bingham from attending the state funeral for Kamehameha II and Kamāmalu.[45]

Boki's middle-way through this tension was to turn to Catholicism as a competing form of Christianity. The Catholic church was newly engaged in missionary work in the Pacific in these years, particularly after 1825 when Pope Leo XII announced the creation of the Prefect Apostolic for the Sandwich Islands, under the auspices of the Congregation of the Sacred Hearts of Jesus and Mary, more popularly known as the Picpus Fathers after the Parisian *Rue de Picpus* upon which their first chapter house was located. To categorize Boki's Catholicism as entirely a response to Protestant power at Hawaiʻi would, though, misread the internal dynamics of power on the islands. Boki's voice was influential in the reign of Kamehameha II, but the governor had been long absent from the Pacific as part of the embassy to London on which the young king died. That Boki accepted Catholic baptism aboard the HMS *Blonde* as he sailed home with the bodies of the dead king and queen, suggests that he understood the changed political situation he would face upon his own return to the Hawaiʻian Islands.[46] Kaʻahumanu and her circle used Boki's absence and the absence of the king to consolidate their power, and Boki's alliance with the new forces of Pacific Catholicism was as much an internal political maneuver as it was a denominational decision. The

---

[43] Ibid., 74.   [44] Quoted in Haley, *Captive Paradise*, location 1492 of 7968.
[45] Haley, *Captive Paradise*, location 1492 of 7968.
[46] Ibid., location 2418–2425 of 7968.

Calvinists from the ABCFM, like Ka'ahumanu, had grown accustomed to dominance, and the opposition from Boki was novel and unwelcome.[47] The dowager queen's response was to order Hawai'ians not to attend Catholic worship. Eventually, she forbade Catholic priests from preaching entirely, going so far, even, as to expel them from the islands.[48]

Boki's resistance to Ka'ahumanu's power and the denominational character of the fight, in particular, direct our attention to the complex, fluid, and transnational nature of Pacific history at this moment. Rather than carving out political spheres in the Pacific, as they would later do in Africa, Euro-American powers favored a comparatively "incremental process" of "*non*-imperialism" in the eighteenth- and early nineteenth-century Pacific.[49] This disengaged and, some might suggest, haphazard model of drawing the Pacific into the imperial framework first established by the Europeans was unacceptable to men like Joshua Hill, who argued for a stronger and more centralized colonial presence in the region. Evangelical imperialism had its possibilities, Hill was certain, but it was not without its limitations. As organizations like the ABCFM and the LMS (or Pope Leo XII's Apostolic Prefecture, for that matter) were not openly imperialist institutions, they wanted for the clearly defined boundaries that framed and, ultimately, secured colonial power in other parts of the globe. Mix in the international communities of whalers, sealers, merchants, and beachcombers, and the Pacific was rife for contested encounters like the one between Boki and Ka'ahumanu – moments when local political context became indistinguishable from global imperial questions.

Elsewhere in the world – in cities like London, Paris, Rome, and Washington, DC – it was these contested and tangled networks of local power and loosely defined spheres of evangelical influence, tinged – as they were – with their respective national flavorings, that drove Western powers to consider establishing more formal ties with protean Pacific kingdoms like Hawai'i and Tahiti. In Tahiti, as we have seen, George Pritchard would eventually be tapped to function as Britain's consul. J. A. Moerenhout would come to represent the Americans. At Hawai'i, two former merchants, John C. Jones and Richard Charlton became the American and British consuls, respectively. Neither was terribly well-suited for the job, as both seemed to hold their own dignity and financial comfort as primary concerns. Charlton, in particular, is remembered as a

---

[47] Ibid., location 1393 of 7968 and Location 1492 of 7968.
[48] Lummis, *Pacific Paradise*, 172.
[49] Joyce E. Chaplin, "The Pacific before Empire, c. 1500–1800," in David Armitage and Alison Bashford, eds., *Pacific Histories: Ocean, Land, People* (New York: Palgrave, 2014), 53–54.

nasty individual, described variously as: a "coarse, choleric, intemperate, violent fellow" and a "rough, obtuse, foul-mouthed and choleric man."[50] Indeed, Charlton's personality was so dastardly Dickensian that Herman Melville could not resist inserting him in his novel *Typee* as an abusive villain.[51]

With such limited consular stock to lean on, was it any wonder that the indigenous princes at Tahiti and Hawai'i turned to men like Bingham, Pritchard, or Hill for assistance? For his part, Joshua Hill was clear that a stronger British imperial presence in the Pacific was to be desired. But, his vision of the Pacific was not without its religious character, and he made use of the moment – the tensions stirred by the arrival of Catholicism at Hawai'i, in particular – to secure his own influence and cement his own view of the region as a substantive part of the broader religio-political conversation taking place.

The arrival of Catholic missionaries at Hawai'i had challenged not only the Protestant ascendancy of Bingham and the ABCFM but also the consolidation of royal authority. That the frontier existed at all was a testimonial to the collapse of an older consensus that European evangelism in the Pacific was best accomplished via a division of labor across the vast ocean.[52] Pope Leo XII's decision to engage in evangelical work in the Pacific is often credited with this shift, for Catholic missionaries paid no heed to the confessional borderlines that had previously been charted across the ocean.[53] In the Catholic world, the upheaval of the Napoleonic years had been unsettling. It took some time for Rome to reassert itself in the global evangelical race, before groups like the Jesuits and the Picpus Fathers could be mobilized across the Pacific.[54] But, as John Ward has observed, both Paris and Rome became convinced that Protestant Anglo-American missionaries were also operating as imperial agents precisely because neither Washington nor London seemed to take any other interest in the South Pacific.[55] Of course, it was never a given that Paris' suspicions about the imperial intentions of ABCFM and LMS missionaries would translate into French colonial aggression in the Pacific, but

[50] Campbell, *A History of the Pacific Islands*, 84; and Samson, *Imperial Benevolence*, 44.
[51] Melville, *Typee*, 255. See also, Howarth, *Tahiti*, 209; and Brantlinger, *Dark Vanishings*, 150.
[52] Jocelyn Linnekin, "New Politics Orders," in Denoon, ed., *The Cambridge History of the Pacific Islanders* 197. See also, Felicity Jensz, "Missionaries and Indigenous Education in the Nineteenth-Century British Empire – Part I: Church-State Relations and Indigenous Actions and Reactions," in *History Compass* 10:4 (2012), 295.
[53] Oliver, *The Pacific Islands*, 116; and John Gascoigne, "From Science to Religion: Justifying French Pacific Voyaging and Expansion in the Period of the Restoration and the July Monarchy," in *Journal of Pacific History*, 50,123.
[54] Gascoigne, "From Science to Religion," 123.
[55] Ward, *British Policy in the South Pacific*, 121.

the intensification of Catholic missionary efforts in the region, frequently led by French religious orders, suggested that both Rome and Paris were beginning to look hungrily at the South Seas.

By the time Leo XII reasserted a Catholic presence in the world and introduced Catholicism to the Pacific in the 1820s and 1830s, the confessional lines that divided the Protestant spheres of influence were entrenched. The only way for a Catholic presence to be felt, particularly on important islands like O'ahu or Tahiti, was for Catholic missionaries to step on Protestant toes.[56]

At Hawai'i, the confessional donnybrook between the Catholic and Protestant worlds also fit itself with the political schisms within the indigenous ruling elites, particularly the internal feud between Governor Boki of O'ahu and the Queen Regent Ka'ahumanu. Their religio-political conflicts took on truly international proportions in 1827 when a party of Picpus priests, led by John Alexis Bachelot, landed at Hawai'i on board two French ships. Almost immediately, Ka'ahumanu ordered the priests to leave the kingdom, but their French transports had sailed before the priests' expulsion could be put into effect. For their first few months, the priests took care to learn the Hawai'ian language and enculturate themselves on the islands. But as she watched them carrying out their liturgical rites, Ka'ahumanu saw much about their piety that reminded her of the pagan traditions she had done away with upon the death of her husband, Kamehameha I.[57]

Hiram Bingham and his associates were no less astonished at Bachelot's arrival than was Ka'ahumanu. As one colleague wrote to Bingham, "we have more to fear in respect to them than in respect to all other foreigners."[58] Of course, the warning was prescient. After all, the most famous European missionary ever to have worked from Hawai'i is Jozef De Veuster, better known at Father Saint Damien of Molokai.[59]

Most historians have, subsequently, credited Hiram Bingham for defusing the tense standoff between Ka'ahumanu, Boki, Bachelot, and the rest of the Catholic missionaries.[60] It is true that Bingham hosted a klatch for the interested parties. Though Catholicism and Catholic evangelization was hardly in his own missionary best interest, Bingham held firm to the notion that it was never a good idea to imprison or banish opponents over matters of conscience. Bingham considered the ecumenical gathering a "triumph of the gospel."[61] People of "every kindred & tongue & people & nation" were present, he recorded. Any peace

---

[56] Oliver, *The Pacific Islands*, 116.   [57] Lummis, *Pacific Paradises*, 172.
[58] Quoted in Gibson, *Yankees in Paradise*, 285.   [59] Hiney, *On the Missionary Trail*, 316.
[60] Haley, *Captive Paradise*, location 2436 of 7968.   [61] Ibid., location 2436 of 7968.

Bingham won, though, was short-lived. Kaʻahumanu wanted the Catholic priests exiled, and, in 1831, some among her supporters took it upon themselves to seize Bachelot and his associates, buffeting them aboard a ship to get them out of the Hawaiʻian kingdom.

Bingham's efforts were not without a personal cost to the missionary. Haggling over confessional differences that, themselves, mapped onto political disagreements within the Hawaiʻian ruling classes was a complex balancing act. Was he doing missionary work? Or, was Bingham being a political agent? The two postures were hardly separable, and the overlap looked unseemly.[62] As we now know, though, Bingham and his ABCFM associates were not alone in Hawaiʻi in 1830 and 1831. In a convenient historical confluence, one of the men who joined Bingham on the bema as a guest at the memorable 1831 prayer service in Hawaiʻi was "an interesting stranger, Capt. J.W. Hill from Liverpool."[63] If we believe Hill's accounts from that same period, he was quite well-known to Bingham and the ABCFM starets. And why not? Here was another Protestant. Though British, Hill, like Bingham, was in the Pacific with missionary aspirations. And, like Bingham, he appreciated the tangled religio-political nature of missionary work with the governing elites of the South Pacific. Indeed, because he was not officially associated with either a missionary outfit or a European government, Hill could operate nimbly on the borderline between religious and political affairs without fearing condemnation for having mixed policymaking with proselytizing.

In a letter to Lord Palmerston dated from Tahiti in November 1831, Hill reflected on the tense standoff at Hawaiʻi. "Just before I left there," he wrote, "the ministers of the Government & principal missionary Mr. Bingham summoned me to give them advice." This was not the first time. Bingham seems to have been particularly keen to know whether or not London could or would be induced to offer firm commitments of protection over Hawaiʻi, perhaps even assigning a British Resident" to the kingdom.[64] Here, Hill argued, the Americans saw something that London had not. They were, he wrote, "wide awake" as to the value and significance of "these beautiful islands." Bingham could see that the Catholic priests were a problem on two simultaneous fronts. Even the Russians saw the situation for what it was worth, Hill noted, as valuable presents had arrived from Russia for the Hawaiʻian royals in the short

[62] Ibid., location 2512 of 7968.
[63] Hiram Bingham, Letter to Jeremiah Evarts in Boston (June 28, 1831). Papers of the American Board of Commissioners for Foreign Missions (ABCFM), Unit 6, ABC 19.1, Reel 796, slide 71.
[64] Hill, Letter to Lord Palmerston (November 20, 1831).

time that he, Hill, had been resident there.[65] Both a vibrant land for evangelical work *and* a strategic boon to any nation with broader ambitions in the Pacific, the Hawai'ian Islands were surprisingly and "imperfectly appreciated" in London.[66]

Here then, we find three things that merit attention. First, we see Hill repeating some of the same claims that we found in his article in the *London Morning Post* so many years before, a vision of British strategic power that included naval mastery as the lynchpin in a global network. Second, we see Hill fusing that geostrategic vision of imperial power to the evangelical fervor that he outlined to the LMS in his letters from the 1820s. Finally, and most significantly, we see a man whose political, religious, and imperial ambitions are perfectly aligned with those of men like Hiram Bingham. He is not the lunatic impostor who has featured in so many Pitcairn histories to date. Rather, he is a man whose global vision, whose political sensibilities, and whose religious zeal all fit into the context of the moment. Hiram Bingham certainly thought so. Ka'ahumanu did too. And so, when Bingham called a meeting to settle the disturbed climate at Hawai'i in 1831, he included our Mr. Hill. Indeed, if we believe Hill's letter, the leadership at Hawai'i "pressed me considerably to remain with them." But, he went on, "I told them I could not, that I had other matters, of more importance to me, to attend to."[67]

Other matters. Matters at Pitcairn Island, no doubt. Those matters, now, seem quixotic, for it is at Pitcairn that Hill lied about his mission or, at least, about his credentials. But, the mission Hill took to Pitcairn – to evangelize and to govern – was the same mission that Bingham was engaged in at Hawai'i. And at Hawai'i, Bingham included Hill in that work. Was Bingham taken in by our South Seas charlatan? It is possible, but it seems unlikely. For, on one hand, Hiram Bingham was hardly your average mark. He was well educated, and he had long been the leading figure amidst the complicated religious and political landscape that dominated the royal court at Hawai'i. And, on the other, Joshua Hill did not engage in any of the jiggery-pokery that he did at Pitcairn. He did not lie. He did not suggest to Bingham or to the Hawai'ians that he had been sent to be the British Resident. He could have, but he did not. Instead, he offered only his credentials – his global connections, his ties to evangelical missionary organizations, his appreciation of international politics. At Pitcairn, we know, Hill would turn haughty and boastful; at Hawai'i, though, he was a model of modesty. He did not have to flaunt his past or lie about his authority to be of value to Bingham, for Joshua Hill seems to

---

[65] Ibid. See also, Kirk, *History of the South Pacific since 1513*, location 1945–1956.
[66] Hill, Letter to Lord Palmerston (November 20, 1831).   [67] Ibid.

have been just the sort of man that Bingham needed to help him walk the high wire that connected religion and politics at Hawai'i in 1831.

Some months later and nearly three thousand miles away, Catholic evangelism was not yet a threat at Tahiti when Joshua Hill landed there. The LMS establishment at Tahiti centered around a small district, at the center of which was a house built for William Bligh during his six-month stay on the island in 1789.[68] As at Honolulu, the LMS missionaries at Tahiti, particularly George Pritchard, had come to be trusted advisors to the Pomare monarchy. Just as was the case in Hawai'i, the arrival of Catholic missionaries threw off the preexisting equilibrium, but the Picpus priests would not arrive there until 1835, well after Hill had left Tahiti to settle at Pitcairn.[69] As had been the case at Hawai'i, the Catholic missionaries at Tahiti would be banished by the Pomares only to attempt to resettle a year later.[70]

Paris and Rome both responded bitterly to the priests' deportation. Standing Tahitian law, they argued, allowed all foreigners to land on the island.[71] Pritchard, that officious Protestant middleman, had no right to secure Tahiti as his evangelical or administrative monopoly.[72] For his own part, Pritchard wrote to the British Foreign Office that he resented the French Catholic intrusion on his work. "It appears to us unreasonable, un-gentlemanly, and un-Christian for a body of Roman Catholics to come on these shores and enter into other men's labours."[73] This was much the same argument Hill and Bingham had made at Hawai'i in 1831. By the time Pritchard faced the "un-gentlemanly" invasion of Catholic priests at Tahiti in 1836, though, Joshua Hill was – for better or worse – not there to offer his council. In Tahiti, the peace fractured. Once the Catholic eye had turned to the Pacific, there was, to quote Alan Moorehead, "never the ghost of a chance" that the LMS missionaries "would be left in quiet possession of Tahiti."[74]

When Hill arrived at Tahiti, though, there was a Catholic presence in the kingdom in the person of Jacques Antoine Moerenhout, the American and later the French consul.[75] Moerenhout was never George Pritchard's biggest champion. By the mid-1830s, even Queen Pomare herself was concerned that the Protestant missionary establishment was no longer

[68] Hiney, *On the Missionary Trail*, 15.
[69] George Pritchard, Letter to Lord Palmerston (Tahiti: November 19, 1836), TNA FO 58/14. See also, Ellis, Letter to Lord Palmerston (November 24, 1837).
[70] Moorehead, *The Fatal Impact*, 91.
[71] Ward, *British Policy in the South Pacific*, 97 and 122.   [72] Newbury, *Tahiti Nui*, 91.
[73] Quoted in Ward, *British Policy in the South Pacific*, 122.
[74] Moorehead, *The Fatal Impact*, 86.
[75] George Pritchard, Letter to Lord Edward Russell (Tahiti: December 25, 1835), SLNSW ML MSS 24–2 – Tahiti British Consulate Papers.

solid enough to stand up to the pressures posed by Catholic evangelism. In a letter from 1834 to William Ellis, then the LMS' Foreign Secretary, Pomare expressed her fear that the LMS missionaries in her kingdom no longer commanded the respect they once had. Attendance at Sunday services was on the wane, she wrote, and the general state of morality in her kingdom was on the decline.[76]

Moerenhout seems to have disliked Protestant missionaries generally. He was happy to see the declining influence of Pritchard and the LMS. He was an early and eager advocate of Catholic missionaries from France, men such as Fathers Caret and Laval, when they arrived from Mangareva. The priests caused trouble, and, as we know, they were expelled. Moerenhout's status as an American diplomat, however, protected him from being banished from the island for his views – at least for the short time that his pro-Catholic positions allowed him to remain in the good graces of his political masters in Washington, DC.[77] We know Pomare IV hated Moerenhout and wanted him removed from her kingdom. She demanded as much of the King of France, to no avail.[78] Indeed, from 1838 onwards, Moerenhout found an ally in Captain Abel Aubert Dupetit Thouars, a French naval officer who championed the rights of French Catholic missionaries in the Pacific during his circumnavigation aboard the *Vénus* between 1836 and 1839. In 1842, it would be Rear-Admiral Dupetit Thouars who oversaw the showdown with Queen Pomare IV that forced the monarch to flee for her own safety to the island of Ra'iatea after having been coerced into deporting her long-time advisor, George Pritchard.[79] Where Hill and Bingham had juggled the tense religio-political balance at Hawai'i in 1831, the tangled nexus of religious evangelism, global imperialism, and political sovereignty at Tahiti in 1843 wanted for calmer voices. By then, though, our Joshua W. Hill had long since left the Pacific.

Much earlier, in April 1832, Hill, writing from Tahiti, explained to Lord Palmerston at the Foreign Office that Pitcairn was in grave danger. At the time, Hill was stranded at Tahiti, in search of passage to Pitcairn. During his unexpected layover, he had seen no fewer than a dozen whale ships, and he had witnessed the moral chaos that landed with every whaling crew. "My detention thus, however contrary to my wish," he explained, "has not been untimely but, as it has enabled me to see things better in their true light. Hence, it is with deep regret I have by a careful development, found the demoralizing condition of these people."[80] The

---

[76] Edmund, *Representing the South Pacific*, 129.
[77] Lummis, *Pacific Paradises*, 179. See also Dodd, *The Rape of Tahiti*, 76.
[78] Dodd, *The Rape of Tahiti*, 94.   [79] Moerenhout, *Travels to the Islands*, 444.
[80] Hill, Letter to Lord Palmerston (April 5, 1832).

chaos at Tahiti, Hill argued, was what had driven the Pitcairners back to their island. "So much for good example, in putting down drunkenness, theft, fornication, &c., which here is the order of the day," Hill lamented.[81]

It merits repeating that Hill's commentaries here – about both Tahiti and Pitcairn – were hardly unique. Indeed, his correspondence with Palmerston hardly seems either deranged or secretive. In his concluding lines, Hill is very open about his plans to go to Pitcairn to oversee affairs there in the wake of the islanders' return from Tahiti. He is equally clear that London needed to take better care of the work being done by the LMS at Tahiti and to keep a closer eye on the work being done by the American missionaries at the Sandwich Islands. Hill was clear that he hoped to go to Hawai'i again after departing from Pitcairn and that he might stay on there for a while if his health permitted. Hill hoped to received "a line in answer" to confirm his plans, and should Palmerston have needed to communicate with him, Hill invited the Foreign Secretary to write him care of the Reverend Hiram Bingham.[82]

Joshua Hill was not, therefore, a raving lunatic. His understanding of the missionary state of the Pacific region was one he shared with many others, among them missionaries from around the globe, politicians in London, and the residents of the Pacific Islands themselves. He did not hide his plans from officialdom. Indeed, he was quite open about his aspirations. J. A. Moerenhout's assessment that Hill's was a "pretended mission" fails to hold up to scrutiny. True, as Moerenhout wrote, Hill "was made fun of" at the end of the day. He was arrogant. He was the sort of man who would stay in your house and leave you with a bill for his laundry upon his departure.[83] But, Hill was not the only one to hold an enthusiastic vision for Pitcairn's place in Pacific history. Indeed, many who shared his enthusiasm also advocated for a plan that looked a great deal like the one Hill was promoting.

In 1819, John Hawtayne of the Society for Promoting Christian Knowledge (SPCK) arranged for a shipment of religious books to be sent on board the *Hercules* from Calcutta to Pitcairn. In addition to sending the SPCK's gifts to the islanders, Hawtayne expressed the Society's earnest prayers "that the books may lead to the advancement of you all in religious knowledge, and in Christian holiness of life." More significantly, though, Hawtayne extended a challenge to the Pitcairners. "At some future time, perhaps not very distant," he wrote, "you may find opportunities of imparting the knowledge which you acquire, to the Natives of other Islands, in which the name of Jesus Christ is not

---

[81] Ibid.   [82] Ibid.   [83] Moerenhout, *Travels to the Islands*, 445.

known." As had Captain Staines and as would Joshua Hill, therefore, the SPCK imagined the Pitcairners as "blessed instruments in the hand of God for extending the kingdom of his Son our Lord."[84]

In 1825, Captain Beechey was pleased to find that John Buffett had landed at Pitcairn. "In this man," he reported, the Pitcairners "have fortunately found an able and willing schoolmaster." But Buffett was not a trained – much less ordained – missionary, though he had "taken upon himself the duty of clergyman, and is the oracle of the community."[85] Beechey repeated this account and reiterated his sense that the island needed an official pastor in a letter to John Barrow at the Admiralty in December 1825.[86] In June 1825, Hiram Bingham made a similar observation in a letter he wrote to George Bunder at the ABCFM's American headquarters. John Adams, it seems, had written to Bingham, noting that Buffett was a fine teacher. But, the Pitcairn patriarch continued to plead for a missionary.[87]

Hill may have been aware of some of these requests when he sailed for Pitcairn. He claims to have been acquainted with Captain Beechey, though there is no proof of that particular bit of his autobiography. Hill would not have been aware that in 1829, the London Missionary Society had become alert to the missionary potential at Pitcairn and to the hazards that the small island faced. In April 1829, Henry Nott posted a letter to the society's headquarters in which he argued that the LMS needed to work more closely with the Admiralty. The navy, he argued, needed to begin more systematic patrols throughout the Pacific, and Pitcairn, in particular, merited attention. Nott was concerned about the arrival of outsiders at Pitcairn. He knew of Buffett, Evans, and Nobbs, and he seems to been suspicious about why somebody from outside Pitcairn would want to settle there. Of Nobbs, Nott was direct. He and Bunker had probably stolen the sloop they used to get to Pitcairn, and Nobbs would "do the people no good but harm."[88]

What Pitcairn needed was "a truly pious man, a man of sound and extensive knowledge a man well acquainted with men and things, and of the best modes of subduing the ground and causing it to yield the most abundant produce."[89] The people of Pitcairn agreed. In October, 1830,

---

[84] J. Hawtayne, Letter to the People of Pitcairn Island (Calcutta: July 15, 1819), Society for Promoting Christian Knowledge, Mfm M 2091–2111.

[85] Quoted in Barrow, *A Description of Pitcairn's Island*, 259–260.

[86] F. W. Beechey, Letter to J. Barrow (Pitcairn: December 21, 1825), TNA FO 58/14.

[87] Hiram Bingham, Letter to George Burder (June 8, 1825), SOAS CWM/LMS – South Seas Box 5A, Folder 4/Jacket A.

[88] Henry Not, Letter to Mission House (Tahiti: April 25, 1829), SOAS CMW/LMS – South Seas Incoming Correspondence – Box 7, Folder 2/Jacket A.

[89] Ibid. Emphasis in original.

fourteen of the island's leading male residents submitted a petition to Tahiti requesting that they be sent "a person capable of preaching to us the Gospel of our Saviour Jesus Christ." The Pitcairn patriarchs noted that they had two men on the island who were vying for the job – Buffett and Nobbs – but they also observed that neither of the two were ordained to their position. Furthermore, hinting at what was to come, the Pitcairners noted that the two outsiders had proven factious within Pitcairnese society, as both were after the same position and the various perquisites that came with it.[90] Only a pastor with clear authority – perhaps even somebody from the LMS – could dislodge these two men and secure an unambiguous claim to moral authority at Adamstown.[91]

At the time the Pitcairners were removed to Tahiti, the dispute between Nobbs and Buffett seems to have been ongoing. When the islanders returned from Tahiti to Pitcairn in 1831, they requested that Nobbs move with them to resume his work among them, but he seems to have refused. Instead of returning immediately, Nobbs issued an ultimatum that, unless the people of Adamstown accepted him as their singular schoolmaster and pastor, he was finished with Pitcairn.[92] Accordingly, the heads of the island's families signed a petition celebrating Nobbs' earlier work and certifying their desire to see him continue. Furthermore, they set out specific terms for what Nobbs would receive in compensation going forward.[93]

Years later, amidst his fight to wrangle power from Joshua Hill, Nobbs would claim that the islanders had urged him to travel with them to Tahiti as their schoolmaster and religious leader in 1830, against his inclination to quit the community at the time of the removal.[94] In 1832, the same community leaders who had requested a new – and authorized – pastor in 1830 – wrote to George Pritchard at Tahiti about the matter again. Pritchard followed up on the communication in a letter to the LMS headquarters noting that the islanders wanted both a teacher and a pastor not only for their education and enlightenment but also to help assuage the infighting between the Europeans who had landed on the island to assume these posts. "Every time Capt. Ebrill has been there," Pritchard recorded, "they have talked to him on the same subject."[95]

---

[90] SOAS CWM/LMS South Seas Incoming Correspondence – Box 8, Folder 2/Jacket D.
[91] Heads of the Pitcairn Families, Letter to Mr. Nott (Pitcairn: October 19, 1830), SOAS CMW/LMS – South Seas Incoming Correspondence – Box 7, Folder 6/Jacket C.
[92] George Stallworth, Letter Mr. Ellis (April 21, 1834), SOAS CWM/LMS – South Seas Incoming Correspondence – Box 9, Folder 5/Jacket B.
[93] See Brodie, *Pitcairn's Island and the Islanders*, 178. See also, Nobbs Papers, SLNSW ML A 2881, 1–4.
[94] Brodie, *Pitcairn's Island and the Islanders*, 180–181.
[95] George Pritchard, Letter to Mission House (Tahiti: November 24, 183), SOAS CWM/ LMS – South Seas Incoming Correspondence – Box 8, Folder 4/Jacket C.

Captain Ebrill was, of course, the merchant trader who landed Joshua Hill at Pitcairn in 1832. For his part, as we have seen, Hill put his plans to the LMS as early as 1829. Pitcairn needed a school. He would establish it, administer it, and function as its exclusive teacher. As an experienced naval officer, he was capable of making his own passage to Pitcairn, and he could do all of this "altogether free entirely of any stipend or charges upon my own acct." Hill anticipated the venture would take three to five years.[96]

The LMS would have to play its part, Hill observed. He would build the school, but the LMS would need to coordinate with its Tahitian missionaries to supply Pitcairn with a pastor. The society would have to put its "hand to the plough," Hill urged, drawing inspiration from Luke 9:62.[97] Joshua Hill was not unlike other missionary agents of empire in this period in as much as he "negotiated quite complex relations with colonial administrations and settlers."[98] Those pursuing missionary goals in the South Pacific – men like Joshua Hill – often "found that they were required to play a wider role than merely spreading the Gospel."[99] Missionary work expanded to include basic medical care and basic political guidance.[100] Joshua Hill had experienced this situation at Tahiti and at Hawai'i. So, when he landed at Pitcairn in 1832 and proposed himself as the island's new chief magistrate, he was doing work that – if unauthorized either by a civil bureaucracy or missionary outfit – was not unlike the work that Hiram Bingham and George Pritchard were doing at Hawai'i and Tahiti respectively.

Indeed, Pitcairn was almost universally held to be an easier evangelical landscape that either Hawai'i or Tahiti. It had no indigenous population and, therefore, no problematic tangle of sovereignty with which to contend. The small Pitcairnese population was also more easily controlled, particularly given the limited geographic scope of settlement on the already small island. At Tahiti, for instance, George Pritchard was forever complaining about his inability to juggle his responsibilities between the missionary establishment, the Tahitian people, and Queen Pomare's court. "There is but one constable on Tahiti," he exploded in a letter from 1827, "and ... I am he."[101]

And, furthermore, because he was not sovereign of the island, Pritchard had very limited control over who came to land at Tahiti. "As a missionary I of course set my face against the vile conduct," he

[96] Hill, Letter to Mr. G. Hodson (May 2, 1829).   [97] Ibid.
[98] Johnston, *Missionary Writing and Empire*, 19.   [99] Ibid., 74.   [100] Ibid., 75.
[101] George Pritchard, Letter to Mission House (Tahiti: January 6, 1827), SOAS CWM/ LMS – South Seas Incoming Correspondence, Box 6, Folder 1/Jacket A.

explained, of Euro-American sailors who came to the island.[102] In some instances, missionaries could consult with and seek assistance from passing naval captains. In 1829, Commander M. Laws landed at Tahiti, where he was asked to intervene to protect the islanders from the "vicious characters that are occasionally left among them by South Sea whalers."[103] This was a legal matter, but one with moral implications. The missionaries assured Laws that these marooned sailors interfered not only with the civil administration of the Pomare monarchy but also with the moral work of the LMS.[104] These were the sorts of complaints that Hill had helped to arbitrate in both Hawai'i and Tahiti. Of course, that the missionaries were willing to play tattletale won them few friends. Pritchard and his allies were, in fact, so unpopular that they – like other missionaries throughout the Pacific – faced threats of physical violence.[105]

At Pitcairn, things could be different. Given the Pitcairners English heritage, they were arguably more likely subjects for the religious, cultural, and proto-colonial administration that Hill hoped to bring to Adamstown. As Hill and others had observed, Pitcairn's population both needed a pastor and was poised to become a fount of evangelical activity in its own right. As Andrew Porter has written, "evangelicals had no ultimate intention of confining activity to colonial territory . . . possessions were no more than toeholds."[106] The expansionist evangelical impulse became more potent, though, in the 1820s and 1830s, particularly after the publication of English translations of Otto von Kotzebue's *A Voyage of Discovery into the South Sea and Bering Straits for the Purpose of Exploring a North-East Passage* and *A New Voyage Round the World* in 1821 and 1830 respectively. The Estonian-born von Kotzebue had used his published accounts from his two voyages to promulgate a harsh critique of both American and British missionary activities in the Pacific.

Von Kotzebue, like Melville and others, worried about the hard moralism of the missionaries. "A religion like this, which forbids every innocent pleasure and cramps or annihilates every mental power, is a libel on the divine founder of Christianity," he explained.[107] In their original Russian, the critiques found only a limited audience. Their English

---

[102] Ibid.
[103] Commander M. Laws, Letter to J. W. Croker (Tahiti: March 11, 1829), TNA FO 58/14.
[104] Ibid.
[105] Pritchard, Letter to Mission House (January 6, 1827). See also, Sturma, *South Sea Maidens*, 5.
[106] Andrew Porter, *Religion Versus Empire?: British Protestant Missionaries and Overseas Expansion, 1700–1914* (Manchester: Manchester University Press, 2004), 64.
[107] Quoted in Moorehead, *The Fatal Impact*, 87.

translations, though, proved scandalous for groups like the LMS and the ABCFM.[108]

As Hill had long feared, British influence in the Pacific was imperiled. Not enough had been done to secure either political influence over or moral authority in the South Pacific, and Pitcairn was the fastest and most obvious place to begin rectifying that mistake. As he wrote to Lord Palmerston in 1832, "in my humble opinion, some thing should be done, in the case of these poor islanders."[109] Knowing that little would be done, Hill followed up on the situation five moths later, writing to Palmerston, that he was eager to be about the business of moving to Pitcairn "to become acquainted respecting [the island's] unfortunate state."[110] Here, then, we find the Hill that historians have given us to this point, a man who was fascinated – even to the point of obsession – with Pitcairn Island. What seems to recede to the background, though, is the image of a madman. Hill's interest in Pitcairn was not – as Ahab's was with the white whale – vengeful or crazy. Rather, Joshua Hill had been at Hawai'i with the ABCFM. He had worked with Pomare IV at Tahiti alongside George Pritchard. He carried with him to Pitcairn a Protestant evangelicalism, part of an internationalist movement in the Pacific, a movement with a religiously based geostrategy that was precariously balanced on a small handful of islands and in need of serious refortification. The Anglo-American evangelical establishment in the region needed new missionaries, and the Pitcairners were, Hill was not alone in believing, best suited to do that work.

But, as we have seen, the Pitcairners were themselves also in need. They were in danger. By almost universal agreement, London was not doing enough for the island and its people. And, where the British had interested themselves about their colonial wards at Pitcairn, Hill seems to have suggested that they had done more harm than good. Hill knew that the arrival of John Buffett and George Hunn Nobbs had not been without its problems on the island. Reports, as we have seen, suggested that these two outsiders divided the Pitcairnese community into factions as they vied with one another for the right to serve as the island's primary educator. Nobbs married Sarah Christian, thus joining the island's most famous clan, hoping, as one biographer would later observe, to inherit "Elijah's mantle" upon Adams' death.[111] Buffett married Dorothy Young in 1824, but he also fathered two children by other women outside of his marriage, undermining so many earlier claims about the chastity of

[108] Porter, *Religion versus Empire?*, 122–123.
[109] Hill, Letter to Lord Palmerston (January 13, 1832).
[110] Joshua Hill, Letter to Lord Palmerston (Tahiti: May 12, 1832), FO 58/14.
[111] Nobbs, *George Hunn Nobbs*, 19.

Pitcairnese women.[112] John Evans, for his part, had married John Adam's daughter, Rachel, within a year of his arrival.

Nobbs, Buffett, and Evans had, thus, injected themselves into Pitcairnese society. They were the only three residents of the island without a hereditary connection to the *Bounty* story. They were, to use Hill's label for them, "Englishmen." At the time of the removal, all three Englishmen traveled with the Pitcairners to Tahiti, and Buffettt and his family were the first to return. That Hill, already certain that exposure to the broader world would pollute the Pitcairnese people, found Nobbs, Evans, and Buffettt engaged in distilling the ti-root plant into liquor, drinking on a Sunday, and sitting idly around at Pitcairn when he arrived there did little to improve his sense that neither London's policies nor the influence of "foreigners" was going to profit Pitcairn. The circumstances he found upon his arrival certainly helped him justify his subsequent actions.[113]

At the Admiralty, John Barrow agreed. "It appears," he wrote, "that no less than three Englishmen have found their way into this happy society."[114] Barrow placed most of the blame for the schisms at Pitcairn at Nobbs' feet. Nobbs, who was "a person of superior talents, and of exceeding great impudence," had, Barrow recorded, stolen Buffett's students and position at the island, becoming "a sufficient cause ... of division and dissension among the members of the little society, which were never known before."[115] Sensing the chaos Nobbs had wrought, J. A. Moerenhout accused Nobbs of pretending at good intentions. Nobbs was, he suggested, guilty of "pharaseeism," though "the good people of Pitcairn thought him a saint."[116]

Recall that Captain Freemantle, who arrived aboard the HMS *Challenger* just months after Hill's arrival at Pitcairn, felt inclined to remove Hill as the educational and religious educator over the island but refused to do so on the grounds that Nobbs had been engaged in the production and consumption of alcohol. Freemantle observed that the visit to Tahiti had changed the Pitcairners "for the worse." Their "Arcadian innocence" was gone.[117] The leadership at the LMS' headquarters in London knew of all of this. George Stallworth reported that the visit to Tahiti "appears to have been prejudicial to [the Pitcairners] in a moral as well as in a physical point of view." The islanders had been

---

[112] Silverman, *Pitcairn Island*, 112. See also, Moerenhout, *Travels to the Islands*, 440 and 448.

[113] Barrow, et al., "Accounts of the Pitcairns Islanders," 159.

[114] Barrow, *A Description of Pitcairn's Island*, 283.   [115] Ibid., 284.

[116] Moerenhout, *Travels to the Islands*, 27.

[117] Nobbs, *George Hunn Nobbs*, 26. See also, Moerenhout, *Travels in the Islands*, 440–441.

distilling alcohol from the ti-root before they left for Tahiti in 1830, but "at Tahiti spirits were more abundant," and the predilection towards drink had grown to be ubiquitous among the Pitcairnese people. The result of this change, Stallworth observed, "could not be otherwise than injurious when under the influence of this liquor they sometimes have quarrels with each other."[118]

Rosalind Amelia Young, one of John Adams' great-granddaughters, later noted in her own history of the island that the period from 1830 to 1833 was hardly Pitcairn's moral zenith. "It is only fair to acknowledge," she wrote,

that at the time of [Hill's] coming the condition of affairs on the island did not witness favorably to the management of those who were the acknowledged leaders.[119]

Indeed, Freemantle was so troubled by the prolific use of spirits at Pitcairn that he recommended to the three Englishmen that they might do well to consider leaving the island at their earliest convenience.[120] Freemantle knew that much of what Hill said about his credentials to govern at the island was not true. He feared that Hill was "some adventurer." But, he also knew that Hill was a man like Hiram Bingham or George Pritchard. He knew that Nobbs, Buffett, and Evans were guilty of public drunkenness.[121] He knew they had divided the community. He also knew that Hill had become a moral Cerberus at the island. He had "succeeded in restoring them to some kind of order, by putting a stop to the intemperance which existed, had broken up all their stills, and had formed them into a Temperance Society," all within seven months of his arrival.[122] All of these changes seemed to verify the claims Hill made to Freemantle that he was "decidedly against the use or ardent spirits, ... tobacco, etc. And as for wine, that only at dinner; it even then ought to be good."[123] Before Hill, Pitcairn seemed to have been a kakistocracy, a colony governed by its most unprincipled citizens. Given the choice of backing Buffett, Nobbs, or Hill, Freemantle was hardly betting on long odds in supporting Hill – at least as things stood in the spring of 1833.

---

[118] Stallworth, Letter to Mr. Ellis (April 21, 1834).

[119] Young, *Mutiny of the* Bounty, 75–76.

[120] Brodie, *Pitcairn's Island and the Islanders*, 182.

[121] Hiney, *On the Missionary Trail*, 100–119. See also, Murray, *Pitcairn*, 145.

[122] Reported in Barrow et al., "Accounts of the Pitcairn Islanders," 165–166. Walter Brodie would also praise Hill on this point after his 1850 visit to the island. See Brodie, *Pitcairn's Island and the Islanders*, 76.

[123] Quoted in Nobbs, *George Hunn Nobbs*, 28.

If we believe a petition to Hill from "the Public Functionaries and others" at Pitcairn dated October 1833, many islanders praised Hill for having saved Pitcairn and for "snatching [its people] providentially, as it were, from the brink of infidelity itself, and as well as other crying and besetting sins (now too painful for us to contemplate), which otherwise must have been our entire and total ruin."[124] The same memorandum further implored Hill not to "think of leaving us yet awhile, or until we become, with the blessed Lord's help, settled somewhat in safety." As long as the three "foreigners" remained on the island, the letter went on, the Pitcairners would never "be able to go on aright, or resist their corrupting or destructive practices."[125]

A similar petition signed by the "principal native inhabitants of Pitcairn's Island" on June 19, 1834 suggested that the islanders were very pleased by Hill's early evangelical accomplishments at Pitcairn. Hill's arrival, they insisted, had to have been "providential." Since Hill landed, the petition read, "we have, the Lord be praised!, had a regular school, and the Church of England service twice every Sabbath, with a lecture on some good subject."[126] The islanders were overjoyed at Hill's new temperance society, "which we very much needed," and the prayer meetings Hill hosted for them.[127]

The seemingly fickle nature of the many "humble petitions" that surround Hill's time at Pitcairn, suggest that both Nobbs and Hill might have been playing family politics with the islanders. As we have seen, similar petitions both certified the islanders' appreciation for Nobbs' work as their schoolmaster *and* asked for somebody to replace him. Petitions for and against Hill have the same back and forth quality. Was this petition Hill's prebuttal to his anticipated discovery? Indeed, both these petitions of support may expose Hill and Nobbs as being guilty of blag, chicanery, and forgery. Freemantle's observations about Hill's early time on the island, therefore, are vital as they confirm the content of Hill's administrative actions at Pitcairn, even if they do not clarify the islander's response to the steps he took to reform the island's morals.

The general impression that this evidence gives us, though, about Joshua Hill's early years at Pitcairn is far removed from the one we get from subsequent historians. Compare the islanders' plea that Hill remain among them to historian David Silverman's description of Hill as "one of those plausible paranoids who punctuate the pages of history with

[124] Brodie, *Pitcairn's Island and the Islanders*, 193–4.   [125] Ibid., 194.

[126] The Humble Petition of the Principal Native Inhabitants of Pitcairn's Island to His Excellency James Townshend (June 19, 1834), in Brodie, *Pitcairn's Island and the Islanders*, 204–205.

[127] Ibid., 205.

blood."[128] To Silverman and other historians, Joshua Hill was a "pretender" who seized control "over every aspect of Pitcairn life, including religious, for several years."[129] His government was "imperious, if not imperial." Hill was a "megalomaniac," and his regime was "a non-benevolent dictatorship."[130]

Context, though, tempers historical judgment. If we reflect that Hill had studied at the knees of both Bingham and Pritchard, men whose first purposes in the Pacific had been evangelical, it ought to come as no surprise that Hill controlled even the religious life of the community at Adamstown. Moreover, it should be even less surprising that Hill's religious leadership at Pitcairn should take on a governmental aspect. The same had proven true for Bingham and Pritchard, men who functioned as veritable prime ministers to their respective monarchs at Hawai'i and Tahiti. Only, at Pitcairn, there was no indigenous monarch. John Adams had been dead since 1829, and neither Buffett nor Nobbs had a legitimate claim to be his heir. John Evans, who had married into the Adams family, seems to have been the weakest of the three men – never truly a contender for the leadership position left up for grabs when the old mutineer died.

At Pitcairn, therefore, there was no division between church and state. Indeed, even under Adams, Pitcairn functioned, as we have seen, as a "Biblical monarchy."[131] During the brief period in which he acted as the chief magistrate at Pitcairn, after having displaced Buffett and before he was himself displaced by Hill, George Hunn Nobbs merged the two roles of magistrate and pastor in a harsh regime of theocratic terror. John Barrow observed that Nobbs "thrust" a code of laws upon the Pitcairners, a code that was predicated upon evangelical moral norms. "He enumerates crimes," Barrow wrote, "such as murder and adultery, unknown and unheard of among these simple people since the time that Adams was the sole legislator and patriarch." Furthermore, Nobbs' punishments were draconian. For adultery, both parties were whipped on their first offense. If the parties refused to marry and were found guilty of a second infraction, they were to forfeit their lands and property and to be banished from the island.[132]

Hill's regime at Pitcairn, of course, would prove no less harsh. But, those who visited the island in the first years of his administration did note, as had Freemantle, that the new Pitcairnese leader was working to impose some semblance of a moral order. One correspondent recalled

---

[128] Silverman, *Pitcairn Island*, 118.　　[129] Ibid., 148.　　[130] Ibid., 173–177.
[131] Lewis, "Pitcairn's Tortured Past," in Oliver, ed., *Justice, Legality, and the Rule of Law*, 48–51.
[132] Quoted in Silverman, *Pitcairn Island*, 155.

that Hill had overseen the construction of a tasteful church, "which in week days serves as the school room."[133] Hill also oversaw the construction of the island's first jail. Susanne Chauvel Carlsson has written that the jail was a distinct penal turning point for the island, "where no formal mode of punishment had been necessary."[134] J. A. Moerenhout would have agreed. When he heard of Hill's jail, he exclaimed, "A prison at Pitcairn! The pen falls from my hand at this thought."[135] Of course, Barrow's descriptions of life at Pitcairn under Nobbs suggests that Carlsson paints too happy a picture of the island before Hill's arrival. Perhaps her assessment, like so many others has been skewed by a failure to contextualize Hill – by an overly ready inclination to see in Hill only a liar, only a "mentally unstable" disciplinarian and a "a smooth-talking, self-made dictator."[136]

Those familiar with Herman Melville will, of course, take refuge in the author's skepticism about missionary activity in the South Pacific. His warnings that Polynesian islands were "authentic Edens in a pagan sea, fresh as at the moment of creation" and best left alone seem *apropos* in the context of Nobbs' and Hill's tyrannical administrations at Pitcairn.[137] Hill and his contemporaries – even George Hunn Nobbs – shared none of those reservations. Morality was the key to the idyllic image conjured about Pitcairn Island, and it had to be enforced.

In 1845, Buffett would recall the role that censorship played in Hill's regime. In the early years of Hill's administration, an American ship brought in a shipment of books, among them some of the writings of Thomas Paine. Hill, Buffett records, was outraged that the book was circulating, and John Evans became a particular target of Hill's ire. Hill became "very angry" at Evans, Buffett remembered, and called him a "Big Fool with the woolen Cap" for having allowed books to be distributed without approval. Going forward "all books coming on shore" were to "undergo his inspection and such as he condemned" were to be "burnt by the common hangman," though Buffett confessed that he did not think the island had an official executioner.[138]

Similarly, Hill warned the island's inhabitants against unauthorized public meetings, which he declared illegal. Those resisting this new regulation would be shot by the authorities. Hill's actions assured that his Sunday services were the only official means to communicate a religious ideology at Pitcairn, and his school sessions were the only educational outlet. As he secured control over the flow of ideas at Pitcairn, Hill

[133] Woolridge, Letter to an Unidentified Recipient (June 18, 1849).
[134] Carlsson, *Pitcairn Island*, 40.   [135] Moerenhout, *Travels to the Islands*, 446.
[136] Carlsson, *Pitcairn Island*, 39–40.   [137] Daws, *A Dream of Islands*, 71.
[138] Buffett, *Twenty Years Residence*, Part V.

also sought to control the island's arms and ammunitions. He ordered all of the weapons on the island gathered, and he had them stored at his residence by his allies while the islanders attended church one Sunday.[139]

Given Pitcairn's reputation for moral excellence, the abject failure of the Tahitian removal and its moral consequences, to say nothing of the seeming failure of leadership under both Buffett and Nobbs, Hill might ought to be forgiven for arguing that it was outside forces that had damaged Pitcairn Island. John Adams' death had, as Greg Dening has written, returned the island to a Hobbesian state of nature; it was time for a Leviathan to take the stage.[140] Writing to the Earl of Ripon in December 1832, just weeks after his arrival at the island, Hill was able to speak of his nascent temperance society as well as the governing committee of elders that he had established to help him administer at Adamstown. But, Hill required help. He needed medical supplies. He needed more books with which to teach and catechize the islanders. He needed public authority over the outsiders. In what is perhaps Hill's most direct admission that he was lying about his authority at Pitcairn, he asked Ripon to help him secure his nomination to be the permanent and official chief magistrate at Adamstown. Only then, he argued, could he build on his successes at the island with any degree of confidence and authority.[141]

In Hill's evangelical administration at Pitcairn, some have found hints of Wesleyanism.[142] What John or Charles Wesley would have found to like about Hill's Sunday services seems unclear. It was an odd sort of Methodism, to have the pastor seated in a chair under which he kept a loaded musket, after all.[143] Still, Rosalind Amelia Young recognized Hill's efforts as a sort of "Reformation."[144] Young was particularly pleased to see that the stills, which had not been unheard of in either Adams' time or under the leadership of Buffett or Nobbs were removed.[145]

Though the next chapter will endeavor to contextualize the broader political aspects of Hill's regime at Pitcairn, it wants noting here that Hill made use of religion in all of his administrative actions. All of Hill's

---

[139] Nicholson, *The Pitcairners*, 138.

[140] Greg Dening, *Mr. Bligh's Bad Language: Passion, Power, and Theatre on the Bounty* (New York: Cambridge University Press, 1994), 337–338.

[141] Joshua Hill, Letter to the Earl of Ripon (Pitcairn Island: December 23, 1832), RGS LMS, Item 4-b: 26.

[142] See Hancock, *Politics in Pitcairn*, 13. See also Brodie, *Pitcairn's Island and the Islanders*, 76–77.

[143] Hancock, *Politics in Pitcairn*, 13. See also, "Pitcairn's Island," in *Daily Southern Cross* 6:336 (September 17, 1850), 4.

[144] Young, *Mutiny of the Bounty*, 76.

[145] Ibid. See also, Hancock, *Politics in Pitcairn*, 3, 10, and 12.

governmental actions hinged on moral judgments. George Nobbs, for instance, inserted the letters "P.S.M." after his signature to indicate he was Pitcairn's pastor and spiritual mentor. Hill reinterpreted the abbreviation, identifying Nobbs as the island's foremost "Public Scoundrel and Miscreant."[146] When a group of women opposed some of his policies, Hill called a community meeting. At the meeting, the truculent Hill insisted that a prayer be said. Pitcairn was, after all, to be a godly colony. But, the prayer Hill uttered was hardly a call to moral reform. Rather, he seemed to want to call down God's wrath on the women, even suggesting they might die for resisting him. "If these women die the common death of all men," he prayed, "the Lord hath not sent me." At the end of Hill's petition, nobody at the meeting – Hill excepted – dared to say "Amen."[147] In yet another moment, Hill threatened Arthur Quintal with a sword for questioning an order. As he brandished the weapon, Hill demanded that Quintal "Confess your sins, for you are a dead man."[148] Like George Pritchard at Tahiti, Hill had come to Pitcairn with a missionary goal in mind. Just as Pritchard had come to view himself as the sole "constable" at Tahiti, Hill's work became civil *and* political, and his administrative vocabulary retained its religious inflection.

On one hand, the people of Pitcairn were not wholly unique. In 1838, the Protestant residents of Valparaíso wrote to John Walpole, the British consul general in Santiago, asking him to help them in their quest to recruit a minister as well as more naval surveillance from London.[149] It was a marvel, Moerenhout would later write, that the missionary societies out of London were so slow about responding to these sorts of requests, particularly at Pitcairn. Like Hill and others, Moerenhout felt that the Pitcairners were the perfect people to develop an "indigenous" Pacific missionary community with strong political ties to London.[150] If ever the flag and the Bible were to be joined in a common evangelical–colonial project, surely these were the people to do the work. To Moerenhout's mind, it was entirely London's fault that the entire set of fiascos – from Buffett down to Hill – had taken place.[151]

The confusion Hill caused at Pitcairn certainly put the small island on the official radar. Administrators from Chilé to London and most everywhere in between scrambled in the mid-1830s to figure out what exactly was going on at Adamstown. Who was Joshua Hill? Why was he at

---

[146] Nobbs, *George Hunn Nobbs*, 32.   [147] Young, *Mutiny of the* Bounty, 77–78.

[148] Ibid., 82–83.

[149] Protestant Residents of Valparaíso, Letter to HM's Consul General in Santiago, John Walpole (Valparaíso: August 1838), TNA FO 16/35.

[150] Moerenhout, *Travels in the Islands*, 446.   [151] Ibid.

Pitcairn? Who, if anybody, had sent him?[152] The crew of the HMS *Blond* were "much grieved" by reports they received of Pitcairn when they landed in Valparaíso in December 1836. Noting that he took "great interest in the spiritual and temporal welfare of the English residents" of the Pacific, Commander Mason could only hope that the recent visit of Captain Seymour of the *Challenger* would have a "good effect," as Seymour was known to be a man of "exemplary manners and conduct."[153] Once he had matters sorted, Commander Mason wrote Pritchard again to inform him that he was "anxious" to communicate with the Pitcairners "to undeceive" them about Joshua Hill and his authority to be their civil and spiritual leader.[154]

In none of the correspondence about the situation at Pitcairn did anybody suggest that Hill's intentions had been wrong. The missionary impulse survived Hill's implementation unscathed. As Brian Stanley has argued, the nineteenth-centruy missionary framework "was born out of a conviction that the church stood on the brink of the last days of history." But, this eschatology was also "incurably optimistic, evangelism was destined to succeed on an unprecedented scale, and as it did so the world would become a better place."[155] As had happened at Hawai'i and Tahiti, Hill's evangelical regime had bound missionary work to colonial governance that was both subjugating and oppressive, but the problem was Hill and his lack of authority.[156] Not the message. Not the domination.[157]

The wider public continued to be interested in Pitcairn Island as the site of religious conversion across the rest of the nineteenth century.[158] As Mary Russell Mitford had indicated in her 1811 poem *Christina, The Maid of the South Seas*, which was the first literary piece published about Pitcairn after news of the island's discovery began circulating in the West, Pitcairn drew people in in ways no other South Pacific island could do. Unlike Hawai'i or Tahiti, Pitcairn was inextricably linked to the West – through history and through ancestry. It was a "corner of the South Pacific which is for

---

152   H.M. Consul General at Chilé, Letter to the Colonial Office (Valparaíso: March 25, 1835), Te Puna, MS-Papers-1009–2/51-Letters and Papers. See also, George Adams, Letter to John White (Tahiti: July 14, 1834), Te Puna, MS-Papers-1009–2/51-Letters and Papers.

153   Francis Mason, Commander HMS *Blond* at Valparaíso, Letter to George Pritchard, dated December 3, 1836. ML MSS 24–2 – Tahiti British Consulate Papers.

154   Commander Francis Mason, Letter to George Pritchard (Callao: April 16, 1836), SLNSW ML MSS 24–2 – Tahiti, British Consulate Papers.

155   Stanley, *The Bible and the Flag*, 74–75.

156   Johnston, *Missionary Writing and Empire*, 19.

157   Bennett, *Narrative of a Whaling Voyage*, 54–55.

158   Maxton, *The Mutiny on HMS* Bounty, 56.

ever England."[159] No doubt, the Hill episode – so often described as "interesting" or "entertaining" in press reports from the period – helped bring the small island and its population to the public's attention. Even while Hill was still in power at Pitcairn, George Nobbs was busy trying to secure a more stable theological structure for the island, one atop which he could sit. The battle with Hill was never far from Nobbs' mind. In 1834, Nobbs wrote to Reverend W. T. Bullock of the Society for the Propagation of the Gospel in Foreign Parts to observe that Pitcairn still wanted for theological supervision from the outside.

Nobbs himself tried, he wrote, to observe some form of Holy Communion on the fourth Sunday of every month, but the island's religious orthodoxy was questionable at best without connections to an external authority.[160] Indeed, Lord Edward Russell, captain of the HMS *Actaeon*, did "not consider [Nobbs] at all a fit person" to serve as the island's pastor. It was Russell who first disabused the islanders about Hill's pretensions to power at Pitcairn and formally reinstated Nobbs as the island's pastor and schoolmaster. But even in his report about those changes at Adamstown to Commodore Mason, Russell noted that the island needed more official help.[161]

Across the 1840s and 1850s, missionary societies and Bible groups throughout the British imperial world would raise funds to send Bibles, prayer books, and other religious reading material to the people of Pitcairn – often along with tools, supplies, and other household items.[162] Using these items, their limited resources, and their own piety, the islanders tried to make due. Outsiders could still land at the island in these years and find the pious characters who had been fashioned in sailors' tales so long before. Captain R. C. Morgan of the *Camden* described seeing the islanders at worship during his visit in the early 1840s. "They all assembled," he wrote, "neat and clean, in a long neat building set apart for worship and for school," a building – ironically – that Hill had ordered built.[163]

[159] Edmond, *Representing the South Pacific*, 79–81.
[160] George Hunn Nobbs, Letter to Rev. W. T. Bullock (Pitcairn Island: October 8, 1834), Te Puna, MS-Papers-1009–2/51 – Letters and Papers.
[161] Lord Edward Russell, Letter to Commodore Mason (February 3, 1837), NMM HTN/68.
[162] Thursday October Christian and George Hunn Nobbs, Letter to Admiral Richard Thomas (Pitcairn Island: July 29, 1844), SLNSW ML MS 2233; Thomas Boyles Murray, Letter to Reverend William Armstrong (November 27, 1850), SLNSW Mfm M 2109; and Sir William Burnett, Letter to George Nobbs (January 28, 1853), in The Pitcairn Island Register, SLNSW C134 (also SLNSW Mfm CY 349).
[163] Captain R. C. Morgan, *Voyage of the Camden*, SOAS CWM Australia – Journals Box 1, File 4. See also Thomas Heath, Visit to the Austral Islands, Pitcairn, and Marquesas, SOAS CWM/LMS – Journals – South Seas, Box 9, File 129.

But, were the islanders safe? Most agreed they were not. The Reverend W. H. Holman wrote to Admiral Fairfax Moresby that the Pitcairners "pressed upon him almost daily" about their desire to "have among them an earnest and well educated English clergyman to whom they could look up with perfect love and confidence as their spiritual guide."[164] The reports sent back to the Admiralty by those who eventually removed Joshua Hill from Pitcairn made a similar point. Captain Bruce of the *Imogene* felt certain that removing Hill – and perhaps Nobbs, Evans, and Buffett – would restore peace at Pitcairn. But, the island would still need an official pastor.[165] One unidentified sailor from the HMS *Thunder* was pleased that Hill was willing to give up his post at Adamstown. "We found Mr. Hill so much disliked by the majority of the inhabitants," the sailor wrote. But removing Hill was, by itself, not the solution. "Can it be expected that these people will long remain uncorrupted when persons with such morals pretend to preach the Gospel?"[166] The Pitcairners were, to quote Raymond Nobbs, "unsophisticated, confiding people," and their "simple believism" left them vulnerable, particularly to somebody as beguiling and dazzling as Joshua W. Hill had been that October morning back in 1832.[167]

Commander Mason, who had been so eager to sort out the Hill situation in 1836, followed up on the situation in an 1838 letter to the Bishop of London. "I have the honor to inform your lordship," Mason observed, that there was still a great need for missionaries in the Pacific. American merchants had too much influence in the region, and they did little more than promote sin. "The Natives of Pitcairn's Island," he went on,

now amount to upwards of 90 and are still a most exemplary population, but they have no minister, nor any person qualified to teach the rising generation, & are therefore exposed to the profligate example of the crews of whale ships which touch there. I believe they are anxious for a minister of the Established Church.[168]

It would take time, but, on October 24, 1852, the Church of England responded to Mason's letter. On that day, at the parish church of St.

---

[164] Emphasis in original. Holman, Letter to Admiral Fairfax Moresby (June 4, 1853), frames 43–87.

[165] Captain Henry William Bruce, Letter to J. Backhouse (December 17, 1839), TNA FO 58/15. See also Captain Henry William Bruce, The Remark Book of the *Conway* and *Imogene*, 1832–1840. UKHO OD 777, 297; Captain Henry William Bruce, Letter to Lord Palmerston (March 24, 1840), TNA FO 58/16; and Bruce Letter to Lady Troubridge (January 2, 1838).

[166] Narrative, Remarks, Statistics, Extract from HMS *Thunder*, Te Puna, Turnbull Collection, MS-2148.

[167] Nobbs, *George Hunn Nobbs*, 27.

[168] Commodore Francis Mason, Letter to the Lord Bishop of London (Wheler Lodge, Welford: April 17, 1838), Te Puna, MS-Papers-1009–2/51 – Letters and Papers.

Mary's, Islington, the Bishop of Sierra Leone, ordained George Hunn
Nobbs an Anglican deacon by special permission of the Bishop of
London. Nobbs was visiting Britain as part of a voyage organized by the
Church Missionary Society and other missionary friends of Pitcairn
Island.[169] One month after having been ordained to the diaconate,
Nobbs was elevated to the priesthood by the Bishop of London, who
gave the now-Reverend Nobbs orders to take up the position of Chaplain
of Pitcairn's Island. Before he sailed back to Pitcairn, Nobbs met with
Queen Victoria and Prince Albert at Osborne House.[170]

The nineteenth-century South Pacific "had an enormous impact on
Britain, enhanced by the images published in exploration narratives and
missionary journals, and eagerly consumed by an increasingly literate
public."[171] As Jane Samson notes, "Sunday school children felt they
knew the King of the Cannibal Islands," and they grieved at the deaths –
particularly the tragic ones – of missionary heroes like John Williams, who
was killed and cannibalized while evangelizing on the island of Erromango
in November 1839.[172] In grand imperial terms, the years after Hill's
disruptive time at Pitcairn made the Pacific interesting in other ways.
France, America, Russia, and other imperial powers would begin to take
a more active interest in the Pacific across the 1840s and 1850s. In this
atmosphere, Britain would begin to translate missionary influence across
the region into more direct colonial control. The elevation of George
Pritchard to the office of consul at Tahiti in 1837 was but the first hint of
this shift in policy.

At Pitcairn, Captain Russel Elliot of the HMS *Fly* helped the
Pitcairners draft a new constitution when he landed in November 1838,
shortly after Joshua Hill departed. Nobbs' trip to London was part of this
same process – the integration of Pitcairn into the British imperial order
and, specifically, into the framework of a British Pacific. Ironically, Hill's
legacy was that London shifted policies vis-à-vis Pitcairn, adopting many
of the same suggestions that Hill had once made – all in order to prevent
another Hill from gaining control at the island in the future.

But it was Nobbs, not Hill, who would be canonized as part of the
British Pacific's religious elite. His ordination at the hands of the Bishop
of London assured that Pitcairn was now safely part of the missionary
network of the establish Church of England. And despite his own cloudy

[169] Minutebook of the Committee for Managing the Pitcairn Island Fund, December 1852-
May 1858, SLNSW Mfm M 2111.
[170] Boyles, *Pitcairn*, 218–220. See also Hoare, *Norfolk Island*, 68.
[171] Samson, *Imperial Benevolence*, 174. See also, Fulton and Hoffenberg, "Introduction," in
Fulton and Hoffenberg, *Oceania and the Victorian Imagination*, 7.
[172] Samson, *Imperial Benevolence*, 174.

background, Nobbs emerged from the trip as the authorized theological leader at Pitcairn. Whether the honor was deserved or not, Nobbs was John Adams' heir, at long last. Writing of his own visit to Pitcairn in 1850, Walter Brodie would record that Nobbs' arrival at the island was "one of the providential occurrences in the History" of this already providential little community.[173] Six years on, as the Pitcairners were removed from their home island for a second time, in this instance to Norfolk Island, it would be the Reverend George Hunn Nobbs who saw to the spiritual welfare of the community in a turbulent time.[174] Though others officially served in the role of the island's chief magistrate – both at Pitcairn and at Norfolk – it would be Nobbs who cast the longest shadow over the story.

When he finally died in November 1884, George Hunn Nobbs was laid to rest in the Norfolk Island Cemetery, where his headstone – like all the others in the cemetery – faces outward from the island, over the waters of Cemetery Bay, and into the vast expanse of the Pacific Ocean. In death, as in life, Nobbs, is surrounded by Christians, and Quintals, McCoys, and Adamses – the names of those families whose mutinous actions onboard the *Bounty* were, so the story tells, redeemed at Pitcairn Island.

---

[173] Brodie, *Pitcairn's Island and the Islanders*, 76   [174] Nobbs, *George Hunn Nobbs*, 41.

4   The Age of Reform

But one man of her crew alive,
What put to sea with seventy-five.
Robert Louis Stevenson, *Treasure Island* (1883)[1]

"Tis too late, I have been in hell for this fortnight past and am determined to bear it no longer."[2]

Such is the exordium. Every account of our story begins here.[3] "I have been in hell." These were the heated words Fletcher Christian strafed across the deck of HMAV *Bounty* to his captain, William Bligh, early in the morning of April 28, 1789. Only an hour or so before, Bligh had been sleeping soundly, no longer, it would seen, troubled by a splenetic shouting match he had had with Christian, his hand-selected master's mate for the *Bounty*'s voyage to Tahiti, the evening before. They had fought over coconuts.

According to Morrison, Captain William Bligh went for a turn on the quarterdeck of the *Bounty* on the afternoon of April 27, 1789. During his walk, the captain noticed that a pile of coconuts he had stashed between the ship's guns seemed smaller than it ought to have been. He concluded that several of his coconuts had to have been stolen, and he mustered all the ship's officers to find out what they knew about the situation. When it came time for him to answer questions about the missing fruit, Fletcher Christian replied that he had no knowledge of its whereabouts, adding that he hoped the captain did not "think me so mean as to be guilty of stealing yours." Captain Bligh's response was shirty and ferocious.[4] "Yes, you damned hound," he fumed,

I do – You must have stolen them from me or you could give a better account of them – God damn you, you scoundrels, you are all thieves alike, and combine with

---

[1] Stevenson, *Treasure Island*, 156.
[2] James Morrison, *After the Bounty: A Sailor's Account of the Mutiny and Life in the South Seas.* Donald A. Maxton, ed. (Washington, DC.: Potomac Books, 2010), 37.
[3] Barrow, *A Description of Pitcairn's Island*, 69.   [4] Dening, *Mr. Bligh's Bad Language*, 9.

the men to rob me – I suppose you'll steal my yams next, but I'll sweat you for it, you rascals, I'll make half of you jump overboard before you get through Endeavour Strait.

He then ordered that the officers should be deprived of their daily grog ration and fed but one half a pound of yams the following day. He had the remaining coconuts moved and secured, and then he went below for the evening.[5]

The boatswain woke Morrison the next morning with the news that Christian had taken the ship during the night. Having secured the *Bounty*'s armory, Christian and his party gathered the crew on the deck, ordered that the ship's small cutter be hoisted over the side, and had Bligh (still dressed only in his night shirt) brought out of his quarters.[6] When it became clear that many of the crew were loyal to the captain to the point of wanting to be cast off with him, several Bligh loyalists begged Christian for the twenty-three-foot-long launch over the cutter, and Christian reluctantly agreed. In all, Bligh took eighteen crewmembers with him. He might have taken more had the launch not been so heavily laden that only a few inches of its gunwales remained above the water line. The nineteen men aboard the *Bounty*'s launch faced what has become one of the most harrowing tales of ocean navigation in all of Europe's Pacific history – an open-boat voyage of nearly 4,000 nautical miles that lasted a remarkable forty-seven days. When Bligh landed the launch at the Dutch East Indian port of Batavia on June 14, 1789, he had lost only one sailor, his quartermaster John Norton, who had been killed by natives on the island of Tofua.

As Bligh sailed back to Britain and into nautical history, Christian, his band of mutineers, and the rest of the *Bounty*'s crew who remained on the ship sailed into the realm of legend. Glynn Christian, himself a distant relative of Fletcher Christian, summarized the myth nicely when he wrote that Christian was the father to "a unique people" led by "a law-breaker, a mutineer, a pirate, a blackbirder, and possibly a fool." There was no getting around the story's criminal origins. Christian had set a tale in motion that would eventually see the settlement of Pitcairn Island, Britain's second (if unofficial) Pacific colony after Australia.[7] And like that larger, authorized colonial setting, most of the inhabitants at Pitcairn – indeed, all of the British men there – were criminals.

---

[5] Morrison, *After the* Bounty, 35. See also Salmond, *Bligh*, 206–209; and Edwards, *The Story of the Voyage*, 137–138.
[6] Danielsson, *What Happened on the* Bounty, 101.
[7] Ward, *British Policy in the South Pacific*, 1.

Aware that the crew were all now wanted men, Christian had to seek an uncharted island where he and the other twenty-three men under his command could live out their lives in hiding.[8] After several false starts, Christian returned to Tahiti one last time. There, sixteen of his crew – including James Morrison – announced their plans to remain at the island, taking their chances there rather than continuing to sail the South Seas aimlessly. That left Christian a crew of only nine, counting himself. He set sail from Tahiti for the last time in September 1789 with six Tahitian men and eleven Tahitian women on board the *Bounty*. In almost every account, these Tahitians sailed as semi-hostages. True, some of the women had developed attachments to the *Bounty* men – particularly Christian's "wife," a Tahitian named Mauatua, though Christian called her either Maimiti or Isabella – but nearly every narrative of the *Bounty*'s final sailing from Tahiti includes a nighttime sailing, a secretive order to up the anchor, and the attempt by one Tahitian woman to jump ship and swim home.

Christian and his men settled at Pitcairn in 1790. By 1793, nearly every man who had landed with the *Bounty* was dead. In part, the conflicts that devastated Pitcairn in those three years were the by-product of Christian's decision to divide the island only among its white inhabitants, leaving the kidnapped Tahitian men to serve as veritable serfs to the English fugitives, a subject that will occupy much of the next chapter. But as we will see in Chapter 6, the conflict was also the result of the gender imbalance on the island. Some of the mutineers had seen to it that their favorite Tahitian women were brought (either willingly, by force, or coercion) aboard the *Bounty*. But, as deaths took the lives of several women, some of the mutineers demanded sexual access to women who had established themselves with the Tahitian men. In the conflicts that ensued, five of the nine mutineers (Christian, Jack Williams, Isaac Martin, John Mills, and William Brown) and all six of the Tahitian men were murdered.

Even those, like Lieutenant Edward Belcher from Captain Beechey's *Blossom* voyage, who were quick to note the faithfulness and religiosity of the Pitcairners, could not help but to comment on the violent past the island had known since the *Bounty*'s arrival in 1790. "Murder has become so common," Belcher wrote, that it could almost be passed over without comment when telling the tale of Pitcairn's post-settlement past.[9] True, some of the deaths since 1790 were accidents. In 1798, for instance, William McCoy either slipped from a cliff or committed suicide in

---

[8] H. E. Maude, "In Search of Home: from the Mutiny to Pitcairn Island (1789–1790)," in *The Journal of the Polynesian Society* 67:2 (June 1958), 104–131.
[9] Belcher, *Private Journal and Remarks* (1826).

a drunken fit.[10] But most of the deaths the island experienced were intentional. In 1799, Matthew Quintal decided to murder Edward Young and Alexander Smith, both of whom had stepped in to fill the power vacuum left by Christian's death six years before. Tipped off to Quintal's plan by Tahitian women, Young and Smith butchered Quintal with a hatchet. This execution horrified Belcher, who was repulsed that Englishmen could so casually decide to murder a companion.[11] Young, who had always been a sickly man, died of asthma related complications in 1800. Of the English mutineers (indeed of all of the adult male settlers on the island), only Alexander Smith remained. "But one man of her crew alive," and he was, to call upon Diana Souhami's blunt phrasing, a mutineer and a serial killer.[12]

It had only been ten years since Pitcairn was settled, and already the island had witnessed the death of more than fourteen of its twenty-six residents – and only one of them was clearly the result of natural causes. As Fletcher Christian laments in Richard Bean's 2014 play, *Pitcairn*, "We had this island! This virgin leaf of velum. So perfect a sanctuary, and what have we done with it? We have stained it."[13] Edward Belcher could only be thankful that, after having partaken in actions that caused moral indignation, Smith/Adams was moved "to consider his state seriously" and to answer the "spark of that honor which seamen, men of war's men, are known to feel."[14] Here again, Smith/Adams' life after 1800 seems poised to propitiate the crimes he might have committed in his first decade at Pitcairn. As a founding father, Adams/Smith would become, Belcher later wrote, "a better Christian than he would have proved under any other circumstances, however favourable."[15] *The Mirror* echoed this sentiment in 1831 when it observed that, "having run the full career of most kinds of vice," Adams/Smith had been "effectually *pulled up* by an interval of leisurely reflection, and the sense of new duties awakened by the heaven-inspired power of natural affections."[16]

The popular narrative of redemption notwithstanding, there was no escaping the fact that Pitcairn was an island of crimes – the last refuge of scoundrels. On that harsh Pacific stage, the mutineers played out a drama of piracy that has become – very literally – the stuff of Hollywood legend. The *Bounty* mission should have been, to quote Patty O'Brien, a largely

[10] Hough, *Captain Bligh and Mr. Christian*, 240.
[11] Belcher, Private Journal and Remarks (1826).
[12] Stevenson, *Treasure Island*, 156; and Souhami, *Coconut Chaos*, 124.
[13] Bean, *Pitcairn*, 63.   [14] Belcher, Journal and Remarks (1826).
[15] Ibid. See also, Topliff, "Pitcairn's Island;" and "Pitcairn's Island," extract from *The Mirror* (1831), 375.
[16] "Pitcairn's Island," in *The Mirror* (1831), 377.

"unsensational" sideshow in British naval history.[17] The loss of the *Bounty*, though a blow to naval authority, was hardly consequential in terms of lost personnel or materiel – nothing of the sort the navy would see in 1797, for instance.[18] The power of the *Bounty* saga, then, emerged not from history but from the tales told about the mutiny, tales that focused on the passions and rash actions of a romantic hero, the viperine authoritarianism of a supposedly tyrannical leader, and the mythology that surrounded a South Sea voyage.

The *Bounty* saga was, after all, frequently set against the age of Atlantic revolutions. The 1789 mutiny happened in the same year that the US Constitution came into effect and the same year that George Washington was sworn in as the chief executive of an experimental new republic. And of course, it is worth remembering that the actual mutiny aboard the *Bounty* was also set against the historical background of the revolution in France.[19] As Rod Edmond has observed, the romantic poet Robert Southey was torn as to what he should make of the mutiny on the *Bounty*. On one hand, he understood the dangerous meaning of mutiny within the British navy. On the other hand, he was smitten with the exciting notions of liberty, equality, and fraternity that were drifting in the air in the late eighteenth century.[20] The *Bounty* story tugged against opposing cultural and political currents.

Joshua Hill's mutiny at Pitcairn, for how else but in terms of mutiny and treason ought we speak of the illicit and unauthorized seizure of a British colony by a British subject from the British crown, was arguably more substantive than Christian's brazen bit of piracy the morning after he went toe to toe with his captain over some missing coconuts. It was, though, obviously less flamboyant. Joshua Hill was something of a schoolmarm, a tweedy sexagenarian with an alopecic scalp, flabby jowls, and vague connections to Britain's evangelical communities. At sixty years old, Hill was, by his own admission, a bit "infirm" and, he suggested, in his senescence. "I must go hence ere long," he wrote to Lord Townshend, suggesting that his time on this side of the grave was

---

[17] O'Brien, *The Pacific Muse*, 121.

[18] Ann Veronica Coats and Philip MacDougall, "Introduction: Analysis and Interpretation," in Ann Veronica Coats and Philip MacDougall, eds., *The Naval Mutinies of 1797: Unity and Perseverance* (Rochester, NY: The Boydell Press, 2011), 1. See also, Morrison, *After the* Bounty, 2; Wahlroos, *Mutiny and Romance*, ix; and Henry Adams and Marau Taaroa, *Memoirs of Arii Taimai E Marama of Eimeo, Teriirere of Tooarai Teriinui of Tahiti, Tauraatua I Amo* (Paris, 1901. Kindle Edition), location 1576.

[19] Salmond, *Bligh*, 237.

[20] Edmond, "The Pacific: Tahiti," in Hulme and Youngs, eds., *The Cambridge Companion to Travel Writing*, 144.

short.[21] This man was hardly well cast to play the part of a nineteenth-century Fletcher Christian. Indeed, if anything, Hill's actions at Tahiti and Hawai'i on his voyage out to Pitcairn had proven him to be something of a law and order man, hardly a mutineer.

In an 1834 letter to Lord Townshend recounting his Pacific adventures, Hill noted that he had fallen out at Tahiti with the LMS missionaries over the question of alcohol. The missionaries had been, Hill wrote, "pleased to consult me on certain points, and I freely and candidly gave them my humble opinion."[22] It is doubtful that there was much humble about any opinion held by Mr. Joshua W. Hill, but, in this instance, the direction he offered was that the LMS should do more to curb the Tahitian use of spirituous drink. The island needed a temperance society. We know that this would be the first key to political and social reform at Pitcairn once Hill tool control there. Sadly, the missionaries "did not relish the antidote."[23] Here, then, Hill was willing to engage in conversations with and between European and South Pacific communities – indigenous islanders and missionaries – about how to reform the social and political landscape of the Pacific islands, even if his suggestions went unheeded.

But Hill's efforts could be more directly political. In January 1832, Queen Pomare of Tahiti wrote to King William IV about the case of Captain Miner of the London-based whale ship *Venilia*, a case we encountered in Chapter 1. Miner, recall, stood accused of disturbing the peace at Tahiti because he had turned out thirteen supposedly mutinous members of his crew, abandoning them at Papeete and to the care of the Tahitian queen.

Joshua Hill, Pomare observed, was the most helpful of the Britons at her court in handling the situation, largely because it was he who most clearly insisted that the law be followed. The queen was deeply impressed by Hill's authority. "It is not at all agreeable to the Laws of Britain," she said to Miner, "that you should discharge or in any manner turn away your men in a foreign land." Moreover, Hill had a clear sense of how best to handle Miner's charges against his crew, even in a complex international context. "You write a document stating clearly the crime for which these men have been turned on shore," he requested, "that these men may be interrogated, that the Governor and Chiefs on shore may know how to act, and that the Chiefs of the

---

[21] Joshua Hill, Letter to Lord James Townshend (Pitcairn Island: June 20, 1834), quoted in Brodie, *Pitcairn's Island and the Islanders*, 202.

[22] Ibid., 199.

[23] Joshua Hill, Letter to Lord James Townshend (Pitcairn Island: June 20, 1834), quoted in Brodie, *Pitcairn's Island and the Islanders*, 199.

land may render your assistance."[24] In a surviving letter from Hill to Captain Miner, we find Hill citing British maritime law by chapter and verse. "As an old sea officer myself," Hill begins, "and I trust a loyal subject of His Britannic Majesty, I herewith enclose to you for your better information, both the Laws of England to wit 'Anno 57 Geo. 3 AD 1817' and those Laws of the Tahitian Government ... immediately in reference to the matter in question."[25]

As he had when the matter of Catholic infiltration into Protestant missionary space was brought before him, Joshua Hill had a balanced sense of how to handle the *Venilia* situation. Months later, as the matter was making its way through the Admiralty, officials there would conclude that Hill's recommendations were not only appropriate but geopolitically astute.[26] The Admiralty's assessment, though, would hardly matter at Tahiti. Captain Miner remained intransigent, even going so far as to return the copies of legal documents Hill had sent him regarding the disposition of English crewmen on a Tahitian beach.[27] He refused to write up a list of charges against his crew to appease the legal demands he owed to British or Tahitian law.[28] George Pritchard, the LMS agent at Pomare's court, was little more help himself. Writing to one of the abandoned crewmen, Pritchard observed that "Captain Hill will readily afford all the necessary information on this unpleasant business."[29] Pritchard's most substantive contribution to the affair seems to have been the time he took translating Pomare's petition into English before it was forwarded to London, as it was Hill, not Pritchard, who forwarded the document to Lord Palmerston. No wonder, then, that the Queen hoped Hill could be appointed as the British consul at her court.[30]

In this instance, Joshua Hill does not appear a likely rule-breaker. Indeed, in sending Pomare's petition on to London, he confessed that he was on his way to Pitcairn, and he expressed his "humble hope" that "the little I have contributed both here, the Sandwich Islands, and what I have done and still have in contemplation for the Pitcairn's people (whence I am abt. going) may meet with the perfect approbation of His Majesty's Government."[31] Here we have it. Hill laid his plans out – in full – to the British government. Hardly secretive, hardly mad. This was

---

[24] Queen Pomare IV of Tahiti, Letter to William IV (January 7, 1832).

[25] Joshua Hill, Letter to Captain G. Miner (Tahiti: December 27, 1831), TNA FO 58/14.

[26] Charles Jones, Letter to George Elliot (June 22, 1832), TNA FO 58/14.

[27] Hill, Letter to Captain G. Miner (December 27, 1831).

[28] Queen Pomare IV of Tahiti, Letter to William IV (January 7, 1832).

[29] George Pritchard, Letter to N. Paterson (Tahiti: December 24, 1831), TNA FO 58/14.

[30] Queen Pomare IV of Tahiti, Letter to William IV (January 7, 1832); and Joshua Hill, Letter to Lord Palmerston (Tahiti: January 12, 1832), TNA FO 58/14.

[31] Hill, Letter to Lord Palmerston (January 12, 1832).

not a man suffering under some Jerusalem syndrome. He actually *had* been helpful and influential in the British Pacific, and he made it very clear that he intended to go on doing so – at Pitcairn Island. An odd sort of muntineer! And yet, like Fletcher Christian's, Hill's actions on October 28, 1832, struck at the power of British imperial might, exposing London's limited capacity to hold firm to the reigns of colonial control, particularly as those reigns reached closer and closer to the ends of the earth. Similarly, Hill's ability to undo British colonial power at Pitcairn hinged on fabrications, just as Christian's post-mutiny anchorages at Tahiti had done. In both instances, London's wafer-thin authority was brought low by simple acts of insubordination and a regime of lies.

Joshua Hill's interest in Pitcairn, though, was not always rooted in deception and deceit. As we have seen, the earliest extant reference from Hill about Pitcairn comes in a letter dated May 2, 1829, from Liverpool in which Hill offered to serve as the *custos morum* of Pitcairn Island on behalf of the London Missionary Society. The letter, which was written to the LMS's George Hodson, indicates a rather comprehensive sense of Pitcairn's history, not surprisingly given some of the political and imperial connections that we now know were part of Hill's social vocabulary. Pitcairn, Hill explained, was in want of a moral leader.[32] To leave the Pitcairners unattended was, Hill argued, to miss a critical evangelical, imperial, and civilizational moment, for Pitcairn was the ideal platform from which to stretch a European missionary net across the South Pacific. The logic behind such a plan, Hill explained, was "too obvious, in my humble view," to require an explanation.[33]

This letter to the LMS was not the first time Hill wrote to the society's leadership about Pitcairn, for it references earlier correspondence in which Hill seems to have outlined his vision for a Pitcairnese mission.[34] The LMS does not appear to have responded to Hill's earlier letters, though letters in the society's archives do indicate that many in its leadership knew of Hill and his eagerness and anxieties about Pitcairn Island.[35] Though ignored, Joshua Hill refused to let go of the Pitcairn question; he remained adamant that the recondite little island mattered against the background of the broader Pacific. And so, he volunteered his own services.[36]

Hill's letter, then, offers an outline of the mutiny he would eventually perpetrate at Pitcairn. Though they were mere puffery and taradiddle in

---

[32] Hill, Letter to Mr. G. Hodson (May 2, 1829).   [33] Ibid.   [34] Ibid.
[35] Stallworth, Letter to Mr. Ellis (April 21, 1834).
[36] Hill, Letter to Mr. G. Hodson (May 2, 1829).

1832, Hill's claims to administrative authority at Pitcairn date back to this 1829 plan to serve as a legitimate agent of the LMS on the island, and, perhaps more significantly, they hinge on his extravagant sense of Pitcairn's providential importance. The Pitcairners, those "most insulated creatures," were so well situated for a greater purpose in the Pacific that it "almost seem[ed] the Grt. & Blessed Providence of God designed [for them] to further His good cause."[37] The LMS had failed to see as much or to respond to Hill's first proposal, leaving him to "beg that your laudable Society may be pleased to further my said views & thus patronize my humble labours & undertaking."[38] Once again, though, the LMS never responded to Joshua Hill's letter.

That the London Missionary Society ignored Hill's unsolicited advice is not surprising. As John M. Ward astutely observed in his *British Policy in the South Pacific, 1786–1893*, missionary societies had little to gain and much to lose as outsiders, outside organizations, and (most significantly) colonial powers like Britain and France turned more and more attention to the Pacific.[39] As we have seen, missionary establishments had, in the absence of strong state-sponsored colonial efforts, been able to insert themselves directly into the political systems of island kingdoms like Tahiti and Hawai'i. In such a world, what was the purpose of direct state influence?

Certainly, though, there were exceptions to this broad rule. The LMS itself argued for the institution of a British protectorate over Tahiti in 1826, but, as Ward notes, that had much more to do with the missionaries' fear at rising French influence on the island at the expense of LMS control over the government there than it did with an actual sense that London would be the best place from which to govern the people of Tahiti.[40] On the whole, then, Euro-American missionary societies in the Pacific operated under the notion that "colonization was inimical to native welfare," and they similarly opposed Pacific traders for being a "debauched" influence throughout the region.[41]

Joshua Hill's suggestions to the LMS, therefore, ran counter to the society's interests. They also ran counter to London's inclinations, for Hill seems to have spent the late 1820s and early 1830s writing to the Admiralty suggesting the same scheme that he had outlined to the LMS. One such letter suggested that the Admiralty ought to authorize the South American squadron with a blanket authority to canvas the South Pacific as regularly as it could to augment the visits then being sent from New

---

[37] Ibid.   [38] Ibid.   [39] Ward, *British Policy in the South Pacific*, 45.   [40] Ibid., 47.
[41] Ibid., 45.

South Wales.[42] As had the LMS, the Admiralty ignored Hill, favoring what Ward called a "policy of minimum interventions."[43]

This policy emerged out of two fundamental assumptions. First, it hinged on the notion that Britain had no real political interest or commercial prospects among the islands of the South Pacific. Second, it assumed that Britain would be obliged to administer and protect any islands that fell under its control, a costly proposition that most in London hoped to avoid. We can get a sense of just how much London hoped to avoid spending precious resources in the Pacific when we review Joshua Hill's requests for orders of soap. Early in his time at the island, Hill communicated that the Pitcairners were doing well and that they were well supplied with almost every necessity of life. Soap, though, was in short supply. Could some be sent? The answer was yes, but the dispatch that London sent out to Governor Richard Bourke in New South Wales was clear that the colonial administration in Sydney was "not intended to incur any great expense on this account."[44]

If the small cost of a bit of soap was a problem, it becomes much easier to see why London seems to have favored a policy of maintaining the status quo among the Pacific's many islands more broadly. The hope was, primarily, to secure Britain's Australian possessions without having to engage with other colonial powers – namely France – throughout the rest of the vast Pacific.[45] Britain's first South Pacific voyage with an articulated and targeted objective was Captain Bligh's mission to bring breadfruit plants from Tahiti as a foodstuff for the slave populations on Caribbean islands. Greg Dening has commented on the irony. Breadfruit, which was a staple food in the diet of a society noted for its "free and unencumbered life" was being taken to the West Indies, which were infamous as "islands of bondage."[46] This was an ironic, even cruel, global balancing act, indeed. If, that is, it was a balancing act at all. As O. H. K. Spate has noted, the purpose of the voyage had more to do with the Caribbean and Atlantic worlds than it did with the Pacific per se.[47]

As we have seen, Hill's 1811 editorial in the *London Morning Post* had argued for a more aggressive policy of protecting Britain's global maritime

---

[42] Ibid., 59; and Hill, Letter to Lord Palmerston (May 12, 1832).

[43] Ward, *British Policy in the South Pacific*, 48. See also, Morrell, *Britain in the Pacific Islands*, 63.

[44] R. W. Hay, Letter to Governor Richard Bourke (Downing Street: June 15, 1832), in Frederick Watson, ed., *Historical Records of Australia, Volume XVI* (Sydney: Library Committee of the Commonwealth Parliament, 1922/23), 667–668.

[45] Ward, *British Policy in the South Pacific*, 48.   [46] Dening, *Mr. Bligh's Bad Language*, 9.

[47] Spate, *Paradise Found and Lost*, 166. See also, Alan Lester, *Imperial Networks: Creating Identities in Nineteenth-Century South Africa and Britain* (New York: Routledge, 2001), 6.

supremacy. London's street lamps were fueled by the whale oil to be found in the waters of the Pacific. The lubricants that smoothed the machines of the industrial revolution came from the same leviathans. Soap and other products that made domestic life better did too. In the early years of the nineteenth century, it was not uncommon for whaling ships to return from a voyage to the Pacific with £20,000 to £30,000 worth of profit in their holds, the boiled blubber of some sixty whales per vessel. The Pacific was the essential ocean, and Britain's claim there could not be taken for granted.[48]

Edmund Burke may have understood something of Hill's argument, though a generation too early. As he laid out the case for conciliation with the North American colonies in March 1775, Burke observed that London had come to be envious of the wealth that its colonies drew from the global oceans. Whale fisheries were of particular concern. Americans, Burke argued, would go anywhere – brave any adversity – to draw out the benefits of the world's seas. "We follow them among the tumbling mountains of ice, and behold them penetrating into the deepest frozen recesses of Hudson's Bay and Davis's Streights," he noted. And "whilst we are looking for them beneath the Arctic Circle, we hear that they have pierced into the opposite region of polar cold." Americans, he continued, "are at the antipodes, and engaged under the frozen Serpent of the south." No part of the globe was "too remote and romantic an object for the grasp of [their] national ambition." No place was too far, too cold, too hot.[49]

Anglo-American whaling in the Pacific first emerged in the 1780s. Captain Samuel Enderby sailed the first whaling ship, the *Amelia*, into the South Pacific in 1789. The *Beaver* soon followed under Captain Paul Worth, whose crew was primarily out of Nantucket. As Donald Freeman has observed, whaling in the Pacific in these years "was outside the legal jurisdiction of any nation."[50] It was hard work. It was dangerous. But, as Burke observed, it was also profitable enough to have inspired the commercial sensibilities of American colonialists. The Americans understood the value of sea power. They understood the Pacific.

In *Moby-Dick*, Herman Melville famously boasted that "Yankees in one day, collectively, kill more whales than all the English, collectively, in ten years."[51] The claim was false, but its intention is clear. The Americans were masters of the seas, and of the Pacific in particular. Lest we have any doubt, we might consider Melville's description of Nantucket and its

---

[48] Hiney, *On the Missionary Trail*, 40.
[49] Edmund Burke, "Speech on Conciliation with the American Colonies," in James Buke, ed., *The Speeches of the Rt. Hom. Edmund Burke* (Dublin: James Duffy, 1854), 82.
[50] Freeman, *The Pacific*, 129–131.   [51] Melville, *Moby-Dick*, 244.

nineteenth-century relationship with the world's oceans from *Moby-Dick*. "And thus have these naked Nantucketers," he wrote,

these hermits, issuing from their ant-hill in the sea, overrun and conquered the watery world like so many Alexanders; parceling out among them the Atlantic, Pacific, and Indian oceans, as the three pirate powers did Poland. Let America add Mexico to Texas, and pile Cuba upon Canada; let the English overswarm all India, and hang their blazing banner from the sun; two-thirds of this terraqueous globe are the Nantucketer's. For the sea is his; he owns it, as Emperors own empires.[52]

The sea is his. As emperors own empires. Hardly a neutral view of things! Whaling, as Melville would note, did not come without connotations of control and ownership.

Furthermore, as Hill warned in a letter to Lord Palmerston dated from Tahiti in 1831, it was not only in the realm of whaling that Americans were entering the Pacific.[53] Americans were spreading their morals, their misbehavior, and their might. They were "wide awake" to the significance of the Pacific Ocean.[54] David Igler has observed that the pro-expansionist senator from Missouri, Thomas Hart Benton, imagined the Pacific "not as a terminus but instead as a crucial step on the longer 'North American road to India'."[55] Benton's contemporary, Daniel Webster, a senator from Massachusetts, was as much an opponent of territorial expansion as Benton was an advocate. In the years before the Mexican-American War in the 1840s, Webster was among the first and most intense critics of President James K. Polk's aggressive policies vis-à-vis Mexico. "And yet," Igler has written,

he consistently lobbied for New England's maritime role in the Pacific, strongly supported the US Exploring Expedition (1838–1842) on behalf of the whaling industry, and authored the Tyler Doctrine (1842) which declared an American sphere of influence over large portions of the Pacific.[56]

As Igler also observes, it was also Webster, in 1842, who urged Congress to apportion funds to purchase San Francisco Bay and the Strait of Juan de Fuca from, respectively, Mexico and Britain.[57]

From ports like San Francisco, then, the Pacific was what Andrew Delbanco has called "the ultimate trip west," and Americans eyed the Pacific with ambitious goals in the first years of the nineteenth

---

[52] Ibid., 65–66. See also Philip Hoare, *The Whale: In Search of the Giants of the Sea* (New York: Harper Collins, 2010), 116.
[53] Hill, Letter to Lord Palmerston (November 20, 1831).   [54] Ibid.
[55] David Igler, *The Great Ocean: Pacific Worlds from Captain Cook to the Gold Rush* (New York: Oxford University Press, 2013), 176.
[56] Ibid., 125.   [57] Ibid.

century.[58] Indeed, it is a mistake to assume that San Francisco was the lynchpin in the US Pacific aspirations. East coast whaling towns like Nantucket, New Bedford, Boston, Edgartown, New London, Sag Harbor, Martha's Vineyard, and Mystic would come to rely on the Pacific for their economies during the nineteenth century, marking them as Pacific ports even if, geographically, they were located along the young nation's Atlantic seaboard.[59]

In Hawai'i, only two American whalers landed in 1819. Three years later, the number soared to roughly sixty vessels, and that number was closer to two hundred by 1829.[60] As Trevor Lummis has put it, "the British Lion may have refused to become involved, the Russian Bear may have been chased out, and the French Cockerel was still crowing beyond their horizon – but the American Eagle was casting an ever-growing shadow."[61] The Americans may have been latecomers to the Pacific Basin, but as Burke had observed, when they did come, they came in force.[62]

Joshua Hill sensed this rising American threat. If the Nantucketers could lay claim to the ocean, what was to prevent America more broadly from doing so, or other powers? Among those who Hill feared had Pacific aspirations, Russia also loomed large. Captain Cook's three voyages into the Pacific had alerted Russia to Britain's growing interest in that ocean, and for a time the two powers cooperated to a degree in their voyaging, particularly in the Pacific's northwestern reaches. Two of Cook's crew on the third voyage went on to serve with the Russian navy. But, as Terrence Armstrong has demonstrated, the window for cooperation was quickly closed. In 1799, the newly formed Russian-American Company articulated a formal Russian claim over the lands now known as Alaska.[63] The company's assertions seemed to drive home the point that the

---

[58] Andrew Delbanco, *Melville: His World and Work* (New York: Vintage eBooks, 2006. Kindle Edition), location 1300.

[59] Gibson, *Yankees in Paradise*, 131. See also Nancy Shoemaker, *Native American Whalemen and the World: Indigenous Encounters and the Contingency of Race* (Chapel Hill, NC: The University of North Carolina Press, 2015), 16; Eric Jay Dolin, *Leviathan: The History of Whaling in America* (New York: W.W. Norton & Company, 2008), 205–213; and Gesa Mackenthun, "Chartless Voyages and Protean Geographies," in Bernhard Klein and Gesa Mackenthun, eds., *Sea Changes: Historicizing the Ocean* (New York: Routledge, 2004), 133; Donald E. Pease, "Introduction," in John R. Eperjesi, *The Imperialist Imaginary: Visions of Asia and the Pacific in American Culture* (Hanover, New Hampshire: Dartmouth College Press, 2005), xi; and Igler, *The Great Ocean*, 181.

[60] Haley, *Captive Paradise*, location 1844 of 7968.   [61] Lummis, *Pacific Paradises*, 101.

[62] Gibson, *Yankees in Paradise*, 93.

[63] Terrence Armstrong, "Cook's Reputation in Russia," in Robin Fisher and Hugh Johnson, editors, *Captain James Cook and His Times* (Seattle: University of Washington Press, 1979), 121–122.

Pacific would fall into other hands if London did not move to secure its own control over both the islands and waters of the great ocean.

Russian interest in the Pacific was hardly just commercial. The Russians were particularly active in the Pacific in these years, and the history of Tsarist imperial ambitions in the region was not fully understood by Western European competitors.[64] Hill, for instance, wrote from Hawai'i to Lord Palmerston to inform him that the Russians were trying to buy influence with the Kamehameha monarch using "valuable presents," activities about which Hill felt London should be concerned.[65] Terry Glavin has argued that the Russian history of the North Pacific challenges North American and European assumptions about the geographic movements of imperial expansion, but in the nineteenth century itself, many were alert to Russia's influence in the region.[66] Captain Cook observed and reported on the Russian activity at all of the significant islands between Unalaska and Kamchatka and on the Kuriel Islands as well.[67] As both whalers and fur traders, Russians were major players in the Pacific from their own coastlines to San Francisco, where their most significant commercial competitor was the Hudson's Bay Company.[68] At issue, though, was what, if anything, Britain could do to curb Russian influence in the region.

London was aware of what was happening in the Pacific.[69] Cook's three voyages of the late eighteenth century had generated spectacular levels of public interest in the South Seas. It was, after all, largely due to British exploratory voyages like Cook's that the notion that the Pacific was a "Spanish Lake" had been broken.[70] After the Spanish, then, the British were, as it has been observed, "early adventurers in the Pacific Ocean." And though they may also have been "tardy settlers" in the Pacific, London-based politicians were not derelict in keeping an eye on the region.[71] Paul Burlin has rightly observed that the United States and Great Britain were commercial rivals in the Pacific in the nineteenth

---

[64] See Ryan Tucker Jones, *Empires of Extinction: Russians and the North Pacific's Strange Beasts of the Sea, 1741–1867* (New York: Oxford University Press, 2014), 16. See also, François Péron, *French Designs on Colonial New South Wales François Péron's Memoir on the English Settlements in New Holland, Van Diemen's Land, and the Archipelagos of the Great Pacific Ocean.* Jean Fornasiero and John West-Sooby, eds. (Adelaide: Friends of the State Library of South Australia, 2014), xvii.

[65] Hill, Letter to Lord Palmerston (November 20, 1831).

[66] Terry Glavin, *The Last Great Sea: A Voyage through the Human and Natural History of the North Pacific Ocean* (New York: Grey Stone Books, 2000), 138.

[67] Glavin, *The Last Great Sea*, 134.   [68] Oliver, *The Pacific Peoples*, 48.

[69] Ward, *British Policy in the South Pacific*, 93.   [70] Ibid., 1.

[71] Richard Landsdown, ed., *Strangers in the South Seas: The Idea of the Pacific in Western Thought* (Honolulu: University of Hawai'i Press, 2006), 231. See also, Chaplin, "The Pacific Before Empire," in Armitage and Bashford, eds., *Pacific Histories*, 61.

century.[72] Politicians at Westminster did have their eyes on Washington. They were alert to the Democratic Party's (occasional) aversion to colonial expansion, and they were also aware that the coming of the Civil War in the 1860s made it more difficult for America to assert itself in the Pacific's distant waters.[73] But how to govern the Pacific from London? The question was not easily answered.

In 1839, Rear Admiral Frederick Maitland wrote to Charles Wood at the Admiralty trying to sort out this very issue. Lawless crews of merchants and whalers were trouble to the missionary establishments across the ocean, he observed. But, as we have seen, the merchants, the whalers, and the missionaries each crossed a host of international boundaries.[74] There was no way to assert sovereign control over such a supranational network without also infringing on the sovereignty of other European – to say nothing of Pacific Islander – powers.[75] From New Zealand to South America, the Pacific played host to so many different political jurisdictions that there was no real jurisdictional clarity at all.[76] To have attempted to consolidate any singular European colonial authority – say British – in the Pacific would have been to provoke a possible war in the region.

Indeed, even in London itself, there were competing interests. As John Ward has observed, the commercial monopolies of the East India Company over everything beyond the Cape of Good Hope presented an impediment to other entrepreneurial or imperial ventures in the broader Pacific.[77] There was little, then, in the Pacific – at least in the 1820s and 1830s – to induce London to make the Pacific a formal sphere of colonial influence.[78] As such, the Admiralty was "slow and halting" about its interest in oceanic discovery outside of the Atlantic basin, even some fifty years after Burke's warnings about the power and wealth to be drawn from sea power. To Joshua Hill, as we have seen, this oversight was no small problem.

Joshua Hill's revolutionary arrival at Pitcairn Island overturned the policy preferences of both the London Missionary Society and the British government. In establishing a strong, centrally administered – if still unauthorized – colony at Pitcairn, Hill perpetrated a mutiny that challenged official imperial policy in the Pacific in favor of his own vision

---

[72] Burlin, *Imperial Maine and Hawai'i*, 268.   [73] Oliver, *The Pacific Islands*, 61.
[74] Eperjesi, *The Imperialist Imaginary*, 18.
[75] Ward, *British Policy in the South Pacific*, 65–66 and 130. See also, Eperjesi, *The Imperialist Imaginary*, 18.
[76] Rear Admiral Frederick S. Maitland, Letter to Charles Wood (HMS *Wellesley*, at sea: March 14, 1839), TNA FO 58/1.
[77] Ward, *British Policy in the South Pacific*, 6–13.
[78] Edmond, *Representing the South Pacific*, 130.

of what the British Pacific could, and perhaps ought to, be. His was nothing more than a simple assertion of power built upon a couple of biographical exaggerations embellished with a lie, but it was an action that, in retrospect, actually called into question the power of British imperialism writ large. What sort of empire was it, after all, that could not control its peripheries? What sort of empire that did not want to do so? What sort of empire that could be so easily bamboozled, so easily manipulated, so easily undone? As the British Empire neared the middle years of the nineteenth century, a moment when its global scope was very near its Victorian zenith, it was still possible for the machinations of one man to loose entire islands from London's grasp. As Dane Kennedy has observed, we do well to pay as much attention to "the limits of empire as" we do to "empire's reach."[79] To hold a global empire, one that spanned the earth's oceans, was like holding water in the palm of your hand.

Viewed against the relative weakness of British power in the Pacific, Joshua Hill's "colonial" policies at Pitcairn offer up an opportunity to reimagine a nineteenth-century British empire in the South Seas. To be certain, Hill's imperial regime was idiosyncratic, and it never became *the* official British vision for the region, at least not fully. But it was a powerful enough counterpoint to London's official policy that it motivated Hill to sail around the globe, to leave behind his wife and family, to risk his life and fortune, and to perpetrate a crime against the very political institutions for which he was, ostensibly, working. Having revisited Hill's biography and having excavated the claims he made about the social, political, and intellectual connectedness of his associates in Britain, it is no longer possible to leave Hill's Pitcairnese administrative experiment at the margins of British imperial history, for, as Kirsten McKenzie has observed, "the view from the margins provides us with a different way of understanding the cultural history of imperial politics."[80] This was not the imperial vision of a lunatic, a madman, or a paranoid schizophrenic. This was, rather, a very serious vision of British imperialism in the Pacific region, an alternative to official policy. And so convinced was Hill of his own vision that he took drastic steps to turn that vision into a reality.

Understanding what Pitcairn was like under the administration of Joshua Hill is, though, nearly as difficult as tracing out Hill's biography.

---

[79] Dane Kennedy, *The Last Blank Spaces: Exploring Africa and Australia* (Cambridge, MA: Harvard University Press, 2013. Kindle Edition), location 139.

[80] Kirsten McKenzie, *Imperial Underworld: An Escaped Convict and the Transformation of the British Colonial Order* (New York: Cambridge University Press, 2016. Kindle Edition), location 337.

The existing records from Hill's time in power at Adamstown are broken, and most reflect animosities and partisan divisions that were themselves the results of Hill's regime. Every account agrees that Joshua Hill was unhappy with the state of affairs at Pitcairn upon his arrival in Adamstown. A letter Hill sent to the Earl of Ripon on December 23, 1831 – hardly two months after his arrival at Pitcairn – indicates that "the state of things upon this little island" was "very unsettled ..., owning principally to the presence of three Englishmen, whom, unfortunately, the natives have allowed to settle among them." These men, Hill recorded, were "runaway sailors" who had introduced "drunkenness, and other bad vices" among the islanders.[81]

It is worth pausing here to reflect upon Hill's hostility towards these three Englishmen, these outsiders. As we have already seen, none of the men – not George Hunn Nobbs, not John Buffett, not John Evans – were that different from Hill himself. They were all Englishmen who had come to Pitcairn. True, the three were drunk when Hill first met them, hardly inclining the tumid Mr. Hill to think they were the sorts of men who might head up his program for Pacific evangelization from Pitcairn. But Hill presented these three as gadabouts. They were foreign and, indeed, pernicious to the island and its "natives." They were a pediculous bunch who had brought fighting, confusion, and wickedness to Pitcairn, a claim that would not have held any real water had it been measured against the island's actual post-settlement history of murder, suicide, and death.

Hill's initial move to undermine any authority that these three Englishmen might have had over the Pitcairnese people was designed, therefore, to elevate himself as the colonial fugleman over the island, a new leader for a new era in Pitcairn's history, but it was also a move that marked his reign at the island as the advent of something that was not linked to England. Not only did Hill's posturing lack any authorized support from London, his decision to frame the Englishmen at the island as outsiders acknowledged that, to the degree that England was in command at Pitcairn, its influences had not been good ones. Hill moved quickly to undo the damage that he thought had been wrought by the three English settlers. He established a temperance society and broke up the stills that were scattered throughout Adamstown and the hinterlands of the island. By late December 1832, Hill happily reported that the majority of the islanders had signed on as members of the society and agreed to a new form of administrative governance. The new law code at Pitcairn placed four elders in charge of the little colony, and the only

---

[81] Hill, Letter to the Earl of Ripon (December 23, 1832).

obstacle to the structure's functioning was, Hill suggested, "the presence of these three bad characters."[82]

In writing to the Earl of Ripon, Hill hoped that he could convince London to send out medicines and other instruments to help the Pitcairners. He needed books, perhaps from the LMS, to help with the education and catechizing of the islanders, and he ardently hoped that some naval vessel could be sent to deport the three quarrelsome characters who had caused so much trouble at Pitcairn. More importantly, though, Hill hoped that Ripon could offer some sanction for the revolution that had occurred in Adamstown. "Although I have, perhaps, effected more than could have been expected in so short a time, under the circumstances, and not possessing any public authority thus to keep in check these men," Hill wrote, "I shall continue to maintain peace and quietness among them to the best way I can, until I have the honour of hearing from your Lordship, as to whether His Majesty's government would not be pleased to nominate me its agent for good here." Hill had, he wrote, already assumed the position of doctor, school-master, and minister over the people, and he was doing such a fine job, particularly of this last, that the small island, with a population of no more than sixty people, already hosted two Sunday services. "I have no doubt," he concluded, "that I could make of these natives one of the most happy people whatever."[83]

Captain Charles H. Freemantle of the HMS *Challenger* landed at Pitcairn, as we have seen, in the days just after Hill's arrival. It was through Freemantle that Hill hoped to get his letter to Ripon and others like it off the island. Like Hill, Freemantle recorded his own assessment of what life was like at Pitcairn, and he too was unimpressed. The island's residents had only just returned from their disastrous removal to Tahiti, and it was, Freemantle concluded, this exposure to the wider world that had brought vice among them. It was at Tahiti, Freemantle recorded, that the Pitcairners learned to distill the ti root into a spirituous liquor. Like Hill, Freemantle seems to have either missed or ignored the fact that William McCoy, one of the island's original *Bounty* settlers, had begun distilling ti root in 1796, two years before he fell to a watery death from a Pitcairnese cliff while in a drunken (and possibly suicidal) frenzy. In both men's account, the people of Pitcairn were an "amiable" lot, particularly, Freemantle reflected, considering that they sprung from "so guilty a stock."[84] Both Hill and Freemantle, then, agreed that Pitcairn

---

[82] Ibid.   [83] Ibid.

[84] Captain Charles Freemantle, Letter to Captain Geor. Elliott (May 30, 1833), RGS-LMS, Item 4-d, 26. Also cited in Brodie, *Pitcairn's Island and the Islanders*, 162.

was being subverted by the outside world, and Freemantle further agreed with Hill about the three outsiders from England. Though Nobbs, in particular, had served the island as a pastor, Freemantle felt he could offer no real support to the three men, all of whom had a history of drunkenness that predated Hill's arrival and all of whom had resisted Hill's efforts to reform the island's manners and morals.

For his part, Hill was an enigma to the visiting English captain, who was initially certain that Hill must have been a pecksniffian "adventurer, more likely to do harm than good." After all, here was an older man of some respectability. What was Pitcairn to him that he should have traveled nearly the circumference of the globe? But, as we have seen previously, Hill showed Freemantle a sheaf of papers that all spoke so clearly to legitimate imperial connections with institutions like the Colonial Office, the Lords Commissioners of the Admiralty, and others of Britain's highest and most influential people that Freemantle "was induced to think that he [Hill] must be interested about them; and as he had succeeded in restoring them to some kind of order," Freemantle moved to support Hill in his various positions over the island.[85]

This one bit of approval from Captain Freemantle seems to have empowered all of Hill's subsequent reign at Pitcairn, dislodging Nobbs, Buffet, and Evans from their perches and securing Hill's sober regime of authoritarian reform. To think of Hill's administration at Pitcairn as "reform" opens up new ways of thinking about a bit of history that has previously gone unseen, for Joshua Hill landed at Pitcairn in October 1832, just four months after the passage in London of the Reform Bill of 1832. To be certain, Hill, who had set sail for Pitcairn in June 1830, could not have known about the Bill, but he could not have been unaware of the push for political reform that had been growing in Britain in these years and which erupted as a major issue in the general elections that were held after the death of King George IV in the same month Hill departed England. As we have previously imagined Joshua Hill's curriculum vitae as something more substantial than a web of lies in order to tease out details of his biography, let us similarly reconceive of the work he did at Pitcairn in the light of broader, utilitarian attempts at political and administrative reform in mid-nineteenth-century Britain.

In the 1841 memorial that Hill forwarded to the Colonial Office in hope of getting remunerated for his work at Pitcairn, a spirit of reform under-scores Hill's history of his time on the island. As we have seen, much of what Hill did at Adamstown had links to the evangelical and missionary

---

[85] Captain Charles Freemantle, Letter to Captain Geor. Elliott (May 30, 1833). Also cited in Brodie, *Pitcairn's Island and the Islanders*, 161–162.

impulses of the moment, and his temperance agendas and his destruction of Pitcairn's stills all feature prominently in his reformist agenda. The same can be said of his rigidly enforced observance of the Sabbath on the island. But it would be wrong to distinguish evangelical moral crusades as something completely apart from political reform in these years, and Hill's work at Pitcairn is no exception.

Linked then to the toppling of the stills and to the mandatory church-going that Hill oversaw among the Pitcairners were a set of political, economic, and social reforms, none of which could have gone unobserved by the island's inhabitants and many of which wrought deep divisions in the otherwise paradisical world that visitors to Pitcairn thought John Adams had built before his death in 1829.

To begin, Hill made a study of life at Pitcairn, carefully detailing the island's "code of rules for the guidance of their social, as well as moral conduct." From this investigation, he set out a rigid plan for the improvement of Pitcairn. At the administrative level, Hill created a governing council from the "best informed of the natives," dividing the group into elders and sub-elders who could assist him as he put his agenda into action. In as much as the island needed infrastructural reform, Hill oversaw the reconstruction of the landing place at Bounty Bay, and he made some improvements to the road up the knaggy Hill of Difficulty into Adamstown. Hill worked to rebuild the public school at Pitcairn and took up the position of the island's schoolmaster. And for the better regulation of the island's economy, he worked with the residents to fix prices of goods within the community so that the trade with visiting whalers and sailors could be carried out more easily, more regularly, and more fairly.[86]

From October 1832 until December 1837, Hill governed, if that is indeed the proper verb, at Pitcairn as the islands "pastor, teacher, and general superintendant [sic] and director of the natives."[87] Many on the island seem to have responded positively to Hill and his reforms. William Quintal, eight members of his family, three members of the Young family, two members of the Christian family, and Sarah McCoy, all submitted a letter to Hill as he neared his first anniversary on the island to invite him to remain with them as a leader and to thank him for the work he had done on their behalf over the previous twelve months. He was, they wrote, responsible "for saving and snatching us so providentially, as it were, from the brink of infidelity itself." They reminded Hill that their island had been plagued by "two cursed stills" before he arrived, that it had had no church and no school. They reminded him that the island was still subject

---

[86] Hill, *The Humble Memorial*, 2–4.   [87] Ibid., 10.

to the nefarious influences of the three "profligate foreigners" who had been "the whole cause of our troubles," and they warned that only Hill kept their bad influence at bay and the flame of reform afire on the island.[88]

That all of the signatories to this letter were descendants of the *Bounty* mutineers is telling, for their participation suggests the divisions that Hill's vision of the island wrought between the original inhabitants and the English newcomers. It is similarly telling that these "native" families, to use their word choice, chose to distinguish Buffet, Nobbs, and Evans as "foreigners" even though the three men had woven themselves into the fabric of the island's community, each marrying into the island's native families and fathering between them some fourteen children who would have had blood connections to the island's original *Bounty* population.[89] Furthermore, denigrating outsiders as "profligate foreigners" was hardly the surest means to praise Joshua Hill who had arrived at Pitcairn from England, just as had the other three men. Was not Hill, Pitcairn's erstwhile savior, just another foreigner?

The native families at Pitcairn – the Christians, the Evanses, the McCoys, and the Quintals – seem, therefore, to have bought into the narrative that their island was a Pacific paradise in danger of being corrupted and corroded by outside influences, the same narrative that made the island so appealing to visitors and evangelicals. As Hill put it, the Pitcairners recognized that they needed an age of reform to save them from "fornication, adultery, and, in fact, every crime but murder."[90] Every crime but murder, indeed. Pitcairn was an island born in mutiny and nursed on blood, but the reformist vision that Hill promulgated and which the islanders seem to have adopted forgot that history, retold the past, and conjured a new legend in line with the popular evangelical narrative that had attracted Hill to the island in the first place. Pitcairn was a paradise, forged by John Adams' hands; and the presence, the leadership, and the infiltration of Englishmen like Buffet, Evans, and Nobbs jeopardized Adams' work. To save the island, Hill had to commit a second mutiny. He had to break the island out of the "foreign" hands of pernicious Englishmen; he had to defy the will of the Colonial Office. In short, he had to make Pitcairn his own personal empire in order to reform it – in order to save it.

---

[88] Ibid., 6. See also, Brodie, *Pitcairn's Island and the Islanders*, 193–194.

[89] The Humble Petition of the Principal Native Inhabitants of Pitcairn's Island to His Excellency James Townshend (June 19, 1834), in Brodie, *Pitcairn's Island and the Islanders*, 209.

[90] Hill, *The Humble Memorial*, 3.

The Pitcairnese imbrication of evangelical impulses with more overtly political schemes to improve communal welfare and better administer a social polity was hardly unique. Patrick Brantlinger has traced similar confluences in domestic reform agendas in Britain in the early 1830s.[91] Hill, like domestic reformers, "spoke the Pentecostal tongues of utopia and apocalypse."[92] Domestic reformers in the early 1830s, Brantlinger has argued, wrote with an optimism and a concomitant hope that the political realm could produce genuine reform.[93] In a world where the upheavals of the French Revolutionary era were still not half a century in the past, people could look to near-current affairs to find examples of the possibilities and the limitations of change, reform, and (perhaps) improvement.[94] Hill's letters to London reflect this air of optimism and expectancy. His administration, he eventually wrote, was founded upon "the hope that the permanent welfare of this little community would by this means be placed on a more certain basis, by creating in themselves a feeling for their own respect."[95]

Writing about the Reform Act of 1867, Catherine Hall has demonstrated that the age of domestic reform ought never be isolated from Britain's nineteenth-century imperial history, and she has successfully argued that questions about political reform become necessarily more complicated when we consider the "different notions of citizen and subject" that existed domestically and across the empire.[96] At Pitcairn, Joshua Hill's mutinous seizure of power interestingly inverted many of the questions about belonging, citizenship, and the political community that played out in other imperial locations. Because his actions specifically broke Pitcairn from any authorized channels of colonial control, it served Hill's reformist purposes to accept the widely agreed upon division between metropolitan British citizens and colonial subjects. His move helped to certify the "foreignness" of the three Englishmen at Pitcairn and, simultaneously, to elevate the significance of the islanders' indigeneity.

Pitcairn belonged to the Pitcairners alone. To them alone, of course, in as much as they agreed to cooperate with Hill's reformist scheme. The posturing here is complicated, for just as Hill needed to break Pitcairn out from under London's less-than-watchful colonial eye and

---

[91] Patrick Brantlinger, *The Spirit of Reform: British Literature and Politics, 1832–1867* (New York: Cambridge University Press, 1977), 1.
[92] Brantlinger, *The Spirit of Reform*, 11.   [93] Ibid., 14.   [94] Ibid., 63–64.
[95] Hill, *The Humble Memorial*, 3.
[96] Catherine Hall, "The Nation Within and Without," in Catherine Hall, Keith McClelland, and Jane Rendall, *Defining the Victorian Nation: Class, Race, Gender, and the British Reform Act of 1867* (New York: Cambridge University Press, 2000), 179.

from the sway of the three Englishmen who had become leaders on the island, he could not elevate the islanders too far above their colonial station. He needed them to accept the imperial dynamic that allowed him to assert authority as an agent of metropolitan power. His was, then, a vision of colonial empowerment mapped onto one of centralized colonial authoritarianism. The results, not unpredictably, were not always tranquil, for Hill's history of mutiny, reform, and even revolution (to use Mark Twain's wording) at Pitcairn all revolved around fraught questions about belonging, about citizenship, and about the boundaries of Pitcairn's civil polity.[97] And, as had been the case in the first three years of the island's post-*Bounty* history, the struggle to establish and administer a new colonial society would see blood spilled.

As the primary targets of Hill's reformist regime, John Evans, John Buffet, and George Nobbs all, not unsurprisingly, spent a good deal of time recording the abusive core that, they felt, rested at the heart of the impostor's administration. The chronology of their reporting is a challenge to decipher. Their tales are purposeful, intended to upset Hill's plans and overturn his administration. Indeed, in places, they are clearly designed to answer some of the charges that Hill made against the three Englishmen. George Nobbs, for instance, went to great pains to explain that he had expended a great deal of his own personal influence at the island trying to convince the *Bounty* families to give up the distillation of alcohol, only to be threatened with violence by members of the Quintal, Young, and Christian families.[98] This story is both history and advocacy, but there is still a narrative core to the stories these men told that merits our attention.

Shortly after Hill's arrival at Pitcairn, all three men agree, he began displacing Nobbs, Evans, and Buffett from any form of social or administrative control that they had previously enjoyed. George Nobbs admitted that he was initially impressed enough by Hill's credentials that he gave the newly arrived gentleman a room in his own home.[99] Before one month had passed, however, Hill's plans for reform began to impinge on his relationship with his host family. Not only did Hill convince the islanders to hire him to replace Nobbs as their pastor and teacher, he had "succeeded by villanous [sic] misrepresentations, atrocious falsehoods, and magnificent promises of presents, to be obtained through his influence from the British Government and several British of Mr. Hill's acquaintance, in ejecting your petitioner from his house."[100]

---

[97] Twain, "The Great Revolution in Pitcairn."
[98] Nobbs, The Humble Petition, quoted in Brodie, *Pitcairn's Island and the Islanders*, 181.
[99] Ibid., 182.   [100] Ibid.

As Hill's stay at the Nobbs' homestead degenerated, quite literally, into a battle for turf, both John Buffett and John Evans record that Hill's broader administrative reform of Pitcairn's government rested on tyranny and repression. Buffet, for instance, omits any reference to the work Hill superintended to construct a school or church at Pitcairn, instead focusing on the construction of a prison in case "any of the natives refuse to obey him, lest his proposals be ever so unjust."[101] John Evans' reports similarly note the construction of a prison, dating the edifice to May 1833.[102] Interestingly, nothing in any of the papers that Hill has left us about his time at Pitcairn speaks to Pitcairn's prison. The coercive mechanisms of penal confinement are absent from his own account of his administrative reform at the island.

If what Evans and Buffett report is accurate, Hill was systematic in suppressing the three Englishmen at Pitcairn. They were denied access to and communication with any passing ships' captains, their children were deprived the right to inherit lands through their mothers because of their fathers' "foreign" status, and all "native" inhabitants above the age of seven were coerced into signing a declaration that they would never intermarry with the community of children born of these outsiders.[103] The question of who could own land at Pitcairn and who had a family claim to belong within the island's demography will be the central questions of the next two chapters.

For his part, though, Captain Freemantle, the first outsider to have communicated with these three Englishmen in the hard first days of Hill's time at Pitcairn, objected to Hill's having labeled them "lousy foreigners," and he "bade him desist from doing so."[104] Though he promised to give up the language of civic exclusion, Hill did not, and as we have seen, he promoted it among those Pitcairners who were partisans of his cause. Even Hill's evangelical work at the island seems to have been mired in violence and coercion. According to Nobbs, Hill rounded up all of the munitions on the island in August of 1833. Once all of the island's weapons and ammunition were in his possession, Hill loaded every weapon and housed them, ready for action, in a locked box in his bedroom – which, recall, was in Nobb's old house. Each Sunday, as he sat at

[101] John Buffett, The Testimonial of J. Buffett, quoted in Walter Brodie, *Pitcairn's Island and the Islanders*, 186.
[102] Evans, The Humble Petition, quoted in Brodie, *Pitcairn's Island and the Islanders*, 192.
[103] Ibid. See also, Nobbs, The Humble Petition quoted in Brodie, *Pitcairn's Island and the Islanders*, 183; and Buffett, The Testimonial of J. Buffett, quoted in Brodie, *Pitcairn's Island and the Islanders*, 186.
[104] Nobbs, The Humble Petition, quoted in Brodie, *Pitcairn's Island and the Islanders*, 183.

the front of the island's church for services, a loaded gun rested on the floor beneath Hill's chair "to intimidate his hearers."[105]

It was amidst this tyrannical state of affairs that the native families of Pitcairn wrote to Hill asking him to stay on as their pastor, pedagogue, and president late in 1833. So moved was Edward Quintal, one of the elders in Hill's new cabinet, by the efficacy of Hill's governance, that he wrote to those off-island, asking that the outside world do more to sustain Hill and his anti-foreign policies. "Our good friend, Capt. Hill, has been, and is doing all in his power for our general welfare," Quintal wrote to George Pritchard at Tahiti in April 1833. "I am sure that his plans are well calculated to insure both our present and future happiness."[106] Nearly a year later, writing again to Pritchard, Quintal continued to suggest that Hill was all that stood between Pitcairn and ruin. "Capt. Hill has all along acted like a father to us all, and we really owe him more than we shall ever be able to discharge."[107] For his part, Hill promised his supporters on the island that he would not "think of leaving you until hearing from home *i.e.* from the British Government, nor until my presence becomes no longer necessary in furtherance of the established welfare of your commonwealth and beloved little island."[108]

As John Adams before him, Hill had become a "father" to the Pitcairnese people.[109] The familial reference point here is telling, for, ultimately, the politics at Pitcairn was always a matter of family alliances. As had been the case when Mayhew Folger arrived at the island and met with Thursday October Christian, the family names at Pitcairn were legendary – the Christians, the Quintals, the Adamses, the McCoys. All those who encountered Pitcairn felt the historical rush of meeting these clans, and they also viewed the island's politics in terms of these family groups.

Captain William Driver, who transported the Pitcairners back to their island "home" (another word that suits our sense that the island's histor-ical narrative is also a family romance) was eager to observe the family alliances at work in the Pitcairnese community. John Buffett was married to Dolly Young. George Nobbs was married into the Christian family.

---

[105] Ibid. See also, Buffett, The Testimonial of J. Buffett, quoted in Brodie, *Pitcairn's Island and the Islanders*, 187.

[106] Edward Quintal, Letter to George Pritchard (Pitcairn Island: April 6, 1833), quoted in Brodie, *Pitcairn's Island and the Islanders*, 195.

[107] Ibid., 195–196.

[108] Joshua Hill, Answer to a Letter from the Public Functionaries and Others of Pitcairn's Island (Pitcairn Island: October 4, 1833), quoted in Brodie, *Pitcairn's Island and the Islanders*, 194–195.

[109] The Humble Petition of the Principal Native Inhabitants of Pitcairn's Island to His Excellency James Townshend (June 19, 1834), in Brodie, *Pitcairn's Island*, 205.

John Evans was wedded to John Adams' daughter.[110] To Driver's eyes, the three Englishmen seemed "quiet men," but it was clear that their arrival at Pitcairn had thrown the family dynamics of the island askew. "The Adams family," he wrote, "seemed very dissatisfied with Nobbs, who had married a Christian." Nobbs, it would seem, spoke of his connection "unreservedly, feeling that their father was an officer of the *Bounty* while Smith was only a seaman, their being the leading family when the Colony was first made."[111]

What determined precedence at Pitcairn? Fletcher Christian had been the obvious mastermind behind the mutiny aboard the *Bounty*. He had led the crew while they searched out their island home. He was the island's first "king," if you will. But when he died? The history of Pitcairn Island suggests that Christian's authority eventually passed to the only European to survive the hostilities of those first years, Alexander Smith/John Adams. But after Adams, as we have seen, power was up for grabs. Did political leadership pass through the Christian family? To Mauatua? To Thursday October? And when Thursday October died at Tahiti? Or, did it continue to reside with the Adams family? Did a family's status on the island hinge on that family's patriarch and his rank on board the *Bounty*? Could other families break into the Christian-Smith/Adams contest? These were the questions that seemed to plague Pitcairnese politics and which only grew more complicated when the likes of John Buffett and George Hunn Nobbs – to say nothing of Joshua W. Hill – entered the picture and tangled themselves into the family dynamics at Adamstown.

As we have seen, George Nobbs ousted John Buffett from his position as schoolmaster and as Adams' heir-apparent at Pitcairn shortly after he arrived on the island.[112] That Nobbs married Sarah Christian, Fletcher's granddaughter, put him in direct line of descent from Pitcairn's founding father, its George Washington. John Buffet's wife, Dorothy (Dolly) Young, though, connected him to the last two European settlers – Young and Smith/Adams. Indeed, in every account, it was Edward (Ned) Young who taught Alexander Smith to read, who instructed him in the *Book of Common Prayer* and the Bible, and who, as a result, trained the man who would become Pitcairn's second "president," literally its John Adams. True, John Evans married Adams' daughter, Rachel, but Evans never seems to have made a play for power in the way that Nobbs and Buffett did at Adamstown. The history, then, frames the period from

[110] William Driver, Letter to Mrs. John Clifton Merrill (Nashville, TN: November 16, 1880), Whaling Log Books, SLNSW PMB 780.

[111] Ibid.

[112] Barrow, *A Description of Pitcairn's Island*, 284. See also, Hancock, *Politics in Pitcairn*, 9.

Nobbs' arrival in 1828 until Hill's in 1832 as something of an interfamily struggle between the Youngs and the Christians.

Consider, for instance, Nobbs' refusal to return to Pitcairn from Tahiti in 1831. As we saw in the previous chapter, Nobbs made it a condition of his return to Adamstown that the Pitcairners accept him as the unquestioned schoolmaster and pastor over the island, a request to which the island's families agreed.[113] Captain William Driver, who delivered the Pitcairners back to their home island, found this arrangement suspicious. Nobbs was a smart man, Driver agreed, but it was clear from the outside that he was also the "self-constituted teacher" at the island.[114] We know that Nobbs had been among the happiest of the Pitcairners about life at Tahiti. As one of the Pitcairnese leaders, he had built a relationship with Queen Pomare. John Buffet, though, was one of the most active in wanting to return to Pitcairn. Nobbs had supplanted Buffett at Pitcairn and was now holding court at Tahiti. That left Pitcairn open for Buffet's return, geographically as well as politically. Indeed, once J. A. Moerenhout was able to arrange for the Pitcairners to return to their home island, Buffett and his family headed up the advance party that sailed first.[115]

What we find here is, then, a personal feud between two men – both carpetbaggers – for power at Pitcairn. The fissures were not new. Neither Fletcher Christian nor John Adams ever identified a pattern of succession – patrilineal or otherwise. Both Buffett and Nobbs seem to have tapped into the island's clannish society, and their personal feud, as a result, spilled over into wider social unrest on the island.[116] When we think of Pitcairn's politics as a set of family dynamics framed by clans and marriages, Nobbs' 1831 demand registers as something of a checkmate on the Buffet-Young claim to authority at Adamstown, an affirmation that it was the Nobbs-Christian line that would serve as Pitcairn's "father" figures – at least until Joshua Hill arrived in October 1832.

Hill's political structure at Pitcairn, stepped outside of the family politics that had governed the island previously. Hill, after all, came from the metropolitan center. He had a wife at home. He had no family connection with or loyalty to any one Pitcairnese clan. He was a product of the age of reform at home, with all of its evangelical and utilitarian impulses. These observations allow us to rethink what we know about Hill's time at Adamstown. We know, for instance, that Hill asserted his

---

[113] See Brodie, *Pitcairn's Island and the Islanders*, 178. For the contract detailing Nobbs' pay for his work as schoolmaster at Pitcairn, see Nobbs Papers, SLNSW ML A 2881, 1–4.

[114] Driver, Letter to His Nephew (March 24, 1877).   [115] Macklin, *Dark Paradise*, 158.

[116] I thank Rick Kleiner for his thoughts on this interfamily dynamic at Pitcairn Island. See also, Nobbs, *George Hunn Nobbs*, 33.

own right to administer the island. Some have suggested that he framed himself as Pitcairn's "president," though no surviving document from Hill himself uses that term.[117] The notion that Pitcairn would be governed by a president, though, marked a sharp turn away from the clannish politics of the Christian, Smith/Adams, and Buffet-Nobbs years. It pointed towards a civil administration at Pitcairn that was bureaucratic rather than familial and that had the potential to reform the administration of the tiny community.[118] What Hill was proposing was a structured political regime that included such reformed constitutional features as a mechanism to assure an easy, orderly, peaceful, and legal succession at Adamstown.

In place of an island "father," then, Hill proposed legally defined administrative offices. After having broken down the stills – to assure that the islanders were sober enough to sustain a reformed civil society – he organized a new government from among the island's elders, forming what he called a "Privy Council."[119] Hill's council was a committee of seven of the island's eldest residents, divided as elders and sub-elders. Among the seven, Edward Quintal rose to be the leading voice of the council in Hill's Pacific "commonwealth."[120] Quintal's rise to prominence fits our sense that family politics played a large role both in the structure of Pitcairnese politics before Hill's arrival and in the opposition to his reforms after 1832.

In the grand narrative of the Pitcairn-*Bounty* saga, the Quintals had never featured prominently. Matthew Quintal was a Cornishman. An able-bodied seaman on the *Bounty*, Quintal was one of the active mutineers against Bligh. The seaman had been the first Bligh had lashed on the *Bounty*'s breadfruit voyage – two dozen lashes for insolence and mutinous behavior. This was a troublesome man. It would be Quintal who unilaterally set the *Bounty* ablaze in Bounty Bay in 1790, trapping himself and the rest of his comrades at Pitcairn Island.

Before his death, Matthew Quintal had had aspirations to power. It was, as we have seen, Quintal who most objected to the power that Ned Young and John Adams took for their own in the wake of Fletcher Christian's death. When the two learned that Quintal planned to overthrow them by force from their Tahitian consorts, they ganged up on Quintal and butchered him with an axe, making him the last of the *Bounty*

---

[117] Lewis, "Pitcairn's Tortured Past," in Oliver, ed., *Justice, Legality, and the Rule of Law*, 52–53.

[118] Hancock, *Politics in Pitcairn*, 10.   [119] Ibid., 12.

[120] See Maud, "The History of Pitcairn Island," 70; and Lummis, *Life and Death in Eden*, 208. See also Nicolson, *The Pitcairners*, 138.

men to be murdered at Pitcairn.[121] Before his death, Quintal, with William McCoy, was one of the most active distillers of alcohol at Pitcairn, and he is most often remembered as a drunken brute. Island legend holds that McCoy died in a fall from one of Pitcairn's cliffs. As Robert Macklin has noted, though, that story originated with John Adams, who "was thoroughly self-serving in his accounts. It is just as likely," Macklin continues, "that McCoy was murdered by some combination of his fellows, most probably Adams and Quintal."[122]

In Pitcairn's genealogy, Matthew Quintal is most often associated with Tevarua, whom he called Sarah. The two had five children together. The lubricious Quintal, though, was also known to bully the island's other Tahitian women. Edward Quintal was Matthew's son by Teraura, whom the *Bounty* men called Susan. In a clannish network that included the Adams family, the Christians, and the Youngs, Edward Quintal was hardly going to rise to the top of the social or political order at Pitcairn. Hill's political revolution, though, was also a social one for the Quintal family. Quintal's acquiescence in Hill's brutal politics makes sense, therefore, because it was in overthrowing the older political order and its concomitant social system that Quintal and his family could claim their day in the Pitcairnese spotlight.[123]

It bears observing that Edward Quintal was joined on the council by his older half-brother, Arthur, and William Young, whose older half-sister was John Buffet's wife. John Quintal, another of Matthew's sons, would later join the council, and three of Hill's four cadets – Arthur Jr., William, and Matthew – were also Quintals.[124] Rosalind Amelia Young would later note that these cadets served as something of a police force for Hill's new regime, marking the Quintals as something of Hill's personal gunsels.[125] Frederick Debell Bennett was suspicious of the disproportional influence that the, to his mind, obsequious Quintals had in Hill's regime. He referred to the family as mere trucklers, "a few of the more ambitious and athletic among their countrymen."[126]

Another of Hill's early administrative reforms at Pitcairn had to do with land ownership and inheritance. At Pitcairn, women had, from the outset, been allowed to inherit and own land. This practice was in keeping with Tahitian customs, though it did not necessarily accord with common law practices from Britain.[127] Hill abolished these features of Pitcairnese law. We will take up the question of land reform and land ownership on a small colonial outpost like Pitcairn in Chapter 5, and we will look at the sexual

---

[121] Macklin, *Dark Paradise*, 90.   [122] Ibid., 89.
[123] Lummis, *Life and Death in Eden*, 208.   [124] Nicolson, *The Pitcairners*, 134.
[125] Young, *Mutiny of the* Bounty, 76.   [126] Bennett, *Narrative of a Whaling Voyage*, 54.
[127] Lummis, *Life and Death in Eden*, 208.

politics of the island in Chapter 6. Here, though, in our reflections on Joshua Hill's efforts to bring Pitcairn into a logical, orderly, and legal relationship with London so as to better enable London to master the Pacific Ocean, Hill's decree may simply have been an attempt to bring Pitcairnese law into line with British law. That it served bigger purposes was an added benefit, for, if the Tahitian founding mothers at Pitcairn could not legally own, inherit, or pass on land, then the island's plotted tracts would forever remain in the hands of the *Bounty* men and their direct heirs by patrilineal descent. In one swift action, Hill had revoked any title that John Evans, John Buffet, and George Hunn Nobbs had to property at Pitcairn Island.

If we believe a petition from the "Principal Native Inhabitants of Pitcairn's Island" to Lord Townshend dated from June 1834, many at Pitcairn were happy with Hill's reforms, at least initially. The British commander in chief of naval forces on the West Coast of South America, Townshend was well-placed to help secure Hill's political power at Pitcairn and to support the reformist regime he was attempting to put in place there. The petition to Townshend, therefore, is an open letter elaborating the good that Hill had done in his first year and a half at Adamstown and requesting that his beneficial administration receive more official support from London and from the Admiralty. In addition to praising the school systems, religious reform, and temperance regime that Hill had implemented, the islanders were clear that the "present government, such as it is, of elders, sub-elders, and cadets" had borne good fruit. Hill had been busy on the islanders' behalf, and they had a new landing place in Bounty Bay to show for it. The road to the village up the scandent Hill of Difficulty had been smoothed, removing some of the deep furrows wrought by rainstorms. The petitioners were all "highly satisfied" by Hill's willingness "to sacrifice his time here for our interest," but he required support.[128]

Pitcairn was vulnerable. The "three lazy men," meaning Nobbs, Evans, and Buffet, had had designs on Pitcairn. They had married into the island's families to secure for their descendants "as much of our land as possible." George Adams had left the island, the petition continued, leaving behind his wife and children. His hope was to contact the three men, discredit Hill in the eyes of London and the Admiralty, and return as the island's governor. Adams' actions were portrayed as a fine bit of

[128] The Humble Petition of the Principal Native Inhabitants of Pitcairn's Island to His Excellency James Townshend (June 19, 1834), in Brodie, *Pitcairn's Island and the Islanders*, 204–210.

jobbery. He wanted to "send off our old teacher" Hill, and restore the wicked triumvirate of Nobbs, Evans, and Buffet.[129]

We know that petitions from Pitcairn are always suspect. The 1834 petition from the island's principal residents seems suspiciously like letters Joshua Hill himself sent to Townshend. Though so much of our story here has hinged on a willingness to believe the liar – to follow the rabbit down his hole – we would be misguided to overlook Hill's lies entirely. We know he was willing to be dishonest, that he had a, shall we say, knavish streak in him. Would it be beyond him to forge a document to Townshend seeking additional support against Nobbs, Evans, and Buffet, particularly at the moment when other indigenous Pitcairners like Adams were voyaging out into the Pacific to find the three men, to bring them home, and to mount a revolt? It is hardly impossible. But there is something to be taken from the 1834 petition that merits our attention, whether the document was written by Hill or by the islanders, and that is the nature and the scope of the institutional reform that was underway at Pitcairn in the year and a half after Hill's arrival. Infrastructure. Governance. Education. Institutions. Nearly every aspect of Pitcairnese life was touched by the political reform that Hill attempted, even if in a moment of fraudulent *gleichschaltung*. This is not a moment in Pitcairn's history that can be dismissed. Rather, it is a major moment of colonial change and the dawn of political reform on the island.

Hill's new political structure could only work, however, if Pitcairners agreed to set aside their older patriarchal and patrilineal notions of governance. And none among the islanders had less reason to give up on those notions than did George Hunn Nobbs, John Buffet, and (to a lesser extent) John Evans. Their very presence on the island – to say nothing of their authority over it – hinged on their having insinuated themselves into the family structures that defined Pitcairnese society. If we accept that Joshua Hill's administrative goals at Pitcairn were aimed at reforming the island's political landscape, then the inevitable power struggles that followed the onset of his revolution take on a new meaning. What has heretofore been framed as a battle between rightful power brokers and a usurper becomes a struggle between traditionalists against a modernizer. This was a struggle in which none of the four primary actors were indigenous to the island. As the geographer O. H. K. Spate has observed about Polynesian societies, Pacifics Islanders lived somewhere between a closed-off world and a connected social network. "The arrival of strangers might be infrequent, but it was far from unknown."[130] Pitcairn was similarly positioned as a liminal island.

---

[129] Ibid., 208.   [130] Spate, *Paradise Found and Lost*, 213.

The islanders had always known about the outside world; they were immigrants to Pitcairn themselves. But they were not accustomed to receiving visitors all that often, and the notion that visitors might stay at the island was all but unheard of until the 1820s. We have to imagine, then, the shock that Pitcairnese society felt at having these – to use Spate's charged adjective – "outlandish" men living (to say nothing of governing) among them at Adamstown.[131] Evans, Nobbs, and Buffett went so far as to secure their own authority through marriage into the island's familial hierarchies. In this light, Hill, whose governing aspirations were much more geo-strategic than they were personal, may actually have been the least objectionable of the adventitious outlanders.

Hill's first order of business, therefore, had to be to rid the island of the three Englishmen who had risen to prominence at Pitcairn as teachers, pastors, and civic leaders and who had cemented those positions by marrying into the island's most prominent families. This need explains why one of Hill's first programs as Pitcairn's leader was to enforce a penal system that included the construction of a prison and the implementation of what W. K. Hancock has called a "Treason Act."[132] Heretofore, these initial steps have been viewed as the usurpations of a deceptive strongman. That assessment may well be true. But our entire journey in this history has been based upon a unique and novel premise. Our narrative has been predicated on the notion that Joshua Hill may have been less a fraud, less sinister, less mad than historians have previously assumed him to be.[133] Our goal, though, has not been to psychoanalyze Joshua Hill. It has been, rather, to see if the story changes when we make a new set of initial assumptions about him, and we have found that, indeed, it does.

To assume that Hill's government at Adamstown was reform-minded, purposeful, and (perhaps even) logical, similarly changes the Pitcairnese story as we have known it until now in several ways. First, we come to see a proactive vision for Britain's imperial activity in the Pacific at a moment when few in London actually wanted such a directed policy. Second, we come to see a vision for Britain's Pacific colonialism that mapped domestic evangelical and utilitarian agendas onto the islands of Polynesia. Indeed, we see a systemic vision for British imperialism in the Pacific in which tiny Pitcairn Island and its five or six dozen residents is *the* central island. And, it is important to note, none of these observations in any way diminishes our sense that Joshua Hill became, at Adamstown, a cruel tyrant, a brutal "president," and a political bully.[134] He hoped to make

---

[131] Ibid.   [132] Hancock, *Politics in Pitcairn*, 12.
[133] McKenzie, *Imperial Underworld*, location 1157.
[134] Hancock, *Politics in Pitcairn*, 14.

significant changes on the island in order to induce larger changes in what we might call "the British Pacific." He was bound to break a few eggs. In this regard, Hill practiced a form of imperialism that was not unlike other despotic regimes across the British Empire in these years. A brutal form of control designed to bring the bounty of British governance and culture to an otherwise benighted people.[135] But Hill did more than break eggs. It was not, it would seem, in his nature to be clement. That his tetchy temperament made him ill-suited to the personal challenges of the work need not, however, blind us to the historical value that we can derive from the plan he had in mind, the aspirations he thought he could achieve, when he landed at Pitcairn on October 28, 1832.

Let us turn, then, to the events at Adamstown – to the competing and contradictory narratives – to see how Hill's plan for political reform at Pitcairn was met with traditionalist challenges and, ultimately, sank into dictatorship. It serves our purposes best, perhaps, to begin with John Evans. Though he was John Adams' son-in-law, Evans never vied for the same status at Pitcairn as did Nobbs or Buffet. Unlike reports from those two men – or from Hill himself – Evans' accounts of what happened on the island after October 1832 may be the most neutral. According to John Evans, in July 1833, Hill promulgated a law outlining the terms of and punishments for high treason on Pitcairn. Evans offered no specific detail about the law itself, though it is tempting to speculate about what the man who illegally wrested Pitcairn Island out of London's control might have had to say on the subject of treason. Evans asked Hill for a copy of the law "as a guide for his future conduct."[136] Hill's response was to rant violently, much as Captain Bligh had done when his stash of coconuts seemed a few fruits smaller than it ought to have been. Hill had Evans dragged to the island's church, called for a public trial in which he served as judge and jury and in which he allowed no witnesses, and ordered that Evans should be given a dozen lashes with a whip.[137] We do not know whom Hill had impose the punishment, though we do have evidence that Hill personally lashed John Buffett on at least one occasion.[138] On still other occasions, we know that both Buffett and Evans were lashed, interestingly, by a member of the Quintal family.[139]

Judge, jury, and executioner all in one person. This was hardly the reformed – to say nothing of enlightened – political system Hill had outlined upon his landing. J. A. Moerenhout is again, here, a valuable primary observer. Joshua Hill, he wrote, demonstrated "an implacable

---

[135] See C. A. Bayly, *Imperial Meridian: The British Empire and the World, 1780–1830* (London: Longman, 1989), see, for examples, 10, 60, and 207.
[136] Evans, The Humble Petition, quoted in Brodie, *Pitcairn's Island and the Islanders*, 192.
[137] Ibid., 102.   [138] Hancock, *Politics in Pitcairn*, 13.   [139] Macklin, *Dark Paradise*, 160.

hatred for whoever dared to contradict or oppose his plans with the least objection in the world." He showed "puerile vanity" and "a fantastic pride."[140] These were not the personal characteristics of a politician who sought to undertake a controversial political reform movement, much less political reform that promised to alter the fabric of a community's social and cultural order. Here, even if we choose to see in Hill's agenda something other than madness, we have to conclude that he was the wrong person to undertake the work he sought to do. Unwilling even to show Evans the text of his first major "act" as Pitcairn's political leader, Hill compromised both the transparency and the judicial objectivity of his new political order. In the course of being punished for his infraction, Evans was, in his own words, "so much hurt about the head, eyes, and ribs as to be confined to his bed for ten days. From this time the state of things became desperate, and your petitioner was under continual alarm for the lives of himself and family."[141]

Evans' part in the Hill drama is interesting, in part, because he seems to have been the most supportive of the three Pitcairnese "foreigners" of the island's new leader. Evans later admitted that he initially believed all of Hill's self-promotional advertising in October 1832. He even treated the new arrival "with all possible respect, also cheerfully contributed to his support."[142] But Hill broke with Evans within three weeks' time when "he attempted to persuade [Evans'] wife to leave him, saying he would take her under his protection, and supply her with everything she wanted."[143] We know, of course, that Hill had a wife in Britain, and we know he was substantially older that Rachel Adams. It makes little sense to assume that he was trying to pry his way between the couple out of any sexual interest in Evans' wife. In all of Hill's odd behaviors, there is nothing to suggest that he was seduced by the South Pacific's mythic sexual opportunities.

Why then alienate Evans, in whom Hill had a potentially powerful ally against both Buffett and Nobbs? Hill's explanation to Rachel (Adams) Evans gives us the answer. He informed the young woman that, should she come to live with him, he would "cause the first captain of a man-of-war who arrives to remove these lousy foreigners from the island."[144] To have used Evans against Nobbs and Buffett or to have used Evans' link to the *Bounty* community through John Adams' daughter would have been to play at the same clannish game that John Buffett had played when he married Dolly Young and that George Nobbs played when he married

---

[140] Moerenhout, *Travels to the Islands*, 445.
[141] Evans, The Humble Petition, quoted in Brodie, *Pitcairn's Island and the Islanders*, 102.
[142] Quoted in Belcher, *The Mutineers of the* Bounty, 198.   [143] Ibid.   [144] Ibid.

Sarah Christian. Hill's governing sensibility always seems to have turned away from the familial and towards an institutionalized administrative system of, by, and for the Pitcairnese people. When Rachel Adams refused to abandon her husband for Hill's cause, the entire Evans family became his "declared enemy."[145] Having been flogged at Hill's command and having had his family threatened and, now, declared public enemies, Evans sought passage to Tahiti. The family sailed from Pitcairn on the *Tucan*, the same whale ship on which Frederick Debell Bennett was employed as a surgeon. Had it not been for the help of the ship's master, Captain Stavers, and Dr. Bennett, Evans later recorded, "murder would have been shortly committed."[146]

Amidst the chaos of the treason law, Hill began to entertain the idea of expelling the three Englishmen and their families. John Buffett leaked word of this plan to the other islanders, and he too fell victim to one of Hill's peculiar legal spectacles. "After Mr. Hill's beating me over the head, breaking it in two places, likewise my finger," Buffett recorded, "I was suspended by my hands in the church, and flogged until I was not able to walk home, and confined to my bed for two weeks." Buffett's family was forbidden from seeing him while he recuperated, and Charles Christian was roughly treated when he tried to offer assistance to the Buffett family in their travails.[147] For attempting to help Buffet, Christian, then Pitcairn's oldest resident, was turned out of his house.[148]

It was Hill's regulation of landownership that John Buffett most resented, and after the Buffets were deprived of the lands they held through Dolly Buffet's Young-family genealogy, Buffett made it clear that he intended to move his entire family from Pitcairn. For this step, he was put on trial, and, on August 5, 1833, he was sentenced (by Hill) to "three dozen lashes with a cat, upon the bare back and breech, together with a fine of three barrels of yams or potatoes, to be paid within one month, or, in default thereof, an extra barrel will be required for this re-iterated contempt of court." Furthermore, in an odd twist for a judicial decision that resulted from Buffet's desire to quit Pitcairn, the court ordered that Buffett "whether with or without your family" was "to leave this island by the first vessel that may present herself thus, for if you do not, punishment and imprisonment will be the consequence."[149]

George Nobbs was similarly intimidated by Hill's administrative abuses. As Evans and Buffett were being physically beaten, Nobbs was

---

[145] Ibid.   [146] Ibid., 199–200
[147] Buffett, The Testimonial of J. Buffett, in Brodie, *Pitcairn's Island and the Islanders*, 186–187. See also, Belcher, *The Mutineers of the* Bounty, 194.
[148] Belcher, *The Mutineers of the* Bounty, 194.   [149] Quoted in Ibid., 196–197.

suffering with dysentery and so avoided being tried and whipped.[150] He was not, though, immune to suffering at Hill's hand. In November 1833, as Nobbs lay sick, Hill refused to grant the former pastor access to any of the island's scarce medical supplies, and he warned of dire consequences to anybody who dared to breech the embargo. "In fact," Nobbs wrote, "it was the declared intent of Joshua Hill and his colleagues to bring about the death of your petitioner, either by hanging, flogging, or starvation."[151]

Since securing his place as the island's effective leader after 1831, Nobbs lived in a house that was put up and maintained, in part, at the public's expense. This arrangement was considered part of his salary. The islanders also supplied Nobbs and his family with foodstuffs, as they could hardly be expected to garden and farm effectively if their *paterfamilias'* attentions were always directed to the education, spiritual welfare, and social organization of the wider community. Initially, George Nobbs had invited Hill to reside in his home, as it was one of Pitcairn's largest and finest – one of the few places a visitor to the island might have stayed in 1832. Had Nobbs ever asked George Pritchard, he might have known better than to take in Joshua Hill, for, within one month, Hill had pushed Nobbs to the side and moved his predecessor out of the house, taking it as his own.[152] Homeless, isolated, and fearing that he too might suffer public punishments at Hill's hand, Nobbs' decision to leave Pitcairn was easily made. Upon the defervescence of his dysentery, Nobbs boarded the *Tuscan* with Buffett and Evans, and sailed from Pitcairn in March 1834.[153] None of the three was particularly healthy at the time, none was allowed to take any property from the island, and none had any money to his name.[154] Hill had won, for the moment. He alone was the executive leader of Pitcairn Island, the self-constituted magistrate of a small Pacific island that he now controlled on his own, absent any authority from or connection to the centers of colonial power in London.

Robert Macklin takes it as "a measure of Hill's bravado that the men left" the island but left their families behind.[155] But putting the three men out to the world, as it were, loosed them to have unfettered access to British naval commanders and to London itself. It also unleashed a torrent of internal pain at Pitcairn, and neither ultimately served Hill's administration well. After having been exiled from Pitcairn, George

[150] Nobbs, *George Hunn Nobbs*, 30.
[151] Nobbs, The Humble Petition, in Brodie, *Pitcairn's Island and the Islanders*, 184. See also Lummis, *Life and Death in Eden*, 211.
[152] Stallworth, Letter to Mr. Ellis (April 21, 1834). See also, Shapiro, *The Pitcairn Islanders*, 81.
[153] Shapiro, *The Pitcairn Islanders*, 83–84.
[154] Nobbs, The Humble Petition, in Brodie, *Pitcairn's Island and the Islanders*, 184–185.
[155] Macklin, *Dark Paradise*, 160.

Nobbs settled at the Gambier Islands alongside his fellow exile John Buffett. The two would soon thereafter be joined by John Evans from Tahiti. Back at Pitcairn, the three men's families were left as sympathetic victims of Hill's regime.[156] In a letter to the British consul at Valparaíso John White, George Adams observed that the departure of Nobbs, Evans, and Buffett had left the island divided. In part to ease the dissatisfaction caused by having divided the three families, Hill allowed Captain Ebril, who had originally brought Hill to Pitcairn, to bring the three exiles back to the island long enough to assist their loved ones in joining them in their exile at the Gambier Islands.[157] At the Gambiers, all three men quickly became influential figures, Nobbs in particular. Having been ousted from power at Pitcairn, Nobbs volunteered his services again as a teacher and community leader to the locals.[158] It is interesting that Nobbs, like Hill, seems to have had the capacity to rise time and time again no matter the environment.

Back at Pitcairn, though, we find that Hill's victory was also the beginning of his undoing. From Tahiti and the Gambier Islands, Evans, Nobbs, and Buffett were able to publicize Hills "malevolence" and to petition the outside world for relief.[159] The reports that have outlined this story here were all part of a network of formal "petitions" that the three exiled men circulated around the globe to win support for their causes. Similarly, some among the anti-Hill faction at Pitcairn itself found ways to disseminate their accounts of life at Adamstown. In July 1834, George Pritchard forwarded a report from Tahiti. He had met with George Adams. Adams, Pritchard wrote, had

been deputed by the greater part of the inhabitants of [Pitcairn Island] to come to Tahiti with hope of meeting here a ship of war, to make known to her Commander their present distressed state and to beg such Commander to remove from Pitcairns Island the person who is the principal cause of their distress.[160]

Pritchard then went on to misidentify the responsible party as "Mr. Joseph Hill," which is odd given that Pritchard had met Hill, something he admitted in the report. "This Gentleman lived with me eleven

---

[156] Maud, "The History of Pitcairn Island," 71.
[157] Adams, Letter to John White (Tahiti: July 14, 1834), Te Puna, MS-Papers-1009–2/51 – Letters and Papers. See also, Nicholson, *The Pitcairners*, 142; and Ralston, *Grass Huts and Warehouses*, location 1019.
[158] Murray, *Pitcairn*, 179.
[159] Evans, The Humble Petition, in Brodie, *Pitcairn's Island and the Islanders*, 193. See also, Nobbs, The Humble Petition, in Brodie, *Pitcairn's Island and the Islanders*, 185; and Buffett, The Testimonial of J. Buffett, in Brodie, *Pitcairn's Island and the Islanders*, 187.
[160] George Pritchard, Letter to an Unidentified Recipient (Tahiti: July 16, 1834), Te Puna, MS-Papers-1009–2/51.

months," Pritchard recalled. "It is impossible to understand his character or his object in coming to these islands," the missionary continued. "It appears to me that he is a broken down Gentleman who cannot live in his own Country & has come out here to live on the charity of others."[161] The description here hardly matches with what we know Pritchard knew of Hill, at least not completely. It is true that Hill was parasitical towards his hosts. He had moved into Pritchard's house at Tahiti without invitation, and he had shunted the cost of his laundry service to Pritchard's accounts during his stay as well. But we also have to recall that, at Tahiti, Hill had worked alongside Pritchard to guide and advise Queen Pomare. If J. A. Moerenhout is accurate, Hill impressed Pritchard.[162] We know for certain that he had impressed the Queen, and, yet, Pritchard's summary from Pitcairn serves to discredit anything the Tahitian monarch might have said that was charitable about Joshua W. Hill. Our characters in this story are, at least, consistent in their self-interestedness.

In addition to these petitions, Hill's own letters out from Pitcairn helped to publicize his presence at the island, and that publicity generated no few questions. Hill, after all, had originally been clear that it was his hope that London would seek a stronger British Pacific strategy and that Pitcairn would be central to that vision. And it was London's failure to do so that drove him to take up the cause himself. It is more than a little ironic then that what finally put Pitcairn on the official radar was the chaos Hill inspired on the island. Letters to and from ships' captains in the Pacific indicate that the British navy was both alert to and puzzled by Hill's presence at Pitcairn as early as the summer of 1833.[163] For its part, the British Consulate at Valparaíso was hard pressed to answer a minor flood of inquiries it received asking "whether Mr. Joshua Hill has any authority from His Majesty's Government to interfere with the affairs of the island."[164] Joshua Hill's mutiny at Pitcairn, then, proved his point. If London did not take better care of its Pacific interests, it stood to lose them.

More pressing, from Hill's perspective, were the steps taken by those who sided with Nobbs, Buffett, and Evans. T. Mason, commander of the HMS *Blonde*, informed the Admiralty that he had heard word from Nobbs and affirmed that "Mr. Hill appears to have assumed a power,

---

[161] Ibid.   [162] Moerenhout, *Travels to the Islands of the Pacific Ocean*, 445.
[163] Rear Admiral Michael Seymour, Letter to Captain George Elliott (Rio de Janero: September 3, 1833), quoted in Brodie, *Pitcairn's Island and the Islanders*, 174–175. See also Captain. J. Townshend, Letter to Read Admiral Sir Michael Seymour (June 3, 1833), quoted in Brodie, *Pitcairn's Island and the Islanders*, 175–176.
[164] J. White, Letter to the Rt. Hon. Lord J. Townshend (Valparaíso: June 24, 1833), quoted in Brodie, *Pitcairn's Island and the Islander*, 176.

and exercised a severity, and even cruelty, at Pitcairn's Island quite unauthorized. It is much to be regretted that that once exemplary and interesting population should be under the influence of such a man."[165] Mason's letter to London included Nobbs' petition and two shorter testimonials from the islanders, both dated to 1831, in which the Pitcairners initially invited Nobbs to serve as their teacher and minister.[166] Official notice of this sort could hardly have been desirable to Joshua Hill as he worked to reform Pitcairn outside of London's official sanction.

It was from the inside, though, and not from overseas, that Hill's Pitcairnese empire eventually collapsed. At some point in late 1833 or early 1834 – no account gives the actual date – Charlotte Quintal, one of Arthur Quintal's seven daughters (Quintal had fourteen children over the course of his two marriages), was accused of stealing yams (again, as on the *Bounty*, it is stolen foodstuffs that begins a revolution), running afoul of Joshua Hill's disciplinary regime.[167] According to Rosalind Young, whose narrative of this moment in Pitcairnese history has defined what we know of this period, Hill's sentence for the theft was to have been Shermanesque. "Hill declared," she reported, "that the offender ought to be executed, or, at least, be made to suffer severely for her fault."[168] Clearly, Joshua Hill was not one for political logrolling. When Quintal refused to allow his daughter to be subjected to an arbitrary punishment, Hill is reported to have felt the resistance as a personal affront as well as a breach of the island's new political systems. Here was one of the island's political elders, a member of the governing council, openly defying the judgment of the community's leader as well as arguing for special exemptions for his family. In any systematic political regime, the recourse might have been easy enough. Quintal ought to have recused himself from this particular case. He could not be objective. Had he still sought to interfere with the proper administration of affairs, he might have been removed from office.

But at Adamstown in the age of Hill, the systematic political regime was tainted by Hill's stroppy inability to brook opposition. In this instance, he was positively wroth. Reports suggest that he responded to the situation by threatening Arthur Quintal with a sword. This is the moment when, as we saw in the previous chapter, Hill demanded that Quintal "Confess your sins or you are a dead man!"[169] The fight that followed was, by

[165] Commander T. Mason, Letter to Captain Geo. Elliott (from HMS *Blonde*: December 4, 1834), quoted in Brodie, *Pitcairn's Island and the Islanders*, 177–178.
[166] Two Testimonials from the Pitcairn Islanders, quoted in Brodie, *Pitcairn's Island and the Islanders*, 178; and Silverman, *Pitcairn Island*, 78 and 120.
[167] Nicholson, *The Pitcairners*, 146.   [168] Young, *Mutiny of the* Bounty, 82.
[169] Ibid., 82–83. This scene is also recorded in Nobbs, *George Hunn Nobbs*, 31.

accounts from both Hill's supporters and his opponents, ferocious. Quintal was dressed only in his trousers, exposing his shoulders and back to Hill's blade. Hill beat Quintal viciously before Quintal was able to grab the sword in his bare hands and force Hill to the floor. In thinking about this scene, we cannot forgo the observation that Joshua Hill would have been nearly sixty-one years old as he wrestled with Quintal, who was a full twenty-two years younger. That it took Quintal as much effort as it did to best Hill in this contest speaks to the elder man's physical stamina and emotional fortitude.[170]

Indeed, even from the ground, Hill could not accept that he had been defeated. After agreeing to discuss the situation regarding what a proper punishment ought to be for the theft of yams "in a Christian manner," Hill was allowed to sit up, but, before anybody knew better, Hill went again for his sword. But for a group of young men whose attention had been drawn to the scene by the noise, Hill might have won the day. He did manage to hit Quintal on the neck and shoulders a few more blows before these newly arrived men grabbed Hill and his sword.[171]

The Pitcairners did not return Joshua Hill's sword to him until he was about to board the HMS *Imogene* in 1837. Deprived of the threat of violence, and, more importantly, deprived of the political support of the disaffected Quintal family, Joshua Hill's "reign" at Adamstown was at an end. A governmental structure that was to have been predicated on institutions like a governing council and on public offices instead of on the power dynamics within and between family clans collapsed when the Quintals turned against Joshua Hill. By September 1834 and over Hill's objections, the three exiled "foreigners" began returning to Pitcairn. John Buffett was the first to return, but George Nobbs' return proved particularly crippling for Hill, for Nobbs returned with a letter from Commodore Mason, the British naval officer commanding the South American station out of Callao in which Mason made it quite clear, on behalf of British officialdom, that Hill "had no right to assume any authority on the island, much less use corporal punishment, or to send any of the inhabitants away."[172]

The fraud was exposed.

As we have seen, of course, the fraud had been obvious from the very beginning, but Mason's letter cemented Hill's fall, though the fallen leader did not stop in his attempts to return to power. In April 1835, he wrote to the British consul at Valparaíso asking for permission to exile Nobbs, Buffet, and Evans once more. He had, he observed, been trying to

---

[170] Nobbs, *George Hunn Nobbs*, 31.   [171] Ibid.
[172] Quoted in Ibid. See also, Nicholson, *The Pitcairners*, 141 and 147.

rid the island of their influence since his arrival in 1832. "But," he went on, "they seem determined to respect nothing … we have daily trouble with them."[173] The letter was a desperate attempt, if ever one has been made. Hill had to have known from Mason's statement that the circulation of information about him throughout the naval networks of the British imperial world and in the official channels of government communication in London itself had turned against him. Still, he made this one last effort.

By 1837, the Admiralty dispatched Captain Lord Edward Russell of the HMS *Actaeon* to conduct a public hearing at Pitcairn. As fate would have it, Russell was the son of the Duke of Bedford, whom Hill had claimed as a boon companion. Russell confirmed that this too was a fabrication on Hill's part, and after a two-day set of interviews with the island's residents, the captain determined that Hill should be banished from Pitcairn. Lacking the authority to carry out the punishment, Russell left Hill in a state of limbo at Pitcairn when he departed. It would fall to Captain Henry William Bruce of the HMS *Imogene* to remove Hill later that year.[174]

The "reform" had failed. And in the wake of his failure, Hill was easily identified not only as the one responsible for all of the chaos that had happened between 1832 and 1837 but also as a manic, if not a completely mad, charlatan – the image that history has held of him ever since. Naval officials, many of whom had been eagerly following the Pitcairn crisis in an attempt to understand what exactly was happening on the island, were quick to judge. One captain lamented that "that once interesting and exemplary colony should be under the influence of such a man."[175] For his part, Nobbs would forever record that his power had been usurped and he had been exiled by the "villainy of a wretched imposter."[176]

In 1847, the residents of Pitcairn submitted a petition to London in which they tried to explain what had happened in their community during the 1830s. Hill was gone, and so he becomes the full villain in this report, "a partially deranged imposter."[177] But, even in the post-1838 assessments, there are hints that the story of a madman and his political coup at Pitcairn hide some of the story. In the remark books of the HMS *Imogene*, the ship that carried Hill from the island, there is a report about the state

---

[173] Joshua Hill, Letter to J. White (Pitcairn Island: April 5, 1835), Te Puna, MS-Papers-1009–2/51.
[174] Young, *Mutiny on the* Bounty, 82–85.
[175] Quoted in Belcher, *The Mutineers of the* Bounty, 198.
[176] George Hunn Nobbs, Letter to an Unidentified Recipient (Pitcairn Island: July 20, 1847), Te Puna, MS-Papers-1009–2/51.
[177] Murray, *Pitcairn*, 206. See also, Ball, *Pitcairn*, 119.

of the island that is more nuanced than what the islanders would remember a decade on. True, the report notes, Hill "had made himself very obnoxious to the Natives" at Pitcairn. True, he had lied to them about his authority to rule over them. But the impulses that drove him to lie and to govern with authoritarian force were not entirely misguided. "His conduct was marked by the strictest moral integrity," and, despite "the seeds of dissension" he had sown, "it is probable however, that he produced more good than evil amongst them." Rosalind Young would agree. Had Hill, she wrote, "been as wise as he was zealous in" reforming the island "there is no question but that he would have accomplished such lasting good among the people as would have continued so long as they had a history."[178] Still, though, the island would be calmer without Hill, Captain Bruce noted, the islanders were also "most desirous to be relieved of the presence of" Evans, Nobbs, and Buffet.[179]

Mark Twain's short story about Hill's time at Pitcairn calls the events from 1832 to 1838 the "Great Revolution."[180] Compared to America in 1776, France in 1789, or Haiti in 1791, the events at Pitcairn in the 1830s hardly seem that revolutionary at all. In Pitcairn's isolated history, however, the 1830s were revolutionary years for the people living in Adamstown. If we accept the assumption that Joshua Hill hoped to bring Pitcairn into the age of reform, his goal was to transform the *gemeinschaft* that marked the island's sociopolitical order into something more modern, a civil polity. To do this, he had to rid the Pitcairners of their patriarchal political system that leaned on the rule of wizened father figures. He had to make the Pitcairners citizens of their own commonwealth within the broader British Empire, indeed a central colonial outpost in a wider and growing British Pacific. If we accept the assumption that this may have been Hill's goal, we also have to accept that, ultimately, he was not the right man for the task, which is why so many observers – both contemporaries and subsequent historians – have judged Hill harshly.

In 1837, Lord Edward Russell, captain of the HMS *Actaeon*, observed that Mr. Hill and Mr. Nobbs had divided the island into two factions, concluding that "Mr. Hill had been the principal cause of all their dissensions."[181] Russell's assessment hinged, as have the conclusions of so many others, on the fact that Hill deceived the islanders about his

---

[178] Rosalind Amelia Young, *Mutiny of the* Bounty, 76.
[179] Bruce, Remarks of the *Conway* and *Imogene*. UKHO OD 777, 296–297. See also Lummis, *Life and Death in Eden*, 215. See also Bruce, Letter to J. Backhouse (December 17, 1839).
[180] Twain, "The Great Revolution in Pitcairn."
[181] Lord Edward Russell, Letter to Commodore Mason (February 3, 1837).

authority to govern at Pitcairn. But as we have seen, Nobbs did much the same. Indeed, the dissension that Hill and Nobbs caused from 1832 until 1838 was but an extension of the dissension that Nobbs had started between himself and Buffett in 1828, dissension that had divided the island into family factions – the Christians against the Youngs. Pacific missionaries as far from Pitcairn as Tahiti knew about the schisms that Buffett and Nobbs had wrought. In 1834, George Stallworth wrote to Reverend Ellis at the LMS's headquarters to observe that two or three families still sent their children to Buffett after Nobbs had established himself as Pitcairn's pastor and teacher.[182] Hill stirred new passions, to be certain. But he cannot be credited with bringing division to Pitcairn's society. That serpent existed in paradise long before Joshua Hill landed on the island.

What Hill did, though, was give in to the revolutionary temptation to turn tyrant. The "Great Revolution" at Pitcairn took the path of the French Revolution, ending with the advent of a demagogue and a dictator. Hill could brook no compromise with his enemies; he could tolerate no objections to his methods or his ends. He was no George Washington; he wielded power (literally) in the form of a sword, and he ceded power only when it was wrested (physically) from his hand. The result is that Hill comes down to us as a madman. We focus on his regime of lies, what Lady Belcher would describe as his "reign of terror on Pitcairn."[183] He is "the Mussolini of Pitcairn," a "czar," or, as George Elliott would put it, the *soi-disant* "King of Pitcairn."[184] We remember that he raged at his enemies, that he flogged and beat them. We forget that George Nobbs' past was just as checkered, recalling only Nobbs' post-Hill years – the successful removal of the Pitcairners to Norfolk, his trip to Britain, his ordination to the Anglican priesthood, and his meeting with Queen Victoria and Prince Albert.[185]

Nobbs' history, therefore, fills the lion's share of any book about the Pitcairnese people. Joshua Hill, in contrast, has never received more than a chapter's worth of attention in this bigger drama. As Lady Diana Belcher had observed, Hill's story more or less ended when he was removed from Pitcairn in 1838. The "aged imposter" had "sunk into the contempt and oblivion he merited by his disgraceful

---

[182] George Stallworth, Letter to Mr. Ellis (April 21, 1834). See also, Nobbs, *George Hunn Nobbs*, 26–28.

[183] Belcher, *The Mutineers of the* Bounty, 206.

[184] Kirk, *Pitcairn Island*, chapter twelve; and Robert Kirk, *Paradise Past*, 63. See also Hall, *The Tale of a Shipwreck*, 89. For Hill as a czar, see Silverman, *Pitcairn Island*, 162. See also, George Elliott, Pencil Sketch of Joshua Hill, in Pitcairn Islanders: Autographs and Pencil Sketches, SLNSW Ap25/Pitcairn Island, Folder 1, Fourth Sketch.

[185] Nobbs, *George Hunn Nobbs*, 11.

conduct."[186] But Belcher was not quite right. Hill himself had vanished. True. But his influence persisted. The 1838 Constitution at Pitcairn, which we will investigate more in Chapter 7, prohibited non-native Pitcairners from becoming the island's chief magistrate.[187] For all of his influence over Pitcairnese history, George Hunn Nobbs would never serve as the community's chief executive. In this regard, the official understanding of what a proper government at Pitcairn ought to be picked up on themes that Joshua Hill had brought with him. Not only did the Constitution mandate that the island needed an elected executive head, it also recognized that there was real value in promoting indigenous leadership, even if it came at the cost of marginalizing educated and dynamic men with George Hunn Nobbs' qualifications.[188]

That Pitcairn needed a constitution was obvious to Captain Edward Russell of the HMS *Actaeon* who landed at Pitcairn in 1837. Russell arrived at Pitcairn after the Quintal family had left Hill's side, and so he encountered the island at a fraught crossroads. It was clear to Russell that Hill had been a tyrant, that he had deceived, and that he had to go. But it was also clear that if Pitcairn did not get some official status in the eyes of the imperial capital, it would forever be prey to vultures like Hill. "I fear," he wrote, "that unless some person with authority from the Government is sent to superintend the internal affairs, there will be constant quarrels & disturbances upon the island."[189] In the 1820s, these same lines might have come from the pen of Joshua W. Hill. When Captain Russell Elliott of HMS *Fly* agreed to help the Pitcairners draft a constitution for the island in November 1838, therefore, he was both repudiating and affirming Joshua Hill's goals for the tiny island.

As much, though, as the Constitution of 1838 reflected some of Joshua Hill's aspirations for Pitcairn Island and as much as the discord he had caused at Adamstown put Pitcairn on London's radar (again, as Hill had wanted), the island continued, after Hill's removal, to have a clannish quality about its leadership and politics. Thomas Heath visited Pitcairn in November 1840. We will return to the island Heath found in Chapter 7, when we come to look at Pitcairn Island as a colonial space. At this juncture in our story, though, it is enough to observe that Heath

---

[186] Belcher, *The Mutineers of the* Bounty, 206.
[187] Regulations for the Appointment of a Magistrate at Pitcairn's Island, 1838, in Nobbs Papers, SLNSW ML A 2881.
[188] Lewis, "Pitcairn's Tortured Past," in Oliver, ed., *Justice, Legality, and the Rule of Law*, 54.
[189] Lord Edward Russell, Letter to an Unidentified Recipient (Valparaíso: February 3, 1837), FO 16/32.

found a "patriarchal simplicity of manners among" the Pitcairners. The island's residents continued to pay "regular attention to religious duties," as well as to their public obligations and their family allegiances.[190] In such a society, one did not need to occupy the top job to play a central part in the small community. As Raymond Nobbs had observed, "it was religion which underpinned the whole fabric of society" at Pitcairn, and George Hunn Nobbs would be the heart of the Pitcairn community from the moment Hill left until the day of his death on Norfolk Island in 1884.[191]

The heart, but never the chief magistrate. Under the new constitutional structures put in place in 1838, the island's first chief magistrate was Edward Quintal, Joshua Hill's foremost macher and, as such, one of George Nobbs' most hostile critics. Quintal would be reelected for a second term as chief magistrate, thereby remaining in office until his death in 1841, when he was replaced by his half-brother, Arthur. The Hill years at Pitcairn had elevated the status of the Quintal family; they had given this clan political clout. Only by tracing Hill's history more centrally than we have before, therefore, can we see that the 1830s – the Age of Hill – did bring about a modicum of reform at Pitcairn. Hill made a difference, and it was a difference that would limit George Hunn Nobbs' political influence and aspirations for the remainder of his life.

---

[190] Heath, "Visit to the Austral Islands."   [191] Nobbs, *George Hunn Nobbs*, 33.

5   The Island

They landed on a wild but narrow scene,
Where few but Nature's footsteps yet had been;
Prepared their arms, and with that gloomy eye,
Stern and sustained, or man's extremity,
When Hope is gone, nor Glory's self remains
To cheer resistance against death or chains, –
   Lord Byron, "The Island" (1823)[1]

In February 1831, Captain Alexander A. Sandilands arrived, per orders from London, off the coast of Pitcairn Island. His ship, HM Sloop *Comet* sailed with a small companion barque, the *Lucy Anne*, from Sydney. Sandilands' orders were ambitious. He was to remove every living inhabitant of Pitcairn Island and resettle them at Tahiti.

After the settlement of the island in 1790, Pitcairn's landscape changed dramatically. The first edition of Robert Michael Ballantyne's *The Lonely Island; or, The Refuge of the Mutineers* includes an illustration entitled "The Landing of the Live Stock" (Figure 5). The picture, one of many that adorned this popular novel for younger readers, gives us some sense of the zoological exchange that took place when the mutineers landed at Pitcairn. Here we see men driving goats into the island's hinterlands with the ship's cat-o'-nine-tails. Sheep are being guided down a wooden plank from the *Bounty*'s decks to the island's rocky shores. One eager sailor has tossed a pig overboard, and at least two cats – Pitcairn's first feline residents – wait on board to be carried to shore.[2]

There is a lot that is wrong about the illustration in *The Lonely Island*, but the types of animals that the *Bounty* introduced at Pitcairn did include those we see in the picture.[3] We know, for instance, that Fletcher Christian did collect a host of animals – thirty-eight goats; eight dozen chickens; many, many pigs; and the bull and the cow that Captain Cook had left at Tahiti – when he sailed from that island, all with an eye towards using this stock to

---

[1] Byron, "The Island," iii, 388.
[2] Ballantyne, *The Lonely Island*, plate found opposite page 63.
[3] Silverman, *Pitcairn Island*, 85; and Crosby, *Ecological Imperialism*, 173.

LANDING OF THE LIVE STOCK—PAGE 63.

Figure 5 *Landing of the Live Stock*. Plate from Robert Michael Ballantyne, *The Lonely Island; or, The Refuge of the Mutineers* (London: James Nisbet and Company, 1880). Published by permission of the New York Public Library.

settle a new land for himself, his mutinous crew, and the Tahitian wives they intended to carry off with them.[4] Ironically, the vessel that was to have been a sailing greenhouse – carrying breadfruit from the Pacific to the Atlantic – became Noah's ark, delivering Western fauna to a Pacific island. The agricultural civilization that the *Bounty* settlers brought with them meant that the island's trees had to be cleared. The *Bounty*'s Western axes and saws made quick work of the island's hardwood trees, converting them into the houses of Adamstown and the community's fishing boats. The goats the *Bounty* settlers had brought to Pitcairn chewed and destroyed their own share of the islands plants and trees.[5] As David Silverman has observed, "[T]oday almost no timber trees remain; an undulating grassy savannah, broken by clumps of pandanus, coconut palms, and bush, covers the top of the island."[6]

Absent trees, the island experienced soil erosion where it had not before, and the soil that washed into the waters around the island changed the nature of fishing in Pitcairn's rough seas. More pressingly, population growth on the island strained Pitcairn's water supply. Recall that Fletcher Christian arrived with only twenty-five other people. By the 1830s, Pitcairn's population was nearing ninety in total – more than a threefold increase in only four decades and quite a large population for an island that was, recall, less than two square miles in area.[7]

As the water table at Pitcairn sank deeper and deeper into the island's volcanic substratum, the springs in and around Adamstown produced less and less water to supply the Pictairners.[8] The matter of water was particularly pressing, noted Captain W. M. Waldegrave of the HMS *Seringapatam*. Waldegrave had been charged with delivering clothes and some farming equipment to the people of Pitcairn during his Pacific voyage of 1830, but it was the plight of the island's erstwhile innocents vis-à-vis the bounded nature of their Pacific paradise that became his deep concern.

Food grew at Pitcairn, Waldegrave observed, as one would expect it to do in a tropical paradise. "They appear to be careless," he reported, when it came to fruits and vegetables, particularly "yams, sweet potatoes, cocoa-nuts, plantains, and bananas."[9] Of course, Waldegrave did not mean to suggest that the Pitcairners were wasting this produce. No – he used "careless" in the sense that the islanders, quite literally, had no care, no cause for concern, about the supply of these foodstuffs. They had, he

---

[4] Wahlroos, *Mutiny and Romance*, 72.   [5] Silverman, *Pitcairn Island*, 86.   [6] Ibid., ix.
[7] Captain Alexander A. Sandilands, Report (March 1831), RGS-LMS, Item 4-a, 26. See also, "Pitcairn Island," in *The Bruce Herald* 23 (May 27, 1892), 4.
[8] Lummis, *Pacific Paradises*, 21.   [9] Barrow et al., "Accounts of Pitcairn Islands," 158.

observed, cultivated only about a twelfth of the island. It would take work to cultivate the craggy remainder, but it could be done if it were needed. Water, though. Water was the issue, and, by Waldegrave's estimation, the population at Pitcairn stood to increase at such a rate that it would be overpopulated by the end of the nineteenth century.[10]

Waldegrave was hardly the first to suggest that the Pitcairners should leave their home island. In 1819, there had been talk of removing the Pitcairnese population to Opunohu Bay on Moorea near Tahiti, though, at that time, the islanders agreed among themselves that they wished to remain at Pitcairn. We know that John Adams was an advocate for at least studying the possibility that the islanders might be relocated. Indeed, within Adams' lifetime, most at Pitcairn agreed that all of the cultivable land on the island was in use.[11] Captain Beechey of the *Blossom* talked to Adams about the demographic limitations that the island imposed on the community at Adamstown, and Beechey passed his concerns along to Sir John Barrow.[12] Pitcairn was nearing what environmentalists now call its "carrying capacity."[13]

Letters from the late 1820s suggest that both the directors of the LMS and leading figures at the Foreign Office and at the Admiralty were thinking about – indeed collaborating on – the question of what should be done at Pitcairn.[14] We know that those who looked into the question considered a host of global destinations for the Pitcairners. New South Wales was one choice; Bathurst Island was another. That planners would settle on Tahiti, though, seems to have been a foregone conclusion. Tahiti was the island homeland for some of the remaining *Bounty* women.[15] Its siren song was strong. It was closer than some of the other choices too. Henry Nott wrote to his superiors at LMS headquarters in London in April 1829 to offer his thoughts on Tahiti as a destination. The directors had wanted to know what the missionaries at Tahiti could say on the question: "How far the ships of Tahiti may be disposed to

[10] Ibid., 160.   [11] Nicholson, *The Pitcairners*, 98.   [12] Ibid., 113.

[13] See Patrick V. Kirch and Jean-Louis Rallu, "Long-Term Demographic Evolution in the Pacific Islands: Issues, Debates, and Challenges," in Patrick V. Kirch and Jean-Louis Rallu, eds., *The Growth and Collapse of Pacific Island Societies: Archaeological and Demographic Perspectives* (Honolulu: University of Hawai'i Press, 2007), 8. See also, Shripad Tuljapurkar, Charlotte Lee, and Michael Figgs, "Demography and Food in Early Polynesia," in Patrick V. Kirch and Jean-Louis Rallu, eds., *The Growth and Collapse of Pacific Island Societies: Archaeological and Demographic Perspectives* (Honolulu: University of Hawai'i Press, 2007), 37.

[14] R. W. Hay, Letter to J. Planta (February 22, 1827), TNA FO 58/14; Beechey, Letter to J. Barrow (December 21, 1825); Unsigned Letter to J. Planta (London: February 28, 1827), TNA FO 58/14; and John Barrow, Letter to Mr. Hay (November 29, 1826), TNA FO 58/14.

[15] Maud, "The History of Pitcairn Island," 67.

receive the people of Pitcairns Island?" Indeed, the directors had warned Nott that the government was eager for his thoughts on the subject too. In reply, Nott was clear. The Pomare monarchy at Tahiti was in need *and* in search of good relations with London. Ministers for the boy king Pomare III had expressed their openness to receiving the Pitcairners before he died in 1827, and his heir, Queen Pomare, had not changed her position.[16] But, Nott cautioned, there was one hurdle, and that was the Pitcairners themselves. "Several vessels which have lately been at Pitcairns Island," he wrote, "have informed me that the people express no wish to remove from that island."[17]

The Pitcairners loved their island home. And, why not? One account of the island now at the Mitchell Library in Sydney, tucked away inside other papers from the Nobbs family, attests to Pitcairn's viridity. The island was "irregularly diversified with hills and valleys through which run several streamlets of the finest water; and the soil, which is of a rich alluvial nature, abounds with evergreen shrubbery among which thousands of aquatic birds make their habitations."[18] Adamstown was perched at "a romantic spot situated on the north side of the Island," on a cliff some three hundred feet above sea level.[19] The *Bounty* settlers had "landed on a wild but narrow scene," according to Lord Byron.[20] Wild and narrow, perhaps, but this was also a particularly beautiful island.

The year 1830, though, brought drought, and any previous concern over the water supply became pressing for the Pitcairners.[21] When he arrived on board the *Comet*, Captain Sandilands reported that Pitcairn had been without rain for fifteen months and that the islanders were "exceedingly distressed for water, what they had even being procured with great difficulty."[22] Barrow and others at the Admiralty had been right to send him to relocate the Pitcairners, but the decision to remove the people of Pitcairn was no small project, hardly the sort of mission that one would have undertaken lightly. The operation required not only that the government organize the transportation but also that it convince the Pitcairners to leave their island home *and* to convince the government of Queen Pomare IV of Tahiti to receive them.[23] Working with the Tahitian

---

[16] Queen Pomare IV of Tahiti, Letter to Mr. Planta (Tahiti: February 20, 1829), TNA FO 58/14.

[17] Nott, Letter to Mission House (April 25, 1829).

[18] Account of the *Bounty*, in Nobbs Papers, SLNSW ML A 2881, 100.   [19] Ibid., 106.

[20] Byron, "The Island," iii, 388.   [21] Belcher, *The Mutineers of the* Bounty, 189.

[22] Barrow et al., "Accounts of the Pitcairn Islanders," 164. See also, Captain Alexander A. Sandilands, Journal from the Voyage of the HMS *Comet* from Sydney to Pitcairn Island, 1830–1831, SLNSW ML MSS 8104/Box 1X.

[23] Murray, *Pitcairn*, 141. See also, Alfred McFarland, *Mutiny in the Bounty!, and Story of the Pitcairn Islanders* (Sydney: J.J. Moore, Publishers, 1884), 125.

monarch proved to be the easier side of the equation. Despite the drought, only about half of the island's population agreed to sail with Sandilands immediately. It took the captain weeks before he was able to cajole and convince the full Pitcairnese population to abandon their homes, to pack their impedimenta, to board his ships, and to sail away from their island.[24] The *Comet* and the *Lucy Anne* did not leave Pitcairn for Tahiti until March 6. They arrived at Tahiti fifteen days later.[25]

The removal to Tahiti, as the voyage is now remembered, was disastrous; the leechdom was worse than the ailment. Fate had suggested that it would be. After fifteen months without rain, Pitcairn Island was drenched by "an exceeding hard shower of rain" the day before Captain Sandilands sailed the Pitcairners away from their island home.[26] Their island, the rain suggested, was on the mend, but, at Tahiti, the Pitcairners found that Queen Pomare had lost control over the administration of *her* island, which was in a veritable state of civil war.[27] More significantly, the Pitcairnese people faced a public health crisis at Tahiti.[28] Though the Pitcairners were descended from Britons – the *Bounty* mutineers – and the Tahitian women the mutineers had kidnapped, and though the Pitcairners had been visited (from time to time) by the outside world since they were found by Captain Folger in 1808, they had lived in ecological isolation for long enough (from 1790 to 1831) that they were vulnerable to diseases when transplanted into the more cosmopolitan world at Tahiti. In the reechy hovels they called home at Tahiti, the Pitcairners saw disease spread among them. Like plants deprived of sunshine, they withered and etiolated. Thirteen Pitcairners – including the forty-one-year-old Thursday October Christian – died within three months of their arrival at Tahiti. Seventeen of the islanders died in all. By June, it was clear to the Pitcairn leadership that the islanders needed to go home, and the first of the emigrants turned immigrants arrived at Pitcairn by the end of that month.[29]

So quick was this turn of events that news of both the Pitcairners' arrival at *and* their departure from Tahiti arrived at London in the same letter.[30] We know that J. A. Moerenhout engaged with the community through their travails at Tahiti, even (circuitously) publishing an article in *The United States Service Journal* that criticized the missionary

---

[24] Shapiro, *The Pitcairn Islanders*, 75.   [25] Belcher, *The Mutineers of the* Bounty, 190.

[26] Sandilands, Journal from the Voyage of the HMS *Comet*.

[27] Murray, *Pitcairn*, 142. See also Pritchard, Letter to Mission House (November 24, 1832); and Moerenhout, *Travels to the Islands*, 442.

[28] Katherine Foxhall, *Health, Medicine, and the Sea: Australian Voyages, c. 1815–1860* (Manchester: Manchester University Press, 2012), 7.

[29] *The Pitcairn Register*.

[30] Richard Charlton, Letter to Lord Palmerston (March 12, 1832), TNA FO 58/6.

establishment at Tahiti for not having done more to support the Pitcairnese community. The Pitcairners had approached the missionaries about returning them to their native island very early on in their time at Tahiti. Moerenhout's essay accused the LMS, and David Darling in particular, of having missed the opportunity to demonstrate Christian charity.[31]

In subsequent letters between Mission House in London and Tahiti, Darling grumbled in explanation. To have helped the Pitcairners, he would have had to have broken off his already planned mission to the Marquesas Islands. Moreover, he was concerned that the diseases that were passing among the Pitcairners seemed communicable. They were hardly suited for the conditions of an open-ocean voyage. Perhaps most callously, Darling also wrote that the English government had spent a great deal of time and money planning this relocation on the Pitcairners' behalf. "I thought as well as many others on the island," he wrote, "that they ought not to be removed to their own island again until they had made a fair trial at Tahiti, by establishing themselves on the land that had been given them."[32]

The Pitcairners were fortunate, then, to know J. A. Moerenhout, for it was Moerenhout who helped the Pitcairnese people arrange to return to Pitcairn, starting first with an advance party that included John Buffett on board a chartered pearling vessel.[33] Those Pitcairners who remained at Tahiti continued to work with Moerenhout to find a way home.[34] On July 17, 1831, Captain William Driver of Salem, Massachusetts, landed at Tahiti in command of the *Charles Doggett*.[35] Driver found that sixty-four Pitcairners were still on the island. They were a "forlorn" bunch, a sorry group of "distressed looking creatures." Though London had supplied them with much that might have been required for life at Tahiti, the Pitcairn émigrés had been shaken by the deaths of more than a dozen of their number. They were "living huddled together in a miserable old thatched 'Brua' on the low lands by a small water run named 'Be By At,' or small water." Driver could not resist their entreaties. "Their tears," he recorded, were "ever too much for a sailor at 27."

---

[31] George Pritchard, Letter to the Directors at Mission House (October 22, 1833), SOAS CWM/LMS – South Seas Correspondence – Incoming Correspondence, Box 9, Folder 2/Jacket B.

[32] David Darling, Letter to the Directors at Mission House (January 4, 1833), SOAS CWM/LMS – South Seas Correspondence – Incoming Correspondence, Box 9, Folder 1/Jacket A.

[33] Maud, "The History of Pitcairn Island," 68.

[34] Moerenhout, *Travels to the Islands*, 444.

[35] William Driver, Letter to Caroline Buswell (Nashville, TN: November 16, 1880), in Whaling Log Books, SLNSW PMB 780.

The trip was only "a short deviation from my intended route," but it would also, Driver knew, void his insurance policy. But helping the Pitcairners was – as Driver would reflect to his family for years to come – the right thing to do. As he departed from Pitcairn, Driver noted, the islanders had tears in their eyes over all he had done for them, and many, he recorded, "paused to write my name on their walls," a touching – if odd – act of appreciation and memorialization.[36]

It was in the lead up to and in the wake of the removal that Pitcairn first became a consistent topic of conversation in Britain, particularly in evangelical and administrative circles. What would otherwise have been a romantic side story became a policy concern when those in London had to spend time mapping a strategy to move a dehydrated population from one island to the other across the Pacific Ocean. It was in this atmosphere, it seems, that Pitcairn became the sort of place that would come to the attention of a man like Joshua Hill.

And, we *have* been a long time without our protagonist.

We know from his correspondence around London in the late 1820s that Joshua Hill knew about the possibility that Pitcairn would be depopulated. Newspaper reports and other accounts about the island had made the debate over the island's water supply and its ultimate human carrying capacity a public one.[37] And, most agreed, the island was stressed to a near breaking point. We know too that Hill volunteered to help oversee the removal of the Pitcairners if either the government or a missionary group decided to undertake such a venture, for he had grave concerns about such a policy.[38]

Hill was not alone in worrying about the removal strategy. Early in 1831, *The Mirror* published a collection of extracted observations about Pitcairn Island, many drawn from reports out of Captain Beechey's earlier visit to the island. The reports focused attentively on the future fate of this unique little community. John Buffett was quoted as being concerned about plans to move the community from Adamstown. "To hear of these innocent creatures," he said, "being transplanted *per saltum* into any of the sinks of wickedness in New South Wales or Van Diemen's Land, would be utterly horrible."[39] Captain Beechey agreed: "It would be a pity," he wrote to John Barrow at the Admiralty, "to separate their little colony, as they are all so much attached to each other and their manners are so different from, and superior to the people whom they would have to mix with" at any other location.[40]

[36] Ibid.   [37] Brodie, *Pitcairn's Island and the Islanders*, 162.
[38] Maude, "The Migration of the Pitcairn Islanders to the Motherland," 112.
[39] "Pitcairn's Island," in *The Mirror* (1831).
[40] Beechey, Letter to J. Barrow (December 21, 1825).

Joshua Hill had had a proverbial bee in his bonnet over Pitcairn Island. As the foreign secretary to the LMS, George Stallworth, confirmed in a letter to Reverend William Ellis, "Captn. Joshua Hill ... is pretty well known in the Society and Sandwich Islands."[41] It might have been unusual for an average British citizen to take as close an interest in the to-ing and fro-ing of Pitcairnese domestic policy as Hill did, but, when we consider the big questions that were driving that policy in the late 1820s and early 1830s, what we find is that Hill's thinking about the island was not outside the mainstream. Like Buffett and Beechey, Hill was con-cerned that removing the Pitcairners would uproot them. Their island was central to the story of redemption that was the center of Pitcairnese history. It was their Eden. If the islanders were to be moved, they had to be sent to just the right spot, and Hill was a staunch opponent of the idea that Tahiti was that place.[42] He was always very clear about Tahiti. It was worse than other Pacific islands and other Pacific ports – places that themselves "suffered from dubious reputations."[43] Tahiti was "the Wapping of the Pacific."[44] And, he agreed that the islanders needed, come what may, to be maintained as a single community. But could they be retained at Pitcairn? Was it possible for these chosen people to carry on in their own Edenic paradise? Those were the questions that seem to have been swirling in Hill's head as he interjected himself into the Pitcairn debates taking place in the last years of the 1820s. These were the questions that Mr. Hill seems to have had in mind when he sailed from Britain in June 1830.

Joshua Hill, then, became interested in Pitcairn as a matter of grand, geopolitical strategy, as a matter of evangelical zeal, and because of specific environmental concerns about the limited resource base of a small South Pacific island that was only about one mile long and two wide. One might argue, of course, that our story has been an environ-mental one from its very outset – a botanical adventure that all began with the breadfruit tree and the British empire's attempts to transplant a Pacific fruit to the Atlantic and Caribbean worlds.[45] As the *Bounty* mission was in its planning stages, Sir Joseph Banks had taken great care to study the breadfruit tree's needs to insure that Bligh's voyage would be a success. He consulted with some of those best placed to

[41] Stallworth, Letter to Mr. Ellis (April 21, 1834).
[42] Barrow, *A Description of Pitcairn's Island*, 287.
[43] Kirsten McKenzie, *Scandal in the Colonies: Sydney and Cape Town, 1820–1850* (Melbourne: Melbourne University Press, 2004), 1.
[44] Hill, Letter to Lord Palmerston (April 5, 1835).
[45] Jennifer Newell, *Trading Nature: Tahitians, Europeans, and Ecological Exchange* (Honolulu: University of Hawai'i Press, 2010), 2.

understand the fruit and its capacities.[46] He mapped out the voyage in detail, even redesigning the interior of the *Bounty* to ensure that the ship was a comfortable home for the breadfruit seedlings – more comfortable for the plants, even, than it was for the master and his crew.[47] Banks even hand-selected William Bligh to captain the expedition.[48]

All of Banks' planning hinged on his faith in the empirical process, in "the belief not only that the environment of new lands could be exactly described and understood but also that it could in a sense be reordered."[49] Banks' vision here was no less evangelical than the Christian messages coming out of Euro-American missionary societies. And, he shared this faith with others, including the likes of Johann Reinhold Forster, the man who had replaced Banks as the naturalist on Captain Cook's second Pacific voyage from 1772 to 1775.[50]

Harry Liebersohn has argued that the relationship between scientists and missionaries was one of conflict in these years, and it is true that the two groups did imagine that they were going about different projects.[51] But it merits our notice that the two projects were not entirely distinct from one another. Scientists and evangelicals alike were selling messages rooted in European notions of progress and improvement.[52] As David Mackay has observed, the "truly remarkable aspect of the [*Bounty*] voyage is the fact that" so many "were prepared to invest in the magnificently

---

[46] George Vancouver, Letter to Sir Joseph Banks (August 1787), in Joseph Banks, *The Indian and Pacific Correspondence of Sir Joseph Banks, 1768–1820*, Neil Chambers, ed. (London: Pickering and Chatto, 2009), ii, 218–220. See also, Lamb, *Preserving the Self*, 105; and Liebersohn, *The Travelers' World*, 103.

[47] Sir Joseph Banks, Letter to an Unknown Correspondent (London: February, 1787), in Joseph Banks, *The Letters of Sir Joseph Banks: A Selection, 1768–1820*, Neil Chambers, ed. (London: Imperial College Press, 2000), 83–85. See also, Thomas Townshend, Letter to Sir Joseph Banks (August 6, 1787), in Joseph Banks, *The Indian and Pacific Correspondence of Sir Joseph Banks, 1768–1820*, Neil Chambers, ed. (London: Pickering and Chatto, 2009), ii, 223; and Sivasundaram, *Nature and the Godly Empire*, 98.

[48] William Bligh, Letter to Sir Joseph Banks (August 6, 1787), in Joseph Banks, *The Indian and Pacific Correspondence of Sir Joseph Banks, 1768–1820*, Neil Chambers, ed. (London: Pickering and Chatto, 2009), ii, 220. See also, Liebersohn, *The Travelers' World*, 101; and Alan Frost, *The Global Reach of Empire: Britain's Maritime Expansion in the Indian and Pacific Oceans, 1764–1815* (Carlton, Victoria, Australia: The Miegunyah Press, 2003), 204.

[49] David Mackay, "Myth, Science, and Experience in the British Construction of the Pacific," in Alex Calder, Jonathan Lamb, and Bridget Orr, eds., *Voyages and Beaches: Pacific Encounters, 1769–1840* (Honolulu: University of Hawai'i Press, 1999), 104.

[50] K. R. Howe, *Nature, Culture, and History: The "Knowing" of Oceania* (Honolulu: University of Hawai'i Press, 2000), 33.

[51] Liebersohn, *The Travelers' World*, 14 and 232.

[52] Sivasundaram, *Nature and the Godly Empire*, 93. See James Beattie, *Empire and Environmental Anxiety: Health, Science, Art, and Conservation in South Asia and Australasia, 1800–1920* (New York: Palgrave, 2011), 73. See also, Wilson, *The Island Race*, 69.

fanciful voyage."[53] But why not believe? Banks' career had (and would) produce major botanical innovations – scientific improvements of natural creation. Strawberries grew better fruit when cultivated in the cushioned comfort of scattered straw. Cranberries floated in watery fields in Britain. Fig trees were forced to produce a second crop in a season. Orchids flowered in hothouses across the cold, gray English countryside.[54] As Sujit Sivasundaram has rightly acknowledged, there was little about these innovations that had to do with faith, not, at least, in Joseph Banks' mind. But, inasmuch as greater control over the natural world generated an improvement in the material wealth humans could extract from nature, these botanical projects had everything to do with salvation.[55]

Some, like the ever-curmudgeonly Horace Walpole, doubted that anything would ever come of scientific explorations in the Pacific. Captain Cook, after all, had sailed the South Seas to fetch the "blood of a great whale called *Terra Australias incognita*, but saw nothing but its tail."[56] It did not help matters that the very first thing that the *Bounty* mutineers did after taking the ship was to toss the breadfruit trees – pots and all – into the Pacific Ocean, a scene that was captured in Robert Dodd's now iconic image of the mutiny (Figure 6). Here was an obvious setback for evangelical science, if ever an example was needed.[57] But Walpole was in the minority in his thinking. Even as he reported news of the *Bounty*'s failure, Joseph Banks was pleased to observe that his botanical planning had been sufficient. The breadfruit plan could be made to work.[58] Indeed, when it was tried again in 1791 aboard a new vessel, the *Providence* (also under William Bligh's command), the mission to transplant breadfruit from the Pacific to the Caribbean was successful.[59] Little could Banks have imagined, at the outset of the first voyage, that what threatened the plants most would be the line of naval command on board the floating Wardian Case that was the *Bounty*.[60]

[53] Mackay, "Myth, Science, and Experience," 111. See also, Kennedy, *Bligh*, 20; and Newell, *Trading Nature*, 142–149.

[54] Sivasundaram, *Nature and the Godly Empire*, 99. See also, Lamb, *Preserving the Self*, 77–80.

[55] Sivasundaram, *Nature and the Godly Empire*, 101. See also, Igler, *The Great Ocean*, 154.

[56] Quoted in Mackay, "Myth, Science, and Experience," 106.

[57] Sivasundaram, *Nature and the Godly Empire*, 97.

[58] James Wiles, Letter to Sir Joseph Banks (Jamaica: April 12, 1799), in Joseph Banks, *The Indian and Pacific Correspondence of Sir Joseph Banks, 1768–1820*, Neil Chambers, ed. (Brookfield, VT: Pickering and Chatto, 2012), v, 70.

[59] George Tobin, *Captain Bligh's Second Chance: An Eyewitness Account of His Return to the South Seas*, Roy Screiber, ed. (London: Chatham Publishing, 2007). See also, N. A. M. Rodger, *The Command of the Ocean: A Naval History of Britain, 1649–1815* (New York: W.W. Norton and Company, 2004), 360; Frost, *The Global Reach of Empire*, 314; and Toohey, *Captain Bligh's Portable Nightmare*, 57.

[60] William Bligh, Letter to Sir Joseph Banks (Batavia: October 13, 1789), in Joseph Banks, *The Indian and Pacific Correspondence of Sir Joseph Banks, 1768–1820*, Neil Chambers, ed.

Figure 6 Robert Dodd, *The Mutineers Turning Lieutenant Bligh and Part of the Officers and Crew Adrift from His Majesty's Ship the* Bounty (London: Benjamin Beale Evans, 1790), BM 1854, 1020.46. Published by permission of the British Museum, London.

The environmental threads that weave through this history, though, are more robust than the mere story of Banks and Bligh and the transplantation of breadfruit from one side of the globe to the other – though reframing that narrative as a history of environmental crossings and of invasive species is an important sea change worth noting here.[61] Pitcairn Island itself offered a unique physical landscape – a specific stage – on which this history unfolded, and that stage fundamentally influenced subsequent events.

(London: Pickering and Chatto, 2010), iii, 60–61. See also. Kennedy, *Bligh*, 82; and Gascoigne, *Encountering the Pacific*, 380–381.

[61] See Freeman, *The Pacific*, 127; Newell, *Trading Nature*, 8; and Kennedy, *Bligh*, 18. See also, Arthur Herman, *To Rule the Waves: How the British Navy Shaped the Modern World* (New York: Harper Perennial, 2005), 321; Crosby, *Ecological Imperialism*, 147; and Richard H. Grove, *Green Imperialism: Colonial Expansion, Tropical Island Edens, and the Origins of Environmentalism, 1600–1860* (New York: Cambridge Unviersity Press, 1995), 339.

The Pacific is bespeckled by some 20,000 islands. Eighty percent of the islands on Earth can be found peeking out from the azure waters of that ocean.[62] But, not every island is the same. Pitcairn, for instance, lacks a coral reef. As nineteenth-century travel reports about the island observed, it "rises abruptly from the depths, with steep and rugged cliffs of dark basaltic lava."[63] A volcanic island, like the Hawai'ian chain, Pitcairn was born of violent earthly processes. Rachel Carson once wrote that "the birth of a volcanic island is an event marked by prolonged and violent travail; the forces of the earth striving to create, and all the forces of the sea opposing."[64]

As we have seen, Fletcher Christian was pleased by Pitcairn's treacherous landings, its lack of beaches, and the infelicitous seas stirred by the island's want of a quiet coral lagoon. As Michael Reidy and Alain Corbin have both argued, early medieval scholars feared the rough sea. Unsettled ocean waters "represented the realm of the unfinished, a vibrating, vague extension of chaos [that] symbolized the disorder that preceded civilization."[65] Christian, though, was looking for something quite different than medieval scholars, and Pitcairn's frightening natural visage suited his needs perfectly. Here again, the environment drives the course of our story.

Islands, of course, conjure images of paradise.[66] The link is "burned into the psyche of the denizens of the western world," as Stephen A. Royle has argued.[67] As Royle observes, the very notion of "bounty" here is telling. The *Bounty* was to have fed the enslaved multitudes of the Caribbean and to have provided food for passing ships at Atlantic islands like St. Helena.[68] Forget the few fishes; forget the five loaves. The breadfruit was to be science's manna. As Lord Byron wrote in his *Bounty*-inspired epic poem *The Island, or, Christian and His Comrades*, the breadfruit tree produced food (seemingly) without effort:

---

[62] Thomas, "The Variety of Physical Environments," 7. Fischer, *A History of the Pacific Islands*, xvi. See also Freeman, *The Pacific*, 9–13; and Dennis O. Flynn, Arturo Giráldez, and James Sobredo, "In Search of Periodization for Pacific History," in Dennis O. Flynn, Arturo Giráldez, and James Sobredo, eds., *Studies in Pacific History: Economies, Politics, and Migration* (Burlington, VT: Ashgate, 2002), 1.

[63] "Pitcairn Island," in *The Bruce Herald* (May 27, 1892), 4. See also, Elwood C. Zimmerman, "Nature of the Land Biota," in F. R. Fosberg, ed., *Man's Place in the Island Ecosystem: A Symposium* (Honolulu: Bishop Museum Press, 1965), 58.

[64] Rachel Carson, *The Sea Around Us* (New York: Oxford University Press, 1951), 83.

[65] Reidy, *Tides of History*, 18; and Alain Corbin, *The Lure of the Sea: The Discovery of the Seaside in the Western World, 1750–1840*, Jocelyn Phelps, trans. (Los Angeles: University of California Press, 1994), 2. See also, John R. Gillis, *The Human Shore: Seacoasts in History* (Chicago: University of Chicago Press, 2012. Kindle edition), 129.

[66] Gibson, *Yankees in Paradise*, 17; and Landsdown, ed., *Strangers in Paradise*, 71.

[67] Royle, *A Geography of Islands*, 16.   [68] Frost, *The Global Reach of Empire*, 196.

The Breadtree, which without the ploughshare, yields
The unreap'd harvet of unfurrow'd fields.[69]

This was to have been a miraculously grand banquet, particularly from such a small island as Tahiti. Bounty, indeed.

Though they both looked at the same set of islands, Byron's romantic conjecturing stands in stark contrast to Joseph Banks' cool and enlightened perspective of South Pacific landscapes.[70] Romantic it might be, but Byron's premise here is, of course, pure applesauce. "There are few, if any, benefits from being of small scale," Royle insists.

Usually being small scale is simply and obviously a problem ... In addition to scale, small islands face specific problems with isolation, which impacts on accessibility to services and to markets as well as bring danger and inconvenience in the necessity to travel over, on, or under the water surrounding the islands. Isolation, together with scale, often distance islands from political power.[71]

Throughout the post-*Bounty* history of Pitcairn, beginning in 1790, resource scarcity has defined much of the island's relationship with the outside world. The historical archives of the British Foreign Office, of the State Library of New South Wales, of the London Missionary Society, and other institutions are all replete with documents recounting efforts to supply the people of Pitcairn Island with tools, books, clothing, seeds, soap, shoes, fuel, and other necessities of modern life.[72] When Captain Beechey landed in the *Blossom* in 1825, his crew were taken by the notion that the Pitcairners were objects of charity, as many of the sailors "donated their breeches to the ill-clothed islanders," an image we can see in sketches that William Smyth made as a member of Beechey's crew (Figure 7).[73]

Worse still was the delay that might be expected as the islanders waited for the outside world to send supplies, as records – most notably from the Foreign Office – indicate that a gap of two to four years was not uncommon as items bounced from port to port in search of a vessel that was headed for Bounty Bay.[74]

---

[69] Quoted in Silverman, *Pitcairn Island*, 3.
[70] Beattie, *Empire and Environmental Anxiety*, 73.
[71] Royle, *A Geography of Islands*, 42–43.
[72] See Christian, *Fragile Paradise*, 11. For the Foreign Office, see, for example, John White, Letter to J. Bidwell (February 1830), TNA FO 16/12A. See also, Pitcairn Extracts, SLNSW F999.7/9; and Pitcairn Extracts, SLNSW AJCP M 1672. See also, "Descendants of the *Bounty*'s Crew," in *The Calcutta Journal* (July 13 and 20, 1819); and Maud, "The History of Pitcairn Island," 63.
[73] Birkett, *Serpent in Paradise*, 177.   [74] See TNA FO 16/27; and TNA FO 16/23.

Figure 7 William Smyth, *Sketches of Several Pitcairn Islanders*, in Sketchbook of Places Visited during the Voyage of the HMS *Blossom*, 1825–1826. SLNSW PXB 55. Published by permission of the State Library of New South Wales, Mitchell Library, Sydney.

Jared Diamond offers us an interesting *longue durée* portrait of Pitcairn's resource limitations. We know from archeological finds on the island that the *Bounty* settlers were not the first to live at Pitcairn.[75] We know too that

[75] Scarr, *A History of the Pacific Island*, 53. See also, Account of the *Bounty*, in Nobbs Papers SLNSW ML A 2881, 100; and Belcher, Private Journal; "Pitcairn Island," in *The Bruce Herald* (May 27, 1892), 4; John Connell and Moshe Rapaport, "Mobility and

nobody had occupied Pitcairn for some time before the *Bounty* settled itself into Bounty Bay in 1790. In his study of societal collapse, Diamond cites recent archaeological work, particularly excavations by Marshall Weisler, that have given us a better sense of what life was like for Pitcairn's first inhabitants. John Donne famously noted that "no man is an island." Weisler's findings seem to suggest that no island is an island either.[76] Pitcairn has always functioned as part of a larger network, including particularly the islands of Henderson, Ducie, and Oeno – a triad of nearby islands now charted together as the Pitcairn Islands group. Beyond these small islands, early Polynesian Pitcairn islanders also forged bonds with more distant lands like Mangareva. Indeed, Diamond argues, instability at Mangareva may well explain the collapse of the first Pitcairn civilization. But how do we know?

Weisler's archaeological findings indicate that Henderson, Pitcairn, and Mangareva functioned in a tight and reliant trading triangle. All three, he suggests, were settled around 800 AD in one of the final – and most easterly – waves of Polynesian expansion over the Pacific. Mangareva was the westernmost of the three islands and the most connected to the rest of Polynesia, islands like Tahiti or the Marquesas.[77] Mangareva wanted for a supply of stone, though, making life there very difficult for Polynesians, who relied on stone for most of their tools. Pitcairn, though much smaller, is a volcanic island. Stone abounds. Indeed, Pitcairn is rich in volcanic glass that can be flaked into razor sharp edges for cutting and slicing tools.[78] Trading with Pitcairn for the stone and glass by-products of the island's volcanic birth made life at Mangareva possible.

But Pitcairn was a steep and mountainous island, and there was not enough flat land on the island to truly sustain an agricultural economy there, certainly not one substantive enough to sustain a sizable population. And, without a coral reef, fishing at Pitcairn was much less robust than it was on a coral island. Henderson Island, further to the east from Pitcairn, is larger than its more famous neighbor. But Henderson is really "the most marginal [of these islands] for human existence."[79] Indeed, all Henderson really *is* is a coral reef that has been tossed up out of the ocean.

Migration," in Moshe Rapaport, *The Pacific Islands: Environment and Society* (Honolulu: University of Hawai'i Press, 2013, Kindle Edition), location 12,479 of 21,398; Kenneth P. Emory, "Stone Implements Of Pitcairn Island," in *The Journal of the Polynesian Society* 37:2 (146) (June, 1928), 125–135; and R. C. Green, "Pitcairn Island Fishhooks in Stone," in *The Journal of the Polynesian Society* 68:1 (March, 1959), 21–22.

[76] Buschmann, Slack, and Tuller, *Navigating the Spanish Lake*, 31.

[77] Jared Diamond, *Collapse: How Societies Choose to Fail or Succeed* (New York: Viking Press, 2005), 121.

[78] Diamond, *Collapse*, 123.   [79] Ibid., 124.

It has no stone or rock to make tools. Indeed, unless we count for "a freshwater spring that bubbles up in the ocean about twenty feet offshore" of the island, its only supply of fresh water is from the puddles that form on the island after a storm.[80]

And yet, we know that Polynesians once lived on Henderson too. How? The archaeological record now suggests that the Henderson islanders sustained themselves on the rich fish, turtle, shellfish, and bird populations that were abundant there.[81] Even today, Diamond observes, Pitcairners enjoy "vacationing" for short periods at Henderson for these same reasons.[82] The stone tools that made this life possible were had from Pitcairn in a trade that saw Henderson's rich maritime food supply sent back to Pitcairn. And, of course, both Henderson and Pitcairn could rely on Mangareva for contact with and trade goods from the rest of the Polynesian Pacific, for Mangareva had to remain in trade contact with Pitcairn for its own livelihood.[83]

This complex web of human civilization sustained itself until Mangareva gave out, for it was "the geographic hub" of the "much larger trade network."[84] Over time, Diamond points out, Mangareva fell victim to deforestation and habitat damage. "With too many people and too little food, Mangarevan society slid into a nightmare of civil war and chronic hunger, whose consequences are recalled in detail by modern islanders."[85] As would be the case in the wake of European infiltration into the Pacific, island commodities were easily thrown out of equipoise. As would happen to the Pacific's sandalwood trees or its whale populations in later centuries, Mangareva's natural bounty could only sustain so much human usage before it was depleted.[86]

We do not know for certain how the history played itself out at either Pitcairn or Henderson, where no indigenous Polynesian society exists into the present era. But we can imagine that life would have been hard, indeed unsustainable, at either island without the life-supporting network that the Polynesians had woven between the Pitcairn Islands and

---

[80] Ibid. See also, Fischer, *A History of the Pacific Islands*, 65–67.
[81] Diamond, *Collapse*, 127.   [82] Ibid., 130.
[83] Ibid., 128. See also, Fogle, *The Teatime Islands*, 185.
[84] Diamond, *Collapse*, 130. See also Katrina Gulliver, "Finding the Pacific World," in *The Journal of World History* 22:1 (March 2011), 100.
[85] Diamond, *Collapse*, 132.
[86] Freeman, *The Pacific*, 132. See also Fischer, *A History of the Pacific Islands*, 99; Nicholas Thomas, "The Age of Empire in the Pacific," in David Armitage and Alison Bashford, eds., *Pacific Histories: Ocean, Land, People* (New York: Palgrave, 2014), 81; and Donald Denoon, "Land, Labour, and Independent Development," in Donald Denoon, ed., *The Cambridge History of the Pacific Islanders* (New York: Cambridge University Press, 1997), 157.

Mangareva and, from there, westward across the ocean and deeper into Polynesia.[87] If we look at Pitcairn through the lens of this delicate Polynesian balancing act, we see, then, something very different than the European myth, the uberous island, the Pacific paradise. Instead, we find something that is unstable and dangerous.[88] Not every island has coconuts. No every island has bananas, breadfruit, or yams. Some islands are rich in birds. Others in fish. At the time of the *Bounty*'s arrival, Pitcarn's only indigenous quadruped was the Pacific rat.[89] As Judith Schalansky has put it, "Paradise may be an island. But it is hell too."[90]

It was possible, then, to find an island that only *partially* supported human existence. And, an island's already limited supply of natural resources could dry up. Humans have a record as "destroyer[s] on the oceanic islands," writes Rachel Carson.[91] Even on the continental island of Australia, some twenty-three native mammal species are known to have gone extinct since the arrival of Europeans.[92] On an island, the consequences of contact are felt even more profoundly. The best-known case study is, of course, Rapanui or Easter Island, but there are others.[93] As Steven Roger Fischer has written,

at least 1000 species of animals have disappeared in Hawai'i as a direct result of Polynesian (and later European) intrusion: they were simply unequipped to withstand the newcomers, especially the feral pig. Among the first to go were twenty species of flightless birds, reminiscent of the disappearance of the *moa* very soon after the Māori had landed in New Zealand.[94]

The disappearance of the moa is one of New Zeland's most famous instances of animal extinction, giving rise to the Māori expression *Ka ngaro i te ngaro o te moa*, which translates as "Lost like the losing of the moa" – the South Pacific's (rough) equivalent of being "dead as a dodo."[95]

---

[87] Diamond, *Collapse*, 133. See also, Patrick Vinton Kirch, *Unearthing the Polynesian Past: Explorations and Adventures of an Island Archaeologist* (Honolulu: University of Hawai'i Press, 2015), 316.

[88] Lynne D. Talley, Gerard J. Fryer, and Rick Lumpkin, "Oceanography," in Jonathan Scott, *When the Waves Ruled Britannia: Geography and Political Identities, 1500–1800* (New York: Cambridge University Press, 2011), 40–43. See also Rapaport, *The Pacific Islands*, location 849 of 21398.

[89] Christian, *Fragile Paradise*, 226–227.

[90] Judith Schalansky, *Pocket Atlas of Remote Islands – Fifty Islands I Have Not Visited and Never Will*. Christine Lo, trans. (New York: Penguin Books, 2009), 24.

[91] Carson, *The Sea Around Us*, 93.

[92] Tim Flannery, *The Future Eaters: An Ecological History of the Australasian Lands and People* (New York: Grove Press, 1994), 237.

[93] Ibid., 253–257.   [94] Fischer, *A History of the Pacific Islands*, 79.

[95] Hirini Moko Mead and Neil Grove, *Ngā Pēpeha a ngā Tīpuna: The Sayings of the Ancestors* (Wellington, New Zealand: Victoria University Press, 2007), 1047. See also, "The Māori and the Moa," in *The Journal of the Polynesian Society* 20:2(78) (June, 1911), 54–59.

To carve out an existence in such an environment could be hard – and decidedly unromantic – work. Polynesians developed sophisticated, if tenuous, networks that made the colonization of Pacific islands possible.[96] At Pitcairn, perhaps more so than on other Pacific islands, the question of how to supply and sustain a human civilization has, then, always been central to the environmental core of the island's history. We will return to this point at the end of the present chapter.

Let us pause here, for a moment though, to think about Pitcairn Island as part of the Pacific more broadly. The field of Atlantic history is now a well-defined historical genre. To speak of the Atlantic World conjures a fixed set of ideas – topical and geographical.[97] The Pacific, though, is harder to pin down. It has a more complex coastline and fewer natural harbors per linear mile of coast.[98] Some have attempted to encompass, literally, the Pacific by speaking of a "Ring of Fire." Can we, though, really speak of a "Pacific World" in the way we do the Atlantic? Matt Matsuda and David Igler have both written of the Pacific, not as a singular world but rather as a collection of "Pacific Worlds."[99]

The making plural of the Pacific Ocean is, I think, a useful idea here. As we saw in the first pages of this history, the Pacific is rightly understood in broadly fluid terms. Arif Dirlik is correct to caution against "the reduction of the very concept of the Pacific."[100] What is called the "Pacific Rim," after all, is a biogeographically diverse space that includes "a full range of arctic, temperate, and tropical ecosystems."[101] To make

---

[96] Donald Denooon, "Pacific Edens," in Donald Denoon, ed., *The Cambridge History of the Pacific Islanders* (New York: Cambridge University Press, 1997), 90.

[97] Gregory T. Cushman, *Guano and the Opening of the Pacific World: A Global Ecological History* (New York: Cambridge University Press, 2013), xiv. See also, David Armitage and Alison Bashford, "Introduction: The Pacific and its Histories," in David Armitage and Alison Bashford, eds., *Pacific Histories: Ocean, Land, People* (New York: Palgrave, 2014), 6.

[98] Flynn, Giráldez, and Sobredo, "In Search of Periodization for Pacific History," 12. See also, Gulliver, "Finding the Pacific World," 90.

[99] Matsuda, *Pacific Worlds*, 2. See also, Matt K. Matsuda, "AHR Forum: The Pacific," in *The American Historical Review* (June, 2006), 758–759; Igler, *The Great Ocean*, 4 and 11; David Igler, "Exploring the Concept of Empire in Pacific History: Individuals, Nations, and Ocean Space Prior to 1850," in *History Compass* 12:11 (2014), 880; and Vaine Rasmussen, "Our Pacific," in Robert Borofsky, ed., *Remembrance of Pacific Pasts: An Invitation to Remake History* (Honolulu: University of Hawai'i Press, 2000), 399–400.

[100] Arif Dirlik, "Introduction: Pacific Contradictions," in Arif Dirlik, ed., *What is in a Rim? Critical Perspectives on the Pacific Region Idea* (New York: Rowman & Littlefield, 1998), 3.

[101] John R. McNeil, "Islands in the Rim: Ecology and History in and around the Pacific, 1521–1996," in Dennis O. Flynn, Lionel Frost, and A. J. H. Latham, eds., *Pacific Centuries: Pacific and Pacific Rim History Since the Sixteenth Century* (New York: Routledge, 1999), 71.

the Pacific into a rim, a region, or a basin is to institutionalize it, which may well undermine the real historical value we get from viewing it as something more open-ended.[102]

Greg Dening once observed that he "would have fewer qualms about the term 'Pacific history' if by it we meant history *in* the Pacific rather than history *of* the Pacific."[103] But the story we have traced of Pitcairn thus far has not been simply history *in* the Pacific. Indeed, the Pacific, as we have seen, has proven too small an ocean, ironically, to contain the history of tiny Pitcairn Island. It is not, as Bronwen Douglas has offered, "an *island sea*."[104] We do better, we might rather argue, to think of the Pacific as the "world ocean."[105] As we saw in the previous chapter, we would not be entirely out of place to re-situate whaling ports on America's Atlantic seaboard within the context of Pacific history, certainly in economic terms though also, clearly, in environmental terms.[106] The American geologist James Dwight Dana realized much the same thing. In his own investigations of the Pacific, he found that the ocean's "importance is not limited . . . for it has an evident connexion with a system that pervades the world."[107]

Herman Melville, then, was right when, in *Moby-Dick*, he called the Pacific "the tide-beating heart of earth," suggesting that the "mysterious, divine Pacific zones the world's whole bulk about; makes all coasts one bay to it."[108] Melville's is a model that embraces both the "actuality" and the "fantasy," echoing (at least in part) Denis Diderot's suggestion that the Pacific was an "ocean of fantasy."[109] But Melville was writing fiction. We have to ask: how is it possible for the historian to conceptualize an ocean as a plurality? What does it mean for the Pacific to be the global ocean? Perhaps we too, as historians, need to embrace fantasy alongside the actual. But how?

Peter Kreeft may best be known as a philosopher and Christian apologist. Kreeft, though, has an abiding interest in the world's oceans that may serve our purposes here. Humans love the sea, Kreeft has written, but more than that, we love "the seaside, the boundary, the beach." It is the

---

[102] K. R. Howe, *The Quest for Origins: Who First Discovered and Settled the Pacific Islands?* (Honolulu: University of Hawai'i Press, 2003), 25. See also, Gulliver, "Finding the Pacific World," 83–85.

[103] Quoted in Gulliver, "Finding the Pacific World," 97.

[104] Bronwen Douglas, "Pasts, Presents, and Possibilities of Pacific History and Pacific Studies: As Seen by a Historian from Canberra," in *The Journal of Pacific History* 50:2 (2015), 227.

[105] Winchester, *Pacific*, location 5455.

[106] Dirlik, "Introduction," in Dirlik, ed., *What Is in a Rim?*, 9.

[107] Quoted in Igler, *The Great Ocean*, 157.   [108] Herman Melville, *Moby-Dick*, 491.

[109] Dirlik, "Introduction," in Dirlik, ed., *What Is in a Rim?*, 9. Diderot quoted in Lamb, *Preserving the Self*, 8.

boundary zone here, Kreeft argues, that makes the sea so intriguing.[110] But what are the boundaries around and within the Pacific and its many worlds? The problems implied by the question are manifold. First, a boundary or borderland "privileges contact between two nation-states," but, as David Chang has argued and as Pitcairn's history thus far has demonstrated, "the emergence of the modern world saw the construction of spaces where global history became local." Moreover, the overlapping map of national histories in the Pacific (and we have to include the indigenous histories of Pacific kingdoms like Hawai'i and Tahiti here too) did not always lend itself to a clear sense of boundary or border.[111]

Frontier is just not the right conceptual metaphor for the history under consideration here. Rather, as Chang has written, "where nations meet, there exists not just a frontier line but also a land, a region where identities, economies, languages, and what we call cultures create new mestizo realities."[112] The island, here, offers us a "microcosmic scale" and a new mode of historical interpretation that Sujit Sivasundaram has called "islanding."[113] This is a model that keeps "the specificity of the island alive, by taking it seriously for itself and by looking at it from multiple points of view from within and without."[114]

In the case of Pitcairn Island, "islanding" alone may not even be enough. Here, the individual human biography may better capture the mobility of what is afoot.[115] As David Chang has observed, "an unremarkable life can reveal things that appear quite remarkable in historical retrospect," a point that has been one of the central impulses behind our willingness to chase Joshua Hill around the globe – and, particularly, into the Pacific.[116] Hill's life has always seemed strange. It has always seemed out of the ordinary, but it has always been recorded as one of history's many footnotes. In that regard, it has been nearly unremarkable. Here, in these pages, we have unwrapped that footnote, and we have found that what may have seemed small and trivial before was, in point of fact, connected to much bigger historical

---

[110] Kreeft, *The Sea Within*, 20.
[111] David A. Chang, "Borderland in a World at Sea: Concow Indians, Native Hawai'ians, and South Chinese Indigenous, Global, and National Spaces," in *The Journal of American History* 98:2 (September 2011), 384–385.
[112] Ibid., 385.
[113] Sujit Sivasundaram, *Islanded: Britain, Sri Lanka, and the Bounds of an Indian Ocean Colony* (Chicago: University of Chicago Press, 2013), 25–26.
[114] Ibid., 336.
[115] Jennifer Ashton, *At the Margins of Empire: John Webster and Hokianga, 1841–1900* (Auckland: University of Auckland Press, 2015), 8.
[116] Chang, "Borderlands in a World at Sea," 399.

processes – processes that both predated and postdated Joshua Hill's Pacific adventures.

Turning our clocks back to 1790, then, and to the moment when Fletcher Christian and the original *Bounty* settlers at Pitcairn decided to divide the island into family plots, allows us a chance to reset our assessment of this story and to reframe Joshua Hill's political aspirations for the island in terms of environmental history – namely, a history framed by a scarcity of land and resources specific (though hardly unique) to this one, small, isolated Pacific island.

When Fletcher Christian headed out for Pitcairn after his final departure from Tahiti, it is important that we remember that he did not even know where Pitcairn was on the Pacific's vast waters. At least, the location he thought he had for the island – from Captain Carteret's voyage in 1766 – was wrong.[117] If the natural world has driven much of our story, here we find that misunderstandings of the natural world can be just as potent, for when he did accidentally find Pitcairn, Fletcher Christian was even happier about the inhospitable little island than he might have been. No beaches. No bays. And hidden in the vast Pacific Ocean by a cartographic error.

As we have seen, the *Bounty* was still functioning as something of a colonial biosphere when Christian landed it at Pitcairn. Clearly, Sir Joseph Banks' plan had taken a bad turn along the way to Pitcairn, but when they landed, the *Bounty* and its crew were still carrying flora and fauna that they intended to cultivate in this new landscape. We will want to hold these introduced species near at hand as we move forward, but let us also consider that the settlers themselves were part of the change that was about to arrive at Pitcairn. Nine English men. Six Polynesian men – three from Tahiti, two from Tubuai, and one from Taiatea. Twelve Tahitian women. There had been no human civilization at Pitcairn for hundreds of years, if not longer. It was, in perhaps the most genuine sense, *terra nullius* – empty and unoccupied land – but Pitcairn was about to be claimed, divided, possessed, and cultivated.[118]

One of Fletcher Christian's first and most consequential decisions was that Pitcairn should be divided into only nine plots. The British mutineers also divided the island's rock pools, which "were essential sources of salt, and convenient places from which to fish."[119] Christian and his compatriots acted "with the gradeur of conquerors," carving out homesteads for themselves on the island, leaving nothing behind for the six Polynesian

---

[117] See Frank McFlynn, *Captain Cook: Master of the Seas* (New Haven: Yale University Press, 2011), 80, 203, and 264. See also, Beaglehole, *The Life of Captain James Cook*, 168 and 339.

[118] Flannery, *The Future Eaters*, 144.   [119] Lummis, *Life and Death in Eden*, 86.

men or the dozen Tahitian women.[120] Because most of the women were attached to the British mutineers, many among the twelve did come to own land, and, in the initial legal vision for the island, these women were allowed to inherit and pass along territorial holdings, a practice that was in keeping, as we have seen, with Tahitian law. But the South Pacific men were left with nothing – no land to cultivate, no prospect for supporting themselves autonomously. Most took to scavenging the island for their food, gathering birds' eggs while they lasted. But, over time, the men had to concede that their only hope was as agricultural laborers for the white landholders at Pitcairn.[121] They had sailed on the *Bounty* as comrades. "In the course of time," they became slaves.[122]

Christian divvied the island's parcels out by lottery. The lines between the plots were very European. Neat lines denoted roughly equal lots, each with its own benefits and its own limitations.[123] To look at a map of the island today is to see place names that mirror the original boundaries and holdings at Pitcairn. McCoy's Valley. Isaac's Valley. These labels mark out the land that once belong to the mutineers – to William McCoy or to Isaac Martin.[124] Not every inch of the island was privately owned. Even today, there is public property at Pitcairn, including the church, the courthouse, the school, roads, the boat landing, and similar pieces of island infrastructure.[125] But, on the whole, the island remains as Christian designated it from the outset – parcels of private land.

Of course, private property would have been nothing new to the mutineers, as the concept is the cornerstone of English Common Law.[126] At Pitcairn, of course, the rule of primogeniture would not have worked. To have left younger sons without land would have left them – as Christian had left the Polynesian men – without means to support themselves.[127] Over time, then, Pitcairn's nine original parcels were subdivided into smaller and smaller plots.

Land was Pitcairn's scarcest resource. To have divided it among fifteen men instead of nine would have brought an impending (and eventual) problem of resource limitations forward in time. Of course, leaving the Polynesian men out of the division of land was not an unpredictable turn in this story. The obviously racialist overtones behind Christian's actions will become more central to our analysis in the next chapter.[128] Suffice it, for the moment, that we quote Glynn Christian, who has observed that "the idea of democracy and the equality of men taking root in the newly independent states of

---

[120] Nicholson, *The Pitcairners*, 44.   [121] Tobin, *Colonizing Nature*, 87.
[122] Nicholson, *The Pitcairners*, 45.   [123] Tobin, *Colonizing Nature*, 82.
[124] Birkett, *Serpent in Paradise*, 165.   [125] Shapiro, *The Pitcairn Islanders*, 171.
[126] Silverman, *Pitcairn Island*, 178.   [127] Ibid.   [128] Ibid., 140.

America, and in France, has no place here."[129] We might reflect that those same ideas were not completely practiced even in the Atlantic World. Let us focus in particular, then, on what being denied land – cut out from a place in the natural landscape of their new island home – might have meant for these six Polynesian men, some of whom were from aristocratic families on their home islands.[130]

Like their contemporaries in Hawai'i or Tahiti, the Polynesians at Pitcairn would have viewed land as a link not only to wordly sustenance but also to historical relevance. Pitcairn's Polynesians had homelands that meant something the European mutineers would not have understood. Polynesian landscapes and seascapes, Epeli Hau'ofa has argued, "are cultural as well as physical. We cannot read our histories without knowing how to read our landscapes (and seascapes)." You cannot remove a people whose historical existence is so deeply linked to a landscape without severing "them not only from their traditional sources of livelihood, but also and much more importantly, from their ancestry, their history, their identity, and from their ultimate claim for the legitimacy of their existence."[131] The sacrilege here, Hua'ofa has argued, is akin to "the complete destruction of all of a nation's libraries, archives, museums, monuments, historic buildings, and all its books and other such documents."[132]

The conclusion we must reach, then, is a hard one. True, but brutal. Fletcher Christian did not *merely* enslave Manarii, Niau, Teirnua, Taroamiva, Oher, and Taruro – though he did effectively enslave them and the choice he made to do so was horrific enough. Christian uprooted these men from the oral traditions and the ancestral memories that defined their very being only to deny them the right to pledge themselves to a new place, to a new belonging, and to a new lineage. "To deny human beings the sense of homeland," Hua'ofa has observed, "is to deny them a deep spot on Earth to anchor their roots."[133] Fletcher Christian had disconnected these men from their natural environment and, in doing so, erased them from history.[134]

Christian's crime left historical scars. In 1831, amid the conflicts between pro-Buffett Pitcairners and those who supported George

---

[129] Christian, *Fragile Paradise*, 160.
[130] Birkett, *Serpent in Paradise*, 211. See also, Newell, *Trading Nature*, 87.
[131] Epeli Hau'ofa, "Epilogue: Pasts to Remember," in Robert Borofsky, ed., *Remembrance of Pacific Pasts: An Invitation to Remake History* (Honolulu: University of Hawai'i Press, 2000), 466–468.
[132] Ibid., 469.   [133] Ibid., 470.
[134] See Klaus Neumann, "Starting from Trash," in Robert Borofsky, ed., *Remembrance of Pacific Pasts: An Invitation to Remake History* (Honolulu: University of Hawai'i Press, 2000), 83.

Nobbs, some of Buffet's indigenous advocates accused Nobbs of wanting "to make slaves of us." As Edward David, the master of the *Nelson*, observed upon witnessing the scene, the islanders were "alluding to their fathers cruel treatment of the Otaheitians (for they told me [that their] fathers, after flogging them would rub salt into the wounds & that it was this cruel treatment that caused them to shoot their fathers)."[135]

So much of the violence that marked the first three years of settlement at Adamstown grew out of Christian's unfair division of Pitcairn. As Menalee (Manarii) explains in Richard Bean's 2014 theatrical *Pitcairn*, Christian's "promises to you of land, and wealth are like the wind."[136] Diana Souhami has echoed this point: "The Polynesians on board knew that *Bounty* was a misnomer."[137] They would not profit from sailing with Christian, and the resulting anger and violence at Pitcairn was sometimes masked in nineteenth-century accounts from and about the island. In July 1845, for instance, *The Dublin Literary Journal*, reporting on the history of Pitcairn and its people, summarized the discord from 1790 to 1793 very quickly. "They quarreled," the journal observed, "and acted very badly."[138] Very badly indeed, for, as Stephen Royle has rightly expressed it, "they slaughtered each other."[139]

Interesting too are reports, like that in the *Dublin Literary Journal*, that downplay the bilateral nature of this violence. Of Christian and his comrades, the *Journal* wrote, "these wicked men treated the Otaheitians so badly that they were all murdered, including Christian, except four."[140] We could overlook a lot of the inaccuracies here. Not all of the men were Tahitian, and not all of the European men who died at Pitcairn were murdered by the Polynesian men. It is hard, though, to read this report without flinching at the failure to record that some of the Tahitian men were killed by the Europeans. Within three years of its settlement, Pitcairn Island was in an all out state of war, a conflict that "seemed like some Old Testament chapter of judgment and nemesis. It scarcely seems credible."[141] As Fletcher Christian observes in Richard Bean's play, "Not yet two years in the Garden of Eden and we have a civil war."[142] That piece of the story, the *Journal*'s report masks. These were "wicked" men. They behaved "badly." That is all.

---

[135] Edward David, Letter to an Unidentified Recipient, in Accusations against John Buffett and George Nobbs by the People of Pitcairn (October 20, 1831), SOAS CWM/LMS – South Seas Incoming Correspondence – Box 8, Folder 2/Jacket D.

[136] Bean, *Pitcairn*, 42.   [137] Souhami, *Coconut Chaos*, 88.

[138] "Pitcairn's Island," in *The Dublin Literary Journal* (July 1, 1845), 443.

[139] Royle, *A Geography of Islands*, 17. See also, Belcher, Private Journal.

[140] "Pitcairn's Island," in *The Dublin Literary Journal* (July 1, 1845), 444.

[141] Souhami, *Coconut Chaos*, 123.   [142] Bean, *Pitcairn*, 70.

The environmental story at Pitcairn Island is, then, one of how the land was divided among the original *Bounty* settlers and what that division meant culturally, historically, politically, and economically for different members of the community. There is also, though, a story of the stress that these settlers put on the island itself. As we have seen, the *Bounty* was loaded with flora and fauna designed to help the settlers establish themselves at their new home when they landed at Pitcairn in 1790. Many of the species they brought with them would be considered "invasive" by today's standards, meaning, as we have observed, that the *Bounty* did eventually succeed in transplanting plants around the British colonial world, even if it was unintended plants to an unintended place.

European infiltration into the Pacific marked a major shift in the demands placed on the resources of Polynesian islands. After long months of travel, crews arrived wanting "fruit, coconuts, fish, shellfish, tubers, chicken, pork. They wanted fresh water from the island's streams and timber from groves of trees."[143] To European captains, it was the islands of the Pacific that supplied everything necessary for life. There was no Captain Nemo among them, no men who saw the sea as everything. The sea was not, as Jules Verne's famous captain would suggest, "a vast reservoir of nature."[144] Captain Nemo was, of course, correct. As Ryan Tucker Jones has observed, "the crucial environmental constraint" to keep in mind regarding the Pacific is the simple fact "that the ocean is far more productive of nutrients than the land."[145] Eighteenth- and nineteenth-century seamen saw it differently. Voyaging the ocean's surface drained them of their supplies, cut them off from life. Life happened on, and was supplied by, the land, which in the Pacific meant the islands.

Initially, at least, most islanders supplied these items, most often in a network of trade that saw European tools traded for the Pacific's natural resources, though we know that in some instances the Polynesians took in other natural and invasive plants and animals. Captain Wallis, for instance, traded away guinea hens, turkeys, a pregnant cat, and a garden of peas to Purea upon his first landing at Tahiti.[146] This exchange altered the geographic space of the Pacific Ocean. As Jennifer Newell has written, "by the end of the eighteenth century, the northern districts of Tahiti were marked by the decades of supplying Europeans with local resources." Reduced animal stocks and a landscape of tree

---

[143] Newell, *Trading Nature*, 7
[144] Jules Verne, *20,000 Leagues Under the Sea*, Mendor T. Brunetti, trans. (New York: Signet Classics, 2001), 77.
[145] Ryan Tucker Jones, "Running into Whales: The History of the North Pacific from Below the Waves," in *The American Historical Review* 118:2 (April 2013), 353.
[146] Newell, *Trading Nature*, 7.

stumps, Newell suggests, would have indicated that a new ecological era had arrived.[147] More than a few commentators observed these changes with concern, noting that contact with Europe was a "fatal impact" that had sullied the innocent purity of the South Pacific.[148] Captain Bligh himself was among this community, as he was able to compare the descriptions of Tahiti he had read from Wallis' landing there in 1767 to Bligh's own visit there with Cook in 1777 and his second arrival there on board the *Bounty* in 1788.[149]

The concerns that Europeans expressed wound morality with ecology. Islanders were drinking more. Their civilizations were crumbling. Venereal disease was spreading among them.[150] Their resources were drying up. All of these evils were linked. We have observed that Pitcairn's moral future was also the subject of a tremendous amount of anxiety in these years, but there was less a sense the environment was part of the problem. The difference here is easily explained. Pitcairn was a unique Polynesian island. The European myth-makers who talked, wrote, and worried about Pitcairn knew its inhabitants to have been a settler community. We will return to this discussion of the Pitcairner's racial and ethnic "stock" in the next chapter. What we will see is that the island was not always understood as a fundamental part of what it meant to be Pitcairnese. Europeans met the Tahitians at Tahiti, binding Tahitian culture and civilization to the physical landscape of the island. That was less the case at Pitcairn.

Pitcairners had built their society accidentally. They literally had not known where to find the island when they set out looking for it. Nobody ever seems, therefore, to have paid much attention to the ways in which settlement changed this island. In this regard, Pitcairn was different from islands like Tahiti, where Europeans were more aware of – if not necessarily concerned about – the ecological, social, and even moral changes that came with contact and the arrival of Europeans. Joshua Hill, as we are beginning to understand, had a different sense of things. Of course, it helped too that many fewer people stopped at Pitcairn than stopped at Papeete or Honolulu to trade and resupply. Pitcairn was out of the way.

[147] Ibid., 18.

[148] See Moorehead, *The Fatal Impact*; and Howe, *Nature, Culture, and History*, 44.

[149] Dodge, *Islanders and Empires*, 105. See also Newell, *Trading Nature*, 51; Withye, *Voyages of Discovery*, 117–122; Howe, *Nature, Culture, and History*, 43–44; and Brantlinger, *Dark Vanishings*, 141.

[150] Edwards, *The Story of the Voyage*, 111. See also Andrew Mitchell, *The Fragile South Pacific: An Ecological Odyssey* (Austin: University of Texas Press, 1989), 201; and A. Grenfell Price, *The Western Invasions of the Pacific and Its Continents: A Study of Moving Frontiers and Changing Landscapes, 1513–1958* (New York: Oxford University Press, 1963), chapter 6.

It was geographically inhospitable. It was too small. The environmental changes that we see at the island, then, were only ever really the result of the small community of residents at Adamstown and the plants and animals that their predecessors had brought to the island.

The changes at Pitcairn were, though, almost instantaneous. In their first days on the island, the *Bounty* settlers constructed temporary housing from the leaves of the *ti* tree. Soon after, they began to fell the island's larger trees to put up their permanent homes in the areas we know now as Adamstown.[151] Like Tahiti, Pitcairn was quickly left with forests of tree stumps. It also saw new animal life and vegetation take control over swaths of the island.[152] The spread of such invasive species was a comparatively new historical phenomenon, particularly in the Pacific. As O. H. K. Spate observed, in the two hundred plus years between the voyage of Ferdinand Magellan and James Cook, Europeans may easily have crossed the Pacific some five hundred times. But "the vast majority of these were by Manilla Galleons on their fixed route, which even on its southern west-bound limb passed north of all the islands except Hawai'i and the Marianas."[153] Even amidst all of these voyages then, there was little land-based contact to introduce new flora or fauna to the islands of the Pacific Ocean. Plants continued to be carried as seeds by birds or by the tide from island to island in a slow and accidental process, and because land-based animals do not easily move by either of these methods, there was little in the way of zoological exchange in these years.[154] The scene we saw described in an image from *The Lonely Island* at the outset of this chapter, then, marked a revolutionary moment in Pitcairn Island's environmental history.

Upon their arrival, as we have seen, the *Bounty* settlers found Pitcairn to be home to one indigenous quadruped – a species of the Pacific rat – as well as a substantive bird population. The island also sustained coconut palms, breadfruit trees, plantain and banana trees, sugar cane, yams, taro, the ti plant, sweet potatoes, ginger, turmeric, and many types of gourds.[155] J. A. Moerenhout would add that Pitcairn was the first island of the Pacific on which he found indigenous banyans (*Ficus Indica*).[156] The *Bounty* crew brought with them, Edward Belcher reported in 1826, better varieties of a number of these plants, including the yam, the sweet potato, and ginger. They also brought watermelons and pumpkins.[157]

[151] Salmond, *Bligh*, 344.
[152] Price, *The Western Invasions of the Pacific and Its Continents*, chapter 7.
[153] Spate, *Paradise Found and Lost*, 56.   [154] Ibid., 33.   [155] Belcher, Private Journal.
[156] Moerenhout, *Travels to the Islands*, 26. See also Bennett, *Narrative of a Whaling Voyage*, 41–46.
[157] Belcher, Private Journal.

Belcher's account of the agricultural production at Pitcairn is helpful, for it gives us a clear sense of how the Pitcairners sustained themselves and their community in the years just before Joshua Hill arrived. The island's women, he tells us, took care of the livestock at the island and tended to the cooking, while the men oversaw the island's agriculture – including the physical work of leveling the island to create enough land for the growing community to farm.[158]

The *Bounty*'s pigs and goats had soon scattered across Pitcairn Island, providing the islanders a supply of meat.[159] Pitcairners never seem to have developed a taste for beef, and they always seem to have favored coconut milk to the bovine alternative. These preferences were just as well, as the topography of Pitcairn was hardly suitable to raising cattle.[160] As we have seen, the Pitcairners could fish the waters off their island, even if those waters were growing less and less productive. And the island was (and still is) home to the frighteningly Brobdingnagian coconut crab, the largest land-based arthropod known to exist.[161] Despite these supplies, though, we also know from Belcher that Pitcairn was not robustly abundant. The men, he reported, had grown strong and fearless about dragging heavy casks of supplies to shore through the treacherous waters of Bounty Bay. The surf in the bay "would make one's hair stand on end," but the Pitcairners were "quite at home" in it. They had to be, for they needed many of the items that came ashore from passing ships. Unlike their Polynesian cousins in places like Tahiti, islanders who traded supplies *to* passing ships, Pitcairn had to be supplied *by* the outside. Between 1813 and 1818, two ships called at Pitcairn. Between 1825 and 1830, that number had risen to twenty-three. All of the ships that landed in Pitcairn recorded that they took fresh water away from the island. Some reported that they bartered for fresh food supplies as well. But all of the ships indicated that they had left goods at Adamstown that were critical to sustaining the community there.[162] Indeed, Belcher was worried about the length of the *Blossom*'s stay at Pitcairn. "Had we remained much longer," he remembered, "I am afraid we should have distressed them much," for the *Blossom*'s crew exponentially increased the rate of food consumption at Pitcairn, particularly on Sundays when the islanders traditionally ate only a simple meal.[163]

---

[158] Belcher, Private Journal. See also, Moerenhout, *Travels to the Islands*, 26–27.
[159] Moerenhout, *Travels to the Islands*, 435.
[160] Silverman, *Pitcairn Island*, 237. See also Bennett, *Narrative of a Whaling Voyage*, 40–41.
[161] Moerenhout, *Travels to the Islands*, 56 and 179.
[162] Lummis, *Life and Death in Eden*, 191.
[163] Belcher, Private Journal. See also Bennett, *Narrative of a Whaling Voyage*, 36–37.

By the time Belcher visited Pitcairn, its bird population was negligible. Moerenhout noted much the same thing. "It's the cats," the Pitcairners explained to Moerenhout. We saw that Ballantyne's *The Lonely Island* was illustrated with a picture that showed two cats disembarking from the *Bounty* at Pitcairn. Those cats, Moerenhout was informed, had been allowed to go wild. They had reproduced. They had hunted the island, devouring the indigenous rat population, and when it began to run thin, they turned their attention to the island's birds as well. "They could even be seen taking away the chickens of the inhabitants," one Pitcairner told Moerenhout. In response, the islanders had taken to trapping and killing the felines.[164]

Settlement at Pitcairn, then, mirrored Rachel Carson's assessment. Where humans brought their cattle and dogs and cats, they unleashed "the black night of extinction."[165] Joseph Banks had predicted this sort of an outcome. In outfitting the *Bounty*, he had ordered that "no Dogs, Cats, Monkies, Parrots, Goats, or, indeed, any animals whatever must be allowed on board, except Hogs & Fowls for the Company's use; & they must be carefully confined to their Coops."[166] In Banks' estimation, the concern was what other plants or animals might do to the *Bounty*'s bread-fruit plants. The expedition under Bligh's command was a costly one, after all. Banks' point, though, resonated more broadly. The science of ecological exchange was delicate; the equipoise of a system could easily be disturbed. That had been true from the very beginning of our story.

Captain Beechey reported in 1825 that the Pitcairners were "all well," though he recorded, as we have seen, John Adams' concerns about the long-term stability of the Adamstown community.[167] Food could be scarce, but, by the late 1820s, water shortages were the most pressing worries.[168] The report from John Adams circulated through the halls of power in London swiftly, a conversation out of which came the policy impulse to relocate the Pitcairners.[169] Here again, we can return to our main character, Joshua Hill, a man who did not want to see the Pitcairners mingled with outside groups who might corrupt their redeemed purity. For Hill, there were two problems. First, the Pitcairners required protection from the outside. Second, they needed to be assured that their small island home could sustain their community. Moving them might solve the second of the two problems, but it did not answer the first challenge at

---

[164] Moerenhout, *Travels to the Islands*, 27.   [165] Carson, *The Sea Around Us*, 93.
[166] Sir Joseph Banks, Letter to an Unidentified Recipient (February, 1787), 83.
[167] Beechey, Letter to J. Barrow (December 21, 1825).
[168] Bennett, *Narrative of a Whaling Voyage*, 30.
[169] Letter to J. Planta (February 28, 1827). TNA FO 58/14; George Canning, Letter to King Pomare III (March 3, 1827), TNA FO 58/14.

all. The key, then, was to find a way to insulate and isolate the Pitcairners at Pitcairn while also stretching the resources of the island.[170] The fastest way to make Pitcairn's limited resources go further was, of course, to reduce the island's population, which we know was artificially bloated in 1832 by the presence of the three outlanders, John Buffet, John Evans, and George Nobbs.

That Hill's policy was rooted in land distribution and insular resource supplies may not, at first glance, appear an obvious thing. The truth is only hinted at in many of the surviving records from Hill's time at Pitcairn. But where the records do direct us to Hill's environmental outlook on the island and its history, they are rather clear. John Buffet, for instance, in a letter he wrote pleading for help against Hill, is explicit. Hill had driven him (Buffet) from Pitcairn because "there is not land sufficient."[171] Not land sufficient. It is an interesting justification for his actions, one rooted in the ecological landscape of Pitcairn Island itself. It is also a frequently overlooked aspect of Hill's thinking about the proper administration of the island.

Interestingly, Raymond Nobbs, whom we have previously identified as George Nobbs' biographer and his great-great-grandson, observed that George Nobbs had had to make "subtle changes" to Pitcairn's administration in the wake of John Adams' death. The theocracy remained, but there were outside pressures that were making "the old patriarchal order" hard to sustain. Among those pressures? An increasing population, the "concentration of inhabitants," and an "increasing value on private property."[172] We saw in the previous chapter that Hill addressed some of these very issues when he altered Pitcairn's law on inheritance, making it impossible for the island's women to pass land. We noted then that this change meant that land could only pass through the line of the *Bounty*'s men, both because only the nine mutineers had been given land at the time of Pitcairn's settlement and because none of the Polynesian men had ever been identified as the father of any of the children born at Pitcairn. Had Hill had his way, Pitcairn's land would today belong exclusively and forever only to people whose last names were Christian, McCoy, Young, Adams, Quintal, Brown, Martin, Mills, and Williams.

Until we consider Hill's land ownership policies at Pitcairn in terms of the island's natural limitations, the changes he invoked look like the erratic actions of a lunatic against Nobbs, Buffett, and Evans – the three targets of his deranged mind. And, it has to be said, we do know that Hill

---

[170] See Ralston, *Grass Huts and Warehouses*, location 1658.
[171] Quoted in Shapiro, *The Pitcairn Islanders*, 85; and Lummis, *Life and Death in Eden*, 211.
[172] Nobbs, *George Hunn Nobbs*, 22.

expressed the belief that he could better govern Pitcairn were the three foreigners removed. He was, to be frank, hostile to these men. Though if we believe Buffet, Hill was also clearly thinking, at least in part, about the island and its carrying capacity.[173] "There is not land sufficient." It was not Hill's only reason, then, for exiling Evans, Buffet, and Nobbs, but it was hardly an illogical reason.[174] Let us remember, the evidence here comes from Buffet, who had no reason to share this justification for Hill's actions with the outside world, for it only really helped Hill's case. In all probability, then, Pitcairn's small size, its limited resources, and its need for insularity *were* part of Hill's thinking as he sailed to, took possession of, and administered over Pitcairn Island in the 1830s.

Some will object here. By adding his own person to the island, did not Joshua Hill increase the population at Adamstown by one? Yes, but let us consider the difference between Hill and his three British adversaries. Joshua Hill, recall, did not marry into the Pitcairnese society. He had left his family in Britain. He was not about the business of establishing a dynasty at Pitcairn, a new bloodline. He moved into the house that the Pitcairners had erected for their schoolmaster, but he was making no claim to the island's land over the long term. Hill took the house as a perquisite of his job, and he had made it clear in every letter he ever wrote about his work at Pitcairn that he only intended to remain on the island for a handful of years. When Nobbs took up residence in the same house after his return from the removal to Tahiti, he had had members of the Young, Adams, and Quintal families sign a deed giving him the land "for his use and his family forever."[175]

In his study of the effects of Western law at Hawai'i, Jonathan Kay Kamakawiwo'ole Osorio has observed that "some western missionaries had no trouble justifying a claim for thousands of acres of the kingdom's lands nor any problem engaging in land sales once they got over whatever initial reluctance they may have possessed."[176] All three of the British settlers at Pitcairn focused intently on the lands that Hill had seized from them in their petitions seeking redress. We cannot make too much of this, for who among us would fail to object at having our lands and our homes

---

[173] Peter Holland and Jim Williams, "Pioneer Settlers Recognizing and Responding to the Climate Challenges of Southern New Zealand," in James Beattie, Emily O'Gorman, and Matthew Henry, eds., *Climate, Science, and Colonization: Histories from Australia and New Zealand* (New York: Palgrave MacMillan, 2014), 81.

[174] Brodie, *Pitcairn's Island and the Islanders*, 202–203.

[175] Deed Gifted by William Young to George Hunn Nobbs, 1832, Nobbs Papers, SLNSW ML A 2881, 5–8. Another deed would grant more land to Nobbs in 1847. See Deed from the Pitcairn Islanders to George Hunn Nobbs, 1847, Nobbs Papers, SLNSW ML A 2881, 23–27.

[176] Osorio, *Dismembering Lāhui*, 96–97.

confiscated? But it merits noting that John Buffet's 1834 complaint about Hill's actions makes more references to the fact that Hill deprived the Buffett family of its lands on Pitcairn than it does to the fact that John Buffet's exile had broken the family apart from one another.[177] John Evans and George Nobbs would make similarly telling complaints in their own petitions.[178] The Buffet, Evans, and Nobbs families were still in their first generation at Pitcairn, and yet the three family patriarchs' petitions make it clear that they, at least, were deeply wedded to their family's claims to land on the island. Foreigner though he was, Joshua Hill was a distinctly different kind of foreigner than Evans, Buffet, or Nobbs.

In the last chapter, we linked Joshua Hill's political reform, if we can call it that, at Adamstown to a broader era of political reform in Britain and its empire. Hill's seeming interest in who owned and inherited what parcels of land at Pitcairn also touches on the larger question of political reform in these years. In the great age of British political reform, Joshua Hill introduced a reformist movement to Pitcairn that was distinctly rooted in an imperialist, evangelical, and Pacific context. At Pitcairn, to Hill's mind, the presence of English authority or foreign English blood-lines was not a public good. Nor were the introduction of new English landholders or new political institutions. In as much as British colonial control from the center allowed these influences to invade Pitcairn, it was to be avoided. Hence we see Hill's proclamation of May 1833 making it illegal for the children of the three "lousy foreigners" to inherit land on the island.[179]

Chris Vanden Bossche reminds us that the Great Reform Act of 1832 did not disassociate the political franchise from property. Though the act reimagined what property qualified a person for active participation in the political process – landownership was no longer the only means to secur-ing a vote, as land leases could now assure one access to the ballot box – the act did nothing to disassociate land from the vote entirely. "In this context," Vanden Bossche writes, "the traditional symbolic power of landownership remained intact, continuing to play an important role in the discourse of social agency."[180] Hill, we have to remember, sailed for the Pacific before the passage of the Reform Act of 1832, so he would not have been aware of even the changes that the act did introduce. His sense that landownership translated into political power at Pitcairn was, there-fore, absolute, and the three outlanders who had married into the

---

[177] See Belcher, *The Mutineers of the* Bounty, 194–195.
[178] See Brodie, *Pitcairn's Island and the Islanders*, 183, 186–187, and 192.
[179] Ibid., 183.
[180] Chris R. Vanden Bossche, *Reform Acts: Chartism, Social Agency, and the Victorian Novel, 1832–1867* (Baltimore: Johns Hopkins University Press, 2014), 75–76.

Pitcairnese community and taken land as their own were changing the nature of the island – its political and its social face. Hill's presence, by contrast, was not permanent; it did not introduce anything new to the lineage of these people whose unique Anglo-Tahitian origins had overcome so many perceived disadvantages – mutiny, sexual libertinage, etc. – to achieve an almost prelapsarian perfection. In this way, then, the land did factor into Hill's sense of how best to promote "the general interest and welfare of our little commonwealth."[181]

"Commonwealth." Pitcairn was not a colony. It was not connected through Hill's rule to the broader structures of British imperial power. As we well know, that was, in part, due to the fact that Hill's sovereignty over the island was fraudulent. But, it was also intentional. Pitcairn and its people were also disconnected from the British Empire more broadly because Hill's entire ideology centered on the island's unique place in a larger salvic history. Pitcairn, in short, had become Hill's private moral empire. He did not want to own land there. He did not want to build a family there. He did not want heirs to take the island after him. He wanted, rather, to drive out those who had sullied the purity he imagined to have defined the island circa its rediscovery in 1808, 1814, and 1825. He wanted to re-secure the ethnic and/or racial lineage of the Anglo-Tahitian population (the topic of our next chapter), and he wanted to enforce the deep-rooted religiosity of the islanders. This plan required that he secure Pitcairn as the exclusive domain of the Pitcairners, and he would accomplish all of this at gunpoint, if necessary. This was his reformist manifesto; this was his imperialist ideology.

Hill's plan for Pitcairn, though, only worked if the island could sustain Adamstown's population. The question of the island's carrying capacity was not removed from the table simply because John Evans, John Buffet, and George Nobbs were removed from the island. Even in Hill's years at Pitcairn, news reports from the island questioned how many people could safely be sustained by Pitcairn's natural and limited resources. In 1834, the Philadelphia-based journal *The Friend* guessed that Pitcairn could *feed* a population of about one thousand people. Water, though, was a different question. The island, in 1834, was home to only seventy-nine inhabitants, the magazine reported, and even with that small population, there was pressure on the few wells then available. "They must dig more reservoirs and wells," *The Friend* concluded.[182] *The Sailors' Magazine* of New York raised similar concerns the following year.[183]

---

[181] Brodie, *Pitcairn Island and the Islanders*, 183.
[182] "The Pitcairn Islanders," in *The Friend: A Religious and Literary Journal* 7:31 (May 1, 1834), 241.
[183] "Pitcairn Island," in *The Sailors' Magazine*, 258.

Captain Bruce of the *Imogene* reported that the island was well-supplied with water when he arrived to remove Hill in 1837. "Water is now in abundance," he wrote, "as they have two large Reservoirs," but the supply was fragile, as "they depende greatly upon the Rain to fill them."[184]

The removal to Tahiti in 1831 had been a disaster. In Joshua Hill's mind, the Tahiti trip proved that the Pitcairners belonged on *their* island as their own community. The ecological evidence, though, suggested that Hill was wrong. Captain Bruce was not alone in imagining that Pitcairn was unsustainable. Even in 1837, he imagined that the Pitcairners might someday in the future need to be moved again to another homeland. It would not be an easy endeavor. The Pitcairners, he reported, "do not now like the thought of leaving their islands, unless to see England, (home as they call it) which all of them would like to do." But time would make emigration necessary, he predicted. Bruce even suggested an alternative island home for the Pitcairners. "Toubouai," he insisted, "would be an advantageous place for the whole Pitcairn's population to be removed to. It had good landing and a harbor for small vessels, wood and water in abundance, a fertile soil." Indeed, Bruce had inquired with Consul Charlton about the island. It could be purchased, he estimated, for about £100 and given to the Pitcairners, should the government want to adopt such a program.[185]

Captain Bruce removed Joshua Hill from Pitcairn, thus ending the imposter's reign at Adamstown. Bruce's predictions about the long-term sustainability of life at Pitcairn and his inquiries into and suggestions about the possible relocation of the Pitcairners were, though, the real death knell for Hill's political plan at the island. When Hill sailed with Bruce on board the *Imogene*, Evans, Buffet, and Nobbs were among the islanders who saw him off. They had to have been pleased to see their nemesis leaving Pitcairn, and Hill had to have been galled that these outsiders had been allowed to resettle among the people of Adamstown. They had no connection to the land; they were a threat to the broader project Hill had hoped to plant at Pitcairn, a plan that was specific to the island, its geography, and its history.

And, as Hill could have predicted, when the notion of relocating the Pitcairners again gained traction in London, it would be one of the out-landers, George Nobbs, who became the central player in the realization of the policy. Even before Hill had left the island, Nobbs had begun to correspond with the outside world, suggesting in his letters that Pitcairn

---

[184] Bruce, The Remark Book of the *Conway* and *Imogene*, 300. See also Bruce, Letter to J. Backhouse (December 17, 1839).
[185] Bruce, The Remark Book of the *Conway* and *Imogene*, 303.

Island was not able to support the Pitcairnese population.[186] "We are becoming very sparse in our agricultural resources," Nobbs reported. "So much so that there may be an emigration shortly, partial or total." Moreover, Nobbs predicted that the emigration from Pitcairn would bring substantive change to the nature of Pitcairnese life. "I do not think there is any place in the world that will suit us as well as this Rock."[187]

The 1856 resettlement of the Pitcairnese people to Norfolk Island, therefore, merits a moment of our time before we end this chapter. The relocation may seem to be well beyond the scope of our history of Joshua Hill and his counterfeit commonwealth, but it is not. The logic of the policy dated back to the 1831 removal to Tahiti, though neither effort would have made sense to Hill. Throughout the 1840s and the 1850s, those who corresponded with Pitcairn became increasingly insistent that there was no way to expect the island to sustain its population much longer. Gone was the sense that Pitcairn was a fertile Eden that had given rise to a community that was both historically and morally significant. In 1849, communication with the Hawai'ian Islands suggested that King Kamehameha III was willing to take the Pitcairners into his kingdom should they need a new home.[188] In 1850, both Walter Brodie and Charles Philippe Hippolyte de Thierry suggested that the island was nearly at the limits of its ecological bounty and that a removal was necessary. As we noted when we first met Walter Brodie back in Chapter 2, history owes much to his ability to capture and record the firsthand accounts from Hill's time at Pitcairn Island. In 1850, Brodie had yet to take his seat in New Zealand's parliament, but he had traveled the globe. Indeed, Raymond Nobbs has hinted that it may have been Brodie who first suggested Norfolk Island to the Pitcairners as a replacement homeland. Norfolk's harsh penal history was coming to an end, as Brodie knew by 1850, and it was situated much nearer to Australia and New Zealand than was tiny Pitcairn.[189]

De Thierry, as we will see in the final pages of this book, was cut from the same cloth as Joshua Hill. As the self-styled king of Nuku Hiva in the Marquessas or the sovereign of a self-proclaimed sovereign state on New Zealand's North Island, de Thierry was one of the Pacific's many other nineteenth-century mountebanks.[190] But, like Brodie, de Thierry felt

[186] Nobbs, Letter to Rev. W. T. Bullock (October 9, 1834).   [187] Ibid.
[188] Consul General William Miller, Letter to G.H. Nobbs (Honolulu: May 28, 1849), Nobbs Papers, SLNSW ML 2881.
[189] Nobbs, *George Hunn Nobbs*, 45.
[190] Kirk, *History of the South Pacific since 1513*, location 2859. See also, particularly Paul Moon, *A Savage Country: The Untold Story of New Zealand in the 1820s* (New York: Penguin Books, 2012. Kindle Edition), see particularly chapter 2.

Norfolk was an ideal location for the Pitcairnese people.[191] In Hill's mind, the island and its people were tied to one another. Their braided interests – those of the island and the people – were peculiar to Pacific history; they had a significant role to play well beyond the shores of their one island, or even of the other small islands nearby. The notion that you could move these people higgledy-piggledy to some other place broke that line of thought. But, by the 1850s, the fracture was almost universal. In a journal entry from January 1853, W. E. Gordon derogated Pitcairn as a "little rock." It was a lovely island, to be sure, that Gordon saw during his visit on board the HMS *Virago*, but it was still only a small rock.[192] Even the islanders seemed to agree. "The time is not far distant when Pitcairn's Island will be altogether inadequate to the rapidly increasing population," wrote the island's leaders in a letter to the Society for Promoting Christian Knowledge in May 1853.[193]

The most important report on Pitcairn's ecological sustainability, though, came in June 1853. It was a letter written by Reverend William Henry Holman to Admiral Fairfax Moresby. Holman could claim to know the island well. During George Nobbs' long voyage to Britain in 1852 (a voyage largely organized by Morseby), Holman remained on Pitcairn as the island's spiritual leader. When he reported on the island in 1853, Holman was a pessimist. "The fact is," he wrote, "that the productions of the Island have of late years been greatly reduced by the quantity of wood which has been already cut down." Pitcairn was situated at a precarious spot in the Pacific. It was about as far north as one could possibly expect tropical fruit to grow, and the island was subject to constant winds that further complicated the growing cycles of many of the foodstuffs that normally supplied a South Pacific diet.[194] Rain, though, was still the biggest problem, as the island had had none throughout the last four months of 1853. Drought had resulted in famine, and Holman was left with only one conclusion. The islanders had to be moved.[195]

When George Nobbs returned to Pitcairn in 1853, now a newly ordained Church of England priest, the first task on his plate as one of the island's most influential civic leaders (to say nothing of its most

[191] Nobbs, *George Hunn Nobbs*, 45.

[192] William Ebrington Gordon, Journal Kept on board HMS *Virago* (September 10, 1851–January 28, 1854) and HMS *Portland* (February 1, 1854–April 25, 1854), SLNSW ML MSS.3091 (also CY 1139).

[193] Letter from the Magistrate and Councilors of Pitcairn's Island to the Society for Promoting Christian Knowledge, dated May 18, 1853, in Pitcairn Island Papers, Society for Promoting Christian Knowledge, M2111. Also quoted in Murray, *Pitcairn*, 232.

[194] Holman, Letter to Admiral Fairfax Moresby (June 4, 1853).   [195] Ibid.

famous resident internationally) was to oversee the planning for the removal to Norfolk. Once Nobbs had returned, the Pitcairn Islanders began their collaboration with B. Toup Nichols, the British consul at the Society Islands, asking for London's help in removing them from their ancestral home. In July 1854, Nichols informed the islanders that they had been granted permission to *settle* at Norfolk Island.[196] Even in allowing the Pitcairn Islanders to make Norfolk Island their home, though, the British government made it clear that the entire island could not be ceded to the Pitcairners. The Pitcairn families would receive grants for parcels of land at Norfolk, but the island would never be theirs by right of ownership as Pitcairn had been.[197] It would never completely be home.

We know from surviving correspondence that the Pitcairners were unhappy at what they saw when they first sailed into view of Norfolk Island. "They missed the rugged beauty of Pitcairn and their cozy little houses embowered in a rich foliage; they wanted the snug security that their own island gave them."[198] Within two years' time, "some considered that the change had not been for the better, and murmurs of discontent were heard."[199] The older generation, in particular, was unhappy at Norfolk. By the end of 1858, two families – that of Moses Young and that of Mayhew Young – left Norfolk on the schooner *Mary Ann*, arriving at Pitcairn on January 17, 1859.[200] In 1863, another group of Pitcairners, joined by an outsider by the name of Samuel Warren, left Norfolk and reached Pitcairn in February 1864.[201]

Today, "Pitcairners" live all around the globe. The greatest concentrations of them, though, still live on two islands that are separated by nearly 4,000 miles of open-ocean. The Pitcairners at Norfolk continue to hold themselves apart from the rest of the community, dividing the island's population into those descended from the Pitcairn/*Bounty* saga and those who have settled at Norfolk in the years since 1856.[202] Among the Pitcairners at Norfolk, we still find members of the Evans, Buffet, and Nobbs families. At Pitcairn, we still find descendants of those who returned from Norfolk. Joshua Hill had imagined a Pacific world in which tiny Pitcairn Island mattered more than its size, its geology, its geography, or its ecology might have suggested it should. His was a frangible dream. Today, as we will see in Chapter 7, the island struggles with a dwindling

---

[196] Hoare, *Norfolk Island*, 68–69.   [197] Ibid., 69.
[198] Shapiro, *The Pitcairn Islanders*, 106.   [199] Hoare, *Norfolk Island*, 80.   [200] Ibid.
[201] Ibid., 82.
[202] "Does Norfolk 'Mutiny' Disguise Bounty of Privilege?" BBC News, May 25, 2016. www .bbc.com/news/world-australia-36376219.

population.[203] A community that was once deeply rooted to its home island and that had existed in a small, closed society in Pitcairn's only village is now a diasporic people, and the island at the center of the diaspora – Pitcairn itself – is again facing existential pressures. There is much that binds the residents of Norfolk and Pitcairn Islands. They remain a conterranean people. But the romantic sense of isolation, the exclusively Anglo-Tahitian bloodlines forged by the *Bounty* settlers, the deep bond to their "native" island – all of the things that Joshua Hill had insisted were so important not only to this island and its people but also to London's influence over the South Pacific – have all been splintered.

---

[203] Lal and Fortune, eds., *The Pacific Islands*, 602. See also, Royle, *A Geography of Islands*, 106.

6   Seduction

Why do you think that beauty, which is the most precious thing in the world, lies like a stone on the beach for the careless passer-by to pick up idly? Beauty is something wonderful and strange that the artist fashions out of the chaos of the world in the torment of his soul.

W. Somerset Maugham, *The Moon and Sixpence* (1919)[1]

It was a weary William Bligh who landed at Timor on June 14, 1789. He had been at sea in the *Bounty*'s launch for forty-seven days. Of the eighteen men who had lived in that cramped twenty-three-foot-long boat with Bligh, only one had lost his life on the otherwise stygian voyage.[2] It was eighteen skeletons, though who washed ashore at Coupang. They had sailed onboard the *Bounty*, but they had come to experience the worst examples of human privation.

"What could be the cause for such a Revolution?" This was the very question on William Bligh's mind as he sat at the Dutch East Indian port of Batavia writing home – to his wife, to Sir Joseph Banks, to the Admiralty – about the mutiny aboard the *Bounty*.[3] What could be the cause? In all of his accounts of the mutiny, Bligh repeated his answer to this pressing question: Tahiti! The island was, he wrote to his wife, Betsy, "the Paradise of the World," an island with "every allurement both to luxury and ease."[4] His crew, he told Sir Joseph Banks, must have "Assured themselves of a more happy life among the Otaheiteans than they could possibly have in England."[5] This island was a place, after all, where bread – or at least breadfruit – quite literally grew on trees.[6]

In particular, Bligh was certain that it was Tahitian women who had been the greatest seduction to mutiny among the *Bounty*'s men. Some of his crew,

---

[1] Maugham, *The Moon and Sixpence*, 91.   [2] Frost, *The Global Reach of Empire*, 6.
[3] William Bligh, Manuscript Account of the Mutiny, SLNSW ML Safe 1/36, 11. See also William Bligh, Voyage of the *Bounty*'s Launch, SLNSW ML MSS Safe 1/37, 18; and Salmond, *Bligh*, 232.
[4] Quoted in Salmond, *Bligh*, 232.   [5] Bligh, Voyage of the *Bounty*'s Launch, 18.
[6] Casid, *Sowing Empire*, 61. See also, Gascoigne, *Encountering the Pacific*, 277.

Bligh reported, had forged "female connections" at Tahiti.[7] Fletcher Christian's relationship with Mauatua was but the most famous of these romantic alliances.[8] History and Hollywood have immortalized Mauatua, whom we also know as Miamiti, Isabella, Mainmast, or Mrs. Christian. She was not, though, a singular figure in this story. The women at Tahiti were, Bligh wrote, all "handsome, mild in their manners & conversation, with sufficient delicacy to make them admired and beloved."[9]

In his letter to his wife, Bligh went further. "What a temptation it is to such Wretches," he wrote,

when they find it in their power (however illegally it can be got at) to fix themselves in the midst of Plenty in the finest Island in the World, where they need not labour, and where the allurements of dissipation are more than equal to any thing that can be conceived.[10]

Still physically shattered from starvation, dehydration, and exposure, Bligh cast his mutinous crew as "wretches," for their behavior had set aside the moral probity he exemplified in favor of hedonism and debauchery.[11] The narrow road of the law seems to have been much thornier for Bligh than was the primrose path chosen by his crew. But who was to blame the mutineers? Only a fool or a prude would choose Britain over Tahiti. Even Bligh – who had suffered so much to get home – accepted Tahiti as the "finest Island in the World."

There is also, in William Bligh's letter to Betsy Bligh, an important, but perhaps insulting, comparison between English and Tahitian women. That Bligh loved his wife has never been doubted. He addressed his letters to "My Dear Dear Betsy," and in this particular letter, there is a real and deep sense of failure when he confesses what has happened.

What an emotion does my heart and soul feel that I have once more an opportunity of writing to you and my little angels, and particularly as you have all been so near losing the best of friends.

Bligh went on, "Know then my own Dear Betsy, I have lost the *Bounty*!"[12] In a world that defined masculinity as physical, violent, militant, and strong, Bligh had been bested.[13] This was a *paterfamilias* who knew he

---

[7] Bligh, Voyage of the *Bounty*'s Launch, 18. See also O'Brien, *The Pacific Muse*, 84.
[8] Hough, *Captain Bligh and Mr. Christian*, 55.   [9] Bligh, Account of the Mutiny, 11.
[10] Quoted in Salmond, *Bligh*, 233.
[11] Toohey, *Captain Bligh's Portable Nightmare*, 161–162.
[12] Quoted in Salmond, *Bligh*, 228–233. See also, Toohey, *Captain Bligh's Portable Nightmare*, 168–169.
[13] Angela Wollacott, "Gender and Sexuality," in Deryck M. Schreuder and Stuart Ward, eds., *Australia's Empire – The Oxford History of the British Empire, Companion Series* (New York: Oxford University Press, 2008), 316.

had disgraced his family, no matter how loyal or faithful or true he had remained through the ordeal. And on top of that? To write to his wife that the women of Tahiti were so easily "admired and loved." Was this the sort of praise a wife really wanted or needed to hear? Bligh had remained physically scrupulous, but in his heart, he understood the mutineers' temptation. As Rudyard Kipling would later observe in his 1892 poem *Mandalay*, English women could look "Beefy face an' grubby" once one had met "a neater, sweeter maiden in a cleaner, greener land!"[14] The observation might have been true, but it is hardly farfetched to assume that Betsy Bligh did not appreciate reading about it.[15]

The causes behind the mutiny on the *Bounty* have made this story famous – even infamous – from the very beginning. As we have seen, the sense that this mutiny was connected in some way to the liberating politics of the age of Atlantic revolutions was articulated even by those who knew the story firsthand. Captain Bligh, though, did not agree. There was revolution, and then there was mutiny. *This* was mutiny. This was a story of men who refused to do their duty to their captain, their king, and their country – indeed, a story of men who went one step beyond refusing. These men were mutineers, and it was Tahitian exoticism and Polynesian sexual promiscuity that had led them astray.

Bligh's charged and sexualized explanations for the mutiny on the *Bounty* have helped to shape our sense of Polynesia and of Polynesians.[16] Eventually, the Orientalist Sir Richard Burton would institutionalize Bligh's descriptions of Polynesian sexual licentiousness, labeling the South Seas as a "sotadic zone."[17] Bligh is not, to be very clear, singularly responsible here, but the mutiny on the *Bounty* quickly became a romantic adventure story and continues to be one of the best-known stories (fictitious or historical) out of the European South Pacific, if not from the Pacific more broadly.

In literature, not surprisingly, we need look no further than Herman Melville to see the influence of Bligh's explanation for the *Bounty* mutiny. In the nineteenth century, as Michael Sheldon, a Melville biographer, confesses, "sexy women and friendly cannibals ... always dr[e]w a crowd."[18] Melville supplied both in his first novel, *Typee* (1846). Half fiction, half travel adventure based on Melville's own experiences as a whaler in the Pacific, *Typee* charmed and titillated Victorian audiences

---

[14] Rudyard Kipling, *Mandalay* (New York: M.F. Mansfield and Company, 1898), unpaginated.

[15] Nicholas Thomas, *Cook: The Extraordinary Voyages of Captain James Cook* (New York: Walker and Company, 2003), 141.

[16] O'Brien, *The Pacific Muse*, 129.   [17] Edmond, *Representing the South Pacific*, 177.

[18] Shelden, *Melville in Love*, location 488.

with descriptions of Fayaway, the beautiful Polynesian woman who joins the book's narrator on some of his travels.[19] Like Tahiti's women, Fayaway had the power to seduce a European visitor. In one of the book's most famous (and certainly one of its most suggestive) scenes, Melville wrote,

One day, after we had been paddling about for some time, I disembarked Kory-Kory, and paddled the canoe to the windward side of the lake. As I turned the canoe, Fayaway, who was with me, seemed all at once to be struck with some happy idea. With a wild exclamation of delight, she disengaged from her person the ample robe of tappa which was knotted over her shoulder (for the purpose of shielding her from the sun), and spreading it out like a sail, stood erect with upraised arms in the head of the canoe. We American sailors pride ourselves upon our straight clean spars, but a prettier little mast than Fayaway made was never shipped a-board of any craft.[20]

We might, here, elaborate on the suggestive meanings that nineteenth-century sailors layered onto the word "spar" – to say nothing about "straight clean spars" – but it hardly takes Sigmund Freud to unpack just how salacious a scene Melville had painted for his readers.

The literary imaginings about Polynesian sexuality were not, however, without their historical antecedents. As K. R. Howe reminds us, "when Bougainville first approached [Tahiti], the vessel was immediately surrounded by canoe-loads of young women most of whom 'were naked, for the men and old women that accompanied them had stripped them of the garments which they generally dressed themselves in'."[21] As would Melville, Bougainville, Cook, Bligh, and other European captains offered this image of beautiful, bare-breasted Tahitian women as the stage for the "sexual trystings" of "willing" Tahitian Dulcineas and "lusty sailors."[22] In this view, Polynesian sexuality was liberated from the moralizing constraints that bound sex in European Christendom. In the South Seas, sex was, to quote Trevor Lummis, "a leisure pursuit."[23]

The history of and literature from the South Pacific are both, then, filled with what Lord Byron called "summer women."[24] These were islands that drew eighteenth- and nineteenth-century European minds back to the Edenic descriptions of paradise found in Genesis.[25] Polynesian women, Patty O'Brien has argued, became a resource in these island paradises – one more among nature's stores (like the whales, the seals, the furs, etc.) to be harvested by European adventurers.[26]

---

[19] Liebersohn, *The Travelers' World*, 289.   [20] Melville, *Typee*, 134.
[21] Howe, *Where the Waves Fall*, 83. See also Matsuda, *Empire of Love*, 3.
[22] Howe, *Where the Waves Fall*, 84. See also, Liebersohn, *The Travelers' World*, 145.
[23] Lummis, *Pacific Paradises*, 113.   [24] Quoted in O'Brien, *The Pacific Muse*, 38.
[25] Ibid., 50.   [26] Ibid., 119.

As O'Brien has astutely observed, many of the products extracted from the Pacific – whalebone, baleen, ambergris, oils, etc. – were used to perfume and to beautify the bodies of wealthy European women.[27] Even the islands themselves were gendered as "markedly feminine," there to be claimed, possessed, had, penetrated, and other verbs of colonial inclination that are loaded with sexual double entendre.[28]

There is more to this part of our story, though, than mere sexual prurience. We are not pausing here for a casual dalliance. These moments – when European crews met South Pacific islanders – were profound instances of cultural contact. They were fraught manifestations of diversity in the making, for the discovery of new people and new cultures had the potential to cut two competing directions simultaneously. In these moments, on one hand, there was the opportunity to relish the cultural diversity of two distinct and different peoples meeting on one beach.[29] The larger history of global expansion and colonization tells us, however, that the first path was only rarely chosen. Rather, these were also moments in which cultural difference had to be explained in order to be understood, and the explaining often yielded to justifications for why and how European civilization was more "advanced" than anything else Europeans found in sailing around the globe.[30]

The opening of the Pacific to this grander narrative of global encounter produced what Glyndwr Williams has called the "Pacific craze" from 1763 to 1793.[31] It might be argued that the craze lasted a good many years longer, for our Joshua Hill was clearly still very much drawn to this ocean in the 1830s. The *Bounty*'s voyage and the Pitcairnese settlement have to loom large in this history precisely because no European crew had previously spent so much time at Tahiti. Bligh's men were the first to form connections and attachments to their Tahitian hosts. Theirs was "something more than . . . a sailor's spree."[32] If, as Nicholas Thomas has argued, Captain Cook's crews were intoxicated by the "bodies, behaviours, and societies" they met with in the South Pacific, what were Europeans to make of a community of South Pacific Islanders who had been born of Anglo-Tahitian parents?[33] Of this mixed-race people? Of the Pitcairners?

Elisa Beshero-Bondar has observed that few actually spent much time worrying about the actual origins of the Pitcairnese people, certainly not in the eighteenth or nineteenth centuries. This omission has not been

---

[27] Ibid., 146.   [28] Edmond, *Representing the South Pacific*, 74.   [29] Ibid., 69.
[30] Glyndwr Williams, *Buccaneers, Explorers, and Settlers: British Enterprise and Encounters in the Pacific, 1670-1800* (Aldershot, New Hampshire: Ashgate Publishing, 2005), 3. See also, Thomas, *Entangled Objects*, 144.
[31] Williams, *Buccaneers, Explorers, and Settlers*, 3.   [32] Moorehead, *The Fatal Impact*, 76.
[33] Thomas, *Cook*, xx. See also, Young, *Mutiny's* Bounty, 114; and Chapter 4 of this book.

corrected in contemporary popular culture. "The twentieth century's film adaptations of the *Bounty* story," Beshero-Bondar writes, "were disinclined to follow the story of Tahitian women and British mutineers much beyond their settlement of Pitcairn." In this regard, Hollywood's *Bounty* films have taken "their cue from [Lord] Byron's *The Island,* which never introduces Pitcairn at all but simplifies the story to a dreamy vision of Pacific bliss and forgetfulness of British identity."[34]

Byron's poem, which we quoted from in the last chapter, was published in 1823. *The Island* pauses the *Bounty* story at the oneiric moment the mutineers settle at Pitcairn, before the dream became a nightmare. In choosing to end the poem there, Byron helped solidify the image of Pacific islands as paradisical promised lands. Let us leave Byron, for a moment, though, and turn to another author, to the English poetess Mary Russell Mitford, for Mitford would make a different choice in her Pitcairnese poem, a piece entitled *Christina, the Maid of the South Seas* from 1811. Unlike Byron, Mitford chose to delve deeply into life at Pitcairn, and her poem "stands out for its depiction of Tahitian women's violence against men and for its perspective on two generations of instability and loss on Pitcairn's Island."[35]

Today, Mary Russell Mitford is much less well known than Lord Byron. In her day, though, she moved in rarefied circles. In 1836, as Joshua Hill was deep into his Pitcairnese years, Mary Russell Mitford met Elizabeth Barrett Browning. The two would go on to become good friends. Years earlier, and inspired by the first suggestive reports that an American vessel, the *Topaz,* had happened upon an island inhabited by the last surviving *Bounty* mutineer and his small community of Anglo-Tahitian devotees, Mitford had published *Christina,* and we know that she consulted with Samuel Taylor Coleridge, author of the well-known *The Rime of the Ancient Mariner* (1798) as she wrote the piece. We know too that she met with James Burney who had been part of the *Resolution*'s crew during Captain James Cook's third voyage.[36]

Like Byron's, Mitford's was a well-researched (and, it merits observation, *earlier*) poetic study of the *Bounty* saga – from breadfruit to mutiny, and from mutiny to Pitcairn. The crucial difference between the two poets and their poems, though, may be Mitford's decision to tell the Pitcairn story using a female character, Fletcher Christian's daughter Christina, as the poem's central figure.[37] As we have observed previously,

[34] Elisa E. Beshero-Bondar, "Romancing the Pacific Isles before Byron: Music, Sex, and Death in Mitford's Christina," in *ELH* 76:2 (Summer, 2009), 285. See also, O'Brien, *The Pacific Muse,* 127; and Silverman, *Pitcairn Island,* xv.
[35] Beshero-Bondar, "Romancing the Pacific Isles," 286.   [36] Salmond, *Bligh,* 466.
[37] Smith, *European Vision and the South Pacific,* 248–249.

few – if any – of those who attempted to sort out the complicated history of the *Bounty* settlers at Pitcairn ever paid much attention to the Tahitian mothers who had co-settled the island.[38] We know that the dozen Tahitian women who landed at Pitcairn Island with Fletcher Christian were not the only Polynesian women to enter into Europe's Pacific history. As David Chappell reminds us, "Oceanian women … spent so much time on ships that they helped in trading and cross-cultural mediation."[39] These women

also traveled on foreign ships. In 1774, an attractive Boraboran woman journeyed with Cook from Tahiti to Ra'iatea, and after his death at Hawai'i in 1779, seven women sailed with his ships as far as O'ahu, helping the British to provision.[40]

In some instances, we know that Polynesian women sailed from home with European men in informal marital relationships.[41]

The Tahitian women at Pitcairn, though, are unique in this history, for they alone stand as "founding mothers," to borrow a phrase from Cokie Roberts and to relocate it to a South Pacific context.[42] These women were not passive passengers in the post-settlement history of the *Bounty* saga.[43] Rather, they actively shaped the early history of Pitcairn Island. They seemed to know that they were living through important events and that, in the future, they would be able to shape the story of what they were experiencing. Twice in the years just after the *Bounty* landed at Pitcairn, the island experienced internal upheaval. In those instances, the Polynesian male population attempted to overthrow the established order led by the European mutineers. We know that the island's female residents directed some of the violence that occurred from behind the scenes – leaking word of the feuding factions' plans one side to the other – when it best suited the needs of the island's female population and the needs of the women's children. That these twelve women never claimed to have borne a single child by the six Polynesian men who settled at Pitcairn has to have been a strategically planned bit of sexual politicking, even if the reasoning behind the design remains unclear.[44] And, of course, once the six Polynesian men and all but Adams/Smith among the Europeans were dead, Pitcairn's adult population was left disproportionately female, a fact that cannot but have influenced the way that Adams/Smith managed the island as patriarch.[45]

---

[38] See Maxton, *The Mutiny on HMS* Bounty, 3; and Trevor Lummis, *Life and Death in Eden*, 84.
[39] Chappell, *Double Ghosts*, 18.   [40] Ibid., 19.   [41] Ibid., 20.
[42] Cokie Roberts, *Founding Mothers: The Women Who Raised Our Nation* (New York: Harper Perennial, 2005).
[43] O'Brien, *The Pacific Muse*, 124.   [44] Ibid., 192–193.
[45] See Chappell, *Double Ghosts*, 96.

Part of our effort to understand Pitcairn's history, then, has to include an attempt to come to terms with the history of these twelve women and the distinctly Pitcairnese racial or ethnic community they gave birth to. We must, therefore, look at this history as Mary Russell Mitford did – through Christina's eyes. In doing so, we will find that the story is often more complicated and frequently less comfortable than we might previously have imagined. Take, for instance, Mitford's willingness to implicate the Tahitian women in the carnage that defined Pitcairn's history, in particular from 1790 to 1793. Mitford does not, for an instant, shy away from the fact that the Tahitian women had blood on their hands. "Christian's brave dame the daggers bore," she writes in one stanza,

> Still dripping with the white men's gore;
> The bright steel caught the silvery gleam,
> Her dark hair floated in the beam,
> Hung round that sad and pallid face,
> And that tall form of loftiest grace;
> Like prophetess in gifted mood,
> Before the widow's eyes she stood, -
> "Revenge! revenge! this life blood cries,
> "The murderers sleep. Arise! Arise!"
> They rose. The soft and gentle fair,
> Who even the creeping worm would spare,
> Who wept kid's gay life to spill,
> Those fearful women rose – to kill![46]

What we get from Mary Russell Mitford, then, is more than twelve Tahitian women acting as historical courtesans. These women add "cultural complexity" to the history.[47] These are beautiful women, sexual women. They intrigue us today – as they did the *Bounty* men in their own day – because they "romanticize the possibilities of native-British fusion." Their relationships with the *Bounty* mutineers were sexual alliances that drew on the exotic image nineteenth-century Europeans held about Tahitian woman, but they also simultaneously cut against the grain of nineteenth-century sensibilities about sex, sexuality, and race. Furthermore, these Tahitian women were also deeply engaged in the making of a new Anglo-Polynesian polity in the Pacific.[48] The image Mitford conjures is not entirely "a triumph of British liberty," nor is it safe.[49] The sexual tension in *Christina* spills into divisive – even deadly – politics.

In Mitford's poem, though, the heroine, Christina, shies away from the violence that marked her mother's generation. She is "characterized

---

[46] Mitford, *Christina*, 131.   [47] Beshero-Bondar, "Romancing the Pacific Isles," 284.
[48] Ibid., 287.   [49] Ibid., 299–300.

as the first-born in a superior new race, the result of the mixing of superlative gender and racial traits, the best of British in Christian and the best of Tahitian in her mother."[50] Pitcairners, Mitford seems to suggest, were something like a new race. Before we assess Russell's claims, it is important that we observe that race was already a challenging topic in the Pacific before the emergence of the Anglo-Tahitian Pitcairners. The racial constitution of Pacific-bound crews in these years was, for instance, something of interest, even if it was never described with any real precision. Melville's Ishmael may have seemed open-minded when he observed of Queequeg that "a man can be honest in any sort of skin."[51] But in actual whaling logbooks, the complexions of sailors were categorized and in a host of different ways – "light, dark, fair, freckled, yellow, copper, Indian, black, swarthy, mulatto, even blue in a few instances."[52]

The population at Pitcairn proved similarly slippery. As Rod Edmond has described it, "traces of Tahitian grace and beauty" survived among the Pitcairners, "but the stock will be predominately English … One small part of the Pacific will have been colonized and redeemed."[53] We might disagree with Edmond's argument that the Pitcairners could be "readmitted to the English diaspora," for we have already seen that they were not imagined as being purely English.[54] Despite their mixed racial and ethnic heritage, though, the Pitcairners were never categorized with the world's less-civilized or savage people. They were rarely denigrated for being the byproducts of South Seas miscegenation. There was always something special about the Pitcairners; they were a chosen people.

How do we explain this assessment of a mixed-race community of thieves, mutineers, drunkards, savages, and murderers – for any of these adjectives might have been applied to the Pitcairners in the nineteenth century? Did "the distinction [turn] upon the transformative power of a Western presence" at the core of the little community at Adamstown?[55] To a degree, yes. But there is more here, for Tahiti itself held a special place in eighteenth- and nineteenth-century understandings about race. Tahiti was

the most civilized nation of the South Seas not only because the people's physical appearance coincided with European taste, but precisely because it seemed to *be* a nation, apparently governed by dynastic kings and queens, possessing both

[50] O'Brien, *The Pacific Muse*, 125.   [51] Melville, *Moby-Dick*, 23.
[52] Shoemaker, ed., *Living with Whales*, 69.
[53] Edmond, *Representing the South Pacific*, 82.   [54] Ibid., 81.
[55] Thomas, *Entangled Objects*, 147.

a priestly class and an aristocratic one, and having a history of civil war and an architectural record of religious buildings to match.[56]

While most Pacific populations were viewed as "living beyond the touch of time," Tahitian civilization suggested forward and progressive historical movement, even if it was not on par with European historical advances.[57]

The question of where South Pacific Islanders originated from was one that had intrigued Europeans from the moment of first contact. The question was directed at the other, but it revealed much about the self.[58] Captain Cook, for instance, had marveled that South Pacific Islanders had been technologically capable of sailing and settling the Pacific in what otherwise seemed very primitive canoes.[59] The construction of history here – the notion of primitive and modern and, pointedly, the concept of "prehistory" – was always an "ideological device."[60] Cook was a rarity. His ability, as a captain from a seafaring people, to view Polynesians as another seafaring community scattered across a South Pacific empire was not something shared by many of his contemporaries.[61] Most Europeans through both the eighteenth and the nineteenth centuries (indeed, even well into the twentieth and the twenty-first) defined history as the study of change over time.[62]

Cook recognized that Polynesians were "historical" people by this European measure. Most, though, limited that recognition to Tahiti, which would eventually benefit the Pitcairners who could be understood as the heirs – through their mothers – of the Pacific's most advanced native society.[63] By this way of thinking, the Pitcairners lived in the Pacific, but they were not really South Pacific Islanders.

What is in a name? Is a South Pacific maiden, by any other name, still just as sweet? We return with these questions to a set of inquires we took up in the previous chapter, for, as Epeli Hau'ofa has observed, in order to

[56] Landsdown, ed., *Strangers in the South Seas*, 18. See also Geoff Quilley, *Empire to Nation: Art, History, and the Visualization of Maritime Britain, 1768–1829* (New Haven: Yale University Press, 2011), 260.

[57] Landsdown, ed., *Strangers in the South Seas*, 18.

[58] Howe, *The Quest for Origins*, 183. See also, Quilley, *Empire to Nation*, 55. See also Robert Borofsky, "An Invitation," in Borofsky, ed., *Remembrance of Pacific Pasts*, 47.

[59] John Gascoigne, *Captain Cook: Voyager between Worlds* (New York: Hambledon Continuum, 2007), 63. See also Davis, *Island Boy*, 62–63.

[60] Howe, *The Quest for Origins*, 23. See also Hau'ofa, "Epilogue: Pasts to Remember," in Borofsky, ed., *Remembrance of Pacific Pasts*, 456.

[61] Gascoigne, *Captain Cook*, 63.

[62] Damon Salesa, "The Pacific in Indigenous Time," in David Armitage and Alison Bashford, eds., *Pacific Histories: Ocean, Land, People* (New York: Palgrave, 2014), 36–37.

[63] O'Brien, *The Pacific Muse*, 125.

develop a regional identity for the Pacific islands, we have to have a collective sense of what it means to be a South Pacific Islander, and vice versa. "What or who is a Pacific Islander?," Hua'ofa has asked.[64] To judge by *The Cambridge History of the Pacific Islanders*, the Pitcairners do not count, for Pitcairn Island receives only one mention in that volume – a reference in one, singular footnote.[65]

It is worth taking a moment here to pause and think back to some of what we have already seen about outsiders' assessments of the Pitcairnese people. Captain Pipon, we will remember, was astonished at the modesty and chastity that prevailed at Pitcairn Island when he arrived in 1814. The island's women were "wonderfully strong" with "pleasing countenances, & a degree of modesty and bashfulness that would do honour to the most virtuous nation."[66] John Shillibeer sailed with Pipon as a lieutenant. In the Marquesas, he observed, "chastity is so little esteemed." At Pitcairn, though, the women were as lovely as any other Polynesians, though "their minds and manners were ... pure and innocent." They avoided any "lascivious looks, or any loose, forward manners which so much distinguished the females of other islands."[67]

These descriptions fit easily alongside everything else we have come to appreciate about nineteenth-century descriptions of the Pitcairn Islanders. Charles Dilke visited Pitcairn in 1867. His sense of the islanders was less positive. Moses Young, the island's magistrate, was "slightly built," like all of the young men of the island. Furthermore, Dilke concluded, the group he met at Pitcairn were a rather lazy bunch. They had opted to return to Pitcairn from Norfolk because they were "indolent half-casts" who "found the task of keeping the Norfolk Island convict roads in good repair one heavier than they cared to perform."[68]

Dilke was writing a good thirty years after the period we are considering – the years when Pitcairn was governed by Joshua Hill. A lot had changed in those years.[69] The removal to Norfolk. Britain's colonial relationship with the Pacific Ocean. European racial attitudes.[70] We cannot, therefore, take Dilke's commentary to have been indicative

[64] Epeli Hau'ofa, "The Ocean in Us," in David Hanlon and Geoffrey M. White, editors, *Voyaging through the Contemporary Pacific* (New York: Rowman & Littlefield Publishers, Inc., 2000), 122.

[65] Denoon, ed., *The Cambridge History of the Pacific Islanders*, 511.

[66] Quoted in O'Brien, *The Pacific Muse*, 125.   [67] Ibid., 126.

[68] Charles Wentworth Dilke, *Greater Britain: A Record of Travel in English-Speaking Countries, during 1866–8* (Philadelphia: J.B. Lippincotte & Co., 1869), 274.

[69] See Brantlinger, *Taming the Cannibals*, 54.

[70] See Peter Clayworth, "Richard Taylor and the Children of Noah: Race, Science, and Religion in the South Seas," in Hilary M. Carey, ed., *Empires of Religion* (New York: Cambridge University Press, 2008), 222.

of early-nineteenth-century attitudes towards Pitcairn, but he does remind us of several salient aspects of this history. First, the Pitcairners were the descendants of mutineers. Had the nine *Bounty* men who landed at Pitcairn ever been tried, they would all have been convicted of mutiny. They were criminals.

And yet, in Dilke's mind, the Pitcairners were not as hard-working as the men at Norfolk; they could not sustain the infrastructure of that island, roads that had been built by Norfolk Island convicts. And it merits remembering that Norfolk Island was well-known as a hard penal establishment even by those living in other penal colonies. It was the penal destination for those convicted of crimes *during* their exile for earlier crimes. When Dilke indicated that the Pitcairners were less capable of sustaining Norfolk's roads and public works than the island's earlier recidivist convicts, he knew he was reminding his audience of the mutinous stock from which the *Bounty* men had been born, and he knew he was making a particularly damning comparison.

Dilke's critique, though, was doubly barbed, for he also reminded his audience that the Pitcairners were half-castes. They were not purely descended from mutineer stock. No. The *Bounty* men had kidnapped Tahitian women, "married" them, and had children with them. Dilke's commentary directs us at the very problematic racial and ethnic origins of the Pitcairn Islanders. Descended from criminals, they were also an entirely mixed-race population, Anglo-Tahitians.[71] Even in the early nineteenth century, "long-term attachments between white men and island women were considered even more threatening than brief encounters."[72] There was no reason why a mixed-race community descended from mutineers ought to have received international praise and support, and yet, as we have seen, Dilke's comments from the 1860s mark a sharp turn from earlier assessments of this unique community.

To understand appreciative, early nineteenth-century assessments of the Pitcairn Islanders requires that we reflect on the idyllic place that Tahiti itself played in the European imagination in the late eighteenth and early nineteenth centuries. Trevor Lummis has observed that "it seems extraordinary that in an age when Europeans were transporting Africans across the Atlantic to work as slaves in their plantations, natives from the Pacific should have been so cared for, even lionized."[73] Lummis overplays his hand here, at least a bit. Not every Pacific island was viewed in the same light in these years. We know, for instance, that Captain Cook was fully able to speak in racialized terms about South Pacific Islanders,

---

[71] See Moerenhout, *Travels in the Islands*, 431.   [72] Samson, *Imperial Benevolence*, 38.
[73] Lummis, *Pacific Paradises*, 116. See also, Wahlroos, *Mutiny and Romance*, 34.

particularly those from Melanesia and Micronesia, comparing the inhabitants of some islands to black Africans and using markers such as "woolly" or "frizzled" hair to suggest racial distance between himself, his crew, and the Pacific Islanders they were encountering on their voyages.[74] An even more ignominious stain on an island's cultural status, of course, was any suggestion that an island's inhabitants practiced cannibalism, something Cook claimed he had found on multiple South Pacific islands.[75]

Cook was able, then, to connect the world he was seeing in the South Pacific to the extraordinary "new" worlds that had been opened to Europeans since 1492. The impulse to compare the exoticism of the South Pacific to the better-known parts of the globe like Africa, after all, seems a typically human exercise. Men like Cook entered the Pacific "with the confidence that Europeans had already seen and absorbed a great deal; and that if Europeans had already once encountered 'natural' societies in America, they could expect to find something similar in the Pacific." But, as Harry Liebersohn notes, "what they found defied their expectations."[76] On one hand, the South Pacific was engaging to Enlightenment thinkers who "were fascinated by societies that lacked anything like Christian sexual morality." Early nineteenth-century Evangelicals would also be drawn to the Pacific because of the region's sexual morality, though this group was more inclined to want to change what they found than to study it.[77] And, finally, late eighteenth-century and early nineteenth-century Romanticism was almost instantly enamored of the Pacific, its "aesthetic attractions" and its "island cultures" – the very things, in short, that the missionaries hoped to alter.[78]

Cook's involvement in the South Pacific was always simultaneously a history of exploration, colonization, and science.[79] Joseph Banks and J. R. Forster were central figures in the dissemination of the Cook voyages throughout the European scientific community, and Banks was almost singularly responsible for the attempt to bring Tupaia, a Ra'iatean priest, from Tahiti to Europe during

---

[74] Captain James Cook, *First Voyage Round the World – Captain Cook's Journal during His First Voyage Round the World, Made in HM Bark* Endeavour, *1768–71* (Nikosia, Cyprus: Verone, 2016), 347; and John Dunmore Lang, *Cooksland in North-eastern Australia: The Future Cotton-Field of Great Britain – Its Characteristics and Capabilities for European Colonization* (London: Longman, Brown, Green, and Longmans, 1847), 344. See also, Campbell, *A History of the Pacific Islands*, 20–23.

[75] Obeyesekere, *Cannibal Talk*, 10. See also, Brantlinger, *Taming the Cannibals*, 28–31.

[76] Liebersohn, *The Travelers' World*, 4.

[77] Johnston, *Missionary Writing and Empire*, 18. See also, Hiney, *On the Missionary Trail*, 96.

[78] Liebersohn, *The Travelers' World*, 5. See also, Brantlinger, *Dark Vanishings*, 142.

[79] See, for instance, David Knight, *Voyaging in Strange Seas: The Great Revolution in Science* (New Haven, CT: Yale University Press, 2014. Kindle Edition).

Cook's first voyage.[80] Though Tupaia died in Batavia while the *Endeavour* was docked there in December 1770, Banks was able to coordinate the passage of Mai (better known as Omai), another Ra'iatean native, to Britain under the guidance of Commander Tobias Furneaux of the HMS *Adventure,* the companion ship to Cook's *Resolution* during the second voyage.[81]

Mai was the second South Pacific Islander to visit Europe. Ahu-toru had traveled with Bougainville to Paris as the first Polynesian to reside on the European continent. The two Pacific Islanders, coupled with the exotic narratives and information (and we have to be clear that those things were not always the same in this history) were deeply intriguing to European thinkers who were themselves deeply engaged in the intellectual exercise of sorting out the many different peoples of the planet. Was the Biblical account of creation accurate? Had all humans descended from a singular and common ancestry? If so, how might Europeans account for the variation in the species that they were finding around the globe?[82] And, pressingly, what did the varying levels of civilization that were to be found suggest about the movement of human culture over time? Did Pacific Islanders and Native Americans, for instance, live in a state of affairs closer to that found at the dawn of time? Had European civilization moved "progressively" forward? Or, had seemingly less advanced people "degenerated" over the course of time?[83]

These were complicated questions, profound questions that would come to shape the nature not only of European colonialism but also of the racial history of the world more generally, for there were obvious implications to be taken from any set of answers one might offer in this conversation.[84] For many engaged in this debate, Adam Smith's four-tiered model of human history and development made sense. Evidence from around the globe seemed to suggest that humans moved in a universal pattern from nomadic communities to pastoralists before becoming agriculturalists and, finally, citizens of

---

[80] Liebersohn, *The Travelers' World,* 149.   [81] Ibid., 150.

[82] Gascoigne, *Encountering the Pacific,* 438–440.

[83] Liebersohn, *The Travelers' World,* 198–207; Johnston, *Missionary Writing and Empire,* 5; and Lamb, *Preserving the Self,* 115.

[84] See Bronwen Douglas and Chris Ballard, "Race, Place, and Civilisation: Colonial Encounters and Governance in Greater Oceania," in *The Journal of Pacific History* 47:3 (September 2012), 245–262. See also J. G. A. Pocock, "Nature and History, Self and Other: European Perceptions of World History in the Age of Encounter," in Alex Calder, Jonathan Lamb, and Bridget Orr, eds., *Voyages and Beaches: Pacific Encounters, 1769–1840* (Honolulu: University of Hawai'i Press, 1999), 39–43; and Adam Smith, *Lectures on Jurisprudence,* R. L. Meek, D. D. Raphael, and P. G. Stein, eds. (New York: Oxford University Press, 1978), 14.

a commercial world.[85] This stadial model allowed Enlightenment thinkers to consider the history of human social development without challenging the Biblical teaching that all human history began with one couple. More significantly, the model not only explained most of the world's varying civilizational patterns, it also suggested that European society had advanced further along an historical scale than had any other society on the planet.[86] This was a model that was at once historically plausible, theologically neutral, and ideologically useful.

It was also a model with deep flaws, some of which were exposed on the waters of the South Pacific. Many South Pacific Island communities were not commercial societies. Some were definitively still agriculturalist. Others were even lower on Smith's stadial scale of human–historical development. How, then, to explain the profound levels of social organization that were required to move a society across the Pacific, across its hundreds of thousands of islands? One could not live as a simple savage on a happy little island if one was not also part of a sophisticated society capable of navigating the global ocean, finding a suitable island, settling it, and sustaining a community there.[87] As Paul Turnbull has observed, it was Pacific paradoxes like this one that so fascinated Enlightenment thinkers.[88] The esteemed German anthropologist Johann Friedrich Blumenbach, for instance, hoped that the *Bounty* voyage would yield a collection of skulls from across the Pacific for his studies in human developmental history. We know from letters between Banks and Blumenbach in 1790 that both men were horrified to hear of the loss of the *Bounty* and, with it, the concomitant delay in Blumenbach's research.[89]

European thinkers in the later nineteenth century would deviate from the initial course of this debate, coming to argue for an evolutionary model in which humans were not a unitary species but rather a set of

---

[85] Smith, *Lectures on Jurisprudence*, 14. See also, Pocock, "Nature and History, Self and Other," in Calder, Lamb, and Orr, eds., *Voyages and Beaches*, 39–43; Wilson, *The Island Race*, 72; Mark Hickford, *Lords of the Land: Indigenous Property Rights and the Jurisprudence of Empire* (New York: Oxford University Press, 2011), 41–42, and Bronwen Douglas, *Science, Voyages, and Encounters in Oceania, 1511–1850* (New York: Palgrave MacMillan, 2014), 111.

[86] See Quilley, *Empire to Nation*, 66–72.

[87] Pocock, "Nature and History, Self and Other," in Calder, Lamb, and Orr, eds., *Voyages and Beaches*, 41.

[88] Paul Turnbull, "Enlightenment Anthropology and the Ancestral Remains of Australian Aboriginal People," in Alex Calder, Jonathan Lamb, and Bridget Orr, eds., *Voyages and Beaches: Pacific Encounters, 1769–1840* (Honolulu: University of Hawai'i Press, 1999), 207.

[89] Ibid., 216–207.

similar but distinct species descended from polygenetic origins. Polygeneticism would mark a sharp break with the Biblical model of humanity's Adamic origins. It would be a profound fissure in human thought, one that carried with it even more profound social implications. But polygenetic theories relied on the evolutionary model set out by Darwin in both *The Origin of the Species* (1859) and *The Descent of Man* (1871).[90] Darwin, it has to be remembered, remained a solidly mono-genetic thinker until his death in 1882.[91] His work, though, would come to be mobilized as evidence for the polygenetic argument, particularly among social Darwinists like his cousin, the eugenicist Francis Galton.[92]

In the late eighteenth century and, indeed, through our entire history of Pitcairn Island, Darwin's theories were, as of yet, unheard of, because, by historical coincidence, Darwin's voyage on the HMS *Beagle* spanned the years 1831 to 1836 – almost exactly the same years that our protagonist, Joshua Hill, spent at Pitcairn Island. As Bronwen Douglas has observed, though, the period from the late eighteenth century onwards did witness the "normalization of a 'science of race'."[93] The Pacific factored into that normalization, particularly as the islands of that great ocean continued to hand up new communities, new populations, and new questions about the origins of humankind.[94] Even from the earliest voyages, European encounters with the people of the Pacific Islands shattered "any fleeting semblance of a system" of racial taxonomy into a "kaleidoscope" of organizational imprecision.[95] To call this a conversation about "race," as we have come to understand the term, would, as Bronwen Douglas has argued, be anachronistic.[96] But, to be certain, the Pacific's anthropological offerings inspired the European scientific mind in an age that witnessed the rise and consolidation of both Linnaean taxonomy and modern racial science.[97] As it would happen, the same ocean that helped Darwin frame *The Origin of the Species* inspired questions about the origin of our species.

In this broader debate about the origins of the human species, Tahiti was marked apart. Forster was particularly attracted to the Tahitians, calling their community "the queen of the tropical societies."[98] The men were tall, Cook reported, "strong limb'd, and well shaped." The Tahitians were "of various Colours," ranging from dark brown to almost white – "almost as fair as Europeans."[99] It was Tahitian women, though, who were the most

[90] Douglas, *Science, Voyages, and Encounters*, 8.
[91] Brantlinger, *Taming the Cannibals*, 132. See also, Douglas, *Science, Voyages, and Encounters*, 108.
[92] Liebersohn, *The Travelers' World*, 285–288.
[93] Douglas, *Science, Voyages, and* Encounters, 8.   [94] Ibid., 15.   [95] Ibid., 61.
[96] Ibid., 65.   [97] Ibid., 104.   [98] Quoted in Howe, *Nature, Culture, and History*, 33.
[99] Cook, *First Voyage Round the World*, 347.

interesting to early European travelers, who were mostly sailors and, therefore, mostly men sailing as homosocial maritime crews. Missionaries would, on the whole, be appalled by Tahitian women's beauty and sexuality. In the missionaries' eyes, these women were lascivious, South Seas Jezebels.[100] The image of Melville's Fayaway, though, was a more common – to say nothing of more appealing – image to the typical sailor.

Tahiti represented what Rod Edmond has called "a golden mean between European over-refinement and South Seas savagery." The island, its people, and its civilization were, as a result, of interest "not only for the sailor but [also for] the philosopher."[101] If ever there had been a living example of Rousseau's "noble savage," many felt they had found it at Tahiti.[102] In a world in which "racial crossing remained an abiding problem," some of the enthusiasm for the mixed-race Pitcairners, then, has to be attributable to the radical racial experiment that was underway at Adamstown.[103] Where else in the world could one find a community whose society – to say nothing of its genetic heritage – was premade as a biological examination of the origins both of the human species and of the genesiological history of human sociology?

The founding mothers at Pitcairn Island were, though, hardly *just* specimens in a global sociology experiment. As we have seen, they were active players in the early history of the island. They planned their pregnancies. They mapped their alliances with the island's founding generation of European mutineers and Polynesian men. Theirs is a history, though, that has always been masked behind the history of John Adams, of Fletcher Christian, and of Captain Bligh. Mauatua, we know, has become a well-known figure, a star of stage and screen, even. But, it is as Mrs. Fletcher Christian more than as a historical actor in her own right that she has stepped into the spotlight. As is the case with Joshua Hill, the twelve women who settled at Pitcairn in 1790 merit more historical attention and contextualization within a broader historical narrative

That these twelve Tahitian women have been largely forgotten in Pitcairn's history says volumes, of course, about both the racism and the sexism that have marked historical narratives from the past.[104] It has

[100] Johnston, *Missionary Writing and Empire*, 141–144.
[101] Edmond, "The Pacific: Tahiti," in Hulme and Youngs, eds., *The Cambridge Companion to Travel Writing*, 143 and 145.
[102] Lummis, *Pacific Paradises*, 119. See also, Brantlinger, *Dark Vanishings*, 9; and Howarth, *Tahiti*, 100.
[103] Damon Ieremia Salesa, *Racial Crossings: Race, Intermarriage, and the Victorian British Empire* (New York: Oxford University Press, 2011), 13.
[104] Silverman, *Pitcairn Island*, 47.

also been confusing to introduce the women to the narrative because so few of them left historical records for us. In some instances, a woman's family tree is her only historical record, though Pitcairn's children, as we will see, have never fully been appreciated for the historical archive that they are. Recording these women's history is complicated by the foreignness of their names to a Western tongue. David Silverman, for instance, has described Teehuteatuaonoa's names as being "mouth-filling" and "vowel-happy."[105] In keeping with the Polynesian practice of taking on multiple names over a lifetime, some of these women had multiple Tahitian names, and it did not make historical record keeping any easier that the mutineers' gave some among the twelve both nicknames and European names.[106] If Joshua Hill is hard to find in the historical archive because of his consistently used and commonplace name, these women slip out of our hands because they are impossible to pin down. Maimiti becomes Mauatua, becomes Isabella, becomes Mainmast. Keeping these stories straight will take some effort on our part, but the effort will be rewarded.

As we saw in Chapter 4, every account of the *Bounty*'s last departure from Tahiti suggests that Fletcher Christian intended to bamboozle at least some of the women he carried with him into the unknown and, eventually, to Pitcairn. Every report of the *Bounty*'s sailing includes the story of one Tahitian woman who dove overboard in an attempt to swim home to Tahiti once she knew that Christian had, effectively, kidnapped her. Some accounts include further reports that other women – possibly as many as six more – were set down from the *Bounty* in a canoe after protesting their captivity.[107] Michael Sturma is right to observe that the coercion that these women experienced has been "repackaged," papered over by the mythology of hypersexualized South Sea libertinism.[108] This coercive violence, though, has to be understood as central to the early history of Pitcairn Island and endemic to the wider history of Pacific exploration and colonization.[109]

The practice of kidnapping South Pacific Islanders, of course, was not limited only to the islands' women, nor was the practice always about access to sex. Perhaps one of the most famous and one of the earliest instances of a European captain taking a hostage came during Captain Cook's first voyage. As Cook readied to sail from Tahiti after a productive stay there, he observed that two of his marines were missing. Reports suggested that the two men had run off with local women.[110]

---

[105] Ibid., xxii.   [106] Wahlroos, *Mutiny and Romance*, 112.
[107] Sturma, *South Sea Maidens*, 40.   [108] Ibid., 23.   [109] Igler, *The Great Ocean*, 94.
[110] Sturma, *South Sea Maidens*, 23. See also George Letsas, "Rights and Duties on Pitcairn Island," in Dawn Oliver, ed., *Justice, Legality, and the Rule of Law: Lessons from the Pitcairn Prosecutions* (New York: Oxford University Press, 2009), 160.

Cook realized that the men were not capable of hiding on the island without the complicity of some of the native Tahitian population, and so he ordered that several islanders, including Purea, whom Cook had dealt with as the Tahitian "queen," be held hostage until the men were found.[111] In other instances, captains picked up Pacific Islanders, most often men, as laborers in a practice that, by the 1860s, would come to be called "blackbirding."[112] We even know that Pitcairn Islanders themselves could be subject to blackbirding, as children's literature from 1829 recounts the sad story of a young Pitcairnese woman who was, by guile and treachery, lured from Pitcairn by a promise of passage to England only to be left "penniless and friendless" in the Hawai'ian chain.[113] One wonders that the female elders at Pitcairn did not warn the young woman of the uncertainty that came with going aboard a ship with a passing European sailor, for that was a lesson that the women of Pitcairn knew only too well.

Since the first moments of European contact in the Pacific, we know that Pacific Islanders boarded and sailed on the visiting Western ships. As John Gascoigne has observed, these Pacific passengers underline "the growing convergence between peoples."[114] Between peoples and, we might add, between histories. European ships. International crews. Global voyages on which "perceptions and practices were *mutually* altered."[115] There is a sense in all of this that the history of the Pacific was coming increasingly to encompass the world, an awareness, to quote Greg Dening, that "each side can only tell its own history by also telling the other's."[116] The Pacific was becoming a global ocean. Pitcairn Island's mixed-race Anglo-Tahitian population offers historians an extraordinary opportunity to think about the planetary confluences at play in this history. At Pitcairn, there was more to the story – much more – than exotic beauty, titillatingly free love, and polygamous *amor*.[117]

It is not to Maimiti, though, that we need to look if we want to get a better historical sense of the history of the twelve Tahitian women who were Pitcairn's founding mothers. Rather, it is to a woman known either by her Tahitian name, Teehuteatuaonoa, or by Jenny, the name the

[111] Sturma, *South Sea Maidens*, 23; and Ward, *British Policy in the South Pacific*, 91.

[112] Samson, *Imperial Benevolence*, 116; and Freeman, *The Pacific*, 140.

[113] Fiske, *Story of Aleck*, 53.

[114] Gascoigne, *Encountering the Pacific*, 326. See also, Kirk, *History of the South Pacific since 1513*, location 689.

[115] Anne Salmon, *The Trial of the Cannibal Dog: The Remarkable Story of Captain Cook's Encounters in the South Seas* (New Haven, CT: Yale University Press, 2003), 10.

[116] Greg Dening, *Beach Crossings: Voyaging across Times, Cultures, and Self* (Philadelphia: University of Pennsylvania Press, 2004), 13.

[117] Wilson, *The Island Race*, 75.

mutineers gave her, that we must turn. From the colonization of Pitcairn in 1790, Jenny seems always to have been the most unsettled among the island's occupants and among the women in particular. The initial arrangements at Pitcairn could not, as Dea Birkett has observed, have been agreeable to the women, nine of whom lived as "wives" with the mutineers. The other three women seem to have been "shared" between the six Polynesian men.[118]

Teehuteatuaonoa's story demonstrates just how completely the women strove to be agents in their own history, despite the constraints that had been placed upon them.[119] Whether or not she sailed from Tahiti as a willing passenger or not, we cannot know for certain. Evidence does suggest that when Fletcher Christian first sailed from Tahiti – on his unsuccessful voyage to colonize Tubuai – Teehuteatuaonoa sailed on the *Bounty* with the colonists. She seems to have been linked to John Adams, who would (at that time) have still been known as Alexander Smith. Later, when the *Bounty* landed at Pitcairn, "Jenny" was clearly connected to Isaac Martin, though we have no evidence to suggest why the group's "living arrangements" might have changed.

We do know, however, that Teehuteatuaonoa was among the first of the Pitcairn settlers to want off the island. Many in the group bristled when Matthew Quintal rashly set the *Bounty* ablaze. The justification was sensible enough. To leave a tall-ship at Bounty Bay was to send up a signal fire that shouted "Come and Find Us Here." The *Bounty* had to be destroyed. But Quintal's actions were unilateral and, perhaps, ill-timed. As they watched the *Bounty* crackle to ash in the rough Pacific waters off Pitcairn Island, few in the group were fully ready to concede that they were to live out the remainder of the lives on this small and isolated island.

Teehuteatuaonoa was not content, though, to accept fate as destiny. For instance, among a community of women who have been described as "healthy reproducers," Teehuteatuaonoa bore no children, despite her romantic connections with two of the *Bounty* mutineers.[120] By the time Mayhew Folger landed at Pitcairn in 1808, the island was already home to twenty-three children. Teehuteatuaonoa's childlessness, then, begins to look a great deal like a regulatory reproductive plan.[121] We know too that Teehuteatuaonoa was not content to be stranded at Pitcairn. Rather, she took it upon herself to construct a boat with which she hoped to escape from the island.[122] Jenny's raft would never be used for its intended purpose.[123] Teehuteatuaonoa stayed on at Pitcairn until

[118] Birkett, *Serpent in Paradise*, 211. See also, Moerenhout, *Travels to the Islands*, 434.
[119] O'Brien, *The Pacific Muse*, 124.   [120] Ibid., 122.   [121] Ibid.   [122] Ibid., 124.
[123] Lummis, *Life and Death in Eden*, 119. See also, Nobbs Papers, SLNSW ML A 2881, 125.

1817, when she was able to secure passage off the island aboard the whale ship *Sultan*, which took her "home" some twenty-seven years after she last sailed from Tahiti.[124]

After her arrival in Tahiti, Teehuteatuaonoa sat down with Peter Dillon, a widely recognized Pacific merchant and explorer from Sydney. The interview she gave to Dillon then appeared in the *Sydney Gazette* on July 17, 1819.[125] It is the only surviving record we have in which one of the *Bounty* women tells her own story, and even it is not directly in her own words.[126] The text of Teehuteatuaonoa's history compels us to reflect on Patty O'Brien's assessment that the *Bounty* mutineers looked on the Tahitian women as commodities, in particular, "sexual commodities."[127] The active grammatical subjects in almost all of Jenny's sentences are "they," meaning the nine mutineers. "They" stripped the *Bounty* of all "they" wanted. "They" debated whether the ship should be burned. "They" divided Pitcairn into parcels; "they" began to build homes and farms.[128]

Still, we do get new details on this history from Teehuteatuaonoa's account. The six Tahitian women who left the *Bounty* after its last departure from Tahiti were, for instance, "ancient."[129] Trevor Lummis has noted that Jenny was the first among the *Bounty*'s passengers to offer an account of what the group had experienced during Fletcher Christian's thousands of miles of wandering in the Pacific between 1789 and 1790.[130] More substantive than this detail, though, is the distinctive angle from which the Tahitian woman is able to reflect on the events at Pitcairn in those earliest years.

At Pitcairn, for instance, we learn that the women worked in cultivating the gardens, a point we observed in the last chapter. Peter Dillon observed that Jenny's "hands are quite hard with work."[131] More importantly, though, we begin to see a better outline of how and, perhaps, why these women regulated their reproductive patterns during the *Bounty*'s voyaging and in the first years at Pitcairn. None of the women, we learn, became pregnant during the months the *Bounty* spent sailing in search of Pitcairn Island.[132] We have already observed that no Tahitian woman

---

[124] Chappell, *Double Ghosts*, 96.
[125] Wahlroos, *Mutiny and Romance*, 260–261; Obeyesekere, *Cannibal Talk*, 193; and Lummis, *Life and Death in Eden*, 140; O'Brien, *The Pacific Muse*, 122.
[126] Silverman, *Pitcairn Island*, xxii.   [127] O'Brien, *The Pacific Muse*, 122.
[128] "Teehuteatuaonoa (or Jenny)," in *Sydney Gazette* (July 17, 1819). Also reported in *Bengal Hurkaru* (October 2, 1826).
[129] "Teehuteatuaonoa (or Jenny)," in *Sydney Gazette* (July 17, 1819). Also reported in *Bengal Hurkaru* (October 2, 1826).
[130] Lummis, *Life and Death in Eden*, 140.   [131] Quoted in Ibid., 171.   [132] Ibid., 165.

ever claimed to have borne a child by any of the six Polynesian men at Pitcairn.[133] Polynesian women, Lummis has written,

> were reputed to have the ability to induce abortion through external massage, and childlessness may well have been a conscious rejection of the fruits of enforced cohabitation, or a determination to remain unencumbered by children and so remain free to seize any opportunity to return to their own island and people.[134]

We hardly need accept Lummis' "may" in all of this. It seems quite certain that the Tahitian women engaged in a sexual politics in which children were the key to empowerment. As Kathleen Wilson has observed, the nature of female sexuality in Polynesia – and in Tahiti in particular – was "destabilizing" to Western social, cultural, and religious norms.[135] That this was the case would be borne out by the missionary impulse to evangelize the Pacific – with a specific eye towards bringing a new sexual order to the region – beginning in the late eighteenth century.[136] The sexual choices that the Tahitian women at Pitcairn seem to have made in these first years framed the early history of the island – its demographics, its social structures, and its political alignments.

As Wilson has observed, the British naval hierarchy was founded on a masculine social order. Anything perceived as unmanliness, in this order, was a threatening possibility, which explains why homosexual sex was one of only eight offenses for which death was a required punishment.[137] The South Pacific offered models that turned this order on its head. At Tahiti and in the Marquesas, for instance, we know of *mahu*, "young boys who were deliberately brought up to dress and behave as women." As adults, *mahu* "openly practiced transvestitism, fellatio, and – perhaps – sodomy."[138] We know too that Polynesians, who always sailed as a heterosocial community of men and women (how else to settle, colonize, and populate a new island at the voyage's end?) were suspicious of European sailors who traveled in impressive ships but as homosocial communities of only men.[139] Captain Cook's astronomer from the *Resolution*, William Wales, recorded that he was pursued by a group of Ni-Vanuatu men "for a purpose I need not mention."[140] In the Pacific, European sailors were, it would seem, in real danger of being "unmanned."

---

[133] Ibid., 90.   [134] Ibid., 118.   [135] Wilson, *The Island Race*, 188–189.
[136] Ibid., 80–81.   [137] Ibid., 177 and 190.   [138] Ibid., 195.
[139] Patrick Vinton Kirch, *A Shark Going Inland Is My Chief: The Island Civilization of Ancient Hawai'i* (Los Angeles: University of California Press, 2012. Kindle Edition), location 306.
[140] Wilson, *The Island Race*, 189.

We need not think of masculinity in the Pacific only in terms of sexuality, though. Bodily integrity was itself at play. Peter Heywood, for example, was quick to observe that he did not get tattooed because *he* wanted to during his voyage as the *Bounty*'s midshipman. "I was tattooed," he wrote in his memoir, "not at my own desire, but for theirs." Thus, in his effort to "acquiesce in any little custom which I though agreeable to them," Heywood gave over his corporeal body to his Pacific Island hosts.[141]

Most of Western political thought – at least that thought coming out of the Enlightenment – hinged on the inviolability of an individual's body. A citizen had a right to his (and the Enlightenment did generally frame the conversation in terms of "him" and "his") mind, his thoughts, and his body. The famous old adage tells us that your right as a free citizen to swing your fist freely ends right where my nose begins. A citizen's freedom can, thus, only be secured when that freedom is balanced against the integrity of an individual body. The female body, of course, has never been an easy fit in this model, for the biological fact of pregnancy calls into question the notion of bodily integrity. Even today, political debates froth over the question of whether a pregnant female body should be spoken of as two civic bodies occupying the same space and form or as a single civic body with unilateral rights regarding the choices made for that body's care.

These debates cannot be disassociated from European cultural, political, social, moral, or religious ideology in the eighteenth and nineteenth centuries. And yet, European sailors entering the Pacific found a world in which none of what was taken as foundational in the West held true. In the South Pacific, as Heywood discovered, tattooing ones body was part of a larger social ritual. His skin did not *belong* to him as it might have in London. My right to tattoo did not end where your skin began. While getting a tattoo might not have destabilized everything Heywood knew about the world, in giving over even his arm or his left breast (where we know Fletcher Christian had been tattooed with a star pattern), Heywood had challenged an epistemology that held his world together.

Polynesian women were lovely. They were seductive. They were tempting. But, when they engaged in sexual activity with European men sailing in the South Seas, they were not merely having sex, or not necessarily so. Take, for instance, the question of what we might call *un*pregnancy. Everywhere one looks, the historical archive is full of accounts of Polynesian women having sex – with Polynesian men, with European

---

[141] Peter Heywood, *Memoir of the Late Captain Peter Heywood* (London, Effingham Wilson, 1832), 83. See also, Wilson, *The Island Race*, 199.

sailors, and with European sailors and Polynesian men at the same time. Where the record is decidedly silent, though, is on the question of pregnant Polynesian women. For all of the records that speak to Polynesian sexuality, a surprising few speak to or describe Polynesian women who are with child.[142] To be certain, European women were able to – and did – abort unwanted pregnancies in the eighteenth and nineteenth centuries.[143] But in Europe, the masculine order of things was buttressed by law and by the intellectual girders of Enlightenment thought itself. Masculinity was written into the code that defined Western citizenship.

In the South Pacific, things were different. Peter Heywood got tattooed. William Wales got pursued. And at Pitcairn, the first generation of female settlers, all of them Polynesian, acted upon a sexual plan that framed the island's history in ways that the island's male population – European and Polynesian alike – seem hardly to have noticed. Or, perhaps it would be more accurate to say of the European men that they hardly commented. For to have commented on the powerful female presence in Pitcairn's early history would have been to admit that Pitcairn Island was founded on a decidedly un-European order and that its first European settlers were unmanned by the Polynesian women they had kidnapped to be their consorts on their South Pacific refuge.

To be sure, the sexual politics at Pitcairn affected both the European and Polynesian men in those first years, if not in the same ways. Denying the six Polynesian men heirs and lineage effectively suffocated a community of men who, as we have seen, had already been denied ownership of land and, with it, any sense of historical belonging in a Polynesian cosmology. For her part, Teehuteatuaonoa left Pitcairn as soon as she could gain passage on the *Sultan* in 1817. The whaler delivered her to the Chiléan coast from which she found passage to the Marquesas Islands before eventually making her way back to Tahiti.[144] Of the twenty-seven *Bounty* passengers to settle at Pitcairn in 1790, Teehuteatuaonoa alone would die off-island.[145] If ever we needed an example of a woman who strategically chose to remain independent (and childless) for the sake of her own geographic mobility, Teehuteatuaonoa is that woman.[146]

[142] O'Brien, *The Pacific Muse*, 192–193. See also, Norma McArthur, "Essays in Multiplication: European Seafarers in Polynesia," in *The Journal of Pacific History* 1 (1966), 91–105.

[143] Lisa Forman Cody, *Birthing the Nation: Sex, Science, and the Conception of Eighteenth-Century Britons* (New York: Oxford University Press, 2005), 46–83.

[144] Topliff, "Pitcairn's Island."   [145] Silverman, *Pitcairn Island*, xxii.

[146] "Teehuteatuaonoa (or Jenny)," in *Sydney Gazette* (July 17, 1819). Also reported in *Bengal Hurkaru* (October 2, 1826). See also, Silverman, *Pitcairn Island*, 111.

In Pitcairnese history, we remember family names that descend from the *Bounty*'s crew manifests – the Christians, the Martins, the Quintals, the Adamses, the Youngs, the McCoys, the Browns, the Mills, and the Williamses. This is the European heritage, the masculine lineage of the Pitcairnese people. Reading the island through its male lines could also be registered as a Polynesian practice. In Polynesian cultures, as elsewhere in the world, women were often "considered to be polluters."[147] Most Polynesian *tapus* suggested as much, as they were a set of religious prohibitions that frequently sequestered women from the broader community. Until the *'Ai Noa*, or breaking of the *Tapu* system by the Hawai'ian *Kuhina Nui* Ka'ahumanu in the reign of her stepson Kamehameha II, women were not even allowed to eat with men.[148] Polynesia was hardly an idyllic matriarchy. But to register Pitcairn's history through the fathers' lines is to miss a critical aspect of Pitcairn Island's story, for this is really not the refuge of the mutineers, as Robert Michael Ballantyne subtitled his novel of 1880. No, the lonely island, as Ballantyne called it, was a feminine island, a woman's world.[149]

Pitcairn Island only had a population because twelve Tahitian women had been taken up – whether coercively or not – from Tahiti into currents of global history that spanned from London to Tahiti, from Tahiti to the Caribbean, and from the Caribbean back to Adamstown. These women – even more than the mutineers – were at the center of a history that circumnavigated the planet, a history so large that only the global ocean – the Pacific – could contain it. Teehuteatuaonoa's story makes it clear: this is a cosmopolitan history. It belongs to these women.

As we have seen previously, the earliest violence at Pitcairn came as a result of the inequitable division of the island's land among its male – European and Tahitian – population. In the eyes of the island's fifteen men, though, the women of the island were as scarce a resource as was property. From the moment of settlement, the imbalance between men and women on the island presented a problem. In her account of life at Pitcairn in these early days, Teehuteatuaonoa describes one of the Tahitian males – Nehou (also known as Niau) – as a "boy." Trevor Lummis has speculated that this description might suggest that Nehou was very young, even prepubescent. We know too that one of the "men" from Tubuai, Tetahiti (also known as Taroamiva) sailed on board the *Bounty* with his uncle Hu (or Oher), so clearly these two men were of different generations; Tetahiti may have been very young as well.[150] Even

[147] Fischer, *A History of the Pacific Islands*, 53 and 55.
[148] Thigpen, *Island Queens and Mission Wives*, 49. See also, Silverman, *Pitcairn Island*, 223.
[149] Ballantyne, *The Lonely Island*.   [150] Lummis, *Life and Death in Eden*, 83.

if we discount Nehou and Tetahiti, there were still thirteen adult males at Pitcairn in 1790 and only twelve adult females.

The island's gender imbalance was thrown further out of alignment when, in October 1793, John Williams' wife, Faahotu (also known as Fasto), died after falling from a rock ledge where she had been gathering bird eggs.[151] Without a wife, Williams grew unsettled at Pitcairn and demanded one of the *Bounty*'s boats so that he could sail for another Pacific island, perhaps one with an indigenous population to live among. When he was denied a boat, Williams made what seemed – to him, at least – the next most reasonable demand. The community had to find him a new female companion. As all of the island's women were attached either (individually) to the other mutineers or (as a group) to the Tahitian men, Williams insisted that a woman be "taken" from the Tahitians and "given" to him.[152]

It will not surprise anyone who has journeyed this far or this deeply into Pitcairn's history to be told that there is some uncertainty about this story. Most of the accounts record the story as we have outlined it above. Williams lost his "wife" to a tragic fall from one of Pitcairn's dangerous cliffs. Teehuteatuaonoa tells us a slightly different story. She records that Williams' wife "died of a disease in her neck, about a year" into the post-settlement history of Pitcairn Island.[153] Some of the accounts from Pitcairn indicate that it was Alexander Smith/John Adams' wife, Obuarei (also known as Puarai) who died while gathering bird eggs and that it was Adams/Smith who demanded a "new woman" from the island's Polynesian men.[154] It is possible, of course, that Adams/Smith scrubbed the story of any mention of his involvement in this episode (as we know he was capable of doing), for it was a turning point in Pitcairnese history – one that sent the island and its people to a very dark place.[155]

Teehuteatuaonoa's version of the story focuses, for what it is worth, on Williams, who, in the wake of his wife's death, drew lots to determine that Toofaiti (also known as Hutia), whom he called Nancy, would be his new companion.[156] Toofaiti, Jenny records, had previously been much attached to Taruro (also known as Talalo), the only Ra'iatean native to have settled at Pitcairn.[157] Threatened with the loss of his companion,

---

[151] Belcher, Private Journal. See also, Peard, *To the Pacific and Arctic with Beechey*, 84.
[152] Barrow, *A Description of Pitcairn's Island*, 261.
[153] "Teehuteatuaonoa (or Jenny)," in *Sydney Gazette* (July 17, 1819). Also reported in *Bengal Hurkaru* (October 2, 1826).
[154] Nobbs Papers, SLNSW ML A 2881, 109–110.
[155] See "Descendants of the *Bounty*'s Crew, on Pitcairn's Island," in *The Calcutta Journal* (July 13, 20, and 25, 1819).
[156] Nobbs Papers, SLNSW ML A 2881, 123.
[157] "Teehuteatuaonoa (or Jenny)," in *Sydney Gazette* (July 17, 1819). Also reported in *Bengal Hurkaru* (October 2, 1826).

Taruro raided Williams' home three days after losing his wife in a lottery and kidnapped Toofaiti, rushing into Pitcairn's mountainous hinterland to hide from the white men who would surely come looking for him.[158]

The male Polynesian community seems to have fractured after Taruro's aggressive resistance to white male rule at Adamstown. Three fled into the hills to be a part of Taruro's insurrection; the rest remained loyal to the political order Fletcher Christian led in the village. In the communal violence that followed, Hu, the leader of the Polynesian faction, was killed. Taruro was executed by the mutineers soon thereafter, and Toofaiti returned to Adamstown to live with John Williams.[159]

Toofaiti's fate may have seemed settled, but the rupture in Pitcairnese society was just beginning. Teehuteatuaonoa records that the Polynesian men began, effectively, raiding into Adamstown to take the agricultural produce that the mutineers were growing on the land that they had denied the Pacific Islanders. Manarii stole a pig from McCoy. Te Moa raided yams out of the community's supplies. According to Teehuteatuaonoa's memory, though, it was the Tahitian women "married" to the white men who reported Te Moa's crimes. Once caught by the white men, the Tahitian man was brutally beaten.[160] This act of arbitrary retaliation, Jenny observed, was the last straw.

The rebellious Polynesian faction determined to murder the white male population at Pitcairn Island. Williams was the first to die. He was shot along the edge of his property. He had been building a fence when he was struck down.[161] The murderous Polynesians next found Fletcher Christian in his garden, and they shot him in the back. He fell face forward into a patch of roots and weeds. George Peard, who sailed as a lieutenant on the *Blossom* with Captain Beechey, reported that the islanders told him Christian's last words in this world were "Oh dear!"[162] According to Jenny's account, the Polynesian men took special care to brutalize Christian's body, as they hatcheted his face until he was unrecognizable. They then moved on, finding William McCoy and John Mills. They were able to surprise Mills, and he was killed. McCoy, though, saw the murderers before they could get to him, and he fled.[163]

Isaac Martin died next. Attacked in his own house, Martin managed to run to William Brown's house before he died, and so Brown was alerted to

[158] "Teehuteatuaonoa (or Jenny)," in *Sydney Gazette* (July 17, 1819). Also reported in *Bengal Hurkaru* (October 2, 1826). See also Nobbs Papers, SLNSW ML A 2881, 125–126.
[159] "Teehuteatuaonoa (or Jenny)," in *Sydney Gazette* (July 17, 1819). Also reported in *Bengal Hurkaru* (October 2, 1826).
[160] Ibid.   [161] Ibid.   [162] Peard, *To the Pacific and Arctic with Beechey*, 87.
[163] "Teehuteatuaonoa (or Jenny)," in *Sydney Gazette* (July 17, 1819). Also reported in *Bengal Hurkaru* (October 2, 1826).

the massacre that was in progress. A second shot killed Martin and alerted Brown to the fact that the enemy was now in his house. For whatever reason, Brown was not shot. Instead, he was clubbed in the head with a rock and left for dead. He would have done well to remain still. When he came to, Brown tried to run, but the rampaging Polynesian men caught him. Brown begged for his life. He wanted to see his wife one more time before he died. He was told that his wish could be granted. The Polynesian men sat him up, as if to let him wait until his wife could be found, and then, as Brown sat quietly, he was shot dead from behind.[164]

Through all of this bloodshed, Alexander Smith had been in his own home. He was found there by the Polynesian men, and he was attacked. Several of his fingers were broken in the violence, and a bullet grazed his neck. He was left wounded, but he would live – nursed to health by several of Pitcairn's Tahitian women. Teehuteatuaonoa is very clear that it was the women who took control over the scene at this point. Smith was wounded and at the mercy of his attackers. He should have died. But, she reports, a group of women had gathered right at the very epicenter of this epochal moment of violence. They threw themselves on Smith's body. They ensured that he would be spared.[165]

What are we to make of this moment of female intervention in what can only be called the Pitcairnese Civil War of 1793? Did the women sense that something dire was about to happen? Perhaps. Teehuteatuaonoa records that even the Polynesian men were turning against one another in all of the violence playing out on the island. Manarii had turned on and killed Te Moa, only to then flee into the hills to hide from the other Polynesian men alongside McCoy and Matthew Quintal. The situation was, clearly, deteriorating – and quickly. Interestingly, it was the Tahitian women, though, who conspired to kill Manarii, for Jenny reports, they went up into the mountains, found McCoy and Quintal, told the two mutineers that Manarii was not to be trusted, and encouraged them to murder the Tahitian, which McCoy and Quintal did that night.[166]

Manarii's death left only two Polynesian men at Pitcairn. According to Jenny, these two went to the hills in search of McCoy and Quintal, fired their guns into what they thought was the mutineers' camp, and returned to report that they had wounded at least one of the white men. The island's women played suspicious, and asked the two Polynesian men to return to the mountain to secure proof of their victories, but, Jenny records, this was all a ruse, as the women were secretly working with McCoy and Quintal to entrap and kill the remaining male South Pacific

[164] Ibid.   [165] Ibid.   [166] Ibid.

Islanders. When McCoy and Quintal failed to accomplish the death of the two men, the women turned to Ned Young and Alexander Smith, who were still residing in Adamstown. The day after making this pact,

about noon, while one of the Otaheite men was sitting outside of the house and the other was laying on his back on the floor, one of the women took a hatchet and cleft the skull of the man on the floor, she had at the same instance called out to Young to fire, which he did and shot the other native dead. Thus ended the whole of the six Tahitians and Tabouaians.[167]

Pitcairn's population, at the end of this war, consisted of eleven Tahitian women and four English mutineers, Alexander Smith, Ned Young, William McCoy, and Matthew Quintal. McCoy, as we have seen, died in a drunken fit – either falling or jumping off of one of Pitcairn's cliffs. Quintal was caught planning the deaths of his two *Bounty* companions and was killed by Young and Smith. Young died of chronic respiratory illness, and Smith went on to become John Adams.

The Pitcairners had once called their island home *fenua maitai*, a Tahitian label meaning "the good or lovely land." Good? Lovely? It would seem not. We have seen that the *Pitcairn Island Register* keeps a rather spotty record of the island's history. An entry for 1793 reads simply, "Massacre of the mutineers by the Tahitians. The Tahiti men all killed, part by jealousies among themselves, the others by the remaining Englishmen."[168] W. K. Hancock records – with a deft understatement – that "these simple entries cover a very wide range of social phenomena."[169] A wide range, indeed. The narrative written into the Pitcairn *Register* is an obvious effort to camouflage the social tensions that wrought the violence of 1793, an obfuscation Teehuteatuaonoa's narrative exposes.

From Teehuteatuaonoa, then, we learn a great deal. Significantly, we learn that Pitcairn's history was, at this crucial moment, driven by the women's intervention. We cannot be sure why, but the Tahitian women decided to plead for Alexander Smith's life. They protected Ned Young. They allied themselves first with McCoy and Quintal and then with Young and Smith. They murdered some of their Tahitian compatriots. Having already chosen to identify their children only as the offspring of the island's European men, the women saw to it that only those men – and, even then, only their hand-selected few – survived to "father" the island's social and political scene. Equally telling, in Teehuteatuaonoa's account, we see that these women were hardly just the seductive, sea-maidens of European sexual fantasies. These were women who

---

[167] Ibid.   [168] Quoted in Hankcock, *Politics in Pitcairn*, 3.   [169] Ibid.

functioned together as a camarilla, and they could be very determined, even violently so, about achieving their ends once they settled on a course of action.

Glynn Christian's book *Mrs. Christian* is a solidly researched, biographical "telling" of his family's founding matriarch. The book is not quite a biography, for Christian has freely woven fabricated dialogue into what seems the most likely historical account of Maimiti's life at Pitcairn Island. In this work of creative nonfiction, Christian is correct to conclude that it was the Pitcairnese women who settled on Alexander Smith/John Adams as their chosen leader for the island. "He was an unpunished mutineer and a reformed drunk, saved only by Pitcairn's women." Adams/Smith "would never have become a leader anywhere else on earth. His influence was largely paternal and over a community of children with no way to judge him."[170] The outside world, as we have seen, would choose to look at Adams/Smith through this same lens. That choice would shape what the outside world came to accept as truth about Pitcairn Island, and it all hinged on the actions of women whose names, with the notable exception of (perhaps) Maimiti, history and popular culture have forgotten.

We should pause here for a moment. We have hit upon a very important juncture in our story. We have recalled from history's attic something that has heretofore been forgotten. Not unknown. Forgotten. This is a moment, then, that begs us to reflect on the very concept of history, of narrative, and of story. Recall that I began by confessing that this was a story I only wished I could tell you in its complete form, though I insisted it was a story that would be well worth the telling. But, what differentiates a story from history?[171] How complete, how accurate, how detailed must a narrative be to cease being a story and to begin being history? Can a history be so inaccurate, so full of forgotten pieces that it ceases to be worthwhile?

Henry Kissinger was famously incredulous about President Richard Nixon's White House taping system. Nixon mistrusted historians. Perhaps he even hated us. The White House tapes, he felt, would narrate his presidency *wie es eigentlich gewesen,* to quote the great nineteenth-century historian Leopold von Ranke.[172] Bob Woodward and Carl Bernstein have described Kissinger's response to the president's

---

[170] Christian, *Mrs. Christian,* 376.

[171] Ann Curthoys and John Docker, *Is History Fiction?* (Sydney: University of New South Wales Press, 2010. Kindle Edition), location 254.

[172] "As it actually happened." Quoted in Peter Novick, *That Noble Dream: The "Objectivity Question" and the American Historical Profession* (New York: Cambridge University Press, 1988), 594.

confidence in the tapes as "contemptuous," for, as Kissinger observed, "To tape eight years of conversation would take eight years to listen to!"[173] History was more than the mere act of recording every word and every detail. Kissinger knew this.

The notion that History can function as a science – or as a social science – suggests a very modern and a very European way of looking at the discipline. Nixon accepted it. History could be captured, recorded, measured – minute by minute. Or, as fate would have it in the president's case, in eighteen-minute intervals. Ann Curthoys and John Docker have observed that the European turn that marked history as a social science – decidedly apart from, say, any literary tradition – can be dated to the 1820s.[174] Interestingly, for our purposes, that is exactly the moment when Joshua Hill began to take interest in the Pacific, in Pitcairn. As Dipesh Chakrabarty has argued, we are wrong to dismiss the value of this turn in historical thinking and in historical inquiry. "European thought" is, Chakrabarty writes, "indispensable . . . in helping us to think through the various life practices that constitute the political and the historical." But, Chakrabarty adds, European thought is not merely "indispensable." Rather, it is "both indispensable and inadequate."[175]

Why inadequate? Here again Curthoys and Docker can help us, for they suggest that the modern, Western tendency to see history and literature in opposition "has left many historians scarcely able to recognize history's inescapably literary qualities."[176] History's "doubleness," they argue, "its divided character from its very beginning means that it is also frequently at war with itself."[177] Has telling the tale of Joshua Hill helped us, at all, to reach a rapprochement? I think the answer is yes, perhaps. To consider Hill's life, we have had to dive deeply into what Curthoys and Docker have described as "the space between history as rigorous scrutiny of sources and history as part of the world of literary forms." This has indeed been a space where we have found "ample room for uncertainty, disagreement, and creativity."[178]

Front and center in this conversation is the question of history's relationship to the truth and to accuracy. Ought a historian offer accurate facts from and about the past? The answer is certainly that a historian not only ought to do so, the historian has an obligation to do so. But, does the

---

[173] Bob Woodward and Carl Bernstein, *The Final Days: The Classic, Behind-the-Scenes Account of Richard Nixon's Dramatic Last Days in the White House* (New York, Simon & Schuster, 1976), 199.

[174] Curthoys and Docker, *Is History Fiction?*, location 1314.

[175] Dipesh Chakrabarty, *Provincializing Europe: Postcolonial Thought and Historical Difference* (Princeton: Princeton University Press, 2000), 6.

[176] Curthoys and Docker, *Is History Fiction?*, location 254.   [177] Ibid., location 264.

[178] Ibid., location 260.

accurate conveyance of facts from the past aggregate to the truth? That is a different question. As with the debates about the life, the voyages, and the death of Captain Cook, the past that we have worked through here has provoked "reflection about the nature of history, and the impartiality of its explanation."[179] Hill's story has shown us that history, more generally, is a process of narrative building, of shaping an account. Historians are editors.[180] History is as much about what we choose to forget as it is about what we decide to remember. Both the forgetting and the remembering, though, are *active* choices in the process. In our story, there is much about Pitcairn Island – and about its founding mothers in particular – that was simply forgotten. Not erased. Not even lost. These were details that were simply set to the side as earlier chroniclers told the story – made their choices about how to tell the tale – and that got left behind as the story took on a life of its own. Why? As we have observed, both racism and sexism play their obvious parts in this process of historical amnesia.

Critical, too, is the European understanding of Tahiti – and of its women in particular. Because the European image of Tahitian women was of noble savages with a libidinous sexual appetite, it was these women's sexual alliances with the male settlers – both European and Polynesian – that came to matter more than any role the women played in Pitcairn's early politics.[181] Only in the eyes of Teehuteatuaonoa do we find an early version of this history that appreciates how fully sex and politics were one in the same. For others, the two were always distinct categories. Take, for instance, some exemplary nineteenth-century accounts of life at Pitcairn. Captain Bruce of the *Imogene* would observe in 1838 that the Tahitian women had been good mates to the *Bounty* mutineers. These women, he wrote, "domesticated" their mutinous, British husbands.[182] Even in 1838, an astonishing forty-eight years after these women landed at Bounty Bay, the two remaining Tahitian women – Maimiti and Teraura (also known as Susanah by her "husband" Ned Young) – were still, Bruce wrote, "strong and healthy-looking."[183] Frederick Debell Bennett had met these two women while sailing aboard the whale ship *Tuscan* under Captain Stavers in 1833. Both were still beautiful.[184] That was to be expected of Tahitian women, after all.

---

[179] Salmon, *The Trial of the Cannibal Dog*, xix. See also Dening, *Beach Crossings*, 234.

[180] Robert Borofsky, "An Invitation," in Borofsky, ed., *Remembrance of Pacific Pasts*, 26–28; Klaus Neumann, "Starting from Trash," in Borofsky, ed., *Remembrance of Pacific Pasts*, 75; Greg Dening, *The Death of William Gooch: A History's Anthropology* (Honolulu: University of Hawai'i Press, 1995), 13; and Howe, *Where the Waves Fall*, xii and 352.

[181] Sturma, *South Sea Maidens*, 23.

[182] Bruce, Letter to Lady Troubridge (January 2, 1838).

[183] Bruce, Remark Books of the *Conway* and the *Imogene*, 301.

[184] Narrative, Remarks, Statistics, Extracts from the HMS *Thunder*.

Though aged, Maimiti's "mental and bodily powers are yet active." She recalled Captain Cook and fascinated the *Tuscan*'s sailors with minor details from the famed navigators visits to Tahiti.[185] Susanah was younger than Maimiti, and she was "short and stout." Still, Bennett was enamored enough to be "flattered" when she insisted that he accept as her gift "a lock of her dark and curling hair, flowing profusely over her shoulders, and as yet but little frosted by the winter of life."[186]

Bennett knew that Pitcairn's Tahitian women had been part of a violent story. Teraura had a "reputation," he noted, "of having played a conspicuous part when the [island's men] were massacred."[187] Not forgotten, you see. Just set aside. Teraura was a murderess, but Bennett played coquettish games with her, asked for a span of her hand-beaten tappa cloth and accepted a lock of her luxuriant hair. The murders? The death? The violence? None of that fit the story.

Pitcairn Island, then, was, to borrow from David Silverman's astute assessment, "an unplanned experiment in the crossbreeding of two disparate races, in cross-culturation."[188] The culture the experiment yielded was to be celebrated. English fathers. Tahitian mothers. Christian morality. Polynesian primitivism. The results were an island of people who were all "modest." "perfectly chaste," and "free from all kinds of debauchery." As Lieutenant Olebar of the *Seringapatam* would observe, something about the commingling had "effected a considerable alteration in a people so proverbially sensual and initiated."[189] The Pitcairners had given up the *laissez-aller* ways of Polynesian life and were, now, hardworking.[190] The children exhibited a preternatural "thirst after scriptural knowledge."[191] The islanders all spoke "a very nautical Tahitian-accented English."[192] They respected Adams' kind and gentle paternalism.[193]

Captain Pipon's description of Thursday October Christian might help us here – focusing our attention not on how outsiders saw the community, but rather on how they saw one specific Pitcairner. Thursday October Christian was, of course, of profound interest to the outside world. Everyone would have loved to have been able to meet and question his father, Fletcher. But, by the time Pipon met Thursday October in 1814, Fletcher Christian had been dead some twenty-one years. Thursday October, Pipon recollected,

[185] Bennett, *Narrative of a Whaling Voyage*, 33.   [186] Ibid.   [187] Ibid.
[188] Silverman, *Pitcairn Island*, xiv and 217–218.
[189] Orlebar, *A Midshipman's Journal*, 32.   [190] Pitcairn Extracts, SLNSW F999.7/9, 10.
[191] Ibid., 375.   [192] Scarr, *A History of the Pacific Islands*, 67.
[193] Hancock, *Politics in Pitcairn*, 5.

was then, when we saw him, about 25 years of age, a tall fine young man, about 6 feet high, dark black hair, a countenance extremely open & interesting; as he wears no cloathes, except a piece of cloth round his loins, a straw hat ornamented with black cocks feathers & occasionally a pancho nearly similar to that worn by the Spaniards in South America tho smaller, he is of course of a brown cast, not however with that mixture of red, so disgusting in the wild Indians. With a great share of good humour, & a disposition & willingness to oblige, we were very glad to trace in his benevolent countenance, all the features of an honest English face . . .[194]

The young man "spoke English in a manner vastly pleasing." He was, Pipon concluded, an "interesting personage" who inspired "feelings of tenderness and compassion."[195]

Clearly, Captain Pipon was not immune to the racial biases of his day. Red skin he found "disgusting."[196] Faced, though, with this mixed-race young Pitcairner, Pipon found in Thursday October admirable reflections of both his English *and* his Tahitian heritage. Indeed, there is reason to believe that the best qualities of each of these two lineages resonated with one another to produce even better offspring than might have been hoped for given Thursday's parentage.[197] In general, the island's children were "stout and shrewd little urchins, familiar and confident, but at the same time well behaved."[198] Pitcairn's young women were the children of lusty mutineers, Captain Pipon conceded, but their mothers were from Tahiti, so the island's daughters were much more modest than the young girls you might meet with, say, in the Marquesas.[199] When Walter Brodie passed at Pitcairn in 1850, he found that the islander's women did not dance, as they were "too modest and shy" to do more than join in "innocent games."[200] Frederick Bennett, again, seems to have put it best. "In person, intellect, and habits," he wrote, "these islanders form an interesting link between the civilized European and the unsophisticated Polynesian nations. They are a tall and robust people, and their features, though far from handsome, display many European traits."[201]

H. B. Willis, a lieutenant with the Royal Navy, toured Pitcairn Island in 1814 while on a Pacific crossing with Captains Staines and Pipon. In Willis' papers, he has left us one large page of text describing what he saw on the island. Willis' lengthy paragraph is largely unexceptional. It would not merit any of our time were it not that Willis illustrated the header of his page with a lively watercolor sketch of Pitcairn.

---

[194] Pipon, *An Interesting Account.*   [195] Ibid.   [196] Belcher, Private Journal.
[197] Lummis, *Life and Death in Eden*, 182.
[198] Bennett, *Narrative of a Whaling Voyage*, 35.   [199] Pipon, *An Interesting Account.*
[200] Lummis, *Life and Death in Eden*, 174.
[201] Bennett, *Narrative of a Whaling Voyage*, 33–34.

Figure 8 H. B. Willis, *Pitcairn's Island in the Southern Ocean*, Te Puna, Turnbull Collection, qMS-2259. Published by permission of the Alexander Turnbull Library, Willington, New Zealand.

Willis' painting shows us a South Pacific Eden, an island graced with tropical apricity and "blessed with innocence, Harmony and peace." This island is home to a community that is "pure, comfortable, happy, and independent."[202] Most interesting, though, is that Willis has appended two additional images, one on each side of his painting of the island. To the observer's left are two women. To the right, a single man. These are, Willis labels them, the "Female Natives" and the "Male Natives" of Pitcairn Island. These figures need to be viewed very closely, for they tell us a great deal about what Willis saw at Pitcairn. The young man to the right of the image is clad only in a wrap around his middle. He is decent, if almost naked. His posture suggests he is engaged in reaching for something, or (perhaps) in a dance of some sort. Could this be Thursday October Christian? Perhaps, though, the lad lacks the dandyish feathered hat that Pipon would describe. Thursday October Christian or not, this man is strong and well-built, a handsome young man with a cordate face. Neither obviously British nor Tahitian. Indeed, he could be called classically Greco-Roman more than anything else.

To the left of the island, we see two equally classical figures. These are Pitcairn's women. Unlike the young man, neither appears to be dancing. In fact, one has her back fully and modestly turned to us, and we see the other woman only in profile. Both have long, black, curly hair, but neither would be identifiable as fully or even half Tahitian from this sketch. That they both wear classically draped togas renders the two Pitcairners even less South Pacific in appearance. It almost goes without noting that these three figures look nothing like the images that William Smyth gave us in

[202] Lieutenant H. W. Willis, Pitcairn's Island in the Southern Ocean, Te Puna, Turnbull Collection, qMS-2259.

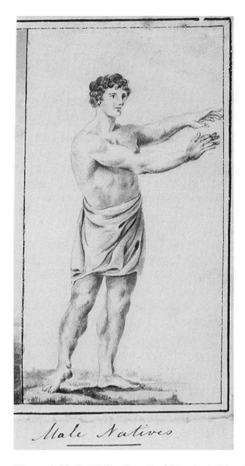

Figure 9 H. B. Willis, Detail of *Pitcairn's Island in the Southern Ocean*, Te Puna, Turnbull Collection, qMS-2259. Published by permission of the Alexander Turnbull Library, Willington, New Zealand.

the previous chapter. These, I might argue, are figures that Willis saw less in front of him than he did in his own mind's eye.

What might we make of Willis' beautiful, if very odd, set of sketches? Why, we have to wonder, did he draw representations that were so obviously *not* realistic? The man had some artistic talent, after all. The painting of the island is romantic and moving. Romantic. Therein, I might suggest, is the key. Romance was at the heart of these first encounters at Pitcairn. Romance told of a noble island called Tahiti, a place that was home to the South Pacific's best possible, if still

Female Natives.

Figure 10 H. B. Willis, Detail of *Pitcairn's Island in the Southern Ocean*, Te Puna, Turnbull Collection, qMS-2259. Published by permission of the Alexander Turnbull Library, Willington, New Zealand.

historically and racially primitive people. Pitcairn's mothers came from that island. They had built a world on this remote (and, until Willis' day, largely lost) island with a crew of revolutionary mutineers on a swashbuckling journey. Their story was the stuff of legend. It was its own sort of mythology in which Pitcairn became a Pacific Olympus and the Pitcairners that ocean's titans.

Having established, then, through verbal *and* visual evidence that visitors to Pitcairn Island in the first half of the nineteenth century *saw* an island, a people, and a history that were much different from any reality and that they promulgated that vision back to Europe where it was eagerly received and widely disseminated, we come to appreciate yet again why somebody with an interest in the Pacific – a man like Joshua Hill – might perseverate on this tiny little place. This was a community that remained "inscrutable" despite having been talked about, written about, and visited, and the inscrutability was, we can now appreciate, by design.[203] These were a special people. They were "custom made," as it were, for a special mission in the wider Pacific Ocean. They had to be tended with great care.[204] And, careful tending is exactly what this community was not getting. Before he settled down in marriage with Dolly Young, John Buffett, for instance, seduced Mary Christian, Thursday October's eldest daughter.[205]

Captain Bruce *could* have been quoting Joshua Hill as easily as he *was* removing Hill when he observed that "Alas! Wherever Englishmen go, there [sic] profligacy and depravity are to be found in their train."[206] Like Hill, Bruce was a persistent critic when it came to these three men. The arrival, Bruce observed, of Buffet, Nobbs, and Evans at Pitcairn had damaged the community at Adamstown. The three had introduced something from the outside, something bad, something English. For, the people of Pitcairn were not English. They were not Tahitian. They were, as we saw in Chapter 2, "a people set apart."[207]

By the 1850s, racial science was predictable on the historical landscape. So too were its calamitous social, political, cultural, and moral implications. But, as Bronwen Douglas has argued, despite these "dire prognostications, much of Oceania remained Indigenous space" well into the middle years of the nineteenth century.[208] The question of indigeneity at Pitcairn is, of course, distinct from the same question at other Pacific Islands. But, it was not as distinct as we might imagine – certainly not to Joshua Hill. The island was home to a unique ethnic community – perhaps even a unique racial one. Outsiders imperiled Pitcairn Island and its people; they were an invasive species.

In Joshua Hill's mind, then, the arrival of Evans, Buffet, and Nobbs was a pressing and acute problem. These men arrived tenebrously at the small island. Their stories had all the scandalous markings of a whaler or beachcomber. They boded nothing but ill. And, worse still, unlike whalers who might stop at an island for a few drinks and a seaside hochle with a fabled South Sea nymph, Nobbs, Evans, and Buffett were gannets.

---

[203] Young, *Mutiny's* Bounty, 310.   [204] Nobbs, *George Hunn Nobbs*, 25.
[205] Silverman, *Pitcairn Island*, 162.
[206] Bruce, Letter to Lady Troubridge (January 2, 1838).
[207] *The Jerusalem Bible*, 1 Peter 2:9–10.
[208] Douglas, *Science, Voyages, and Encounters*, 292.

They wanted more. They were intent on settling at Pitcairn – owning it, controlling it.[209] Lieutenant Belcher of the *Blossom* would note that Evans, who, according to Belcher, had no friends in England, was lazy at Pitcairn. "He has not turned out as quite a character as they would have wished." Even though he had only been at Pitcairn a couple of years by the time Belcher met him, Evans had already been subject to the community's collective approbation on several occasions. He was, Belcher concluded, "a great nuisance." It was only to be hoped that marriage into the Adams family might "perhaps reform him."[210]

For their parts, Nobbs and Buffett had done little more than introduce factionalism to the island. These men were a problem. They were, to quote Joshua Hill, "foreigners."[211] We have spent time reflecting on Joshua Hill's word choice earlier. Foreigner. He too was a "foreigner" at Pitcairn, no? Indeed, he was. But, as we have seen, Hill lived in a different sort of outsider's relationship with the community at Adamstown than did Evans, Buffet, and Nobbs. Even in the 1840s, observers of the Pitcairnese community would view these three men as "intruders" at the island.[212] Even the idea that familial inbreeding – which always surfaces in any discussion of the small and, more importantly, isolated Pitcairn Island – posed less of a threat to these people than did the outlanders. As one observer noted, "the popular idea, that families intermarrying causes a degeneration of the Human species, here received a contradiction as finer children I never saw."[213]

The three earliest outsiders to settle at Pitcairn wanted to marry into the island's families, and, though their DNA might have augmented the small community's biodiversity, there was still much to worry about. Sexual relations with passing sailors was not something that eighteenth- and nineteenth-century Pacific Islanders celebrated as a tool for genetic diversification. Rather, in many instances, sexual contact with the outside world had meant the spread of venereal diseases on Pacific islands, diseases that brought with them the pain of "infertility, infant mortality, and brutal assaults on immune systems," to say nothing of death.[214] So common was the link between passing Euro-American sailors and sexually transmitted disease that Pacific Islanders labeled any passing argosy as a "disease boat."[215] Hill, though, promised something different.

---

[209] Amelia Rosalind Young, Letter to Captain and Mrs. Gibbons (April 15, 1882), in Young, Letters to Captain and Mrs. Gibbons, 6.

[210] Belcher, Private Journal.   [211] Brodie, *Pitcairn's Island and the Islanders*, 183.

[212] Woolridge, Letter to an Unidentified Recipient (June 18, 1849).

[213] Ibid. See also, Young, *The Mutiny of the* Bounty, 231.

[214] Igler, *The Great Ocean*, 45. See also, Crosby, *Ecological Imperialism*, 198–199.

[215] Igler, *The Great Ocean*, 65.

He did not marry into the Pitcairnese storyline. That difference, set against this narrative of Pitcairn's story as Teehuteatuaonoa would have us know it, is crucial to our fully understanding what Hill hoped to accomplish at Pitcairn vis-à-vis the island's special place in the Pacific's broader history.

Let us recall that Hill's most focused policy initiative – at least as it related to the dynastic history of Pitcairn Island – was to pass a law that forbade those not associated with the *Bounty* saga from owning land at Pitcairn. Furthermore, the law included a signed pledge that was distributed to all of the islanders – the "genuine natives," that is – who were seven years old and older in which they promised never "to intermarry with the foreigners."[216] Hill's law, as we have seen, disconnected Nobbs, Buffet, Evans, and the eight children the men had already fathered in the years before Hill arrived on the island not only from Pitcairn the place but also from the Pitcairnese community more generally. And, as we have seen, Hill was no milksop. He was willing to enforce these edicts at gunpoint if necessary.[217]

Joshua Hill's land reallocation schemes at Pitcairn, then, synthesized two currents that have to be central to any history of a South Pacific island in the middle years of the nineteenth century. As we saw in the previous chapter, Hill seems to have been alert to the ecological limitations of a small island; he understood Pitcairn's paradisical lifestyle to be a delicate harmony. His administrative reforms on the island had the potential to render the precarious way of life that had developed at Adamstown more sustainable in the long term, if not, admittedly, forever. Hill's reforms also demonstrated his familiarity with the racial or ethnic history of this small island and its unique people. Seizing property from Evans, Nobbs, and Buffett was just the beginning here. It was the promise that none of the "genuine" Pitcairners would marry among those men's offspring that really secured the Pitcairnese lineage, for it was that promise that isolated the three men whom Hill saw as the island's royal road to ruin.

We might read Hill's inducements towards Rachel Adams in a similar light. Adams, we will remember, married John Evans. Soon after Hill arrived, he approached Rachel Adams about leaving Evans. In his complaints about Hill's behavior, even Evans admitted that Hill had not had sexual designs on John Adams' daughter. Rather, Hill merely hoped to drive a wedge between the young couple, to get Adams away from Evans.[218] Adams and Evans had two children together when Hill arrived

---

[216] Belcher, *The Mutineers of the* Bounty, 199.   [217] Shapiro, *The Pitcairn Islanders*, 83.
[218] Ibid., 87.

at Pitcairn. Before Hill was removed, they would have three more, making five children in all. They would have a sixth the year after Hill left the island. Tony Ballantyne and Antoinette Burton have argued intimacy was often "a crucial instrument of colonization."[219] At Pitcairn, though, Joshua Hill saw the politics of intimacy as being as much about who partnered with whom as it was about who got put to the side. If the three "foreigners" had arrived in hopes of pouncing on and preying upon Pitcairn's indigenous people, Hill was ready to exungulate the tiger.

Though Rachel Adams defied Hill early on, we know that the Evans, Buffet, and Nobbs families were eventually broken apart when the three outlanders were driven from Pitcairn by the end of Hill's first year in Adamstown.[220] Hill was determined about his program of limiting how much access these ugsome foreigners had to the Pitcairnese people. Indeed, the idea that Joshua Hill might break apart a family seems to have been almost universally terrifying at Pitcairn. In July 1834, George Adams reported to John White, the British Consul at Tahiti, as the amanuensis for a large group of Pitcairners. Even some Pitcairnese wives whose husbands supported Hill, Adams reported, feared that the island's new administrator would divide their families as he had done to the Evans, Buffet, and Nobbs households.[221] Understanding what it meant to be a Pitcairner – in Hill's mind and in the minds of others like H. B. Willis – we can now see that the Evans/Adams children were not truly Pitcairners, and that, at least in Joshua Hill's mind, was a problem that had to be contained, even if it could not be repaired.

Of course, we know that Hill was not able to isolate Pitcairn's genetic stock to that select community of Anglo-Tahitians who were direct heirs to the *Bounty* settlement. As he left the island with Captain Bruce on the HMS *Imogene*, Hill had to have choked, as we observed earlier, to see that John Evans, John Buffet, and George Hunn Nobbs remained behind him on the island. The three outlanders had not only returned, they had been reunited with their families. After Hill's removal, Evans would, as we have seen, have one more child – for a total of six – with Rachel Adams. John Buffett and Dolly Young would have five children together. George Hunn Nobbs and Sarah Christian's dozen children could have populated a small island of their own. Three outlanders. Twenty-three children!

[219] Tony Ballantyne and Antoinette Burton, "Introduction: The Politics of Intimacy in an Age of Empire," in Tony Ballantyne and Antoinette Burton, eds., *Moving Subjects: Gender, Mobility, and Intimacy in the Age of Global Empire* (Chicago: University of Chicago Press, 2009), 6.

[220] Stallworth, Letter to Mr. Ellis (April 21, 1834).

[221] Adams, Letter to John White (July 14, 1834).

The social consequences for Pitcairn's genetic isolation would be insurmountable.

Not all of the Buffet, Evans, and Nobbs lines remained at Pitcairn, as we now know. All of the Pitcairners moved to Norfolk in 1856, and only some of the community's families returned to Pitcairn in the years that followed. That the Warrens and other families like them entered into the Pitcairn story at Norfolk in the 1860s would have troubled Hill, though the problem itself was nothing new. Evolution, changing bloodlines, genetic biodiversity: These, Joshua Hill had predicted, would ruin the island. He never used those words. He could not have. Science had yet to articulate or popularize such concepts. Hill was at Pitcairn decades before Charles Darwin published the scientific insights he made during his visitation to the Galápagos, that harsh and primitive archipelago that would help the world sort its way into modernity. But, like Darwin at the Galápagos, Hill saw something happening at Pitcairn.

The notion that social change came through biology was deeply entrenched in his thoughts on and his administrative policies at Pitcairn Island. Hill hoped to contain that change, but, as Darwin would demonstrate, natural selection will have its way. Like Darwin's Galápagos finches, both the Norfolk Islanders and Pitcairners continue to be identified with Pitcairn or, at least, with the *Bounty* saga even to this day. They live thousands of miles apart on two distinct islands, but they are all still one people – the Pitcairners. Still finches, just with different beaks.[222] That would not have been enough for Joshua W. Hill.

---

[222] Rececca Tansley, *Big Pacific* (Princeton, NY: Princeton University Press, 2017), 120–121. See also, J. R. McNeill, "Of Rats and Men: A Synoptic Environmental History of the Island Pacific," in *Journal of World History* 5:2 (Fall, 1994), 301–302; and Henry Nicholls, *The Galápagos: A Natural History* (New York: Basic Books, 2014. Kindle Edition), Chapter 6.

7   Colonization

> Populous and independent – warrens of men, ruled over with some
> rustic pomp – such was the first and still the recurring impression of
> these tiny islands.
>
> Robert Louis Stevenson, *In the South Seas* (1896)[1]

The SS *Ancon*'s passage as the first vessel to officially cross the
Panamanian isthmus through the newly opened Panama Canal
on August 15, 1914 was a historical earthquake for the Chiléan city of
Valparaíso, a shift in the sands as severe the actual earthquake in 1906
that killed thousands of Valparaísians. After having traversed the Strait of
Magellan at Tierra del Fuego, sailors had once been charmed by
Valparaíso. It was a welcoming and cosmopolitan port of call after the
hard passage from the Atlantic to the Pacific Ocean. Valpaŕiso was the
queen city of the Spanish Lake. People called it "Little San Francisco"
and "The Jewel of the Pacific."[2] The Panama Canal, though, rendered
Valparaíso irrelevant.

The Panama Canal opened seventy-six years after Joshua Hill was
banished from Pitcairn Island and landed in exile at Valparaíso.
The city was still booming when he arrived there. A decade earlier,
Valparaíso was where the Chiléan constitutional convention had met to
draft the Constitution of the Republic of Chilé in 1828. The city's principal newspaper, *El Mercurio de Valparaíso*, established in 1827, was already
widely read and on its way to becoming, in the twenty-first century, the
world's oldest circulating Spanish language newspaper.[3] Like Rome in
Italy, Valparaíso, Chilé blankets itself across a handful of steep hillsides.

---

[1] Stevenson, *In the South Seas*, 245.
[2] Buschmann, Slack, and Tueller, *Navigating the Spanish Lake*, 3 and 6. See also, Elizabeth
Quay Hutchinson, Thomas Miller Klubock, Nara B. Milanich, and Peter Winn, eds.,
The Chilé Reader: History, Culture, Politics (Durham, NC: Duke University Press, 2014.
Kindle Edition), location 2563; and John L. Rector, *The History of Chilé* (New York:
Palgrave MacMillan, 2003), 127.
[3] Simon Collier and William F. Sater, *A History of Chilé, 1808–2002* (New York: Cambridge
University Press, 2004. Kindle Edition), locations 905 and 1517.

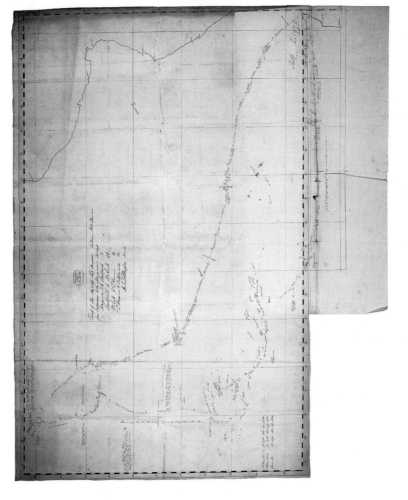

Figure 11 Captain William Henry Bruce, R.N., *Track Chart of the HMS* Imogene's *Voyage across the Pacific, c. 1840.* UKHO L1972. Published by permission of the United Kingdom Hydrographic Office through the National Archives, Kew.

The result is a picturesque city, a distinct cityscape, and a labyrinthine web of small stone streets that run uphill and downhill past and between the city's gracious public buildings as well as its almost magically, multi-colored housing blocks. Unlike Rome, though, which gazes out over the Tyrrhenian Sea, Valparaíso's vista is the global ocean. It might be hard to imagine for those visiting today, but nineteenth-century Valparaíso was a global hub, a major port city, and a metropolitan home to European immigrants who could have lived anywhere in the world.[4]

We do not know what Joshua Hill thought of Valparaíso when Captain Henry Bruce landed him there on January 2, 1838.[5] The circumstances of his arrival at Valpariso in 1838 were certainly novel, for we know that Hill arrived in South America a defeated man. His Pitcairnese dreams, indeed his vision for a broader British Pacific, had collapsed around him at Adamstown. Six years after his arrival at Pitcairn, and almost a decade after he had first set out on his "philan-thropic tour among the islands of the Pacific," Joshua Hill's avowed enemies were living at Adamstown with their families. They were having more children. They were leaders within the Pitcairnese community.[6] Hill, meanwhile, was back on the mainland, seemingly without a friend on the flat side of the grave. His had been a peripeteia of classical proportions.

The circumstances surrounding Hill's removal from Pitcairn are murky at best. Nobody who has spent time with this story will be surprised, of course. Many, over the years, have reported that Captain Bruce was sent to Pitcairn as a primary goal, that he had specific orders to remove Joshua Hill from Adamstown. We know, though, that Bruce's mission across the Pacific was much wider than that.[7] Pitcairn was still not – indeed, it never was – the central and sole focus of London's colonial attention. The chart of the HMS *Imogene*'s Pacific mission itself tells us how much Pitcairn matters. Bruce set out from Valparaíso in 1836, and his first target was the Hawai'ian Islands in the North Pacific. Having sailed above and through that archipelago, the *Imogene* set a course southward on what the Hawai'ians called *Ke Ala ki Kahiki*, or "the Way to Tahiti," where Bruce would give George Pritchard the papers cre-dentialing him as the British consul to Queen Pomare IV's court.[8]

---

[4] Bach, *The Australia Station*, 3. See also, Collier and Sater, *A History of Chile*, location 767.

[5] Journal of the Proceedings of the HMS *Imogene*, July 6, 1831–December 6, 1839, TNA ADM 51/3259. See also, *Imogene* Log Books from 1836–1839, TNA ADM 53/697.

[6] Hill, Letter to Lord Palmerston (January 13, 1832).

[7] Nicholson, *The Pitcairners*, 149.   [8] Davis, *Island Boy*, 67.

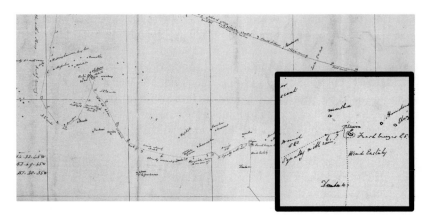

Figure 12 Captain William Henry Bruce, R.N., Detail of *Track Chart of the HMS* Imogene*'s Voyage across the Pacific, c. 1840*. UKHO L1972. Published by permission of the United Kingdom Hydrographic Office through the National Archives, Kew.

From Tahiti, Bruce looped south again with Pitcairn as his heading and Joshua Hill on his agenda.[9]

For those of us who have spent so much time in search of Joshua Hill, Captain Bruce has left us with a rather thin description of what he found at Pitcairn. Mr. Hill, he wrote in one dispatch, "had made himself very obnoxious to the natives, having assumed power and control over them."[10] Fair enough. On the other hand, Bruce also noted that Hill's conduct and rule at Pitcairn had been "marked by the strictest moral integrity."[11] Far harsher, as we have seen, was Bruce's assessment of Evans, Nobbs, and Buffett: "But for the fact that [these] three strangers have misconducted themselves, the little community of natives forms a social circle not to be met with elsewhere on the face of the globe." Like Hill, Bruce admonished the three as "delinquent foreigners."[12] Bruce might well have been channeling Hill when he wrote that vice and crime were

unknown among the children of these Mutineers until the settlement of the 3 English sailors I have mentioned on the island; and they are altogether without excuse, but the clove foot is among them, and they have set iniquity stalking abroad in the very worst shapes and the most baneful to society that can instigate

---

[9] Chart of the Voyage of the HMS *Imogene*, 1836–1839. RHO L1972. See also Captain W. H. Bruce, Letters, NMM TRO 120/3.

[10] Quoted in Kirk, *Pitcairn Island*, 87.   [11] Ibid.

[12] Bruce, Extract from a Letter to Lady Troubridge (January 17, 1838).

it, I do not speak from <u>hearsay</u> but from knowledge of the vices of these men, for which I called them to account, and they vowed and promised amendment, acknowledging with apparent contrition, how guilty they had been, but such pests should not be suffered to remain in a comparatively innocent and, except by them, uncontaminated community and I hope that from my representation the 3 may be withdrawn from the island, where the state of society is not all calculated for the residence of persons so devoid of moral firmness and principles.[13]

Bruce, then, seems to have resettled on the notion that Pitcairn was a Pacific paradise. Bruce often recalled later in his life that he "should like to have passed some days on shore with the natives of this most interesting Christian Community, but my time was too limited for that."[14] Bruce had a job to do – to remove Joshua Hill.

Perhaps the most remarkable thing about Bruce's reflections on his visit to Pitcairn are to be found in the notes he made about Joshua Hill, notes that were limited to the simple observation that he had brought Hill "away at his own request."[15] The novelist James Norman Hall (who, with Charles Nordhoff, would coauthor the now famous *Bounty* trilogy of novels that have captivated readers' imaginations since the first novel was published in 1932) once observed that Hill was "the Mussolini of Pitcairn," but Bruce and his crew seem to have experienced a different man entirely.[16] John C. Dalrymple Hay, later to be knighted and elevated to the rank of Admiral in the Royal Navy, sailed with Bruce aboard the *Imogene* as a midshipman. Later in his career, Dalrymple Hay reflected back on his voyage to Pitcairn, noting that "we deported from the island a gentlemen, a member of an English University, who, having spent all his money, had obtained a passage in an American whaler and landed about two years before." Here again, we see the hugger-mugger about Hill's arrival at Pitcairn – this time on board an American whale ship circa 1834 – as well as his willingness to tell tales about himself – this time an unsubstantiated claim to belong to the Oxbridge elite.[17]

Captain Bruce seems to have talked at some length with Hill about the plans that the now-deposed dictator had had for Pitcairn Island, and the captain seems to have approved of Hill's ambitious endeavor. "Mr. Hill's absence will I think be of benefit to the Community," Bruce recollected.

[13] Bruce, Letter to Lady Troubridge (January 2, 1838).

[14] Bruce, Extract from a Letter to Lady Troubridge (January 17, 1838). See also Captain H. W. Bruce, Record of the Voyage of the HMS *Imogene*, TNA FO 16/34; and Captain H. W. Bruce, Letter to Viscount Troubridge (Valparaíso: March 21, 1838), NMM TRO 119/2(2).

[15] Quoted in Kirk, *Pitcairn Island*, 87. See also, Nicholson, *The Pitcairners*, 152.

[16] Nordhoff and Hall, *The Bounty Trilogy*. See also, Hall, *The Tales of a Shipwreck*, 89.

[17] Admiral Sir John C. Dalrymple Hay, *Lines from My Log-Book* (Edinburgh: David Douglas, 1898), 66–67.

"Tho' his object was to do good, he does not seem to have gone judiciously to work about it."[18] Hay confessed that Hill "had persuaded the islanders to maintain him and appoint him their schoolmaster, but he was not well calculated for the post, and his wants were found to be a heavy tax upon the inhabitants," but he also noted that Hill was charismatic and, simply put, fun. "On the passage to Valparaíso he regaled us with anecdotes of high life, and would seem on his own showing to have been a boon companion of Frederick, Duke of York, beginning many of his stories with 'When I was sipping my Clos Vougeot with His Royal Highness.'"[19] Hill was, it would seem, the life of the party. But, scoundrels often are.

By both Bruce and Hay's accounts, the *Imogene* landed Joshua Hill at Valparaíso as a passenger rather than a prisoner. They did not see or hear anything more of him. When the *Imogene* sailed for Callao on January 6, 1838, Hill was no longer on board.[20] Where did he go? Why was he permitted to go? We simply do not know. Indeed, history loses all sight of Hill again until 1841, when Hill petitioned the British government for payment for the services he rendered to their colony at Pitcairn. We will return to Hill later, in our final pages together. For the moment, though, we do well to leave Joshua Hill mysteriously marooned at Valparaíso. We need to return to Pitcairn. There is work yet to be done there, for, in the wake of Joshua Hill's removal from the island, much happened at Adamstown. Much happened, as history would have it, across the Pacific more broadly, and there is reason for us to connect those larger narratives, as we have been doing for some time now, to Mr. Hill's fraudulent reign at Pitcairn.

In the wake of Joshua Hill's departure from Adamstown, the great fear among the Pitcairnese population was, not illogically, that they might once more become victims to some South Seas charlatan. In his critique of Nobbs, Buffet, and Evans, Captain Bruce admitted that London ought to be worried, for the Pitcairners were still *and* already being duped by outsiders. "I hope," he wrote in a letter to Viscount Troubridge, "the government will take my advice and send a competent head" to Adamstown before the island was overrun by "vice and corruption."[21] In his account of the history of Norfolk Island – a story that has to begin, as we have seen, on Pitcairn – Robert Macklin records that Pitcairn was visited, soon after the departure of the *Imogene* by an American whaling

---

[18] Bruce, Record of the Voyage of the HMS *Imogene*.
[19] Hay, *Lines from My Log-Book*, 66–67.
[20] Bruce, *Imogene* Log Books from 1836 to 1839.
[21] Captain H. W. Bruce, Letter to Viscount Troubridge (Valparaíso: July 17, 1838), NMM TRO 119/2(6).

vessel. The crew remained off Pitcairn's coast for two weeks, during which time they harassed the islanders for supplies and, more ominously, sexual access to Pitcairn's women. The island's men, Macklin writes, "defended the community with their firearms."[22]

The "Hill imbroglio," as David Silverman has described this period, "brought home the vulnerable position of Pitcairn." More and more sailors were targeting the island. More and more visitors wanted to meet these celebrated islanders. And the islanders had no army or navy to defend themselves from any outside abuse. They were "up for grabs."[23] It was not just physical danger, though, that threatened Pitcairn. The islanders were so naïve. They had fallen for and been flimflammed by Joshua Hill.[24] The Pitcairners needed some form of support. Recent history suggested that London's policy of benevolent colonial neglect – of distance and disengagement – was no longer suitable to Pitcairn's requirements.

These were the arguments that the islanders placed before Captain Russell Elliott of HMS *Fly*, who arrived at Pitcairn on November 29, 1838. On the *Fly*, Elliott and his crew had valuable supplies for the people of Adamstown, donations sent from Valparaíso. More importantly, though, Elliott was deeply interested to hear about the island's recent history and its troubles with outsiders, in particular.[25] Captain Elliott had no official authority to engage in Pitcairnese politics. He was simply to have visited the island as part of his Pacific inspection.

In the wake of Captain Bruce's report and in the wake of the Hill affair, it seems that the Admiralty had come around to the idea that Pacific patrols were essential if London was to retain any semblance of authority over its possessions in the global ocean.[26] Sir John Barrow, at the Admiralty, had only recently published his history of the mutiny on board the *Bounty*, and so he was predisposed in these years to play "the role of 'fairy godmother' to the Empire's smallest and most romantic outpost."[27] It was, moreover, mud in the eye that Hill had been able to land at and govern over Pitcairn for so long while colonial British officials in London and naval leaders around the globe spent years trying to sort out what was going on.[28] Supervising Pitcairn was an easy decision in 1838.

---

[22] Macklin, *Dark Paradise*, 177.   [23] Silverman, *Pitcairn Island*, 179.

[24] Hancock, *Politics in Pitcairn*, 11–12.

[25] Pitcairn Register. SLNSW DLMSQ7, CY 294.

[26] Ward, *British Policy in the South Pacific*, 79. See Hay, Letter to Charles Wood (July 22, 1835). See also, Young, *Mutiny on the* Bounty, 91.

[27] Nobbs, *George Hunn Nobbs*, 25.

[28] Commodore Francis Mason, Letter to Lord James Townshend (Callao: June 2, 1836), quoted in Belcher, *The Mutineers of the* Bounty, 204–205. See also Admiralty, Letter to

Captain Elliott, though, did more than simply visit and inspect Adamstown. He listened to the Pitcairners, heard their concerns, and heeded their arguments. They needed a "national allegiance." It was "essential that the British Government take them in, so to speak."[29] Writing in 1870, Lady Diana Belcher recorded that "to belong to England, to be looked upon a subjects of the Queen, was the height of their ambition."[30] Theirs was a decidedly odd ambition for the descendants of a clutch of mutineers. If Pitcairn Island was, indeed, an actual part of Britain's colonial empire, the island was an imperial stepchild at best. Illegitimate even. It had been born in mutiny, founded by furacious mutineers. Its very existence depended upon a rejection of London's authority, a repudiation of the global reach of Britain's power.[31] And yet, here were the Pitcairners petitioning to be brought under London's formal control. Here they were presenting themselves as loyal subjects of the British crown.

Captain Elliott was moved. Without permission but with pomp and ceremony, Elliott presented the people of Adamstown with a Union Jack.[32] It was an almost cinematic reversal. "You are now under the protection of the English flag," Elliott is reported to have announced.[33] The island's piratical history would be masked, the metaphoric skull and crossbones replaced by the red and white crosses of the Union Jack. As Thomas Boyles Murray would later observe, the Pitcairners were profoundly loyal. "The English union-jack is hoisted on all grand occasions."[34] Perhaps more enduring than the gift of a flag, though, was the help Elliott also gave the islanders in outlining a new legal code for the proper governance of their small community.[35] Officially, it would be the British Settlements Act of 1887 that annexed Pitcairn into Britain's colonial structure.[36] For the islanders, though, Elliott's 1838 "constitution" marked the moment that Pitcairn Island became part of the British Empire.[37] In 1847, George Hunn Nobbs outlined the islanders' sense of

---

Rear Admiral Sir G. Hammonds (London: August 7, 1835), Te Puna, MS-Papers-1009–2/51.

[29] Silverman, *Pitcairn Island*, 179.   [30] Belcher, *The Mutineers of the* Bounty, 191.

[31] See George Letsas, "Rights and Duties on Pitcairn Island," in Oliver, ed., *Justice, Legality, and the Rule of Law*, 160.

[32] Captain R. Elliott, Letter to Rear Admiral C. B. H. Ross (Callao: January 25, 1839), quoted in Brodie, *Pitcairn's Island and the Islanders*, 82–83.

[33] Young, *Mutiny on the* Bounty, 91.   [34] Murray, *Pitcairn*, 152.

[35] Elliott, Letter to Rear Admiral C. B. H. Ross (January 25, 1839), quoted in Brodie, *Pitcairn's Island and the Islanders*, 82–83.

[36] Carlsson, *Pitcairn Island*, 176.

[37] Macklin, *Dark Paradise*, 178. See also, Nicholson, *The Pitcairners*, 162; and Nobbs, *George Hunn Nobbs*, 34 and 57; and Maud, "The History of Pitcairn Island," in Ross and Moverley, *The Pitcairnese Language*, 73.

themselves. "We are British subjects," he wrote, "I believe our Island is an anomaly within the precincts of Polynesia. We are members of the Protestant Episcopalian Church of England."[38]

Before we look at the Elliott constitution, let us pause for a moment to think about the situation at Pitcairn in 1838. Joshua Hill had just left the island. He had attempted to fashion an orderly form of government at Adamstown, to replace the patriarchal system that John Adams had left in place upon his death in 1829. He had done so, though, by force and from the outside. In pursuing his agenda as he did, Joshua Hill made two things obvious to the Pitcairn Islanders. First, they needed political reform. Second, they needed protection from the outside. Both of those needs would be met by Elliott's actions. They would be met in response to Joshua Hill's time at the island, and they would, ironically, fulfill many of the goals Hill had had for the island.

The year 1838 marked a dramatic turn in Pitcairnese history.[39] Many have made this observation. To dismiss Joshua Hill from Pitcairn's history, as so many have before, is to miss that Hill was critical to the turn. He was the catalyst for and intellectual force behind the new Pitcairn that emerged from Captain Elliott's visit in 1838, even if he was not – as he had hoped to be – the one responsible for implementing the changes.

The "constitution" that Captain Elliott helped devise has sometimes been described as little more than a handful of "hasty regulations."[40] The term "constitution" may overplay the political theory that went into Elliott's regulations for Pitcairn. It may overestimate the political structure that the code imposed. Nonetheless, Pitcairn was a small island. It did not really need much in the way of courts and congresses to function. The framework that Elliott helped the islanders flesh out in November 1838 met the island's needs, even if it was rudimentary and simple. The code did, though, institute political reforms at Pitcairn that need to be recorded in the global history of political practice. The case needs to made, too, that the Pitcairnese "constitution" of 1838 was a legal milestone in the British Pacific, for the framework Elliott and the islanders cobbled together at Adamstown that late November afternoon marked a substantial shift in the way Britain interacted with its possessions in and its subjects from the Pacific Ocean.

At the structural level, Elliott's regulations largely collected and organized preexisting Pitcairnese laws and legal practices.[41] The island needed an executive leader, and so the new code established the office

---

[38] Quoted in Nobbs, *George Hunn Nobbs*, 57.   [39] Shapiro, *The Pitcairn Islanders*, 96.
[40] Nicholson, *The Pitcairners*, 162.
[41] Lewis, "Pitcairn's Tortured Past," in Oliver, ed., *Justice, Legality, and the Rule of Law*, 53.

of the island magistrate, to be elected annually on January 1.[42] Only those older than the age of thirty were eligible for this post.[43] After having been elected, the magistrate was then responsible for nominating a councilor and a committee of assistants, who could be no younger than twenty-five, to help in the administration of the island.[44] The magistrate was to "preside on all public occasions, and if any case should be brought to his notice, he is to hear both sides of the question and to decide and pass judgment accordingly."[45] There was even an oath the magistrate was to swear upon being elected in which the island's chosen leader swore fidelity to "Her Majesty the Queen of Great Britain as her Representative."[46]

To this point, Elliott's administrative framework at Pitcairn looks very much like Hill's. Indeed, acting as the island's detached lawgiver, Captain Elliott was operating in much the same role that Hill had occupied when he played solon six years before. Elliott's law code did, though, diverge from Hill's. Should disputes arise within the governing council, Elliott provided that the unanswered matter should be taken to the broader community for a vote or held over to be adjudicated by the next passing British sea captain.[47] Hill, of course, had never allowed disagreements within his council. His word had been final. Unlike Hill, who had always suggested that being Pitcairnese was regulated by *jus sanguinis*, Elliott effectively outlined a Pitcairnese immigration policy, allowing any adult who had lived on the island for at least five years to vote in island elections.[48]

As we have seen, Elliott's law code was not a complete concession to open borders at Pitcairn. George Hunn Nobbs was deeply involved with Captain Elliott in the formulation of the 1838 laws, but Nobbs would never serve as Pitcairn's magistrate. Edward Quintal assumed that position in a unanimous vote supervised by the crew of the *Fly*.[49] Nobbs was ineligible, for only native-born Pitcairners could stand for election to be the island's magistrate.[50] The new legal system welcomed immigrants like George Nobbs, and that would, we know, have upset Joshua Hill. But the code also recognized Hill's concern about the influence of immigrants on

[42] Ibid. See also, "Pitcairn's Island," in *The Dublin Literary Journal* (July 1, 1845), 444.

[43] Laws and Regulations of Pitcairn Island. RGS-LMS P.26, Item 3.

[44] M. Wooldridge, Letter to an unidentified recipient (June 18, 1849). Te Puna. MS-Papers -1009–2/51. See also, Laws and Regulations of Pitcairn Island. RGS-LMS P.26, Item 3.

[45] Laws and Regulations of Pitcairn Island, RGS-LMS, Item 3, 26.

[46] Ibid. See also, George Hunn Nobbs, Regulations for the Appointment of a Magistrate at Pitcairn's Island, SLNSW ML A 2881, 9–15.

[47] Wooldridge, Letter to an Unidentified Recipient (June 18, 1849).

[48] Brodie, *Pitcairn's Island and the Islanders*, 84.   [49] Nicholson, *The Pitcairners*, 162.

[50] Nobbs, *George Hunn Nobbs*, 33–34.

the fragile social order at Adamstown. Hill had hoped to prevent change of any sort. Elliott curtailed change, favoring instead social evolution.

Despite these divergences, the 1838 law code was no less moralizing than had been Joshua Hill's reign at Pitcairn. There was still, here, a sense that the purpose of government at the island was to forge a better social union among the island's residents than might be achieved through any accidental and haphazard cohabitation on the island. Violence, theft, and illicit sex were forbidden. So too was profanity, which was a finable offense. In the main, though, the laws in Elliott's code were simple instructions designed to assure that the Pitcairners were good neighbors one to the other. The island's dogs were to be kept in check by their owners so that the stock of sheep and goats could be kept safe in their pastures. Those canine companions that did chase the island's livestock were to be destroyed. If one family's fowl did damage to another family's property, the offending party owed the other family compensation. Hogs could never run free for the sake of public health.[51]

It was at the social level, however, that the Pitcairnese constitution was the most surprising. Two provisions stand out in the document.[52] First, every adult resident of Pitcairn Island over the age of twenty-one was to be eligible for the franchise in Pitcairnese elections, making Pitcairn's electorate the first in the world to boast of universal suffrage for both men *and* women.[53] Second, Pitcairn's law code established that every Pitcairnese child would be compelled to attend school, and a Pitcairnese education was established as a free public service.[54]

Certifications signed or marked by the residents at Pitcairn demonstrate that all of the islanders read the new "constitution" (or had it read to them) and consented to it.[55] When word of Elliott's actions filtered back to London, however, many were dumbfounded at the captain's audacity. At the Admiralty, even John Barrow who was otherwise so fond of Pitcairn Island, wrote,

I confess I know not how anything can be done for the inhabitants of Pitcairn's Island. It is impossible to establish an independent Govt or Colony there, nor do I know how the Island could with any propriety be annexed to the Govt. of New South Wales, which has no sort of connection with it.[56]

---

[51] Laws and Regulations of Pitcairn Island.
[52] Maud, "The History of Pitcairn Island," in Ross and Moverley, *The Pitcairnese Language*, 73. See also, Nobbs, *George Hunn Nobbs*, 34.
[53] Lewis, "Pitcairn's Tortured Past," in Oliver, ed., *Justice, Legality, and the Rule of Law*, 53.
[54] Ibid.
[55] Nobbs, Regulations for the Appointment of a Magistrate at Pitcairn's Island, 25–26.
[56] Quoted in Lewis, "Pitcairn's Tortured Past," in Oliver, ed., *Justice, Legality, and the Rule of Law*, 53.

Dawn Oliver has pondered the same set of questions that haunted Barrow. "How does a colonial power establish and maintain *authority* over a colony," she has wondered. "What continuing authority does a colonial power which neglects its colony have over that land?"[57]

W. David McIntyre has argued that Pitcairn became, in 1838, a "primitive pioneer democracy," which is true.[58] The legal changes that Captain Elliott put into effect at Adamstown were more than "a constitutional façade" layered "over the framework of a theocracy."[59] Yes, Nobbs remained as the islands "pastor" after 1838. And yes, in his capacity as pastor, Nobbs would cast a shadow over Pitcairn that stretched across more than six thousand miles of ocean to Norfolk Island. Sir John Barrow, though, would hardly have been as concerned as he was had Elliott's efforts to sure up the government at Pitcairn, his promise of British protection over the island, and his engagement with the deep social questions that divided the island community at Adamstown not marked a startling turn in London's engagement with Pitcairn and, indeed, with the Pacific more broadly.

As we have observed before, the Pitcairners are often omitted from books about South Pacific Islanders. Having inquired into what we might call "the Hill Affair," we see that Pitcairn Island and its inhabitants are actually quite central to the history of the global ocean. Pitcairn sits at the intersection of a number of distinct though interrelated Pacific histories – the history of European exploration, the history of European missionary activity, the history of colonization, the history of global ecology, and the history of Pacific Islanders and their pan-oceanic settlements. In none of these histories is Pitcairn paramount. That has never been the argument behind or the justification for telling Joshua Hill's story. Rather, Joshua Hill's interest in Pitcairn, his time on the island, and the historical wake he caused there (and throughout the Pacific) have helped us reframe Pitcairn as part of the Pacific Ocean region and to identify the Pitcairners as Pacific Islanders (if islanders of an idiosyncratic sort). It simply has not been historically accurate to remove Pitcairners or their island from these histories because it or they stand apart. When Joshua Hill targeted Pitcairn in his earliest letters about the Pacific – letters dating from the 1820s – he was thinking about the history of Euro-American missionary work in the Pacific, and he did not exempt Pitcairn from that history.

---

[57] Dawn Oliver, "Preface," in Dawn Oliver, ed., *Justice, Legality, and the Rule of Law: Lessons from the Pitcairn Prosecutions* (New York: Oxford University Press, 2009), x.

[58] W. David McIntyre, *Winding Up the British Empire in the Pacific Islands : Oxford History of the British Empire – Companion Series* (New York: Oxford University Press, 2014), 9.

[59] Hancock, *Politics in Pitcairn*, 14.

When Joshua Hill imagined the Pitcairners as uniquely qualified to disseminate British culture, religion, and colonial power throughout the Pacific, he settled his attention on the Pitcairnese people precisely because they were a bridge between the British and the Polynesians. Because the Pitcairners descended from both lineages, anything that happened in their history belonged in *both* the history of the Pacific *and* the history of the European West. It has never been because Pitcairn is central to Pacific or European history that it has been a meaningful place to study. Rather, it is a meaningful historical subject because it crosses between those two distinct narratives. To do so, it has had to sit on the edge of both. The Pacific, we have said, is the global ocean. Pitcairn, as it turns out, is something of a global island.

As we have seen earlier, policymakers in London – in the government, at the Admiralty, and throughout Euro-American missionary societies – were slow to want to see a formal commitment to Pacific colonization in the eighteenth and nineteenth centuries. Each group had its own reasons. The missionaries enjoyed more power on Pacific islands if the government remained aloof. Those in government did not want to see themselves engaged in "a war in the [English] Channel over an island in the Pacific."[60] None of these alignments quite worked vis-à-vis Pitcairn, where the inhabitants were half-English. Pitcairn could not, as Captain Elliott and Joshua Hill saw, be left exposed to the privations of passing sailors and imported scoundrels. The Pitcairners were also half-Tahitian, and so a commitment to them inclined London down a slippery path to broader engagement with other Pacific islands, most notably Tahiti. As Barrow observed upon learning about Elliott's constitution, Pitcairn was too small to make it on its own, too distant to be administered from New South Wales, and, now, too implicated in London's administrative planning to be overlooked and neglected as it had been in the years before Joshua Hill arrived there in 1832.

It is possible, then, to read Joshua Hill's legacy in broad and substantive ways. In the years after he left Pitcairn, the small island would be wrapped (unofficially) in the loosest folds of London's colonial mantle. Hill had argued that Britain, like the Moirai of Greek mythology, held Pitcairn's fate in its hands. Elliott had actualized that argument, but it was Hill who was the visionary, Hill who saw that the history of the European Pacific was changing in the 1820s. He urged London to adjust to the changes he saw, and nobody listened. The changes, though, came anyway.

As we might expect from the world ocean, many of the changes that Britain would make in its Pacific policies in the mid-nineteenth century

---

[60] Ward, *British Policy in the South Pacific*, 137.

were the result of events that happened well beyond London, or even the limited boundaries of the Pacific itself. One such event took place in the small town of Titusville, in the northwestern corner of Pennsylvania on August 27, 1859.[61] Nobody could quite have predicted the global consequences of what happened there that day, when a steam-powered drill pierced some seventy feet into the earth and found a pocket of liquefied organic matter. Crude oil. What had once necessitated the exploration and exploitation of the high seas – what could only have been boiled out of the bodies of the ocean's leviathans – could now be milked from the planet itself.[62] The Earth's whale populations were already well depleted by the 1850s, so the discovery of petroleum reserves inside our planet was a much-needed revolution in the history of humanity's energy usage.

The United States, William Henry Seward once observed, chased "the whale over his broad range of the universal ocean" in search of fuel.[63] By 1895, the US whaling fleet, which had boasted some two hundred vessels at its peak in the 1850s, had been reduced to just fifty ships out of America's four remaining whaling ports. In the second half of the nineteenth century, then, fewer and fewer libidinous whalers would enter the Pacific Ocean or plague Pacific islands. The end of whaling, though, did not equate to an end in Euro-American involvement with the great ocean. Indeed, if anything, once whaling ceased to cast its nets over the ocean, the impulse towards more directed governmental involvement in the Pacific increased, and from capital cities around the globe.

In Tahiti, as we know, the changes came early on. Even before the accession of Queen Pomare IV, her brother King Pomare III had urged London to appoint a consul to his island – "to hoist the British flag" as an agent to help secure his power by means of a strategic alliance with the powerful British Empire.[64] By 1838, Joshua Hill was obviously not going to be London's man on the ground at Tahiti, though it was increasingly clear to London that Britain needed an agent on the island. Hill had been right. If Britain did not tend to its own interests in the Pacific, others

---

[61] Hoare, *The Whale*, 128. See also, Delbanco, *Meville*, location 1104.

[62] D. Graham Burnett, *The Sounding of the Whale: Science and Cetaceans in the Twentieth Century* (Chicago: University of Chicago Press, 2012. Kindle Edition), location 517. See also, Greg Bailey, ed., *The Voyage of the F.H. Moore and Other Nineteenth-Century Whaling Accounts* (Jefferson, NC: McFarland and Company, Inc., 2014), 1. See also, John F. Richards, *The World Hunt: An Environmental History of the Commodification of Animals* (Los Angeles: University of California Press, 2014. Kindle Edition), location 3608.

[63] Quoted in "The Pacific Age: Special Report," in *The Economist* (November 15, 2014), 3.

[64] Charles Wilson, Letter to Mission House (October 3, 1825), SOAS, CWM/LMS – South Seas – Box 5A, Folder 4/Jacket A.

would seize on the power vacuum. The American appointment of J. A. Moerenhout as its consular officer at Tahiti seemed to prove the point. The question in London, though, had always been whom to assign to be the British agent in Pomare's court. As we have seen, the question of whether it was suitable to tap George Pritchard while he was simultaneously employed as a missionary for the LMS was a vexing question both for Pritchard's bosses at Mission House and for the politicians at Whitehall.

In the years between Hill's departure from Tahiti for Pitcairn and Bruce's arrival at Tahiti on board the *Imogene* with Pritchard's consular credentials, the debate about how to elevate the missionary to a diplomatic post whirled in London, and, indeed, around the globe.[65] In the absence of an official British agent on the island – indeed, even in the region – Pritchard felt that "the duties of a Consul have devolved upon me."[66] Letters from this period indicate that Pritchard saw the advantages of being tapped for the post officially, not the least of which would be the double income he might earn as both a consul and a missionary.[67] At Mission House, the directors argued that the "combination of the consular and clerical characters in the same individual is undesirable and incompatible with the claims of the missionary office." Though the LMS would be sorry to see Pritchard step down after his long years of dedicated service at Tahiti, they were fully confident that he would understand that stepping down would be the only way for him to take the new post being offered by the British government.[68] Pritchard did agree. Tellingly, though, soon after assuming his position as consul, he informed the government that he would continue to preach at Tahiti, just not as an agent of the LMS.[69]

George Pritchard, then, was not the perfect consular officer. We cannot, though, overlook what a revolutionary policy shift it was for London to have appointed such an officer – imperfect or not – in the first place. Recall that Joshua Hill had, on March 7, 1811, likely published an essay in the *London Morning Post* arguing that his nation needed to be more jealous of its naval power. Even if he had not written the piece, we know for certain that Hill was so taken by its argument that he recalled the essay some twenty years on. In 1832, Hill was willing to serve as the

---

[65] Memorandum (January 1, 1837).

[66] George Pritchard, Letter to Mission House (Tahiti: March 11, 1836), SOAS CWM/ LMS – South Seas Incoming Correspondence – Box 10B, Folder 5/Jacket B.

[67] Elijah Armitage, Letter to LMS missionaries (March 25, 1836), SOAS CWM/ LMS– South Seas Incoming Correspondence – Box 10B, Folder 5/Jacket B.

[68] Lord Henry J. Palmerston, Letter to George Pritchard (London: February 14, 1837), TNA FO 58/15. See also, Ward, *British Policy in the South Pacific*, 95–96.

[69] Charlotte Haldane, *Tempest Over Tahiti* (London: Constable, 1963), 68.

British consul at Tahiti. The Queen there wanted him for the post. It was not, however, because London objected to Hill per se that the appointment did not happen. In 1832, London did not want a consul at Tahiti at all.[70] By 1835, London's tune had changed. American interest in the Pacific had become more focused. French Catholic activity was on the rise. And, as everyone seemed to know, Pitcairn was a mess, and nobody in power had any real sense of why. For all of these reasons, London was beginning to appreciate what Joshua Hill had seen in 1811. Britain's naval hand needed a firmer grasp on the Pacific Ocean.

Australia, of course, was the obvious center of power for Britain's colonial interests in the Pacific. By the 1820s, "Sydney, in particular, was firmly integrated into global maritime networks."[71] After the signing of the Treaty of Waitangi in May 1840, Britain could boast that New Zealand was its first contractually claimed imperial holding in the Pacific.[72] In the Hawai'ian Islands, too, Britain became more assertive about its presence in the middle years of the nineteenth century. There had been a British consular officer posted at Honolulu since 1825, the year that Richard Charlton had arrived to assume the post. Charlton was a controversial figure.[73] Kamehameha II, though, had been warm to a British alliance throughout his short reign. American power was simply not enough to secure the Kamehameha monarchy against external threats.[74] The young king's policy leanings were the reason behind his ill-fated diplomatic trip to London in 1824.[75] Kamehameha's death in London while on his mission did not end the pro-British policies at Honolulu, and Charlton continued to be prized for the diplomatic alliances he symbolized well into the reign of King Kamehameha III. Despite being ill suited to his job, Charlton remained as the British diplomat at the Kamehameha Court until 1843, when he was replaced by Major-General William Miller.[76]

Charlton's influence, though, was hardly limited to the Hawai'ian Islands. Until Pritchard's appointment at Tahiti in 1837, it was to Charlton whom Britons looked for guidance from across the Pacific. But, in his long stint as British consul at Honolulu (1825–1843), Richard Charlton only rarely left his homeport to tour the wider Pacific basin over which his consular authority extended.[77] In 1832, for instance, Charlton had to oversee the resolution of the infamous case of the schooner

---

[70] Samson, *Imperial Benevolence*, 42.   [71] Foxhall, *Health, Medicine, and the Sea*, 24.

[72] Landdown, ed., *Strangers in the South Seas*, 235.

[73] Melville, *Typee*, 255. See also, Howarth, *Tahiti*, 209; and Brantlinger, *Dark Vanishings*, 150.

[74] Lummis, *Pacific Paradises*, 124–125.

[75] J. Susan Corley, "The British Press Greets the King of the Sandwich Islands: Kamehameha II in London, 1824," in *The Hawai'ian Journal of History* 42 (2008), 69–103.

[76] Ward, *British Policy in the South Pacific*, 139.   [77] Samson, *Imperial Benevolence*, 12.

Truro. Lieutenant Cole, master of the *Truro*, had first contacted Charlton to report that his vessel had been seized and plundered at Pukarua (Cole called it "Buckerow") in the Tuamotu Archipelago, some eight hundred miles from Tahiti. Cole argued that the Pomare monarchy had been behind the assault. In order to sort the case, Charlton was forced to arrange transport for himself from Hawai'i on board the HMS *Challenger.* Similarly, Charlton was called upon to adjudicate the question of whether a vessel stranded at Tahiti continued to belong to its British owner, the same Captain Ebril – as fate would have it – who carried Joshua Hill to Pitcairn, or had been *de facto* ceded to Queen Pomare.[78] To hear both cases, Charlton had to travel over an unimaginable distance of more than three thousand miles. The trip from Hawai'i to Tahiti literally carried the British diplomat from winter in one hemisphere to summer in the other. No wonder, then, that, by the 1830s, London was beginning to see that one agent was not enough to secure British rights and interests in an ocean that spanned almost half of the planet.[79]

These changes in British diplomatic policy in the Pacific reflected a new sense of the colonial possibilities of that ocean in Europe more generally. In 1843, Charlton would be brought down when he was implicated in the Paulet Affair, a five-month period in which a British naval officer, Captain Lord George Paulet of the HMS *Carysfort*, occupied the Hawai'ian Islands, claiming them as British colonies, on the grounds that British sailors were not being treated fairly – at least not as Captain Paulet defined that word – in sovereign Hawai'ian law courts.[80] So upset were American missionaries and merchants at Hawai'i that they floated the idea of holding the island chain under a joint Franco-American protectorate. The United States dispatched the USS *Boston* to Honolulu to protect American interests.[81] The age of "gunboat diplomacy," as Gavin Daws has written, had reached the Pacific.[82]

The mid-nineteenth century, to quote Brett Bennett, "witnessed a watershed in the governance of the British Empire" as Britain along with those other nations that had formerly evangelized, whaled, and traded in the Pacific converted their activities into networks of colonial power.[83] Empire had not "smoothly followed" the European "discovery" of the Pacific, but, as Joyce Chaplin has suggested, the "transformation of

[78] Ward, *British Policy in the South Pacific*, 63–65.
[79] Letter to John Backhouse (December 19, 1836), TNA FO 58/14.
[80] Daws, *A Dream of Islands*, 79–80. See also, Haley, *Captive Paradise*, location 2522–2583 of 7968; and Beechert, *Honolulu*, 54–56.
[81] Beechert, *Honolulu*, 55.
[82] Daws, *A Dream of Islands*, 79. See also, Barry M. Gough, "The Records of the Royal Navy's Pacific Station," in *The Journal of Pacific History* 4 (1969), 146–147.
[83] Brett Bennett, "The Consolidation and Reconfiguration of 'British' Networks of Science, 1800–1970," in Brett M. Bennett and Joseph M. Hodge, eds., *Science and Empire:*

the Pacific's natural worlds" did eventually translate into "formal empire."[84] As Katherine Foxhall has so pointedly put it, "voyages did not just deliver emigrants and convicts, they made them into colonists."[85] Britain's colonization of the Pacific, of course, was not always successful; it was often contested. As the 1843 Paulet Affair demonstrated, Pacific monarchs like the Pomares or the Kamehamehas could be protective of their sovereignty.[86] The same Paulet Affair also demonstrated the lengths to which both America and France might go to secure their own power in the Pacific. The American annexation of Hawai'i in 1898 was not an unprecedented imperialist move.[87]

Until now, the story of Joshua W. Hill has almost always been categorized among other accounts of history's great impostors. I can confess that that is exactly where the research for this book began. A would-be king at Pitcairn Island seemed a sound traveling companion for Louis de Rougemont, another gimcrack teller-of-tales. De Rougemont's yarns included tales of thirty years spent among an aboriginal tribe in the Australian outback – a tribe, mind you, who worshiped him as a god. They included flying wombats and giant sea turtles that allowed de Rougemont to ride on the backs of their shells.[88] In Donald Margulies' play *Shipwrecked: The Amazing Adventures of Louis de Rougemont (as told by himself)*, de Rougemont extolls the virtues of telling tales. "What is truth," he asks. "Can one *hold* it? Is it a rock: Is it a bone? If I am guilty of anything, it is of dabbing a few spots of color on the drab canvas of life."[89] Was Hill just another de Rougemont? If so, Hill was the more sinister of the two. De Rougemont put on a show, a spectacle, perhaps taking a crowd or two for the cost of a ticket of admission. Hill, though, seized

     Knowledge and Networks of Science across the British Empire, 1800–1970 (New York: Palgrave, 2011), 30. See also, Fischer, *A History of the Pacific Islands*, 194.

[84] Chaplin, "The Pacific Before Empire," in Armitage and Bashford, eds., *Pacific Histories*, 61. See also, Miles Taylor, "Introduction," in Miles Taylor, ed., *The Victorian Empire and Britain's Maritime World, 1837–1901 – The Sea and Global History* (New York: Palgrave, 2013), 5–6; Edmond, *Representing the South Pacific*, 131 and 265; and Dodge, *Islanders and Empires*, 52.

[85] Foxhall, *Health, Medicine, and the Sea*, 1.

[86] Matthews and Travers, "Introduction," in Matthews and Travers, eds., Islands and Britishness, 6. See also, Deryck Scarr, Fragments of Empire: A History of the Western Pacific High Commission, 1877–1914 (Honolulu: University of Hawai'i Press, 1968), 1.

[87] Dane A. Morrison, *True Yankees: The South Seas & The Discovery of American Identity* (Baltimore: Johns Hopkins University Press, 2014), 95, 139, and 145.

[88] Louis de Rougemont, *The Adventures of Louis De Rougemont* (London: George Newnes, Limited, 1899. Kindle Edition). See also, Iain McCalman, *The Reef: A Passionate History – The Great Barrier Reef from Captain Cook to Climate Change* (New York: Farrar, Straus, and Giroux, 2013. Kindle Edition), 119–120.

[89] Donald Margulies, *Shipwrecked: The Amazing Adventures of Luis de Rougemont (as Told by Himself)* (New York: Theatre Communications Group, 2009. Kindle Edition), location 1244 of 1476.

an island, tossed people from their homes, broke up families, administered beatings. The dabs of color he painted in were dabs of blood.

Louis de Rougemont was not, of course, the only nineteenth-century fraud. Mark Twain was as captivated by the celebrated case of the Tichborne claimant as he was of the Hill affair in Pitcairn.[90] As had the Hill imbroglio, the Tichborne case hinged on the question of proving identity and credentialing in the nineteenth-century British imperial world. How, if their son was assumed to have died in a shipwreck in 1854, was the Tichborne family to winkle out the truth when a heavy-set butcher from Wagga Wagga, Australia stepped forward in 1866 claiming to be the heir to the Tichborne baronetcy?[91] Anybody, as Joshua Hill had proven, could make a claim. They could even bring evidence. Getting at the truth, though, was a different matter. Similarly, there was the case of Mary (Willcocks) Baker who charmed Samuel Worrall and his wife, Elizabeth, for several months in the spring and summer of 1817. Speaking in a cryptic language mixed with broken and heavily accented English snippets, Baker claimed to be Princess Caraboo from the Indian Ocean island of Javasu. The Worralls were pleased to host such an august guest at Knole Park, their estate in Gloucestershire. Only when a boarding-house keeper recognized the pinchbeck princess' picture in the *Bristol Journal* did the true nature of her hoax come to light. The Worralls had been hosting a guileful friend, not South Asian royalty.[92]

Like de Rougemont's, then, Princess Caraboo's story seems an entertaining bit of monkeyshine, a tale told a by *luftmensch* with a talent for fabricating fibs. What we have found in Joshua Hill's life, however, is that his story is hardly just a tale of raw imposture. It fits into the history of the Paulet Affair at Hawai'i. It is even more akin to the life and times of Charles de Thierry, who in 1835 declared himself king of Nuku Hiva in the Marquesas Islands and, then, in 1837, assembled a community of colonists at Sydney to travel with him to New Zealand's north island where he anticipated establishing his own sovereign state three years before the Treaty of Waitangi made Britain's annexation of that island official. As Charles St. Julian has observed,

[90] Rohan McWilliam, *The Tichborne Claimant: A Victorian Sensation* (London: Hambledon Continuum, 2007), 88–89.

[91] Ibid.

[92] John Matthew Gutch, *Caraboo: A Narrative of a Singular Imposition, Practiced Upon the Benevolence of a Lady Residing in the Vicinity of the City of Bristol, By a Young Woman of the Name of Mary Wilcocks, alias Baker, alias Bakerstendht, alias Caraboo, Princess of Javasu* (London: Baldwin, Cradock, and Joy, 1817).

the Pacific in the nineteenth century attracted more than its share of European romantics, ill-assorted men who found in this area, so remote from the mainstream of political events, an opportunity to act out their private dreams and aspirations.

The Pacific's many small islands were perfectly suited for these charlatans and their dramatic biographies. "On such a small stage," St. Julian continues,

the individual had more freedom of action, and could write for himself not only the subsequent scenes of his own drama, but also, if the mood took him, his own prologues to the play. No one could disprove the script.[93]

The French Pacific had its own share of men like Hill and de Thierry. In 1877, for instance, Charles Marie Bonaventure du Breil, better known as the Marquis de Rays, sailed to the Pacific seeking to glorify both France and the Catholic Church. In the Pacific, de Rays declared himself the "King of New France," an Oceanic empire of his own imagining.[94] It has now been nearly eight decades since Josephine Niau published her biography of de Rays, and it has, similarly, been almost forty years since J. D. Raeside published what remains as the most comprehensive account of de Thierry's exploits in New Zealand.[95] There may be reason to think that these two impostors and their Pacific adventures deserve an historical recrudescence, for like Captain Hill, de Rays and De Thierry have sat for some time at the historiographic margins. Like Hill's story, the stories of both de Rays and de Thierry appear, on the surface, to be the stories of Pacific bubblers and cheats, but there is reason to believe that their biographies too might contain historical secrets that have yet to percolate to the surface.

It is possible that de Thierry and de Rays are more like Joshua Hill than they seem. It is possible that they two are part of some much bigger and much more substantial history of Euro-American colonial engagement with the Pacific and within the global ocean. As we have discovered, Joshua Hill was not all that different than Hiram Bingham or George Pritchard. His story was not as simple as Caraboo's or de Rougemont's, for Hill was not just a peripatetic unkard pretending to be as wise as a goat

---

[93] Charles St. Julian, "Alternative Diplomacy in Polynesia," in Deryck Scarr, editor, *More Pacific Island Portraits* (Norwalk, CT: Australian National University Press, 1978), 19.

[94] Josephine Hyacinthe Niau, *The Phantom Paradise: The Story of the Expedition of the Marquis de Rays* (Sydney: Angus & Robertson, Ltd., 1936). See also, Tim Flannery, *Among the Islands: Adventures in the Pacific* (New York: Atlantic Monthly Press, 2011. Kindle Edition), location 1106–1125 of 3320; and Kirk, *History of the South Pacific since 1513*, 4761.

[95] J. D. Raeside, *Sovereign Chief: A Biography of Baron de Thierry* (Christchurch, New Zealand: Caxton Press, 1977).

in the hope that he could beguile some Pacific Islanders, swindle them of their fortunes, abuse their generosity, and cause a bit of chaos. For that matter, we might liken Joshua Hill to other Pacific rascals-turned-colonists. There are more than a few of these fastuous xenophiles to be found in the Pacific archives. Take, for instance, Shirley Waldemar Baker, who began his career as a Wesleyan missionary at Tonga, only to rise, eventually, to the rank of prime minister to the court of King George Tupou I. Baker served the king from 1881 until 1890, when reproving authorities from the Australasian Wesleyan Methodist General Conference arrived at Tonga to remove him from the island for having exceeded his initial missionary mandate.[96]

We might also consider the even better known Walter M. Gibson, a missionary at the Hawai'ian Islands from the Church of Jesus Christ of Latter-day Saints (LDS), better known as the Mormons. In the 1860s, Gibson forged an independent colony in the archipelago for the islands' existing Mormon community. He even purchased the small island of Lanai, which he renamed for himself, for the community. When it was discovered that Gibson had used peculated church funds for the scheme, he was excommunicated by the LDS church. In 1873, Gibson established a small, self-promotional newspaper, the *Nuhou*, in which he built himself a new empire, quickly catching the approving eye of the Hawai'ian monarch, King Kalakaua. By 1886, Kalakaua offered Gibson the post of prime minister at Hawai'i. Together the monarch and the prime minister made terrible decisions, including a misguided effort to build a Pacific empire with Hawai'i at its center. In 1887, the two men were faced with a political rebellion that was led by familiar names like Sanford B. Dole, Peter Cushman Jones, and Lorrin A. Thurston. These men presented Kalakaua with no choice but to accept what is now called the "Bayonet Constitution," a document that both stripped the king of much of his political sovereignty and drove Gibson, as penniless as he now was powerless, to San Francisco, where he died in 1888.[97]

Joshua Hill's story has obvious connections to these Pacific tales from Hawai'i and Tonga. For the individuals involved in our story, though, it was not at those more distant islands but rather at Tahiti that the global competition for colonial power in the Pacific was most directly felt. Given Tahiti's long history with Britain – from Captain Cook to the London Missionary Society – the island is easily marked as one of the most likely places to have been a British colony, perhaps on the face of the planet,

[96] Oliver, *The Pacific Islands*, 121.   [97] Osorio, *Dismembering Lāhui*, 197 and 228–231.

and, yet, today Tahiti is part of *French* Polynesia.[98] The outcome of this colonial story hinges on the narrative we have been investigating. Queen Pomare IV, as we have seen, leaned on George Pritchard and other British missionaries as advisors. In 1836, French Catholic missionaries landed at Tahiti, and Pomare, on the advice of her missionary councilors, ordered the priests from her kingdom. This was the same sort of scene we saw play out under Hiram Bingham's care at Hawai'i earlier in this book and earlier in the 1830s. Joshua Hill had helped defuse the situation and avert a crisis at Honolulu. George Pritchard did not manage the same outcome at Tahiti, for, in 1838, the French admiral, Abel Aubert Dupetit-Thouars, arrived in the South Pacific on board his flagship, the *Vénus*, to secure an apology for the insult France had sustained. The official French position on the matter was that George Pritchard had been deeply involved in the expulsion of the French priests.[99]

In 1842, Dupetit-Thouars returned to the Pacific as captain of *La Reine Blanche*, and his second voyage exposed Paris' truly expansionist impulses, for it was during this voyage that the admiral announced the formal annexation of the Marquesas Islands as French colonies. Later that same year, Dupetit-Thouars arrived offshore of Tahiti. At the moment of Dupetit-Thouars' return to Tahiti, France and Britain were engaged in a European diplomatic standoff over Morocco. Queen Victoria was on the cusp of a state visit to Paris to attempt a de-escalation of that crisis when France decided to provoke this secondary situation in the Pacific. The queen, then only five years into her reign and only twenty-three years old, was reluctant to instigate a fight with France over something as seemingly remote as Tahiti.[100] The policy of "minimum intervention" had its last stand at Tahiti.[101] Dupetit-Thouars was able to annex Tahiti with only minimal protest from British authorities. George Pritchard was expelled from Tahiti by the French and placed under the administrative authority of the consul at Honolulu by the British Foreign Office. Queen Pomare IV was coerced into accepting a French protectorate over her kingdom. Pomare's efforts to sustain Tahitian independence lasted only through the three years of what some call the Tahitian War of Independence (1844–1847) after which time the queen acquiesced to the notion of reigning as a figurehead under the French protectorate. It was an arrangement she would sustain until her death on September 17, 1877.[102]

[98] Dodge, *Islanders and Empires*, 169. See also, Howarth, *Tahiti*, 214.
[99] Ward, *British Policy in the South Pacific*, 97.   [100] Howarth, *Tahiti*, 213.
[101] Ward, *British Policy in the South Pacific*, 97.
[102] Ibid., 133–137. See also, Dodge, *Islanders and Empires*, 169.

But, what of tiny Pitcairn in this much larger history of Pacific Island kingdoms and Euro-American empires? Does it matter at all in light of this much bigger story? I would answer, of course, that it does. Pitcairn's history is telling in this larger framework. We have observed on multiple occasions that Pitcairn Island was Britain's second colony in the Pacific, after only Australia.[103] Australia, though, is something of an anomaly in the history of British non-interventionism and non-imperialism in the Pacific in the first half of the nineteenth century. It is the (very large) exception to the rule, for it was a planned venture. It had to be. How else could a nation mobilize a fleet of eleven ships with more than one thousand people over a distance of some ten thousand miles without extraordinary planning? Australia could hardly be called a land of accidental imperialism.

Pitcairn, though, fits the Pacific model. There was no plan to settle there, to colonize there. Indeed, even if Fletcher Christian did intend the island as his destination in 1790, he did not actually know how or where to find it when he first set sail. The people who landed at Tahiti were mutineers. True, the nine men had named the fort they attempted to build on the island of Tubuai "Fort George," but their choice of name hardly suggested any real commitment either to Britain's monarch or its national mythology.[104] Arguably, these men settled Pitcairn Island to be rid of London's authority, not to spread it. And, finally, the island's population was so isolated and so small that it seemed to merit, and often got by on, very little interventionist attention from London. Until the 1830s, then, one can make the case that Pitcairn Island was London's ideal colonial possession in the Pacific. It cost little; it required little; it risked little. But, a low-cost, low-risk colony paid no real dividends, either. The island could do so much more, which is exactly why Joshua Hill targeted it from the 1820s onwards.

We need to pause here and reflect upon the importance of Captain Bruce's voyage on board the *Imogene* from 1837 to 1838. There had been other Pacific transits before Bruce's, and there would be many afterwards. But, Bruce's voyage marks a turning point. As John M. Ward has observed, Bruce's Pacific inspection is one of the best recorded of the British navy's Pacific voyages, certainly to the 1830s.[105] Bruce's visit to Pitcairn was a minor moment in this voyage, to be sure, but it is telling that the Admiralty included Pitcairn in the voyage in the first place, particularly given how minor it would otherwise seem. Bruce inspected the situation in the Hawai'ian Islands, life under Charlton's diplomatic

---

[103] Landsdown, ed., *Strangers in the South Seas*, 9.   [104] Salmond, *Bligh*, 249.
[105] Ward, *British Policy in the South Pacific*, 62.

hand. He passed what was, in his day, called Independence Island, though it is now better known as Malden Island, part of the Republic of Kiribati. He navigated between Maupihaa Island (also known as Mopelia) and the coral atoll of Suwarrow. He sailed to the Austral Islands of Rimatara and Rurutu, near Tubuai.

Bruce's voyage, in short, was an ambitious circuit of the Pacific at precisely the moment when London saw the geostrategic landscape of the region changing. It was the sort of surveillance that Hill was urging upon the Admiralty in his letters of the 1820s and the sort of attention to global naval affairs that he had either written of or approved of from as early as 1811. It was a superintendent lap around the Pacific that included Pitcairn because Pitcairn was visibly and importantly part of the changing tide in Pacific history. That Joshua Hill happened to have been at Pitcairn when Bruce arrived, that he was to be collected from Pitcairn as part of Bruce's Pacific circumnavigation, that he had predicted the need for more attention to the Pacific Ocean, and that he was himself the reason for some of the newfound attention being paid to the Pacific broadly (and to Pitcairn in particular) were all coincidences that end up being very significant in this history, for it is these coincidences that help us make the claim that Pitcairn was – particularly under the misguided guiding hand of its self-constituted dictator – an influential, if previously overlooked, feature of this larger historical narrative.

As we have observed, the Pitcairnese "constitution" of 1838 rendered the small island as a protean democracy even as it suggested that the island was also, if informally, connected to London in a colonial relationship. In keeping with the history of colonization in the broader Pacific in these years, Pitcairn was a colony of sorts. It would continue to require colonial supervision from London, and it would continue to beg questions about the actual nature of Britain's colonial relationship with the Pacific in general. How committed was London to Pacific imperialism? What costs would London accept to secure power in the global ocean? We know that in the 1830s, the answer to these questions was that London did quite a bit for Pitcairn. The removal to Tahiti in 1831 may have been misguided and unsuccessful, but it marked an unprecedented level of planning and commitment on London's part, whether from the Foreign Office, the Admiralty, or private organizations and societies.

The initial result of the Tahitian removal may not have been to cement a bond of trust and affection between Adamstown and the metropolitan core of empire. In the wake of Joshua Hill's dictatorship at Adamstown, though, the islanders seem to have been deeply committed to London and very interested to see their new constitutional democracy affiliated with the security of British global power. The connection was to prove profitable. We have observed previously that small islands are, as often as not, unsuitable for the permanent sustenance of human society.[106] Utopia was only an island in the mind of Thomas More. Before the Tahitian removal and afterwards – indeed through Joshua Hill's years at Pitcairn and after – both the British government and nongovernmental groups from London endeavored to keep the people of Pitcairn supplied with everything they needed to sustain life on their small Pacific outpost. The island would continue to need staple items – shoes, clothing, books, blankets, glass, tools, and the like – across its history.[107] Transporting these items was still tedious and slow, and, in some cases the time lag in requesting and receiving goods from the outside could be costly for the people at Adamstown. In 1842, for instance, George Nobbs wrote to Admiral Richard Thomas hoping that the Admiralty could supply the island with medical supplies to help fight an outbreak of smallpox, hardly the sort of request that could wait the many months – if not years – it might take to be fulfilled.[108]

In the years after Hill's departure from Pitcairn, the small island was a faithful colonial outpost. In 1869, Charles Dilke, who – as we have seen – did not much care for the Pitcairners generally, observed that the island was of interest "as a solitary British post on the very border of the French dominions."[109] In an age of aggressive imperial competition in the Pacific, Pitcairn was indisputably British. When Dilke arrived at Adamstown, the Pitcairners eagerly asked for news from Britain. "How's Victoria?," they asked him. "There was no disrespect," he observed, "in the omission of the title 'Queen;' the question seemed to come from the heart."[110] For his part, George Hunn Nobbs would develop a deep and personal relationship with British colonial administrators and officials from the Admiralty. In September 1835, he named his newborn son Francis Mason Nobbs after Rear-Admiral Francis Mason, who was the naval commander-in-chief at Valparíso at the time and, as such, one of Pitcairn's most loyal patrons.[111] As Captain Bruce would report in 1838, the Pitcairners thought of Britain as "home."[112]

---

[106] Robert Aldrich and John Connell, *The Last Colonies* (New York: Cambridge University Press, 1998), 34 and 137.

[107] Communication from the General of the Medical Department of the Navy to the Rev. G. H. Nobbs (January 28, 1853), SLNSW C134 (Mfm CY 349). See also, Descendants of the *Bounty*'s Crew, in *The Calcutta Journal* (Tuesday, July 12, 1819); and Pitcairn Island Extracts from *The Illustrated London News* (November 6, 1852), SLNSW F999.7/9, 373.

[108] George Hunn Nobbs, Letter to Admiral Richard Thomas (November 9, 1842), SLNSW ML MSS 2233.

[109] Dilke, *Greater Britain*, 276.   [110] Ibid., 274.

[111] Mason, Letter to George Hunn Nobbs (August 17, 1836).

[112] Remark Book of the *Imogene*, 303.

But, as Dilke noted, it was also expensive to maintain Pitcairn Island.[113] In August 1844, Captain Jones of the HMS *Curaçao* observed that Pitcairn needed more attention. It needed more direct colonial regulation, particularly a detailed revision of the law codes that Elliott had drafted so quickly in 1838.[114] When Admiral Fairfax Moresby, the commander-in-chief of Britain's Pacific station, landed at Pitcairn on a Pacific inspection in 1853, he saw a more dire situation than what Jones had observed nearly a decade before. The Pitcairners were once again outgrowing their island home.[115] But, what could be done? By 1856, it was clear that the only answer would be to attempt a second transplantation. George Nobbs, still a leading figure in the community at Adamstown, was suspicious. "I do not think there is any place in the world that will suit us as well as this Rock," he wrote. If the Pitcairners had to move, though, he could trust the decision, for it would have been made "under the auspices of the British Government."[116] In the years since Hill had been exiled from Pitcairn, Nobbs had come to appreciate that his status on the island hinged upon his connections with elites in London and at the Admiralty. All of the work required to prepare the Pitcairners for a second removal would allow him unprecedented access to his colonial patrons throughout the navy, in government, and within religious societies.[117] The Archbishop of Canterbury himself led the efforts of the Pitcairn Fund Committee, whose purpose it was to raise revenue and support for the small community at Adamstown, support both to sustain them at Pitcairn and, if necessary, to help relocate them to a more sustainable home.[118]

We know, of course, that the Pitcairners would be transported to Norfolk Island – a former penal colony – in 1856. Once again the islanders packed their lares and penates, locked the doors to their houses, and abandoned their fields at Pitcairn to set out for a new island home. Thomas Boyles Murray estimated that the cost of relocating the Pitcairners to Norfolk approached £5,500.[119] Was such a cost worth it, or was this second Pitcairnese removal just wastefulness? The expense was no small token, given that it was spent on only 193 souls. Given that fifteen of those moved from Pitcairn to Norfolk in 1856 returned to their native island within two years' time (in the first of what would be two

---

[113] Dilke, *Greater Britain*, 276.

[114] Captain Charles Jones, Letter to an Unidentified Recipient (August 30, 1844), Te Puna, MS-Papers-1009–2/51.

[115] Young, *Mutiny on the* Bounty, 118.

[116] Nobbs, Letter to Rev. W. T. Bullock (October 9, 1834).

[117] Hancock, *Politics in Pitcairn*, 16.   [118] Macklin, *Dark Paradise*, 231.

[119] Murray, *Pitcairn*, 378.

significant waves of repatriations to Pitcairn from the settlement at Norfolk), the expense seems even more unthrifty.[120]

Pitcairn and the Pitcairners, then, had become the subjects of government largesse, which was not to say, of course, that the Pitcairners were not still also the subject of evangelical dreams. When the first wave of returning Pitcairners landed at Adamstown in 1858, they found that their abandoned community was far from overrun by the creepers and vines that ought to have overtaken the village in their absence. When the islanders had returned to Pitcairn after the earlier Tahitian removal, they returned to a tatterdemalion landscape. Adamstown had been covered in vines; their run-down homes had a feeling of desuetude about them. Now, however, Adamstown was in good repair. Some of the village's buildings showed clear signs of having been occupied, while others had been carefully dismantled. In the Pitcairnese school, the returning islanders found a note from a Captain J. N. Knowles explaining the mysterious findings.

Josiah N. Knowles, the note explained, had been captain of the *Wild Wave*, a vessel out of San Francisco that had floundered at nearby Oeno Island not long after the Pitcairners had departed for Norfolk. The *Wild Wave*'s crew had come to Pitcairn, obviously hoping to find help from the islanders and obviously disappointed to find that Pitcairn had been depopulated. Knowles had overseen the use of the timber taken from the disassembled homes, which were converted to a new boat. The crew of the *Wild Wave* sailed on that vessel from Pitcairn to Tahiti, from whence they were rescued.

Two decades on, Knowles returned to Pitcairn, carrying with him a collection of evangelical materials from a new – though growing – religious movement known as Seventh-Day Adventism. Accustomed to receiving religious literature from the outside world, the Pitcairners must have read this new material with some degree of zeal, for when John Tay, an Adventist missionary, arrived at Pitcairn in 1886, he was able to convert the entire community at Adamstown to his faith within a two month period.[121]

The Pitcairnese conversion to Seventh-Day Adventism is an unpredicted and, perhaps, fittingly epic moment in the story of this, well, *storied* little island. An accidental shipwreck on nearby and uninhabited Oeno.

---

[120] Young, Letter to Captain and Mrs. Gibbons (April 15, 1882), in Young, *Letters to Captain and Mrs. Gibbons*, 7–8.

[121] Herbert Ford. *Island of Tears: John I Tay and the Story of Pitcairn* (Nampo, ID: Pacific Press Publishing Association, 1990. Kindle Edition), particularly locations 69–82 and 1062. See also, Birkett, *Serpent in Paradise*, 109–110. See also, Young, *Mutiny of the Bounty*, 230–233; and Shapiro, *The Pitcairn Islanders*, 113, 117–118, and 163.

The voyage to seek salvation from John Adams' heirs, a community so acutely connected to salvation in their own right. The historical accident of the Pitcairners' being entirely absent from their home at the instant of Knowles' landing. The note in the schoolhouse. The conversion of the entirety of the island's population. The image we might conjure of Pitcairn's islanders running all of their island's pigs – those descendants of the ones we saw in that illustration from *The Lonely Island* in Chapter 5 – over the edge of a cliff so that they would not be tempted to the sin of eating polluted flesh. If this were not all part of a true story – a tale of the South Pacific the way it actually was, to borrow from James Michener – then even the best of authors would have trouble imaging it all as part of one story. But Pitcairn has not always been so fanciful and storybook a place, particularly in the eyes of the colonial administrators who have had to run it.

Pitcairn Island, we have to remember, is today one of the last remaining fourteen British overseas territories.[122] Given its small size, its isolation, and its need for outside supply-lines to sustain a twenty-first-century sense of life on the island, Pitcairn is likely to remain dependent. There is no path forward by which this colony will achieve the sort of independence from its colonial masters that we so relish in the "post-imperial" world. If Pitcairn was once the model of British colonial engagement in the nineteenth-century Pacific, it is now just as much an anomaly, a postcolonial colony.[123] Even administering Pitcairn is something of a problem. The same British administrative structures that were once loath to engage too deeply in colony-making in the Pacific are now pressed to find ways for its Pitcairnese commissioner to stay in contact with Pitcairn. Since the 1970s, Queen Elizabeth II's representative at Pitcairn "has been, *ex officio*, the British high commissioner in New Zealand. Few have ever visited Pitcairn."[124]

From London, it is a challenge just to juggle the concept of a colony in the twenty-first century. As W. David McIntyre has observed, the entire history of decolonization in the Pacific was its own set of problems.[125] As Jodie Matthews and Daniel Travers have written, even forging a sense of state identity on some of the Pacific's islands was an improbably slow proposition.[126] To make matters more complicated, there were the

---

[122] Morrell, *Britain in the Pacific Islands*, 193.
[123] Aldrich and Connell, *The Last Colonies*, 1.   [124] Ibid., 32.
[125] McIntyre, *Winding up the British*, 111.
[126] Matthews and Travers, "Introduction," in Matthews and Travers, eds., *Islands and Britishness*, 6. See also, Stephen A. Royle, "Identity and the Other British Isles: Bermuda and St. Helena," in Jodie Matthews and Daniel Travers, eds., *Islands and Britishness: A Global Perspective* (Newcastle upon Tyne: Cambridge Scholars Publishing, 2012), 14.

logistics. The region was replete with small islands that either did not or could not be granted their independence as nation-states. Some were small islands that could not sustain themselves. Some were too distant from other islands to be constituted as a group. Others were too thinly populated.[127] Pitcairn suffered from all three problems.[128] Such un-decolonizable spaces were an affront, though, to internationalist institutions in the second half of the twentieth century. Nowhere was this affront felt more deeply than at the United Nations. Chapter I, Article I, Section 2 of the UN's founding charter famously commits that organization to the notion of the "self-determination" of the world's peoples.[129] Attempting to "wind up" British imperialism in the Pacific, was like squaring the circle. It was not going to be an easy venture, if it were even a possibility in the first place.[130]

British policy makers in London eventually settled on four categories into which to group their Pacific holdings. The first group included two subsets – those colonies that could be granted independence as distinct states or inside federations as well as those that could be granted independence through treaty relationships with Britain. The second category was those colonies that might opt for Free Association with Britain. A third collection of colonies were those that might seek full integration into Britain or some other state. Finally, there were those colonies that would require continuing association with London in a dependent status for the indefinite future. Pitcairn, of course, fell into this last category.[131] This framework was not, obviously, a complete answer, but decolonization in the Pacific really was a Hobson's Choice from the outset. One took what one could whenever and wherever a decent solution presented itself.[132] These balances have, of course, always defined life at Pitcairn Island.

In the first two decades of the twenty-first century, the British governments of first two Labour prime ministers and, now, two Conservatives as well have had to face the challenges of how to administer Pitcairn Island. Fletcher Christian, John Adams, Joshua Hill, and George Nobbs all cast very long shadows indeed. Today, though, the challenges of colonial control are less about authority and more about survival. Pitcairn Island's population peaked in 1937 at 233 people. In an article from

---

[127] Epeli Hau'ofa, "Epilogue: Pasts to Remember," in Robert Borofsky, editor, *Remembrance of Pacific Pasts*, 453.

[128] McIntyre, *Winding up the British Empire*, 111. See also, Aldrich and Connell, *The Last Colonies*, 1.

[129] *The Charter of the United Nations and Statute of the International Court of Justice* (New York: The United Nations, 1985), Chapter 1, Article I, Section 2.

[130] McIntyre, *Winding up the British Empire*.   [131] Ibid., 116–117.

[132] Aldrich and Connell, *The Last Colonies*, 162.

1964 on the status of "Pitcairn Island Today," one author observed that the Pitcairners received countless requests every year from people who hoped to settle at Adamstown.[133] If that was the case in the 1960s, in the days of Alec Douglas-Home, it was no longer so in the age of Margaret Thatcher. By 1980, the Pitcairnese population had dropped to just over sixty people. That number has only declined since then.[134]

From the 1980s, few could have imagined that demographic collapse would be one of the brighter of Pitcairn's existential crises. By the final years of the twentieth century, worrying stories were emerging from the island about the sexual exploitation of the island's underage female population.[135] By 2004, these cases had erupted onto the world's stage in a series of criminal trials that would thrust Pitcairn into the global spotlight. The scene the world would see was an intimate portrait of a community that had grown intensely private, and it was an image that would forever shatter the sense that this was an island where mutineers could make good, where redemption seemed to grow in the fertile volcanic soil of a South Pacific island.

Other authors and other books have detailed the history of the Pitcairnese sexual assault trials that began in 2004 and that, by 2006, had cost more than NZ$14 million (the equivalent of more almost £10 million) and which saw six of the island's male population, including the mayor of Adamstown, convicted of sexual offenses. This painful moment in the island's history – a moment whose memory continues to tear at the social cohesion of the Pitcairnese community – is not the focus of our story. We cannot, though, spare our story from at least a glancing intersection with this excruciating ordeal, for the world learned many things about Pitcairn Island in the years from 2004 to 2006, and much of what we learned had roots in the history we have been tracing in these chapters.

We know, for instance, that the seven Pitcairnese defendants – one of the six men would eventually be acquitted – offered several possible lines of defense that drew on our history. At the level of culture, the accused men suggested that Pitcairn Island's sexual practices descended directly from the community's Tahitian founding mothers. This was an argument made from cultural relativism. As one observer has suggested, this line of argumentation leaves us with very little of a ledge on which to set our morality. Mutiny, in this way of thinking, gets multiplied into "a multiplicity of different claims of cultural distinctiveness."[136] That such an

---

[133] E. Schubert, "Pitcairn Island Today," in Alan S. C. Ross and A. W. Moverley, *The Pitcairnese Language* (New York: Oxford University Press, 1964), 27.
[134] Aldrich and John Connell, *The Last Colonies*, 102.
[135] Winchester, Pacific, location 3404.
[136] Colm O'Cinneide, "'A Million Mutinies Now': Why Claims of Cultural Uniqueness Cannot Be Used to Justify Violations of Basic Human Rights," in Dawn Oliver, ed.,

argument even entered into the trials in 2004 is arguably a consequence of history. As Michael Sturma has observed, one "feature that was commonly omitted in accounts of early European visits to Tahiti is the extreme youth of many of the females who engaged in sexual relations."[137] Commonly omitted and deeply disturbing. As Sturma notes, Captain Henry Ibbot of the *Dolphin* was shocked to find that many of the young women who sailed to greet his crew when it landed at Tahiti were merely "girls." George Forster concurred with Ibbot's assessment. Most of the Tahitian women who offered sex to Captain Cook's sailors were hardly ten years old, few demonstrated "the least marks of puberty."[138]

As we saw in the previous chapter, Europeans were eager to talk about the sexual appetites of Tahitian women. For sailors, these stories offered the promise of heterosexual company – and more – after months on board a ship with only men as companions. For evangelicals, these same stories outlined the South Pacific peccability that was the target of nineteenth-century religious reform. That both communities invoked Polynesian sexuality for their own ends while also masking underage sexuality on islands like Tahiti paved the way for the sexual abuse of underage victims on Pitcairn. Of course, sex-related crimes abounded at Pitcairn, even if they have not always been pointed out. They have never really been hidden. We know that Fletcher Christian and the other eight mutineers who settled at Pitcairn with him kidnapped at least some of the dozen Tahitian women they took with them to that island.[139] We know too that the mutineers "traded" those women among themselves and "stole" them from the Polynesian men who were among the *Bounty* settlers at Pitcairn.

The world was only shocked in 2004, then, because the trials forced a global awakening to history that had been hidden beneath romantic tropes. Recall that history is as much about what we choose to forget as it is about what we select to remember. "Memory and forgetting are not," as Bill Schwartz has written, "separate practices, but are interlinked, the one a function of the other."[140] The problematic mismatch between Western and Polynesian sexuality – to say nothing of the criminally aggressive ways that Euro-Americans approached sex in the Pacific – was not simply hard to figure into the mythology of the South Pacific. It was impossible to figure in, and so it was set to the side. There was never an attempt to tell

---

Justice, Legality, and the Rule of Law: Lessons from the Pitcairn Prosecutions (New York: Oxford University Press, 2009), 133.
[137] Sturma, *South Sea Maidens*, 23.   [138] Ibid.
[139] Lewis, "Pitcairn's Tortured Past," in Oliver, ed., *Justice, Legality, and the Rule of Law*, 45.
[140] Schwartz, *Memories of Empire*, 6.

this story as it actually was. No. The truth would have compromised the romance of Bali Ha'i, that unattainable island paradise of Rodgers and Hammerstein's 1949 musical, *South Pacific* – itself an adaptation of Michener's *Tales of the South Pacific*. Something had to be forgotten, but the act of forgetting came at a cost.

At the juridical level, the seven Pitcairnese defendants also tried to suggest that they were not British subjects and, so, not bound by any age-of-consent laws passed in London. Mutiny, after all, was Pitcairn's founding impulse.[141] According to this argument, the nine mutineers who settled at Pitcairn had renounced their connection to the British crown when they mutinied against Captain Bligh, and, in doing so, they had disassociated themselves from the Common Law precedent that English subjects carried the Common Law with them wherever they chose to settle.[142] The Common Law, obviously, had never applied to the island's founding mothers. The Supreme Court, a group of judges from New Zealand who had been empaneled by London for the purposes of hearing these cases, took very little time in swatting aside this protestation. Pitcairn was a colony and, as such, was subject to the Sexual Offences Act passed by the Parliament at Westminster in 1956.[143]

As we have seen, Joshua Hill had a great deal to do with this conclusion. True, there was legal wiggle room to suggest that Pitcairn had only *officially* been incorporated into the British Empire in 1887, and true it may have been that Pitcairn had been only casually, distantly, and infrequently governed from London throughout the nineteenth and twentieth centuries.[144] But the fact remained, the judges ruled, that Pitcairners had a long tradition of viewing themselves as British subjects *and* of actively seeking out protection from the British crown, most notably in 1838 when the islanders begged Captain Elliott to give them both a Union Jack to fly over their island and a constitution to regulate their internal affairs. They

---

[141] Dino Kritsiotis and A. W. B. Simpson, "The Pitcairn Prosecutions: An Assessment of their Historical Contexts by Reference to the Provisions of Public International Law," in Dawn Oliver, ed., *Justice, Legality, and the Rule of Law: Lessons from the Pitcairn Prosecutions* (New York: Oxford University Press, 2009), 96–97. See also, Letsas, "Rights and Duties on Pitcairn Island," in Oliver, ed., *Justice, Legality, and the Rule of Law*, 182; and Dawn Oliver, "The Pitcairn Prosecutions, Paper Legal Systems, and the Rule of Law," in Dawn Oliver, ed., *Justice, Legality, and the Rule of Law: Lessons from the Pitcairn Prosecutions* (New York: Oxford University Press, 2009), 24.

[142] Dawn Oliver, "Problems on Pitcairn," in Dawn Oliver, ed., *Justice, Legality, and the Rule of Law: Lessons from the Pitcairn Prosecutions* (New York: Oxford University Press, 2009), 2.

[143] Dawn Oliver, "The Pitcairn Prosecutions," in Oliver, ed., *Justice, Legality, and the Rule of Law*, 25.

[144] Dawn Oliver, "Problems on Pitcairn," in Oliver, ed., *Justice, Legality, and the Rule of Law*, 11. See also, Lewis, "Pitcairn's Tortured Past," in Oliver, ed., *Justice, Legality, and the Rule of Law*, 61.

asked for both of these things to help them secure themselves and their community from the fraudulent intrusions of subsequent interlopers like the recently exiled Joshua Hill.[145]

As with their argument about their Tahitian ancestry and the relativity of sexual praxis across cultures, the defendants were, here, making an argument rooted in our story, for they were questioning the very nature of the British presence in the Pacific. What, they were asking, was Pitcairn Island? Founded in mutiny, it had been governed neglectfully. Joshua Hill, the men might have suggested, was correct. London had never paid any real or persistent attention to the island, so how could a law regulating sexual consent be passed in London and enforced some nine thousand miles away at Adamstown? Ultimately, though, it was not the neglect that Hill so abhorred that won the day during the trials at Pitcairn. Rather, it was the colonial administration that Hill sought – the colonial attention that he drew to the island – that convicted six of the seven defendants.

Hill had argued that Pitcairn should receive more colonial attention. Britain had to be mindful of its naval power, its global empire, and its Pacific might. And, in taking it upon himself to tend to what London would not, Joshua Hill, rather ironically forced London to do exactly what he had argued for – namely, to incorporate Pitcairn into a formal network of colonial control – in order to rid itself of Joshua Hill and others who might follow in his footsteps. The 1838 Pitcairnese constitution, in effect, marked the end of Hill's reign at Adamstown, the success of many of his policy goals for the island, and the undoing of the legal defense that six Pitcairners would offer more than one hundred and sixty years after Hill last cast his eyes upon that small Pacific island.

None of these historical connections will, of course, salve the wounds left in the wake of the 2004 trials. A third of Pitcairn's male population was convicted as sex offenders in those cases. Families were torn apart over what ought to have been done about the allegations and the crimes. Lives were left in ruins. We have had to reopen these painful scars, though, because these early twenty-first-century trials echoed so many of the global issues – matters of law, culture, and colonialism – that were always at the heart of Pitcairnese history, matters that, we might argue, are always intertwined and always at work in any history set upon and within the world's ocean. We have only been able to make these

---

[145] See Dawn Oliver, "The Pitcairn Prosecutions," in Oliver, ed., *Justice, Legality, and the Rule of Law*, 26. See also, Gordon Woodman, "Pitcairn Island Law: A Peculiar Case of Diffusion of the Common Law," in Dawn Oliver, ed., *Justice, Legality, and the Rule of Law: Lessons from the Pitcairn Prosecutions* (New York: Oxford University Press, 2009), 80–81; and Kritsiotis and Simpson, "The Pitcairn Prosecutions," in Oliver, ed., *Justice, Legality, and the Rule of Law*, 113.

connections because we have taken Joshua Hill seriously, because we have recollected a history that had been left to be forgotten. As Bill Schwartz has argued, "when something is forgotten from an individual consciousness, or is pushed aside in the stories a society tells about itself, then chances are that something important is happening."[146]

Items lost in the historical past, though, need not remain forgotten or, as Schwartz has suggested might be the case, "repressed." Hints of the forgotten past "may enter the popular consciousness through ... surreptitious means."[147] Pitcairn's story, of course, was never truly forgotten. The romantic epic that is the *Bounty* saga is not likely to fade from historical memory any time soon. The time is drawing near when we are due for a new film adaptation of this story from Hollywood. It has been more than three decades now, after all, since Orion Pictures released the most recent screen version of the story, *The Bounty* (1984), starring a young Mel Gibson as Fletcher Christian and Anthony Hopkins as Captain Bligh.

The story, though, has more pop-cultural resonance than just a handful of old films. Tell a passing acquaintance, for instance, that you are reading a book about the *Bounty*'s history (or writing one, for that matter), and you are apt to be met with a growling impersonation of a grumpy Captain Bligh. "Mr. Christian!," your friend may well shout at you. Even in that response, however, we are alert to the reality that Pitcairn is never really viewed as the central stage for this drama. Most of the poems, movies, and novels that tell the tale of Christian, Bligh, and the *Bounty* end just as the mutineers land at Pitcairn. Even the historian Stephen Royle has written that there has been no real need to detail the history of a place where the "day-to-day management of" the island "must have been a humdrum existence."[148]

We can, I think, take exception to the notion that anything in this story was truly "humdrum," even beyond the settlement at Pitcairn and the immolation of the HMS *Bounty*. This was, as newspapers reported throughout the nineteenth century, an "extraordinary history."[149] Pitcairn is microscopic almost to the point of being insignificant, particularly in the history of an empire – the British Empire – that once spanned a fourth of the earth's terrestrial surface and administered a fifth of the world's human population. The scope, though, cannot be

---

[146] Schwartz, *Memories of Empire*, 203.   [147] Ibid., 54.

[148] Stephen A. Royle, "Health and Health Care in Pitcairn Island in 1841: The Report of Surgeon William Gunn of HMS *Curaçoa*," in *The Journal of Pacific History* 35:2 (September 2000), 213.

[149] "Descendants of the *Bounty*'s Crew, on Pitcairn's Island," in *The Calcutta Journal* (Tuesday, July 12, 1819).

what we are measuring here, for there is a great deal of historical importance at work in the history of Pitcairn Island and its colonial status within
the British Empire. Pitcairn's history, as we have seen, pulled Britain
more fully into the imperial history of the Pacific. It was, in a profound
and ironic way, mutiny – the resistance to central authority – that poured
the foundation for British imperialism in the mid-Pacific, just as it was
convicts and criminals who populated that more official bit of colonial
terrain at Port Jackson in Australia.

Pitcairn's history, then, has a David and Goliath quality to it, or Jack
and the Beanstalk, if you prefer a less biblical metaphor. The historical
substance of Pitcairn's history is to be found, as is the case in these other
two examples, in the meaning drawn from the *stories* we tell about those
young heroes – David and Jack – or about tiny Pitcairn Island, and
I invoke the word "story" here very intentionally. Here is a history of
one very small island situated in what we have come to respect as a global
ocean. It is a small island bound to another island – an island nation –
situated in another ocean just off the coast of the European continent. For
us to conceive of these two histories as distinct simply because they are so
far removed one from the other or because they find their homes in
different oceans is, we have discovered, simply wrong. The story of each
island is braided to the story of the other. They are bound by the history of
the global ocean, which, as we have seen earlier, is not limited merely to
the actual footprint of the Pacific Ocean per se or to historical events that
happen within the space of the Pacific basin. The global ocean encom-
passes more widely.

Writing about Britain, Jonathan Scott has observed that London functioned as something of a "gateway to the world" over the course of its
imperial history. We see this aspect of Britain's historical past, he argues,
when we assume "an island-centered view of global political space."[150]
In our story, Pitcairn has turned out to be a gateway to much bigger
histories in its own unique way. As Jill Franks has written,

islands are the place *par excellence* of dreams, so universal a symbol that Melville
wrote, "in the soul of man there lies one insular Tahiti," and Dea Birkett echoed
him, a century and a half later, with the words, "We all hold a place within our
hearts – a perfect place – which is in the shape of an island."[151]

Islands, it turns out, sit not on the postcolonial periphery.[152] Melville and
Birkett had it right. Islands reside at the center and in our soul. Pitcairn
Island, in short, cannot be written off in the history of Britain's global

---

[150] Scott, *When the Waves Rules Britannia*, 175–176.
[151] Franks, *Islands and the Modernists*, 4.   [152] Ibid., 6.

empire simply because it is an island, because it is small, or because it is a small island. From its peripheral coordinates deep within the Pacific Ocean, Pitcairn merits a place in the central narrative.

That notion sounds profoundly romantic in its own right. It is not intended to be. This history, I would argue, has demonstrated that there is far less room for romance on an island than we might have expected when we began our tale. In an essay in *The Pacific Islands*, Lamont Lindstrom mourned the passing of "a castaway existence," citing Pitcairn as the ideal case study. "Even the few surviving families on isolated Pitcairn Islands," Lindstrom observed, "get mail and radio transmissions."[153] In Lindstrom's view, the world is getting flatter and more interconnected, a change that, he predicts, will consume Pitcairn's salad days. Of course, as we have seen, Pitcairn was always connected, and the salad days were always less palatable than Lord Byron, Herman Melville, and others might have had us believe.

Pitcairn's history, particularly since the age of Joshua Hill, has been an obviously important and intricately connected piece of Britain's much larger – and shifting – colonial history in the Pacific. Pitcairn's history in the age of Joshua Hill is also, though, a history of the global ocean, a story that is woven into narrative historical currents that span from the Pacific to Britain, from Britain to France, from France to America, from America to India, and from India back to the Pacific. And, there are countless stops to be made in a myriad of locations all along those routes. This is, we have come to understand, a brutal story. It is hardly romantic. But, this is also a story that is, I might argue, too big to be contained by history alone. Perhaps that is why the poetry, and the fiction, and, yes, the lies have all always mixed so easily with the truth. Did Joshua Hill appreciate that this was the case? It would be frustraneous to try to say for certain. What we can know is that, far from trying to disentangle fact from fiction at Pitcairn, Hill further bound the two together.

That Hill wound fact and fiction together at Pitcairn and that he tied his "yarn" to the narrative thread of British colonial history in the Pacific – indeed, across the globe – is revelatory. When Joshua Hill landed at Pitcairn Island in 1832, he was not there to brabble over insignificant affairs on a small island. No. He had a sense of what Britain's global power ought to be. It was a deeply held sense, so deeply held, in fact, that Hill would do whatever he had to do to see his vision through. He was, without a doubt, a zealot, and it was overzealousness, in the end, that did

---

[153] Lamont Lindstrom, "Social Relations," in Moshe Rapaport, ed., *The Pacific Islands: Environment and Society* (Honolulu: University of Hawai'i Press, 2013. Kindle Edition), location 7925 of 21398.

Joshua Hill in. But, before he told his lies, Joshua Hill had had no influence on any aspect of British colonial policy, and not for want of trying.

We have to conclude – and this is the crucial point – that it was the same misguided fervor and the same set of lies that drove Hill to go to Pitcairn and to birdlime its inhabitants that, eventually, triggered action in London (at the Admiralty, at Mission House, and at Whitehall) as well as throughout the British imperial world. To quote the prize-winning, Sri Lankan-born novelist and poet Michael Ondaatje, "a well-told lie is worth a thousand facts."[154] The lie can be power. It was for Joshua Hill, a man who – without any authority to do so – helped build an empire in the Pacific with a well-told lie.

---

[154] Michael Ondaatje, *Running in the Family* (New York: Vintage, 1982), 206.

Epilogue: The Self-Constituted King of Pitcairn

> All we discover has been with us since the sun began to roll; and much we discover, is not worth the discovering.
>
> Herman Melville, *Mardi, and A Voyage Thither* (1849)[1]

On October 28, 1832, after sailing for how many days history will likely never know, an enigmatic man, then aged fifty-nine, landed at Pitcairn Island. It was a Sunday...

Like Captain Ahab in his quest for vengeance against the great, white whale, we have chased Joshua W. Hill "round Good Hope, and round the Horn, and round the Norway Maelstrom, and round perdition's flames." We have been persistent. We have not given up.[2] Here at our journey's end, we have to ask a pressing question, one inspired not by *Moby-Dick*, however, but by Melville's earlier (and widely panned) novel *Mardi: And a Voyage Thither* of 1849. What have we learned by taking this voyage with Joshua Hill? Do we end with the discovery that "all we discover has been with us since the sun began to roll"? And, if we have discovered anything new, has it been "worth the discovering"?[3]

Perhaps here, at the end of our yarn, it is a time for introductions. Perhaps, after everything, you might wish to meet Captain Joshua W. Hill. As we have found, it is not easy to find this man. Maybe Herman Melville – how often we return to Herman Melville in the Pacific! – described him best in Typee when the author introduced his fellow castaway Toby Greene. "He was," Melville wrote,

one of that class of rovers you sometimes meet at sea, who never reveal their origin, never allude to home, and go rambling over the world as if pursued by some mysterious fate they cannot possibly elude.[4]

A rover. Mysterious. Pursued. These are all suitable ways to frame Joshua Hill's life and his time in the Pacific. But, can we know more? There is only one known picture purporting to be an image of our

---

[1] Herman Melville, *Mardi, and A Voyage Thither* (Boston: The St. Botolph Society, 1923), 509–510.
[2] Melville, *Moby-Dick*, 167.   [3] Melville, *Mardi*, 509–510.   [4] Melville, *Typee*, 32.

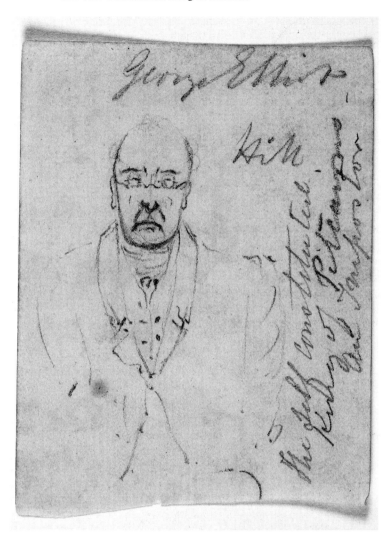

Figure 13 George Elliot, *Pencil Sketch of Joshua Hill*, in Pitcairn Islanders: Autographs and Pencil Sketches. SLNSW Ap25/Pitcairn Island. Folder 1. Fourth Sketch. Published by permission of the State Library of New South Wales, Mitchell Library, Sydney.

protagonist.[5] It is a small pencil sketch, hardly bigger than a passport photograph. It is old, and it is faded. In the image, we see the face of

[5] Elliot, Pencil Sketch of Joshua Hill, in Pitcairn Islanders: Autographs and Pencil Sketches.

a weathered pilgarlic. Beneath the bald half-circle of his head, Hill has a deep and furrowed brow. He is wearing a pair of small, wire-rimmed glasses that give him a double-dome or professorial appearance. But, oddly, the artist who sketched the picture did not draw in Hill's eyes. Like a puppet from Jim Henson's studios, the man in this drawing has only open ovals from which to see the world.

This singular picture of Joshua Hill shows him to be more than a little mumpish. The drawing only gives us Hill from the waist up, and, for the most part, what we see below Hill's neck is – at best – only thinly penciled in. What we can make out, though, shows no signs of a man who would be king, no real signs of grandeur. This is the Gospel-hauler, the evangelical, the missionary we have met already. There is no foofaraw here. Hill does wear an ascot and a waistcoat, but neither is hoity-toity. Rather, they demonstrate a domesticated propriety, a sense that a stern schoolmaster, and not a self-styled king, has come to Pitcairn Island.

In the center of Hill's face, we see a sharp, thin nose. It is Hill's mouth, though, that is his most delineated feature in this sketch. Not quite a snarl, this man's mouth suggests a rictus-like moue. There is no abundance of generosity in this face. No sense of humor. Perhaps, no sense of kindness, though that may be taking things too far. Even the picture's identifying label, though, suggests austerity. This is not Joshua Hill, or Joshua W. Hill, or Captain Joshua W. Hill. This man requires only one name. He is simply "Hill." This is, one suspects, the sort of man who might frighten babies just by peeping into their prams.

We have this one small image of Joshua Hill thanks to Sir George Elliot. The second son of the First Earl of Minto, George Elliot had the good fortune to serve onboard the HMS *Victory* under the famed Lord Horatio Nelson. Having caught the eye of prominent political patrons, Elliot was promoted to the office of Secretary to the Admiralty in November 1830. He remained at the post until 1834. At the end of that year, as Lord Melbourne prepared to assume the British premiership, George Elliot knew that he too was poised to be given a new job, for the new Prime Minister asked Elliot's older brother Gilbert, the Second Earl of Minto to serve the new administration as First Lord of the Admiralty. In the sort of nepotism that was, in the nineteenth century, as of yet permissible, George Elliot was tapped by his older brother to serve as the Lord Commissioner of the Admiralty, the third highest ranking office in the British naval chain of command.[6]

---

[6] "Sir George Elliot," in *The Dictionary of National Biography – Volume VI* (New York: Oxford University Press, 1921, 669–671).

Figure 14 George Elliot, Detail of *Pencil Sketch of Joshua Hill*, in Pitcairn Islanders: Autographs and Pencil Sketches. SLNSW Ap25/Pitcairn Island. Folder 1. Fourth Sketch. Published by permission of the State Library of New South Wales, Mitchell Library, Sydney.

Elliot's biography explains why it was that he would have been interested in Pitcairn Island and in our Mr. Hill. The large, scrawling "George Elliot" across the top of the Hill sketch, though, does not tell us that Elliot drew the picture. Indeed, he almost certainly did not, though the Mitchell Library in Sydney (where the image is now held) attributes the sketch to Elliot. Joshua Hill, remember, was on Pitcairn Island. George Elliot was in London, at the Admiralty. More likely, then, is a scenario in which the Hill drawing, as well as the others now collected with it in a folder there in the archives in Sydney, was made *for* rather than *by* Elliot. George Elliot is not signing his art; he is labeling his property, a picture that came into his hands because of his job, a job that – in the 1830s – required him to sort out a confusing political squabble on a small and seemingly insignificant South Pacific island.

If we turn the Hill drawing on its edge – a ninety-degree flip to the right – we see that this picture of "Hill" did require some description, for there on the picture's edge is written "The Self-Constituted King of Pitcairn's – An Impostor." Did Elliot label the picture? Did the artist who sketched it for Elliot? We cannot know for sure. What we can know, though, is that the person who labeled this small picture wanted everybody who saw it to know that Joshua W. Hill was a fraud, a bumptious Dogberry who had honeyfuggled the Pitcairn Islanders and caused no small amount of trouble for Britain and its navy as a result. That is not an inappropriate or, even, ahistorical interpretation of Joshua Hill's biography or of the events that transpired at Pitcairn Island between 1832 and 1838.

As we have seen, historians, of both the professional and armchair persuasions, have largely accepted this narrative about Hill and his time at Pitcairn. Today, of course, only a few really know anything about the story to begin with. Even the majority of *Bounty* enthusiasts focus largely on the *Bounty*'s voyage up to the arrival at Pitcairn rather than upon the story that happened once the *Bounty* settlers climbed the Hill of Difficulty. In the nineteenth-century, Hill's name had a bit more cultural purchase. That Mark Twain took up this peculiar moment in Pitcairnese history in his short story "The Great Revolution in Pitcairn" of 1879 ought to give us some comfort that we have indeed been looking at a substantive, if unconventional, chapter in Pacific history. Even Twain, though, read Joshua Hill as a hingkponk – an impostor, a fraud.[7]

Twain's is not, though, the story I have told. Twain and others had obsessed over Hill's great lie. I, though, have asked that we use Joshua Hill's story to explore what Robert Zoellner has called "alternative ways of seeing things."[8] I have asked that we be more suspicious of the fine line between truth and fiction. Charles Haddon Spurgeon, one of Britain's most celebrated, nineteenth-century Baptist preachers, once wrote that "a lie will go round the world while the truth is pulling its boots on."[9] Spurgeon's observation – often attributed, interestingly, to Mark Twain – seems a particularly appropriate epithet for Joshua Hill's brief dictatorship at Pitcairn Island at multiple levels. On one hand, we have here the story of one man and his big lie – that London wanted him to govern Pitcairn. That singular lie has heretofore been the only thing historians have wanted to tell us about Joshua Hill; the lie has gone round the world more than once. But, Hill's lie need not blind us to the broader truths that are buried in his biography, within his "philanthropic tour of the Pacific" and his tyrannical rule at Pitcairn. Indeed, the lie itself is telling. It is part of the tale. It speaks to Hill's hubris and to the hubris of the empires that were beginning to reach out into the Pacific in the early nineteenth century.

At the same time, Hill's great lie *has* obscured the truth of the story for far too long. Because Hill lied about the legitimacy of his authority at Pitcairn, historians have assumed that he lied about everything else as well. While the one lie has been going round and round the world, the truth has not even had a pair of boots to pull on. By taking the rest of Hill's autobiography seriously, we have woven a new pattern in the fabric of this *yarn*. We have accomplished several historical ends. First, and most basically, we have developed a better picture of this idiosyncratic man – this ghostly figure whose face we will probably only ever know from one small, faded pencil sketch. After all, Joshua Hill is interesting. He decided

---

[7] Twain, "The Great Revolution in Pitcairn."
[8] Robert Zoellner, *The Salt-Sea Mastodon: A Reading of Moby-Dick* (Los Angeles: University of California Press, 1973), 266.
[9] Charles Haddon Spurgeon, *Gems from Spurgeon; or, Extracts from the Note-Book of a Non-Professional Reporter* (London: Partridge and Company, 1858), 74.

that one small island of mixed-race South Pacific Islanders were so deeply in danger of losing their godly character that he got on a boat and sailed around the world only to lie to his chosen people and hold them in fear of his wrath for the better part of a decade. Second, and more significantly, by taking Mr. Hill's biography more seriously, we have exposed a set of global connectivities that better enable us to understand the complex nature of Pacific Ocean history in the nineteenth century and, perhaps, beyond.

"Blubber is blubber, you know." So, once, wrote Herman Melville to Richard Henry Dana. Whale fat was not worth much. You had "to cook the thing up" to give it value. Melville's observations were, of course, true with regard to the production of whale oil. But the great author was not talking about whale oil when he wrote to Dana. He was talking about his greatest sea yarn (arguably *the* greatest sea yarn), *Moby-Dick*, a novel that, on its surface, was merely about a man and a whale. But, in Melville's hands, the novel became something more. It did so because Melville knew that he had "to cook the thing up, one must needs throw in a little fancy." The result was a powerful book, a tale that was larger even – if we can imagine that to be possible – than its title character, the great white leviathan of the depths. It was a book filled with "fancy" and yet a book that "g[a]ve the truth of the thing."[10] Joshua Hill's story has had a similar purpose. What has heretofore been left aside as mere "blubber" has proven to be more once we cooked it up and added a bit of fancy. It has, perhaps, given us a new sense of truth about the bigger history of the Pacific.[11]

But, what became of Joshua Hill? You will recall that we last left Hill at Valparaíso in Chilé. Had he become such a boon companion to Captain Bruce and to Midshipman John C. Dalrymple Hay that he went down to the port to see them off as they sailed onboard the *Imogene* for Callao? Was he forbidden passage any further than Valparaíso? We simply do not know. Likely, we never will. We do know that Hill returned to London. In 1841, remember, he submitted a memorandum to the British government outlining the work he had done at Pitcairn – among other "services" he claims to have rendered to his nation – and he asked, without any obvious sense of irony, to be paid for his efforts. Three years later, Hill published one more small piece, an attack on the morality of contemporary missionaries.[12] There was nothing white-livered about Joshua Hill.

---

[10] Melville quoted in Erik Hage, *The Melville-Hawthorne Connection: A Story of the Literary Friendship* (Jefferson, NC: McFarland and Company, Inc., 2014. Kindle Edition), 119. See also, Delbanco, *Melville*, location 1064.
[11] McKenzie, *Scandal in the Colonies*, 32.   [12] Nicholson, *The Pitcairners*, 152–153.

Up to the end, he was ready for the attack, if and when he felt it was justified.

There are tantalizing personal details in Hill's memorandum. The toing and froing in and around the Pacific had destroyed his constitution, and he had developed a diabetic disorder as a consequence. That was the least of his worries, though, for when he returned home to Liverpool, Hill found that his wife had left him, running away to continental Europe. This is a man who had suffered for a cause and whom, he suggests, deserved compensation.[13] It goes almost without saying that Joshua Hill was never paid for his supposed services. According to census data, we know that Hill was living in London when he submitted his petition for remuneration. He was, in that period, in his late sixties, and the only member of his household at the time was a woman by the name of Harriet Beech, then age twenty-two.[14] Beech, we might assume, was his housekeeper. Subsequent demographic records indicate that Joshua Hill died in January 1848, at the age of seventy-five. He was buried on the last day of the year in the cemetery at St. Pancras Old Church in central London.[15]

In the 1860s, as London's rail network was expanding, parts of the old St. Pancras churchyard had to be dug up to make way for new terminals and new rail lines. At the time, a young architect from the office of Arthur Bloomfield by the name of Thomas Hardy, who was still in his twenties and not yet a famous author, was the overseer on the project to exhume and relocate those who had been buried in the cemetery. Hardy's was a difficult, even gruesome, task, but, as if predicting his future artistic talents, the young architect decided that the uprooted headstones from the graveyard should not be tossed unceremoniously into the Thames. Rather, Hardy decided to place the grave markers in a lovely circular pattern around a young ash tree growing on the outer edge of the cemetery, far enough removed from the rail and engineering works that they would never again be "in the way." The tree, of course, has now grown quite large, and it is widely known as the "Thomas Hardy Tree." No records were kept to indicate whose names are on the headstones now grouped under that tree, but it is tempting to imagine that somewhere in the blooming arrangement of stone slabs at the base of that sturdy, English ash tree, might be a simple gravestone with the name "Joshua W. Hill" etched on its surface. What else, we have to wonder, did Hill have carved on the

---

[13] Hill, *The Humble Memorial,* particularly pages 11–12.
[14] England Census, 1841, TNA HO 107/686/15.
[15] St. Pancras Parish Church, Register of Burials, London Metrpolitan Archives, P90/PAN1, Item 189, 90.

stone? What else, there at the end, did he want the world to know about himself?

Joshua Hill died three years too early to have read Herman Melville's *Moby-Dick*. Given the lackluster reviews the massive tome received when it was first published, Hill might have passed by the book without reading it anyway. Most people did, after all. Hill, though, would have liked Captain Ahab. At least, I like to think he would have. There was not an ounce of cowardice in either man. Neither was a poltroon. On board the *Pequod*, Ahab expected that his word would be law. As C. L. R. James observed in his literary analysis of Melville's now-classic novel, Ahab "never speaks but in the imperative mood. He commands even the sun. For when the noon observation is taken, it is officially twelve o'clock only when the captain says '*Make* it so'."[16] At Pitcairn, Hill governed the same way, with the same absolute authority. Or, at least, he sought to govern that way, for, like Ahab, he was a man on a mission.

Ahab would let nothing stand in the way of his work. Hill was the same. In the novel, we see the fictitious captain smash the *Pequod*'s sextant, that key scientific tool for determining the ship's location, course, and direction. Even science, he demands, will answer to him and his cause, the destruction of the white whale. "What I've dared, I've willed," Ahab exclaims, "and what I've willed, I'll do!"[17] That sentence could easily have come from Hill's mouth. Both men were monomaniacal, to use one of Melville's favorite adjectives, and those around them thought that both Captain Hill and Captain Ahab were a bit deranged. There was something of the moon flaw in both men. Both were dreamers, some might even say lunatics. Nobbs saw it in Hill. Evans saw it. Buffett saw it. On board the *Pequod*, Ahab's chief mate, Starbuck, saw it too. When there was a white whale to hunt, though, a little madness might be forgiven. "I'm demoniac," Ahab confessed. "I am madness maddened!"[18]

To know Joshua Hill has required that we reconstruct something of his world. It was, as we have seen, a very big world. We have trusted a man who, we know, was not always honest with us in the historical record. But every historian, Dening has argued, "is engaged in some form of reenactment."[19] What we have done with Mr. Hill is nothing different than what any other historian would do with any other subject. We have

[16] C. L. R. James, *Mariners, Renegades, and Castaways: The Story of Herman Melville and the World We Live In*, Donald E. Pease, ed. (Hanover, NH: University Press of New England, 2001), 79.

[17] Melville, *Moby-Dick*, 172. [18] Ibid.

[19] Dening, "Deep Time, Deep Spaces," in Klein and Mackenthun, eds., *Sea Changes*, 21. See also, Greg Dening, *Performances* (Chicago: University of Chicago Press, 1996), xiv.

reconstructed his world. We have been privileged to experience his "present moment," at least to the degree that we can.[20]

But, knowing Hill has also left us with a profound sense of historical humility, for there is a good deal more that we cannot know and will never know about this tale. How did Joshua Hill pay for his voyage to Pitcairn? How did he manage to get from Valparaíso to London again? What became of Hill's wife after her move to Europe? These are all very good questions, and I can confess that they sit heavily on my mind. It is hard to know that we will not know, but I rather think it has become clear in all of the tales we have told that our knowledge of Joshua Hill's life need not be cyclopedic in order to be historically valuable. Paul Lyons has argued that we do well to pay attention to the root verb buried inside the word "ignorance." That root, of course, is "ignore." Ignorance, Lyons posits, is a "resistance to knowledge."[21] Ignorance and not knowing are not the same state of affairs. In the case of Mr. Hill's history, we can take pride in our endeavors, even though we know that there is so much more that we do not and will not know about this man. We can say that we have not been and are not now ignorant. We have insisted that Joshua Hill not be ignored any longer.

At a certain level, of course, Joshua Hill's biography will always belong on the library shelf with accounts of other hucksters, frauds, and cheats. As we have seen, unpacking the simplicity of that categorization has demonstrated that the very category of *imposter* is both historically problematic and intellectually useful. All of the cases we have used as comparison in the course of this book – de Thierry, Tichborne, de Rougemont, and Caraboo – leave us begging for the historical "truth." Of course, as Partha Chatterjee has observed, these stories frequently end at a moment when "the truth turns out to be undecidable."[22] These "histories," if we want to call them that, require quasi-judicial verdicts. We have to decide what is fact and what is factious. The challenge comes, of course, when we accept that verdicts are never, to quote Australian novelist Michael de Kretser "a matter of fact but a point of view."[23]

More important, as Sara Burton has argued, than the simple truth of who an imposter was as compared with the claims that he or she might have made is the simple ability these men and women had to sustain their

[20] Dening, "Deep Time, Deep Spaces," in Klein and Mackenthun, eds., *Sea Changes*, 21.

[21] Paul Lyons, *American Pacificism: Oceania in the U.S. Imagination* (New York: Routledge, 2006), 10.

[22] Partha Chatterjee, *A Princely Imposter?: The Strange and Universal History of the Kumar of Bhawal* (Princeton, NJ: Princeton University Press, 2002), xii.

[23] Michael de Ketser, *The Hamilton Case* (New York: Back Bay Books, 2003), 302.

claims in the face of the wider world's incredulity.[24] In order to convince, the story that an imposter sets out to tell has to resonate with and within its contemporary world. A lie does not work if it does not seem plausible. "I have been sent from London to be your governor." The claim seems so obviously spurious to us today, but it was not so clearly false in 1832. No Pitcairner, you see, would have believed that declaration had they not known that Pitcairn had been in a state of disquiet in the years before Hill's arrival, had they not just been moved to Tahiti by London's authority, had they not been aware that London was beginning to pay more heed to its small possessions across the wide waters of the Pacific Ocean. And, as Burton has reminded us, the historical imposters we know of are, by definition, *not* history's best liars. We know who these people are precisely because they got caught.[25] Be assured, there are others like Joshua Hill out there whom we will never meet – men and women who got away with it!

We have spent time with Joshua Hill, and, for our effort, we know him better now than we did before. We also know that there is much left to be known that is forever out of our reach. Like Sir Isaac Newton, we feel like little children "playing on the sea shore ... while the great ocean of truth lay all undiscovered before" us.[26] What we have discovered is that Philip Snow, editor of the collection *Best Stories of the South Seas*, was wrong. Snow argued that the South Pacific "needs little fiction" added to it because it was so fraught with "inherent drama."[27] The Pacific has been the stage for a trove of great (and another trove of not-so-great) literature. It has been home to some of history's best authors and most storied artists. The Pacific has inspired fiction; it *has* needed fiction. As this account of Joshua Hill's time at Pitcairn has demonstrated, we cannot tell the history of the Pacific as it actually was unless we are willing to integrate the fictions, the lies, and the slippery details that are neither true nor false into one narrative.

Of course, to weave these yarns together into a tale is not to equate the acceptance of fact and fiction as the same thing. In Glynn Christian's *Mrs. Christian*, the Pitcairn Islanders face hard choices about how to tell the outside world what has happened in the early years of their colonial settlement. Ultimately, they decide that truth and fiction amounted to the same thing. "When you live on an island like this," they argue, "so far away, truth is often ... Well, sometimes truth has to be what is most convenient."[28] Joshua Hill's story has never suggested that we should

[24] Sarah Burton, *Imposters: Six Kinds of Liar* (New York: Penguin Books, 2001), 2.
[25] Ibid.   [26] Quoted in Kreeft, *The Sea Within Us*, 87.
[27] Philip Snow, ed., *Best Stories of the South Seas* (London: Faber and Faber, 1967), 9.
[28] Christian, *Mrs. Christian*, 417.

accept lies as truth. It has, though, suggested that we have to appreciate that lies have a place in historical memory.

In Joshua Hill's biography, we have discovered something bigger than the history of one life, though the humanist training that undergirds my historian's mind suggests to me that, even in exploring *one* life we have undertaken something meaningful. In Hill's life, we have validated David Lambert and Alan Lester's assertion that

each colonial life provides insight not only into the heterogeneity of the empire and the multiple subject positions that arose from this "variegated terrain," but also how ideas, practices and identities developed *trans-imperially* as they moved from one imperial site to another.[29]

Lambert and Lester's effort has been to reframe the way we think about empire, focusing on the complex and web-like circuit of empire rather than models that posit a spoke-like structure that emphasizes the connections between colonies and the metropole directly.[30] Older models for thinking about empire, of course, started at the center and looked outwards – down the spokes of the wheel. More recently, efforts have tried to reverse the polarity of that model, starting from the periphery and working backwards to the center of the wheel, as it were. What Lambert and Lester advocate, and what I think Hill's life suggests, is a network – a "constant process of the making and breaking of links."[31]

The diverse colonial landscapes of the nineteenth century forged different kinds of British imperialism and, indeed, different kinds of British identity.[32] In our story, Joshua Hill has offered us a glimpse at a different kind of British imperialism, a different model for the British Pacific. That nobody – initially, at least – agreed with Hill's proposals for the Pacific has mattered to this point. The LMS ignored him. Whitehall ignored him. And, ignored by officialdom, Joshua Hill has been adjudicated to be a madman. But, we have seen that Hill's sense of what Pitcairn Island was and what it might be for the British Empire in the

---

[29] David Lambert and Alan Lester, "Introduction: Imperial Spaces, Imperial Subjects," in David Lambert and Alan Lester, eds., *Colonial Lives across the British Empire: Imperial Careering in the Long Nineteenth Century* (New York: Cambridge University Press, 2006), 2.

[30] See also, Tony Ballantyne and Antoinette Burton, "Introduction: Bodies, Empires, and World Histories," in Tony Ballantyne and Antoinette Burton, eds., *Bodies in Contact: Rethinking Colonial Encounters in World History* (Durham, NC: Duke University Press, 2005), 3.

[31] Lambert and Lester, "Introduction," in Lambert and Lester, eds., *Colonial Lives across the British Empire*, 9–13 and 15.

[32] Lester, *Imperial Networks*, ix. See also, Hickford, *Lords of the Land*, 5; and John L. and Jean Comaroff, *Of Revelation and Revolution: The Dialectics of Modernity on a South African Frontier – Volume II* (Chicago: University of Chicago Press, 1997), 19.

Pacific had context. We have seen, moreover, that large parts of Hill's plans for the island were adopted in the wake of his removal in the late 1830s. What has been called filibustering and imperial adventurism in other histories must, we now see, be included as parts of the larger imperial story, as simply another kind of British imperialism by a different sort of British imperialist.

Lambert and Lester, though, were thinking specifically of the British Empire. Hill's life allows us to step beyond a single imperial frame, for the networks and circuits he connected to were international.[33] In as much as we have identified the Pacific as an international ocean before it truly became a national space, the networks and circuits of Hill's life were Pacific. Histories of the sort we have endeavored at here do not look at the Pacific as a center. Rather, they appreciate the Pacific as "a water hemisphere," a space that floods ever outwards with uncontainable force.[34] Hill's life belongs to this global ocean, and this historical sense of a global Pacific history is the true discovery of this book. What started as one man's biography has become something much bigger, and we see, therefore, the real value in picking up what Klaus Neumann once called "the trash of history," the value in taking that flotsam – stories like Joshua Hill's dictatorship at Pitcairn Island – and bringing it into the light. As Neumann has said, it is these "unspectacular" and "nonmomentous" odds and ends that "disrupt the continuous flow of history" and show us something new.[35]

Nicholas Thomas once observed that "stories are told, and should be told, simply because storytelling is a good thing to do – but particular stories are never innocent of wider agendas."[36] As we reflected earlier, historical narration is always a matter of choices. Jean and John Comaroff have rightly observed that "postmodernist doubt" and "various forms of deconstruction" have made it hard even "to establish the terms in which [a] story is to be told."[37] I would argue that Joshua Hill has been helpful here; he has assuaged some of the doubt. We have not been able to tell Hill's story in exactly the same way we would have done had his been a solidly "Western" or "European" life. Rather, Hill voyaged in and

---

[33] Lester, *Imperial Networks*, 6.

[34] Armitage and Bashford, "Introduction: The Pacific and its Histories," in Armitage and Bashford, eds., *Pacific Histories*, 1.

[35] Klaus Neumann, "Starting from Trash," in Robert Borofsky, ed., *Remembrance of Pacific Pasts*, 71.

[36] Quoted in Katerina Martina Teaiwa, *Consuming Ocean Island: Stories of People and Phosphate from Banaba* (Bloomington: Indiana University Press, 2015), 65.

[37] Jean and John Comaroff, *Of Revelation and Revolution: Christianity, Colonialism, and Consciousness in South Africa – Volume I* (Chicago: University of Chicago Press, 1991), 13. See also Comaroff, *Of Revelation and Revolution – Volume II*, 11.

among a world that was itself "becoming" something new. At islands like Tahiti and on archipelagos like Hawai'i, Hill participated in a decidedly Pacific history. Here again, the Comaroffs can help us. In the West, they have written, history is understood "as an account of 'actual' persons and processes – a notion based on the distinction between 'reality,' the material occurrence of events, and 'representation,' the terms in which the story is told and acts on."[38]

History on the South African frontier (for that was the Comaroff's field of geographic study), required "poetics."[39] The same, we have discovered, is true of the Pacific; the same has been true for Joshua Hill. The ambiguousness and doubt, here, are not rooted in any sense of postmodern doubt. Rather, they constitute a frontier between two different historical epistemologies that are in the process of coming to terms with one another. As the Comaroffs have written relative to missionaries in South Africa, "the most self-scrutinizing description of an evangelist's calling gives us only limited insight into how … he was interpellated as a colonizing subject." There is a second half to the missionaries' history, and it is a half told by the evangelical subject for whom "narrative realism" was decidedly less relevant.[40] The biographical specifics of Hill's life – even the specifics of his "mission" – are, then, less relevant in the bigger story that we have explored here. As much as this has been a story about Joshua Hill, a couple dozen descendants from the mutiny aboard the *Bounty,* and Pitcairn Island, it has also always been the history of Pitcairn as a fulcrum for British imperialism in the Pacific more broadly. It has simultaneously also been the history of global networks and historical confluences. To get at all of this, we have had to "move the everyday to center stage" and to find a "means for mapping the unmarked and justifying the trivial."[41] The result, to borrow again from the Comaroffs, has not been an "ordinary epic." Rather, it has been "an epic of the ordinary."[42]

I am reminded of the last pages of Yann Martel's 2001 Booker Prize–winning novel, *The Life of Pi,* another maritime adventure – another Pacific story. For those not familiar with the book, *The Life of Pi* tells the fanciful tale of an Indian boy who finds himself alone on a lifeboat after the Japanese shipping vessel carrying him, his family, and all of the animals from his family's zoo from Pondicherry in India to Canada was sunk in a tsunami. On the lifeboat with Piscine Molitor "Pi" Patel are a wounded zebra, a hyena, an orangutan, and a Bengal tiger by the name of Richard Parker. After some 227 days on the lifeboat with Parker – days

[38] Comaroff, *Of Revelation and Revolution – Volume I,* 34.   [39] Ibid., 35.   [40] Ibid.
[41] Comaroff, *Of Revelation and Revolution – Volume II,* 31.   [42] Ibid., 29.

in which the hyena ate the zebra and the orangutan only then to be eaten by the tiger – Pi and Richard Parker land in Mexico, where the tiger walks into a jungle, never to be seen again.

It is the novel's final scene that interests us here. Pi is still recuperating – not unlike Captain Bligh at Coupang after his own open-boat ordeal – in a Mexican hospital when he is visited by two men from the Japanese Ministry of Transport. They have been assigned the task of investigating the sinking of the freighter that had been carrying Pi and his family, the *Tsimtsum*. Of course, they find Pi's story bizarre and hard to believe. Pressed with their suspicions, Pi tells them another story, a version of the same tale, only without the animals – if *only* is the right word for such a substantive change in the narrative. In place of the wounded zebra, we have a Taiwanese sailor. In place of the hyena, we have the *Tsimtsum*'s cook. In place of the orangutan, we have Pi's mother. In this second telling of the voyage, Pi never mentions Richard Parker, leaving it to the investigators to see that he, Pi, is the tiger. He is the only survivor of a brutal voyage that has included pain, suffering, deprivation, and cannibalism.

As the two Japanese men sit and stare blankly at the young man, Pi observes, "You can't prove which story is true and which is not. You must take my word for it." And, then, he adds two deeply meaningful and profoundly historical questions. "So tell me," he asks, "since it makes no factual difference to you and you can't prove the question either way, which story do you prefer? Which is the better story, the story with animals or the story without animals?"[43]

Which is the better story? To bind Joshua Hill's life's story to that of fictional Pi Patel is, of course, a purely metaphoric turn, but there is a place in our thinking about this history, I would argue, for metaphoric thought.[44] Like Pi, I have two stories to offer. In one, a muzzy madman lands on a small Pacific Island. He terrorizes the people there for six years, give or take, and he is removed. In the second, a zealous man with global connections arrives at the same small island. He is not there randomly. He has come because he has a world-encompassing vision, an evangelical vision, and an imperial vision. He has shared (and continues to share) his vision for this small island with prominent leaders around the world and in the Pacific Ocean in particular. He has worked alongside men on other islands – not unlike the small island he has selected for his mission – and he has helped those men do their work at those other islands.[45]

[43] Yann Martel, *The Life of Pi* (New York: Harcourt Books, 2001), 317.
[44] See Matsuda, "AHR Forum: The Pacific," 762.
[45] Daws, *A Dream of Islands*, xii–xiii. See also Igler, "Exploring the Concept of Empire in Pacific History," 879.

I confess, I rather like the second story better. It is an oceanic story, and as Greg Dening has written,

Oceans are not easily encompassed. They are voyaged. They are mapped. They are narrated in story and odyssey. They are imaged in song and painting. They are taken possession of by empires, blessed by priests and haunted by pirates. There will be no one songline for an ocean.[46]

Note that Dening is clear. The ocean is not ahistorical. It does have a history, one that is compound rather than singular.[47] No one songline, indeed. We have one man, one island, and two stories. I do not, therefore, say which is true, only rather that I like the second the best of the two.

Which is the better story? Both stories are true. Both begin on October 28, 1832. Both begin that Sunday. Both can be narrated from the historical record, properly footnoted, and verified in an archive. So, I do not ask which story is more "truthful."[48] This is truly a question of which story is *better*. I, obviously, am partial. I prefer the story that is Brobdingnagian, too big to fit on its Lilliputian stage, too grand even to be contained by the Pacific basin. I prefer the telling that connects hemispheres and links civilizations, the version of the story that is both liminal and "paradoxically encompassing."[49] I choose to share with you a biography that transcends empires, nations, and boundaries of all sorts. I favor the story that is small and local but which cannot be contained except in the grand and global, the biography that blurs lines but highlights intersections.[50]

The madman's biography has in it a hint of whimsy, cruel whimsy, but whimsy nonetheless. The second biography, though, has substance. It is a European biography. But, was Hill's a "thoroughly" European life"?[51] After all, much of what made Hill's life historically important happened

---

[46] Dening, *Performances*, 209.

[47] Bernhard Klein and Gesa Mackenthun, "Introduction: The Sea Is History," In Bernhard Klein and Gesa Mackenthun, eds., *Sea Changes: Historicizing the Ocean* (New York: Routledge, 2004), 2. See also, Freeman, *The Pacific*, 99; and Mack, *The Sea*, 21.

[48] Nicholas Thomas and Richard Eves, *Bad Colonists: The South Seas Letters of Vernon Lee Walker and Louis Becke* (Durham, NC: Duke University Press, 1999), 87.

[49] Jonathan Lamb, Vanessa Smith, and Nicholas Thomas, eds., *Exploration and Exchanges: A South Seas Anthology, 1680–1900* (Chicago: University of Chicago Press, 2000), xxv.

[50] Nicholas Thomas, *Colonialism's Culture: Anthropology, Travel, and Government* (Princeton, NJ: Princeton University Press, 1994), 66. See also Hau'ofa, "Epilogue," in Borofsky, ed., *Remembrance of Pacific Pasts*, 454; and Marie Avellino Stewart, "Britain in Aspic: Tourists Visits to Malta," in Jodie Matthews and Daniel Travers, eds., *Islands and Britishness: A Global Perspective* (Newcastle upon Tyne: Cambridge Scholars Publishing, 2012), 62.

[51] Harriet Guest, *Empire, Barbarism, and Civilisation: Captain Cook, William Hodges, and the Return to the Pacific* (New York: Cambridge University Press, 2007), 24.

outside of Europe. His is a life lived in the world. This is also, though, a Pacific biography in as much as Hill's life forces us to recognize, as did the peoples of Oceania, "that the sea was a map, not a barrier, and that sailing routes, like highways, connected the world."[52] This version of the biography is the story of a Pacific life, a global life, for, as Peter Miller has observed, "thalassography as a kind of microhistory is not about water, but about people."[53] It is a story that spans time and place – from the new American republic to Josephine Bonaparte's dinning table, from the East India Company's fleet to the frenetic wars of independence in Spanish South America, and from Hawai'i to Tahiti and on to Pitcairn Island. The second story is a Pacific history, a tale of that ocean in global terms – a tale of the Pacific, I want to suggest, as it actually was.

> Home, wanderer, home again! The spell is past,
> Which lur'd thee, Fancy, to that Southern isle;
> The silent lyre from the high plantain cast,
> Unvocal now, no longer would beguile
> A gentle lady's tear, or critic's smile.
> Fancy, why lingerest thou? Thy pleasing pain
> Is all gone by; return and rest awhile;
> Again perchance to wake the echoing strain
> With firmer, bolder hand. Home, wanderer, home again!
>   Mary Russell Mitford, *Christina, the Maid of the South Seas: A Poem*
>   (1811)[54]

---

[52] Chappell, *Double Ghosts*, 173.

[53] Peter N. Miller, "Introduction: The Sea Is the Land's Edge Also," in Peter N. Miller, ed., *The Sea: Thlassography and Historiography* (Ann Arbor: The University of Michgan Press, 2013), 18.

[54] Mary Russell Mitford, *Christina, the Maid of the South Seas: A Poem* (London: A.J. Valpy, 1811), 185–187.

Bibliography

Primary Sources

Adams, George. Letter to John White. Tahiti: July 14, 1834. Te Puna. MS-Papers-1009–2/51-Letters and Papers.

Adams, Henry, and Marau Taaroa. *Memoirs of Arii Taimai E Marama of Eimeo, Teriirere of Tooarai Teriinui of Tahiti, Tauraatua I Amo*. Paris, 1901. Kindle Edition.

Adams, John. Manuscript Narrative of the Mutiny on the *Bounty* Given by John Adams to Captain Beechey in December 1825. SLNSW ZA 1804, Microfilm Reel CY 3991.

Admiralty. Letter to Rear Admiral Sir G. Hammonds. London: August 7, 1835. Te Puna. MS-Papers-1009–2/51.

American Board of Commissioners for Foreign Missions. Papers. Harvard University, Houghton Library. Unit 6. ABC 19.1. Reel 796.

Anonymous. An Account of the Bounty. SLNSW ML A 2881.

Anonymous. Chart of the Voyage of the HMS *Imogene*, 1836–1839. RHO L1972.

Anonymous. *The Charter of the United Nations and Statute of the International Court of Justice*. New York: The United Nations, 1985.

Anonymous. Communication from the General of the Medical Department of the Navy to the Rev. G.H. Nobbs. January 28, 1853. SLNSW C 134 (also Mfm CY 349).

Anonymous. Deed from the Pitcairn Islanders to George Hunn Nobbs, 1847. Nobbs Papers. SLNSW ML A 2881.

Anonymous. Deed Gifted by William Young to George Hunn Nobbs, 1832. Nobbs Papers. SLNSW ML A 2881.

Anonymous. "Descendants of the *Bounty*'s Crew, on Pitcairn's Island." In *The Calcutta Journal, or, Political, Commercial, and Literary Gazette*. July 13, 1819.

Anonymous. "Descendants of the *Bounty*'s Crew, on Pitcairn's Island." In *The Calcutta Journal, or, Political, Commercial, and Literary Gazette*. July 20, 1819.

Anonymous. "Does Norfolk 'Mutiny' Disguise Bounty of Privilege?" BBC News. May 25, 2016. www.bbc.com/news/world-australia-36376219.

Anonymous. England Census, 1841. TNA HO 107/686/15.

Anonymous. *Imogene* Log Books from 1836 to 1839. TNA ADM 53/697.

Anonymous. "Joshua Hill of Delaware and Shelburne, Nova Scotia." In *Loyalist Claims for Losses* (MG14). National Library of Canada. A012. Volume 41. Reel B-1164.

Anonymous. "Joshua Hill of Delaware and Shelburne, Nova Scotia." In *Loyalist Claims for Losses* (MG14). National Library of Canada. A012. Volume 58. Reel B-1168.

Anonymous. "Joshua Hill of Delaware and Shelburne, Nova Scotia." In *Loyalist Claims for Losses* (MG14). National Library of Canada. A012. Volume 95. Reel B-1176.

Anonymous. "Joshua Hill of Delaware and Shelburne, Nova Scotia." In *Loyalist Claims for Losses* (MG14). National Library of Canada. A013. Volume 96. Reel B-2200.

Anonymous, Journal of the Proceedings of the HMS *Imogene*, July 6, 1831–December 6, 1839. TNA ADM 51/3259.

Anonymous. Laws and Regulations of Pitcairn Island. RGS-LMS. Item 3.

Anonymous. Letter to John Backhouse. December 19, 1836. TNA FO 58/14.

Anonymous. Letter to J. Planta. London: February 28, 1827. TNA FO 58/14.

Anonymous. *Letters from Mr. Fletcher Christian, Containing a Narrative of the Transactions on Board His Majesty's Ship* Bounty, *before and after the Mutiny, with His Subsequent Voyages and Travels in South America.* London: H.D. Symonds, 1796.

Anonymous. Memorandum. January 1, 1837. TNA FO 58/15.

Anonymous. Minutebook of the Committee for Managing the Pitcairn Island Fund, December 1852–May1858. SLNSW Mfm M 2111.

Anonymous. Narrative, Remarks, Statistics, Extracts from HMS *Thunder.* Te Puna. Tunrbull Collection. MS-2148.

Anonymous. Newspaper Extracts. SLNSW DL MSQ 342.

Anonymous (likely Joshua W. Hill). "On Naval Power: Its Use, Fluctuations, and Present State." In *The Morning Post.* London. March 7, 1811.

Anonymous. Pitcairn Extracts. SLNSW AJCP M 1672.

Anonymous. Pitcairn Extracts. SLNSW F999.7/9.

Anonymous. "Pitcairn Island." In *The Bruce Herald* 23 (May 27, 1892).

Anonymous. "The Pitcairn Islanders." In *The Friend: A Religious and Literary Journal* 7:31 (May 1, 1834).

Anonymous. "Pitcairn's Island." Extracted from *The Mirror* (1831). In Pitcairn Extracts, SLNSW F999.7/9.

Anonymous. "Pitcairn's Island." In *Daily Southern Cross* 6:336. September 17, 1850.

Anonymous. "Pitcairn's Island." In *The Dublin Literary Journal and Select Family Visitor* 28:3 (July 1, 1845): 443–444.

Anonymous. "Pitcairn's Island." In *The New Zealander* 6:467. October 5, 1850.

Anonymous. "Pitcairn's Island." In *The Sailor's Magazine and Naval Journal* 7:81. May 1835.

Anonymous. *Pitcairn's Island: Being a True Account of a Very Singular and Interesting Colony.* Amherst, MA: J.S. and C. Adams, 1829.

Anonymous. The Pitcairn Island Register, 1790–1854. NMM Rec/61.

Anonymous. Pitcairn Registrar. SLNSW DLMSQ7, CY 294.

Anonymous. Royal Guest Logs. Brighton Pavilion. The Royal Archives. Windsor Castle. RA MRH/MRHF/Guest/Brighton.

Anonymous. St. Pancras Parish Church. Register of Burials. London Metropolitan Archives. P90/PAN1. Item 189.

Anonymous. "Teehuteatuaonoa (or Jenny)." In *Bengal Hurkaru* (October 2, 1826).

Anonymous. "Teehuteatuaonoa (or Jenny)." In *Sydney Gazette* (July 17, 1819).

Armitage, Elijah. Letter to LMS Missionaries. March 25, 1836. SOAS CWM/LMS – South Seas Incoming Correspondence – Box 10B. Folder 5/Jacket B.

Banks, Joseph. *The Banks Letters: A Collection of the Manuscript Correspondence of Sir Joseph Banks, Preserved in the British Museum (Natural History), and Other Collections in Great Britain.* Warren R. Dawson, editor. London: British Museum, 1958.

Letter to an Unknown Correspondent. London: February, 1787. In Joseph Banks, *The Letters of Sir Joseph Banks: A Selection, 1768–1820.* Neil Chambers, editor. London: Imperial College Press, 2000: 83–85.

Letter to an Unknown Correspondent. February 25, 1810. In Joseph Banks, *The Indian and Pacific Correspondence of Sir Joseph Banks, 1768–1820.* Neil Chambers, editor. Brookfield, VT: Pickering & Chatto, 2013: vii, 476.

Barrow, John. *A Description of Pitcairn's Islands and Its Inhabitants.* New York: Harper and Brothers, 1845.

Letter to Mr. Hay. November 29, 1826. TNA FO 58/14.

Mutiny! The Real History of the H.M.S. Bounty. New York: Cooper Square Press, 2003.

Barrow, John, A. A. Sandilands, and Joshua Hill. "Accounts of the Piticarn Islanders." In *The Journal of the Royal Geographical Society of London* 3 (1833): 156–168.

Baugniet, Charles. *Lithograph Portrait of George Pritchard.* London: Day and Haghe, 1845. NPG D40760.

Beechey, Captain F. W. (R.N.). *Landing in Bounty Bay, Pitcairn Island, December* 1825. Te Puna A-188–009.

Letter to J. Barrow. Pitcairn: December 21, 1825. TNA FO 58/14.

Narrative of a Voyage to the Pacific and Bering's Strait to Co-Operate with the Polar Expeditions. Two volumes. London: Henry Colburn and Richard Bentley, 1831.

Belcher, Lady Diana (née Joliffe). *The Mutineers of the* Bounty *and Their Descendants in Pitcairn and Norfolk Islands.* London: John Murray, 1870.

Belcher, Lieutenant Edward. Private Journal and Remarks. December 4, 1825. Te Puna, Turnbull Collection, MC Copy Micro 12 (also MSX-8774).

Private Journal and Remarks. 1826. Te Puna, Turnbull Collection, MC Copy Micro 12 (also MSX-8774).

Bennett, Frederick Debell. *Narrative of a Whaling Voyage Round the Globe.* London: Richard Bentley, 1840.

Bidwell, John. Letter to George Pritchard. London: February 14, 1837. TNA FO 58/15.

Bingham, Hiram. Letter to George Burder. June 8, 1825. SOAS CWM/LMS – South Seas Box 5A. Folder 4/Jacket A.

Letter to Jeremiah Evarts. Honolulu: June 28, 1831. Papers of the American Board of Commissioners for Foreign Missions (ABCFM), Unit 6, ABC 19.1, Reel 796, slide 71.

A Residence of Twenty-One Years in the Sandwich Islands. New York: Praeger Publishers, 1969.

Selected Writings of Hiram Bingham, 1814–1869: Missionary to the Hawai'ian Islands – to Raise the Lord's Banner. Clar Miller, editor. Lewiston, NY: The Edwin Mellen Press, 1988.

Blagden, Dr. Sir Charles. Letter to Sir Joseph Banks. Paris: July 19, 1802. BL MS ADD 33272.

Bligh, William. Letter to Elizabeth (Betsy) Bligh. Coupang: August 19, 1789. SLNSW ML Safe 1/45.

Letter to Sir Joseph Banks. August 6, 1787. In Joseph Banks, *The Indian and Pacific Correspondence of Sir Joseph Banks.* Neil Chamber, editor. London: Pickering and Catto, 2009, ii, 220.

Letter to Sir Joseph Banks. Batavia: October 13, 1789. In Joseph Banks, *The Indian and Pacific Correspondence of Sir Joseph Banks.* Neil Chamber, editor. London: Pickering and Catto, 2010, iii, 60–61.

Log and Proceedings of the *Bounty*, Volume 2. SLNSW ML Safe 1/47.

Manuscript Account of the Mutiny. SLNSW ML Safe 1/36.

Papers. SLNSW ML MSS Safe 1/43.

Voyage of the *Bounty*'s Launch. SLNSW ML MSS Safe 1/37.

Bligh, William, and Edward Christian. *The Bounty Mutiny.* New York: Penguin Books, 2001.

British Residents at Tahiti. Letter to William Ellis. Tahiti: November 19, 1827. TNA FO 58/14.

Brodie, Water. *Pitcairn's Island and the Islanders, in 1850.* Uckfield, East Sussex: Rediscovery Books, 2006.

Bruce, Captain Henry William (R.N.). *Extract from a Letter to Lady Troubridge.* Valparaíso, Chilé, January 17, 1838. NMM TRO 119/9.

Letter. Valparaíso. February 2, 1838. TNA FO 16/34.

Letter to J. Backhouse. December 17, 1839. TNA FO 58/15.

Letter to Lady Troubridge. Valparaíso: January 2, 1838. NMM TRO/119/4.

Letter to Lord Palmerston. March 24, 1840. TNA FO 58/16.

Letter to Viscount Troubridge. Valparaíso: July 17, 1838. NMM TRO 119/2(6).

Letter to Viscount Troubridge. Valparaíso: March 21, 1838. NMM TRO 119/2(2).

Letters. NMM TRO 120/3.

Record of the Voyage of the HMS *Imogene*. TNA FO 16/34.

The Remark Book of the *Conway* and *Imogene*, 1832–1840. UKHO OD 777.

Track Chart of the HMS Imogene*'s Voyage across the Pacific, c. 1840.* UKHO L1972.

Buffett, John. Diary Kept on Norfolk Island and Pitcairn Island, 1856–1892. SLNSW ML PMB 123.

"Twenty Years Residence on Pitcairn's Island." In *The Friend* 4:7 (April 1, 1846).

Burder, George. Letter to the Directors of the London Missionary Society. Undated. SOAS CWM/LMS – Home Incoming Correspondence, Box 3.

Burke, Edmund. "Speech on Conciliation with the American Colonies." In *The Speeches of the Rt. Hon. Edmund Burke*. James Burke, editor. Dublin: James Duffy, 1854: 71–122.

Burnett, Sir William. Letter to George Hunn Nobbs. January 28, 1853. In The Pitcairn Island Register. SLNSW C134 (also SLNSW Mfm CY 349).

Busby, James. *Our Colonial Empire and the Case of New Zealand*. London: Williams and Norgate, 1866.

Canning, George. Letter to King Pomare III. Foreign Office: March 2, 1827. SOAS CWM/ LMS – South Seas – Incoming Correspondence, Folder 1/Jacket A.

Letter to King Pomare III. London: March 3, 1827. TNA FO 58/14.

Chamberlain, Rev. Levi. Letter to William Ellis. Honolulu: November 3, 1825. SOAS CWM/LMS Box 6.

Letter to William Ellis. Honolulu: November 3, 1825. TNA FO 58/14.

Charlton, Richard. Letter to George Canning. October 4, 1826. TNA FO 58/4.

Letter to Lord Palmerston. March 12, 1832. TNA FO 58/6.

Letter to Lord Palmerston. Tahiti: September 8, 1834. TNA FO 58/8.

Christian, Thursday October, and George Hunn Nobbs. Letter to Richard Thomas. Pitcairn Island: July 29, 1844. SLNSW ML MSS 2233.

Coleman, Joseph. Affidavit. July 31, 1794. SLNSW DL MSQ 163.

Cook, Captain James. *First Voyage Round the World – Captain Cook's Journal during His First Voyage Round the World, Made in HM Bark* Endeavour, *1768–71*. Nikosia, Cyprus: Verone, 2016.

Dana, Richard Henry. *Two Years before the Mast and Other Voyages*. New York: The Library of America, 2005.

Darling, David. Letter to the Directors at Mission House. January 4, 1833. SOAS CWM/ LMS – South Seas Correspondence – Incoming.

Dashwood, George Frederick. *View in Pitcairn's Island, Janry. 1833*. In Sketchbooks, 1830–1835. SLNSW PXA 1679, 58b.

David, Edward. Letter to an Unidentified Recipient. In Accusations against John Buffett and George Nobbs by the People of Pitcairn. October 20, 1831. SOAS CWM/LMS – South Seas Incoming Correspondence – Box 8. Folcer 2/Jacket D.

Delano, Amasa. *A Narrative of Voyages and Travels in the Northern and Southern Hemispheres: Together with a Voyage of Survey and Discovery in the Pacific Ocean and Oriental Islands*. Boston: E.G. House, 1817.

De Rougemont, Louis. *The Adventures of Louis De Rougemont*. London: George Newnes, Limited, 1899. Kindle Edition.

Dilke, Charles Wentworth. *Greater Britain: A Record of Travel in English-Speaking Countries, during 1866–8*. Philadelphia: J.B. Lippincotte & Co., 1869.

Dodd, Robert. *The Mutineers Turning Lieutenant Bligh and Part of the Officers and Crew Adrift from His Majesty's Ship the* Bounty. London: Benjamin Beale Evans, 1790. BM 1845, 1020.46.

Driver, Charles. Letter to His Nephew. Nashville, TN: March 24, 1877. In Whaling Log Books SLNSW PMB 780.

Driver, William. Letter to Caroline Buswell. Nashville, TN: November 16, 1880. In Whaling Log Books. SLNSW PMB 780.

   Letter to Mrs. John Clifton Merrill. Nashville, TN: November 16, 1880. Whaling Log Books. SLNSW PMB 780.

   Logbook and Memoir. SLNSW PMB 39.

Edwards, Captain Edward, and George Hamilton, Surgeon. *Voyage of the HMS* Pandora. London: Francis Edwards, 1915. Kindle Edition.

Elliot, George. Pencil Sketch of Joshua Hill. In Pitcairn Islanders: Autographs and Pencil Sketches. SLNSW Ap25/Pitcairn Island. Folder 1. Fourth Sketch.

Ellis, William. Letter to George Canning. Tahiti: February 28, 1827. TNA FO 58/14.

   Letter to George Canning. Tahiti: March 29, 1827. TNA FO 58/14.

   Letter to Lord Palmerston. November 24, 1837. TNA FO 58/15.

Ferguson, James, and David Brewster. *Lectures on Select Subjects in Mechanics, Hydrostatics, Hydraulics, Pneumatics, Optics, Geography, Astronomy, and Dialling – in Two Volumes.* Edinburgh: Stirling & Slade and Bell & Bradfute, 1823.

Fiske, N. W. *Aleck, and the Mutineers of the* Bounty; *or, Thrilling Incidents of Life on the Ocean. Being a Remarkable Illustration of the Influence of the Bible.* Boston: John P. Jewett and Company, 1855.

   Aleck; The Last of the Mutineers; or The History of Pitcairn's Island. Amherst, MA: J.S. and C. Adams, 1845.

   Story of Aleck: Pitcairn's Islands: Being a True Account of a Very Singular and Interesting Colony. Amherst, MA: J.S. and C. Adams, 1829.

Foreign Office. Letter to George Pritchard. London: June 27, 1840. TNA FO 58/16.

Freemantle, Captain Charles (R.N.). Despatch of the HMS *Challenger*. May 30, 1833. Reprinted in *The Sydney Morning Herald.* October 2, 1834.

   Letter to Captain Geor. Elliot. May 30, 1833. RGS-LMS. Item 4-d.

Gordon, William Ebrington. Journal Kept on board HMS *Virago* (September 10, 1851–January 28, 1854) and HMS *Portland* (February 1, 1854–April 25, 1854). SLNSW ML MSS.3091 (also CY 1139).

Gutch, John Matthew. *Caraboo: A Narrative of a Singular Imposition, Practiced Upon the Benevolence of a Lady Residing in the Vicinity of the City of Bristol, By a Young Woman of the Name of Mary Wilcocks, alias Baker, alias Bakerstendht, alias Caraboo, Princess of Javasu.* London: Baldwin, Cradock, and Joy, 1817.

Hawtayne, J. Letter to the People of Pitcairn Island. Calcutta: July 15, 1819. Society for Promoting Christian Knowledge. Mfm M 2091–2111.

Hay, Admiral Sir John C. Dalrymple. *Lines from My Log-Book.* Edinburgh: David Douglas, 1898.

Hay, R. W. Letter to Charles Wood, Esq. London: July 22, 1835. Te Puna. MS-Papers-1009–2/51.

   Letter to J. Planta. February 22, 1827. TNA FO 58/14.

Heads of the Pitcairn Families. Letter to Mr. Nott. Pitcairn: October 19, 1830. SOAS CWM/LMS – South Seas Incoming Correspondence – Box 7. Folder 6/Jacket C.

Heath, Thomas. Visit to the Austral Islands, Pitcairn, and Marquesas. SOAS CWM/LMW – Journals – South Seas. Box 9, File 129.

Heywood, Peter and Nessy Heywood. *Innocent on the Bounty: The Court-Martial and Pardon of Midshipman Peter Heywood, in Letters.* Donald A. Maxton and Rolf E. Du Rietz, editors. Jefferson, NC: McFarland and Company, Inc., 2013.

Heywood, Peter. *Memoir of the Late Captain Peter Heywood*. London: Effingham Wilson, 1832.

Hill, Joshua W. *The Humble Memorial of Joshua Hill*. London: May 27, 1841.

    Letter to Captain G. Miner. Tahiti: December 27, 1831. TNA FO 58/14.

    Letter to the Duke of Wellington. London: August 15, 1846. TNA HO 44/39.

    Letter to the Earl of Ripon. Pitcairn Island: December 23, 1832. RGS LMS, Item 4-B: 26.

    Letter to J. White. Pitcairn Island: April 5, 1835. Te Puna. MS-Papers-1009–2/51.

    Letter to Lord Palmerston. Tahiti: April 5, 1832. TNA FO 58/14.

    Letter to Lord Palmerston. Tahiti: December 12, 1831. TNA FO 58/14.

    Letter to Lord Palmerston. Tahiti: January 12, 1832. TNA FO 58/14.

    Letter to Lord Palmerston. Tahiti: January 13, 1832. TNA FO 58/14.

    Letter to Lord Palmerston. Tahiti: May 12, 1832. TNA FO 58/14.

    Letter to Lord Palmerston. Tahiti: November 20, 1831. TNA FO 58/14.

    Letter to Mr. George Hodson. Liverpool: May 2, 1829. SOAS CWM/LMS Home Office Extra Box 2. Folder 3/Jacket C.

Holman, Rev. W. H. Letter to Admiral Fairfax Moresby. June 4, 1853. SLNSW CY 352.

HM Consul General at Chilé. Letter to the Colonial Office. Valparaíso: March 25, 1835. Te Puna. MS-Papers-1009–2/51- Letters and Papers.

James, J. A. Letter to George Burder. July 11, 1818. SOAS CWM/LMS – Home Incoming Correspondence, Box 3.

The Jerusalem Bible. New York: Doubleday, 2000.

Jones, Charles. Letter to George Elliot. June 22, 1832. TNA FO 58/14.

    Letter to an Unidentified Recipient. August 30, 1844. Te Puna. MS-Papers-1009–2/51.

Lang, John Dunmore. *Cooksland in North-eastern Australia: The Future Cotton-Field of Great Britain – Its Characteristics and Capabilities for European Colonization*. London: Longman, Brown, and Green, and Longmans, 1847.

Laws, Commander M. Letter to J. W. Croker. Tahiti: March 11, 1829. TNA FO 58/14.

The London Gazette. March 19, 1811.

London Missionary Society. South Seas – Incoming Correspondence. SOAS CMW/LMS Box 6.

    South Seas – Incoming Correspondence. SOAS CWM/LMS Box 8.

Magistrate and Councilors of Pitcairn's Island. Letter to the Society for Promoting Christian Knowledge. Pitcairn Island: May 18, 1853. Pitcairn Island Papers. Society for Promoting Christian Knowledge. SLNSW M2111.

Maitland, Rear Admiral Frederick. Letter to Charles Wood. HMS *Wellesley*, at sea: March 14, 1839. TNA FO 58/1.

Mason, Commodore Francis. Letter to George Hunn Nobbs. Valparaíso: August 17, 1836. SLNSW ML A 2881.

    Letter to George Pritchard. Callao: April 16, 1836. SLNSW ML MSS 24–2 – Tahiti, British Consulate Papers.

    Letter to George Pritchard. Valparaíso: December 3, 1836. ML MSS 24–2 – Tahiti British Consulate Papers.

    Letter to the Lord Bishop of London. Wheler Lodge, Welford: April 17, 1838. Te Puna. MS-Papers-1009–2/51 – Letters and Papers.

McFarland, Alfred. *Mutiny in the Bounty!, and Story of the Pitcairn Islanders*. Sydney: J.J. Moore, 1884.

Miller, Consul General William. Letter to the G. H. Nobbs. Honolulu: May 28, 1849. Nobbs Papers. SLNSW ML 2881.

Miscellaneous. Nobbs Papers. SLNSW ML A 2881.

Miscellaneous Papers. TNA FO 16/23.

Miscellaneous Papers. TNA FO 16/27.

Missionaries at Tahiti. Letter to the LMS Secretary in London. Tahiti: December 15, 1826. TNA FO 58/14.

Moerenhout, J. A. *Travels to the Islands of the Pacific Ocean.* Arthur R. Borden, Jr., Translator. New York: University Press of America, 1993.

Morgan, Captain R. C. *Voyage of the Camden.* SOAS SWM Australia – Journals Box 1. File 4.

Morrison, James. *After the* Bounty: *A Sailor's Account of the Mutiny and Life in the South Seas.* Donald A. Maxton, editor. Washington, DC: Potomac Books, 2010.

Murray, Thomas Boyles. Letter to Reverend William Armstrong. November 27, 1850. SLNSW MFM M 2109.

    Pitcairn: The Islands, the People, and the Pastor. London: The Society for Promoting Christian Knowledge, 1860.

Nobbs, George Hunn. Letter to Admiral Richard Thomas. Norfolk Island: November 9, 1842. SLNSW ML MSS 2233.

    Letter to Rev. W. T. Bullock. Pitcairn Island: October 8, 1834. Te Puna MS-Papers-1009–2/51.

    Letter to Rev. W. T. Bullock. Pitcairn Island: October 9, 1834. Te Puna MS-Papers-1009–2/51.

    Letter to an Unidentified Recipient. Pitcairn Island: July 20, 1847. Te Puna. MS-Papers-1009–2/51.

    Regulations for the Appointment of a Magistrate at Pitcairn's Island. SLNSW ML A 2881.

Nott, Henry. Letter to Mission House. Tahiti: April 25, 1829. SOAS CWM/LMS – South Seas Incoming Correspondence – Box 7. Folder 2/Jacket A.

Orlebar, R.N., Lieutenant J. *A Midshipman's Journal on Board HMS* Seringapatam, *during the Year 1830; Containing Observations of the Tonga Islands and Other Islands in the South Sea.* San Diego, CA: Tofua Press, 1976.

Palmerston, Lord Henry J. Letter to George Pritchard. London: February 13, 1837. TNA FO 58/15.

Peard, George. *To the Pacific and Arctic with Beechey: The Journal of Lieutenant George Peard of HMS* Blossom, *1825–1828.* Barry M. Gough, editor. New York: Cambridge University Press, 1973.

Péron, François. *French Designs on Colonial New South Wales: François Péron's Memoir on the English Settlements in New Holland, Van Diemen's Land, and the Archipelagos of the Great Pacific Ocean.* Jean Fornasiero and John West-Sooby, editors. Adelaide: Friends of the State Library of South Australia, 2014.

Pipon, Captain J. *An Interesting Account of the Mutineers of HM Ship* Bounty *Under Command of Captain Bligh.* SLNSW DLMSQ 341.

    Letter to John Dyer. Jersey. December 20, 1817. SOAS CWM/LMS –Home Incoming Correspondence, Box 3.

Pomare IV, Queen of Tahiti. Dispatch Sent Via Capt. Robert Fitzroy. Tahiti: December 19, 1932. TNA FO 58/14.

    Letter to King William IV of Great Britain. Tahiti. January 7, 1832. TNA FO 58/14.

    Letter to Mr. Planta. Tahiti: February 20, 1829. TNA FO 58/14.

Pritchard, George. Letter to the Directors at Mission House. October 22, 1833. SOAS CWM/LMS – South Seas Correspondence – Incoming Correspondence. Box 9. Folder 2/Jacket B.

    Letter to the LMS. September 26, 1825. SOAS – CWM/LMS South Seas Box 5A. Folder 2/Jacket B.

    Letter to Lord Edward Russell. Tahiti: December 25, 1835. SLNSW ML MSS 24–2 – Tahiti British Consulate Papers.

    Letter to Lord Palmerston. Tahiti: November 19, 1836. TNA FO 58/14.

Letter to Lord Palmerston. Tahiti: December 24, 1839. TNA FO 58/15.

Letter to Mission House. Tahiti: January 6, 1827. SOAS CWM/LMS – South Seas Incoming Correspondence – Box 6. Folder 1/Jacket A.

Letter to Mission House. Tahiti: March 11, 1836. SOAS CWM/LMS – South Seas Incoming Correspondence – Box 10B. Folder 5/Jacket B.

Letter to Mission House. Tahiti: November 24, 1832. SOAS CWM/LMS – South Seas Incoming Correspondence – Box 8. Folder 4/Jacket C.

Letter to Missionary House. January 9, 1826. SOAS CWM/LMS 5B – South Seas Incoming Correspondence. Folder 5/Jacket A.

Letter to Missionary House. Tahiti: October 19, 1826. SOAS CWM/LMS 5B – South Seas Incoming Correspondence. Folder 7/Jacket B.

Letter to N. Paterson. Tahiti: December 24, 1831. TNA FO 58/14.

Letter to Rev. W. Orme. Tahiti: December 26, 1828. SOAS CWM/LNS 6 – South Seas – Incoming Correspondence. Folder 7/Jacket B.

Letter to an Unidentified Recipient. Tahiti: July 16, 1834. Te Puna. MS-Papers-1009–2/51.

Queen Pomare and Her Country. London: Elliot Stock, 1878.

Protestant Residents of Valparaíso. Letter to HM's Consul General in Santiago, John Walpole. Valparaíso: August 1838. TNA FO 16/35.

Revue de Paris. Paris: 1837.

Richards, William. Letter to Rev. W. Ellis. Northampton: October 5, 1837. In SOAS CWM/LMS Incoming Correspondence – South Seas – 11A, Folder 3/Jacket A.

Russell, Lord Edward. Letter to Commodore Mason. Valparaíso: February 3, 1837. NMM HTN/68.

Letter to an Unidentified Recipient. Valparaíso: February 3, 1837. FO 16/32.

Sandilands, Captain Alexander A. Report. March 1831. RGS-LMS. Item 4-a.

Journal from the Voyage of the HMS *Comet* from Sydney to Pitcairn Island, 1830–1831. SLNSW ML MSS 8104/Box 1X.

Shillibeer, J. *A Narrative of the Briton's Voyage to Pitcairn's Island*. Taunton, NJ: J.W. Marriott, 1817.

Smith, Adam. *Lectures on Jurisprudence*. R. L. Meek, D. D. Raphael, and P. G. Stein, editors. New York: Oxford University Press, 1978.

Smith, Alexander. *The Life of Alexander Smith, Captain of the Island of Pitcairn; One of the Mutineers on Board His Majesty's Ship* Bounty; *Commanded by Lieut. Wm. Bligh – Written by Himself*. Boston: Sylvester T. Goss, 1819. Kindle Edition.

Society for Promoting Christian Knowledge. Society Work in Pitcairn, 1853. SLNSW MfM M 2091–2111.

Smyth, William. Sketchbooks of Places Visited during the Voyage of the HMS *Blossom*, 1825–1826. SLNSW PXB 55.

Spurgeon, Charles Haddon. *Gems from Spurgeon: or, Extracts from the Note-Book of a Non-Professional Reporter*. London: Partridge and Company, 1858.

Stallworth, George. Letter to Mr. Ellis. April 21, 1834. SOAS CWM/LMS – South Seas Incoming Correspondence – Box 9. Folder 5/Jacket B.

Stevenson, Robert Louis. *Letters and Miscellanies of Robert Louis Stevenson – Letters to His Family and Friends – Volume 27*. Sidney Colvin, editor. New York: Charles Scribner's Sons, 1901.

Tobin, George. *Captain Bligh's Second Chance: An eyewitness Account of His Return to the South Seas*. Roy Screiber, editor. London: Chatham Publishing, 2007.

Topliff, Samuel. "Pitcairn's Island." In *New-England Galaxy*. Friday, January 12, 1821.

Townshend, Thomas. Letter to Sir Joseph Banks. August 6, 1787. In Joseph Banks. *The Indian and Pacific Correspondence of Sir Joseph Banks, 1768–1820*. Neil Chambers, editor. London: Pickering and Chatto, 2009: ii, 223.

Following the Equator and Anti-Imperialist Essays. New York: Oxford University Press, 1996.

Vancouver, George. Letter to Sir Joseph Banks. August 1787. In Joseph Banks, *The Indian and Pacific Correspondence of Sir Joseph Banks.* Neil Chambers, editor. London: Pickering and Chatto, 2009: ii, 218–220.

Watson, Frederick, editor. *Historical Records of Australia, Volume XVI.* Sydney: Library Committee of the Commonwealth Parliament, 1922/23.

White, John. Letter to J. Bidwell. February 1830. TNA FO 16/12A.

Wiles, James. Letter to Sir Joseph Banks. Jamaica: April 12, 1799. In Joseph Banks, *The Indian and Pacific Correspondence of Sir Joseph Banks, 1768–1820.* Neil Chambers, editor. Brookfield, VT: Pickering and Chatto, 2012: v, 70.

Willis, Lieutenant H. B. *Pitcairn's Island in the Southern Ocean.* Te Puna. Turnbull Collection. qMS-2259.

Wilson, Charles. Letter to Mission House. October 3, 1825. SOAS. CWM.LMS – South Seas – Box 5A. Folder 4/Jacket A.

Wilson, C., G. Pritchard, and D. Darling. Letter to Mission House. Tahiti: November 20, 1826. SOAS CWM/LMS 5B – South Seas Incoming Correspondence. Folder 7/Jacket C.

Wolfe, James. *Journal of a Voyage in HMS* Blossom, *1825–28.* SLNSW PMB 538.

Wood, Jn. Letter to George Burder. October 23, 1818. SOAS CWM/LMS – Home Incoming Correspondence, Box 3.

Woodmason, Mathias. Letter to Rev. Josiah Pratt. Dublin: June 21, 1817. SOAS CWM/LMS – Home Incoming Correspondence, Box 3.

Woolridge, M. Letter to an Unidentified Recipient. June 18, 1849. Te Puna MS-Papers-1009–2/51.

Young, Rosalind Amelia. Letters to Captain and Mrs. Gibbons. Pitcairn Island: 1882–1891. SLNSW PMB 225.

   Mutiny of the Bounty *and Story of Pitcairn Islands, 1790–1894.* Honolulu: University Press of the Pacific, 2003.

   "Pitcairn Islanders, 1859–1880." In *Scribner's Monthly* 22. May 1881: 54–63.

Fiction

Anonymous. *L'ils de Pitcairn.* Unpublished Manuscript: c. 1830. SLNSW ML B803.

Ballantyne, Robert Michael. *The Lonely Island; or, The Refuge of the Mutineers.* London: James Nisbet and Company, 1880.

Bean, Richard. *Pitcairn.* London: Oberono Books, Ltd., 2014.

Bryant, William Cullen. "A Song of Pitcairn's Island (1825)." In Henry Wadsworth Longfellow, editor. *Poems of Places: An Anthology in Thirty-One Volumes – Oceanica* (Volume XXXI). Boston: J.R. Osgood and Company, 1876–1879: 65–66.

Byron, Lord George Gordon. "The Islands, or Christian and His Comrades." In *The Poetical Worlds, in Six Volumes.* London: John Murray, 1879: iii, 345–392.

De Kester, Michael. *The Hamilton Case.* New York: Back Bay Books, 2003.

Golding, William. *To the Ends of the Earth: A Sea Trilogy.* New York: Farrar, Straus, and Giroux, 2006.

Goodrich, Samuel Griswold (Peter Parley). *Peter Parley's Tales about the Islands in the Pacific.* Philadelphia: Thomas, Cowperthwait, and Co., 1841.

Hack, Maria. "The Adventures of Captain Bligh, Part I." In *Adventures by Land and Sea.* Maria Hack, ed. New York: George Routledge and Sons, 1877: 113–166.

   "The Adventures of Captain Bligh, Part II." In *Adventures by Land and Sea.* Maria Hack, ed. New York: George Routledge and Sons, 1877: 167–185.

"Pitcairn's Island." In *Land Ice and Deserts*. Maria Hack, ed. New York: George Routledge and Sons, 1877: 154–172.

Hall, James Norman. *The Tales of a Shipwreck*. New York: Houghton Mifflin Company, 1934.

Hauʻofa, Epeli. *Tales of the Tikongs*. Honolulu: University of Hawaiʻi Press, 1983.

Kipling, Rudyard. *Mandalay*. New York: M.F. Mansfield and Company, 1898.

London, Jack. *South Sea Tales*. New York: Modern Library, 2002.

Marguiles, Donald. *Shipwrecked: The Amazing Adventures of Luis de Rougemont (as Told by Himself)*. New York: Theatre Communications Group, 2009. Kindle Edition.

Martel, Yann. *The Life of Pi*. New York: Harcourt Books, 2001.

Maugham, W. Somerset. *The Moon and Sixpence*. New York: Vintage Books, 2000.

McDemid, Val. *The Grave Tattoo*. New York: St. Martin's Paperbacks, 2006.

Melville, Herman. *Billy Budd and Other Stories*. New York: Bantham Books, 2006. Kindle Edition.

The Confidence-Man: His Masquerade. New York: W.W. Norton & Company, 2006.

Mardi, and A Voyage Thither. Boston: The St. Botolph Society, 1923.

Moby-Dick, or, The Whale. Los Angeles: The Arion Press, 1979.

Omoo: A Narrative of Adventures in the South Seas. New York: Penguin, 2007.

Typee: A Peep at Polynesian Life. New York: Penguin, 1996.

Michener, James A. *Tales of the South Pacific*. New York: Fawcett, 1973.

Mitford, Mary Russell. *Christina, the Maid of the South Seas: A Poem in Four Cantos*. London: A.J. Valpy, 1811.

Naslund, Sena Jeter. *Ahab's Wife, or, The Star-Gazer*. New York: Harper Perennial, 1999.

Nordhoff, Charles and James Norman Hall. *The Bounty Trilogy*. New York: Little, Brown, and Company, 1964.

Faery Lands of the South Seas. Garden City, NY: Garden City Publishing Co., 1921.

Ondaatje, Michael. *Running in the Family*. New York: Vintage, 1982.

Parley, Peter (Samuel Griswold Goodrich). *Peter Parley's Tales About Islands in the Pacific*. Philadelphia: Thomas, Cowperthwait, and Co., 1841.

Poe, Edgar Allan. *The Narrative of Arthur Gordon Pym of Nantucket*. Buffalo, NY: Broadview Press, 2010.

Stevenson, Robert Louis. *In the South Seas*. New York: Scribner's Sons, 1905.

Treasure Island. New York: Barnes and Noble Classics, 2005.

Twain, Mark. "The Great Revolution in Pitcairn." (1879) In Mark Twain, *Collected Tales, Sketches, Speeches, & Essays, 1852–1890*. New York: The Library of America, 1992: 710–721.

Verne, Jules. *20,000 Leagues Under the Sea*. Mendor T. Brunetti, Translator. New York: Signet Classics, 2001.

Yeats, W.B., "The Statues." In W.B. Yeats. *The Poems*. Richard J. Finneran, editor. New York: Macmillan Publishing Company, 1983: 336–337.

Secondary Sources

Aldrich, Robert and John Connell. *The Last Colonies*. New York: Cambridge University Press, 1998.

Alexander, Caroline. *The Bounty: The True Story of the Mutiny on the Bounty*. New York: Viking, 2003.

Allward, Maurice. *Pitcairn Island: Refuge of the Bounty Mutineers*. Stroud, Gloucestershire: Tempus Publishing Limited, 2000.

Anonymous. "The Māori and the Moa." In *The Journal of the Polynesian Society* 20:2.78 (June 1911): 54–59.

Anonymous. "The Pacific Age: Special Report." In *The Economist* (November 15, 2014).

Anthony, Irvin, editor. *The Saga of the* Bounty: *Its Strange History as Related by the Participants Themselves*. New York: G.P. Putnam's Sons, 1935.

Armitage, David and Alison Bashford. "Introduction: The Pacific and Its Histories." In *Pacific Histories: Ocean, Land, People*. David Armitage and Alison Bashford, editors. New York: Palgrave, 2014: 1–28.

Ashton, Jennifer. *At the Margins of Empire: John Webster and Hokianga, 1841–1900*. Auckland: University of Auckland Press, 2015.

Archer, Christon I. *The Wars of Independence in Spanish America*. Wilmington, DE: Scholarly Resources, 2000.

Armitage, David, and Alison Bashford, editors. *Pacific Histories: Ocean, Land, People*. New York: Palgrave, 2014.

Armstrong, Terrence. "Cook's Reputation in Russia." In *Captain James Cook and His Times*. Robin Fisher and Hugh Johnson, editors. Seattle: University of Washington Press, 1979: 121–128.

Bach, John. *The Australia Station: A History of the Royal Navy in the South West Pacific, 1821–1913*. Kensington, NSW: The New South Wales University Press, 1986.

Bailey, Greg, editor. *The Voyage of the F.H. Moore and Other Nineteenth-Century Accounts*. Jefferson, NC: McFarland and Company, Inc., 2014.

Ball, Ian M. *Pitcairn: Children of Mutiny*. Boston: Little Brown and Company, 1973.

Ball, Randy, and Rodney Ferrell. *Rogersville: Then & Now*. Charleston, SC: Arcadia Press, 2009.

Ballantyne, Tony. *Webs of Empire: Locating New Zealand's Colonial Past*. Toronto: University of British Columbia Press, 2012.

Ballantyne, Tony, and Antoinette Burton. "Introduction: Bodies, Empires, and World Histories." In *Bodies in Contact: Rethinking Colonial Encounters in World History*. Tony Ballantyne and Antoinette Burton, editors. Durham, NC: Duke University Press, 2005: 1–15.

"Introduction: The Politics of Intimacy in an Age of Empire." In *Moving Subjects: Gender, Mobility, and Intimacy in the Age of Global Empire*. Tony Ballantyne and Antoinette Burton, editors. Chicago: University of Chicago Press, 2009: 1–30.

Banner, Stuart. *Possessing the Pacific: Land, Settlers, and Indigenous People from Australia to Alaska*. Cambridge, MA: Harvard University Press, 2007.

Batterby, Paul. *To the Islands: White Australians and the Malay Archipelago since 1788*. New York: Lexington Books, 2010.

Bayly, C. A. *Imperial Meridian: The British Empire and the World, 1780–1830*. London: Longman, 1989.

Beaglehole, J. C. *The Life of Captain James Cook*. Stanford: Stanford University Press, 1974.

Beattie, James. *Empire and Environmental Anxiety: Health, Science, Art, and Conservation in South Asia and Australasia, 1800–1920*. New York: Palgrave, 2011.

Beechert, Edward D. *Honolulu: Crossroads of the Pacific*. Columbia: The University of South Carolina Press, 1991.

Bennett, Brett. "The Consolidation and Reconfiguration of 'British' Networkds of Science, 1800–1970." In *Science and Empire: Knowledge and Networks of Science across the British Empire, 1800–1870*. Brett M. Bennett and Joseph M. Hodge, editors. New York: Palgrave, 2011: 30–43.

Bentley, Jerry H. "Sea And Ocean Basins as Frameworks of Historical Analysis." In *Geographical Review* 89:2 (April 1999): 215–224.

Beshero-Bondar, Elisa E. "Romancing the Pacific Isles before Byron: Music, Sex, and Death in Mitford's Christina." In *ELH* 76: 2 (Summer 2009): 277–308.

Birkett, Dea. *Serpent in Paradise*. New York: Doubleday, 1997.

Blainey, Geoffrey. *Sea of Dangers: Captain Cook and His Rivals in the South Pacific*. Chicago: Ivan R. Dee, 2009.

Borofsky, Robert. "An Invitation." In *Remembrance of Pacific Pasts: An Invitation to Remake History*. Robert Borofsky, editor. Honolulu: University of Hawai'i Press, 2000: 1–34.

Bossche, Chris R. Vanden. *Reforms Acts: Chartism, Social Agency, and the Victorian Novel, 1832–1867*. Baltimore: Johns Hopkins University Press, 2014.

Brantlinger, Patrick. *Dark Vanishings: Discourse on the Extinction of Primitive Races, 1800–1930*. Ithaca, NY: Cornell University Press, 2003.

   Rules of Darkness: British Literature and Imperialism, 1830–1914. Ithaca, NY: Cornell University Press, 1988.

   The Spirit of Reform: British Literature and Politics, 1832–1867. New York: Cambridge University Press, 1977.

   Taming the Cannibals: Race and the Victorians. Ithaca, NY: Cornell University Press, 2011.

Breitenbach, Esther. "Religious Literature and Discourses of Empire: The Scottish Presbyterian Foreign Mission Movement." In *Empires of Religion*. Hillary Carey, editor. New York: Cambridge University Press, 2008: 84–110.

Brown, Matthew. *Adventuring through Spanish Colonies: Simón Bolívar, Foreign Mercenaries, and the Birth of New Nations*. Liverpool: Liverpool University Press, 2006.

   "Gregor MacGregor: Clansman, Conquistador, and Coloniser on the Fringes of the British Empire." In *Colonial Lives across the British Empire: Imperial Careering in the Long Nineteenth Century*. David Lambert and Alan Lester, editors. New York: Cambridge University Press, 2006: 35–57.

Buck, Peter H. *Vikings of the Pacific*. Chicago: University of Chicago Press, 1938.

Burlin, Paul T. *Imperial Maine and Hawai'i : Interpretative Essays in the History of Nineteenth-Century American Expansion*. New York: Lexington Books, 2008.

Burnett, D. Graham. *The Sounding of the Whale: Science and Cetaceans in the Twentieth Century*. Chicago: University of Chicago Press, 2012. Kindle Edition.

Burton, Sarah. *Imposters: Six Kinds of Liar*. New York: Penguin Books, 2001.

Buschmann, Rainers F., Edward R. Slack Jr., and James B. Tueller. *Navigating the Spanish Lake: The Pacific in the Iberian World, 1521–1898*. Honolulu: University of Hawai'i Press, 2014.

Camerson, Ian. *Lost Paradise: The Exploration of the Pacific*. Topsfield, MA: Salem House Publishers, 1987.

Campbell, I. C. *A History of the Pacific Islands*. Los Angeles: University of California Press, 1989.

Carlsson, Susanne Chauvel. *Pitcairn Island: At the Edge of Time*. Rockhampton, Queensland: Central Queensland University Press, 2000.

Carey, Hilary M. *God's Empire: Religion and Colonialism in the British World, c. 1801–1908*. New York: Cambridge University Press, 2011.

Carson, Rachel. *The Sea Around Us*. New York: Oxford University Press, 1951.

Carter, Paul. *The Road to Botany Bay: An Exploration of Landscape and History*. Minneapolis: University of Minnesota Press, 1987. Kindle Edition.

Casid, Jill H. *Sowing Empire: Landscape and Colonization*. Minneapolis: University of Minnesota Press, 2005.

Chakrabarty, Dipesh. *Provincializing Europe: Postcolonial Thought and Historical Difference*. Princeton: Princeton University Press, 2000.

Chang, David A. "Borderlands in a World at Sea: Concow Indians, Native Hawai'ians, and South Chinese Indigenous, Global, and National Spaces." In *The Journal of American History* 98:2 (September 2011): 384–403.

Chaplin, Joyce E. "The Pacific before Empire, c. 1500–1800." In *Pacific Histories: Ocean, Land, People*. David Armitage and Alison Bashford, editors. New York: Palgrave, 2014: 53–74.

Round About the Earth: Circumnavigation from Magellan to Orbit. New York: Simon and Schuster, 2012.

Chappell, David A. *Double Ghosts: Oceanian Voyagers on Euro-American Ships*. London: A.E. Sharpe, 1997.

Chatterjee, Partha. *A Princely Imposter?: The Strange and Universal History of the Kumar of Bhawal*. Princeton, NY: Princeton University Press, 2002.

Christian, Glynn. *Fragile Paradise: The Discovery of Fletcher Christian, Bounty Mutineer*. Boston: Little, Brown, and Company, 1982.

Mrs. Christian: Bounty Mutineer. Long Rider's Guild Press, 2011.

Clark, Thomas Blake. *Omai: First Polynesian Ambassador to England*. San Francisco: The Colt Press, 1941.

Clayworth, Peter. "Richard Taylor and the Children of Noah: Race, Science, and Religion in the South Seas." In *Empires of Religion*. Hillary Carey, editor. New York: Cambridge University Press, 2008: 222–242.

Coats, Ann Veronica, and Philip MacDougall. "Introduction: Analysis and Interpretation." In *The Naval Mutinies of 1797: Unity and Preserverance*. Ann Veronica Coats and Philip MacDougall, editors. Rochester, NY: The Boydell Press, 2011: 1–16.

Cody, Lisa Forman. *Birthing the Nation: Sex, Science, and the Conception of Eighteenth-Century Britons*. New York: Oxford University Press, 2005.

Cohn, Margaret. *The Novel and the Sea*. Princeton: Princeton University Press, 2010.

Coldham, Peter Wilson. *American Migrations, 1765–1799: The Lives, Times, and Families of Colonial Americans Who Remained Loyal to the British Crown before, during, and after the Revolutionary War, as Related in Their Own Words and through Their Own Correspondence*. Baltimore: Genealogical Publishing Co., 2000.

Collier, Simon and William F. Sater. *A History of Chilé, 1808–2002*. New York: Cambridge University Press, 2004. Kindle Edition.

Comaroff, John L. and Jean. *Of Revelation and Revolution: Christianity, Colonialism, and Consciousness in South Africa – Volume I*. Chicago: University of Chicago Press, 1991.

Of Revelation and Revolution: The Dialectics of Modernity on a South African Frontier – Volume II. Chicago: University of Chicago Press, 1997.

Connell, John, and Moshe Rapaport. "Mobility and Migration." In *The Pacific Islands: Environment and Society*. Moshe Rapaport, editor. Honolulu: University of Hawai'i Press, 2013. Kindle Edition.

Corbin, Alain. *The Lure of the Sea: The Discovery of the Seaside in the Western World, 1750–1840*. Jocelyn Phelps, translator. Los Angeles: University of California Press, 1994.

Corley, J. Susan. "The British Press Greets the King of the Sandwich Islands: Kamehameha II in London, 1824." In *The Hawai'ian Journal of History* 42 (2008): 69–103.

Crosby, Alfred W. *Ecological Imperialism: The Biological Expansion of Europe, 900–1900*. New York: Cambridge University Press, 1986.

Crowley, John E. *Imperial Landscapes: Britain's Global Visual Culture, 1745–1820*. New Haven: Yale University Press, 2011.

Curthoys, Ann and John Docker. *Is History Fiction?* Sydney: University of New South Wales Press, 2010. Kindle Edition.

Cushman, Gregory T. *Guano and the Opening of the Pacific World: A Global Ecological History*. New York: Cambridge University Press, 2013.

D'Alleva, Anne. "Christian Skins: Tatau and the Evangelization of the Society Islands and Samoa." In *Tatoo: Bodies, Art, and Exchanges in the Pacific and Europe*. Anna Cole and Bronwen Douglas, editors. London: Reaktion Books, 2005. Kindle Edition: Locations 1556–1900 of 5676.

Danielsson, Bengt. *What Happened on the* Bounty. Ala Tapsell, translator. London: George Allen & Unwin, 1963.

Daughan, George C. *The Shining Sea: David Porter and the Eopic Voyage of the USS* Essex *during the War of 1812*. New York: Basic Books, 2013. Kindle Edition.

Davidson, J. W., and Deryck Scarr. *Pacific Island Portraits*. Canberra: Australian National University Press, 1970.

Daws, Gavin. *A Dream of Islands: Voyages of Self-Discovery in the South Seas*. New York: W. W. Norton and Company, 1980.

"The High Chief Boki." In *The Journal of the Polynesian Society* 75:1 (1966): 65–83.

Delbanco, Andrew. *Melville: His World and Work*. New York: Vintage eBooks, 2006. Kindle Edition.

Dening, Greg. *Beach Crossings: Voyaging across Times, Cultures, and Self*. Philadelphia: University of Pennsylvania Press, 2004.

"Deep Time, Deep Spaces: Civilizing the Sea." In *Sea Changes: Historicizing the Ocean*. Bernhard Klein and Gesa Mackenthun, editors. New York: Routledge, 2004: 13–35.

The Death of William Gooch: A History's Anthropology. Honolulu: University of Hawai'i Press, 1995.

"Encompassing the Sea of Islands." In *Common-place: A Common Place, and Uncommon Voice* 5:2 (January 2005): www.common-place-archives.org/vol-05/no-02/.

Mr. Bligh's Bad Language: Passion, Power, and Theatre on the Bounty. New York: Cambridge University Press, 1994.

Performances. Chicago: University of Chicago Press, 1996.

Denoon, Donald. "Human Settlement." In *The Cambridge History of the Pacific Islanders*. Donald Denoon, editor. New York: Cambridge University Press, 1997: 37–79.

"Pacific Edens." In *The Cambridge History of the Pacific Islanders*. Donald Denoon, editor. New York: Cambridge University Press, 1997: 80–118.

Diamond, Jared. *Collapse: How Societies Choose to Fail or Succeed*. New York: Viking Press, 2005.

Dirlik, Arif. "Introduction: Pacific Contradictions." In *What Is in a Rim?: Critical Perspectives on the Pacific Region Idea*. Arif Dirlik, editor. New York: Rowman & Littlefield, 1998: 3–13.

Dodd, Edward. *The Rape of Tahiti*. New York: Dodd, Mead, and Company, 1983.

Dodge, Earnest S. *Islanders and Empires: Western Impact on the Pacific and East Asia*. Minneapolis: University of Minnesota Press, 1976.

Dolin, Eric Jay. *Leviathan: The History of Whaling in America*. New York: W.W. Norton & Company, 2008.

Douglas, Bronwen. "Pasts, Presents, and Possibilities of Pacific History and Pacific Students: As Seen by a Historian from Canberra." In *The Journal of Pacific History* 50:2 (2015): 224–228.

"Religion." In *Pacific Histories: Ocean, Land, People*. David Armitage and Alison Bashford, editors. New York: Palgrave, 2014: 193–215.

Science, Voyages, and Encounters in Oceania, 1511–1850. New York: Palgrave MacMillan, 2014.

Douglas, Bronwen, and Chris Ballard. "Race, Place, and Civilisation: Colonial Encounters and Governance in Greater Oceania." In *The Journal of Pacific History* 47: 3 (September 2012): 245–262.

Dunmore, John. *Where Fate Beckons: The Life of Jean-François de La Pérouse*. Wallombi, NSW: Exisle Publishing, 2015. Kindle Edition.

Durrans, Brian. "Ancient Pacific Voyaging: Cooks' Views and the Development of Interpretation." In *Captain Cook and the South Pacific (The British Museum Yearbook 3)*. London: British Museum Publications, 1979: 137–166.

Edmond, Rod. "Missionaries on Tahiti." In *Voyages and Beaches: Pacific Encounters, 1769–1840*. Alex Calder, Jonathan Lamb and Bridget Orr, editors. Honolulu: University of Hawai'i Press, 1999: 226–240.

"The Pacific: Tahiti – Queen of the South Sea Isles." In *The Cambridge Companion to Travel Writing*. Peter Hulme and Tim Young, editors. New York: Cambridge University Press, 2002: 139–155.

Representing the South Pacific: Colonial Discourse from Cook to Gauguin. New York: Cambridge University Press, 2005.

Edwards, Philip, *The Story of the Voyage: Sea-Narratives in Eighteenth-Century England*. New York: Cambridge University Press, 1994.

Emory, Kenneth P. "Stone Implements of Pitcairn Island." In *The Journal of the Polynesian Society* 37:2(146) (June 1928): 125–135.

Eperjesi, John R. *The Imperialist Imaginary: Visions of Asia and the Pacific in American Culture*. Hanover, NH: Dartmouth College Press, 2005.

Etherington, Norman. "Introduction." In *Missions and Empires – Oxford History of the British Empire, Companion Series*. Norman Eitherington, editor. New York: Oxford University Press, 2005: 1–18.

Farrington, Anthony. *A Biographical Index of East India Company Maritime Service Officers, 1600–1834*. London: British Museum, 1999.

Fischer, Steven Roger. *A History of the Pacific Islands*. New York: Palgrave, 2002.

Flannery, Tim. *Among the Islands: Adventures in the Pacific*. New York: Atlantic Monthly Press, 2011. Kindle Edition.

The Future Eaters: An Ecological History of the Australasian Lands and People. New York: Grove Press, 1994.

Fleming, Fergus. *Barrow's Boys*. New York: Atlantic Monthly Press, 1998.

Flynn, Dennis O., Arturo Giráldez, and James Sobredo. "In Search of Periodization for Pacific History." In *Studies in Pacific History: Economies, Politics, and Migration*. Dennis O. Flynn, Arturo Giráldez, and James Sobredo, editors. Burlington, VT: Ashgate, 2002: 1–22.

Fogle, Ben. *The Teatime Islands: Journeys to Britain's Faraway Outposts*. London: Michael Joseph, 2003.

Ford, Herbert. *Island of Tears: John I Tay and the Story of Pitcairn*. Nampo, ID: Pacific Press Publishing Association, 1990. Kindle Edition.

Foxhall, Katherine. *Health, Medicine, and the Sea: Australian Voyages, c. 1815–1860*. Manchester: Manchester University Press, 2012.

Franks, Jill. *Islands and Modernists: The Allure of Isolation in Art, Literature, and Science*. Jefferson, NC: McFarland & Company, Inc., 2006.

Freeman, Donald B. *The Pacific*. New York: Routledge, 2010.

Frost, Alan. *The Global Reach of Empire: Britain's Maritime Expansion in the Indian and Pacific Oceans, 1764–1815*. Carlton, Victoria: The Miegunyah Press, 2003.

"New Geographical Perspectives and the Emergence of the Romantic Imagination." In *Captain James Cook and His Times*. Robin Fisher and Hugh Johnson, editors. Seattle: University of Washington Press, 1979: 5–19.

Fulton, Richard D. and Peter H. Hoffenberg, "Introduction." In *Oceania and the Victorian Imagination: Where All Things Are Possible*. Richard D. Fulton and Peter H. Hoffenberg, editors. Burlington, VT: Ashgate, 2013: 1–7.

Gascoigne, John. *Captain Cook: Voyager between Worlds*. New York: Hambledon Continuum, 2007.

Encountering the Pacific in the Age of the Enlightenment. New York: Cambridge University Press, 2014.

"From Science to Religion: Justifying French Pacific Voyaging and Expansion in the Period of the Restoration and the July Monarchy." In *Journal of Pacific History* 50: 109–127.

Joseph Banks and the English Enlightenment: Useful Knowledge and Polite Culture. New York: Cambridge University Press, 1994.

Gerson, Noel B. *Sad Swashbuckler: The Life of William Walker*. New York: Thomas Nelson, Inc., 1976.

Gibson, Arrell Morgan. *Yankees in Paradise: The Pacific Basin Frontier*. Albuquerque: University of New Mexico Press, 1993.

Gillis, John R. *The Human Shore: Seacoasts in History*. Chicago: University of Chicago Press, 2012.

Glavin, Terry. *The Last Great Sea: A Voyage through the Human and Natural History of the North Pacific Ocean*. New York: Grey Stone Books, 2000.

Gough, Barry M. "The Records of the Royal Navy's Pacific Station." In *The Journal of Pacific History* 4 (1969): 146–153.

Green, R. C. "Pitcairn Island Fishhooks in Stone." In *The Journal of the Polynesian Society* 68:1 (March 1959): 21–22.

Grove, Richard H. *Green Imperialism: Colonial Expansion, Tropical Island Edens, and the Origins of Environmentalism, 1600–1860*. New York: Cambridge University Press, 1995.

Guest, Harriet. *Empire, Barbarism, and Civilisation: Captain Cook, William Hodges, and the Return to the Pacific*. New York: Cambridge University Press, 2007.

Gulliver, Katrina. "Finding the Pacific World." In *The Journal of World History* 22:1 (March 2011): 83–100.

Hage, Erik. *The Melville-Hawthorne Connection: A Story of the Literary Friendship*. Jefferson, NC: McFarland and Company, Inc., 2014. Kindle Edition.

Haldane, Charlotte. *Tempest Over Tahiti*. London: Constable, 1963.

Haley, James L. *Captive Paradise: A History of Hawai'i*. New York: St. Martin's Press, 2014. Kindle Edition.

Hall, Catherine, Keith McClelland, and Jane Rendall. *Defining the Victorian Nation: Class, Race, Gender, and the British Reform Act of 1867*. New York: Cambridge University Press, 2000.

Hancock, W. K. *Politics in Pitcairn and Other Essays*. London: MacMillan and Co., 1947.

Hau'ofa, Epeli. "Epilogue: Pasts to Remember." In *Remembrance of Pacific Pasts: An Invitation to Remake History*. Robert Borofsky, editor. Honolulu: University of Hawai'i Press, 2000: 453–471.

"The Ocean in Us." In *Voyaging through the Contemporary Pacific*. David Hanlon and Geoffrey M. White, editors. New York: Rowman & Littlefield Publishers, Inc., 2000: 113–134.

We Are the Ocean. Honolulu: University of Hawai'i Press, 2008.

Helu, I. F. "South Pacific Mythology." In *Voyages and Beaches: Pacific Encounters, 1769–1840*. Alex Calder, Jonathan Lamb and Bridget Orr, editors. Honolulu: University of Hawai'i Press, 1999: 45–54.

Herbermann, Charles G., and Edward A. Pace, Condé B. Pallen, Thomas J. Shahan, John J. Wynne, et al., editors. *The Catholic Encyclopedia: An International Work of Reference on the Constitution, Doctrine, Discipline, and History of the Catholic Church*. 15 Volumes. New York: The Universal Knowledge Foundation, 1907–1912.

Hereniko, Vilsoni. "Indigenous Knowledge and Academic Imperialism." In *Remembrance of Pacific Pasts: An Invitation to Remake History*. Robert Borofsky, editor. Honolulu: University of Hawai'i Press, 2000: 78–91.

Herman, Arthur. *To Rule the Waves: How the British Navy Shaped the Modern World*. New York: Harper Perennial, 2005.

Hickford, Mark. *Lords of the Land: Indigenous Property Rights and the Jurisprudence of Empire*. New York: Oxford University Press, 2011.

Hiney, Tom. *On the Missionary Trail: A Journey through Polynesia, Asia, and Africa with the London Missionary Society*. New York: Grove Press, 2000.

Hoare, Merval. *Norfolk Island: An Outline of Its History, 1774–1968*. St. Lucia, Queensland: University of Queensland Press, 1969.

Hoare, Philip. *The Whale: In Search of the Giants of the Sea*. New York: Harper Collins, 2010.

Holland, Peter and Jim Williams. "Pioneer Settlers Recognizing and Responding to the Climate Challenges of Southern New Zealand." In *Climate, Science, and Colonization: Histories from Australia and New Zealand*. James Beattie, Emily O'Gorman, and Matthew Henry, editors. New York: Palgrave MacMillan, 2014: 81–98.

Holway, Tatiana. *The Flower of Empire: An Amazonian Water Lily, the Quest to Make It Bloom, and the World It Created*. New York: Oxford University Press, 2013. Kindle Edition.

Hough, Richard. *Captain Bligh and Mr. Christian: The Men and the Mutiny*. New York: E.P. Dutton and Co., 1973.

The Last Voyage of Captain James Cook. New York: William Morrow and Company, 1979.

Houston, Robert. "Forward." In *The War in Nicaragua*. William Walker, editor. Tucson: The University of Arizona Press, 1985.

Howarth, David. *Tahiti: A Paradise Lost*. New York: The Viking Press, 1983.

Howe, K. R. *Nature, Culture, and History: The "Knowing" of Oceania*. Honolulu: University of Hawai'i Press, 2000.

The Quest for Origins: Who First Discovered and Settled the Pacific Islands? Honolulu: University of Hawai'i Press, 2003.

Where the Waves Fall: A New South Seas Islands History from First Settlement to Colonial Rule. Honolulu: University of Hawai'i Press, 1984.

Hubbard, *An Account of Sa-go-ye-wat-ha, or, Red Jacket, and His People, 1750–1830*. Albany, NY: Joel Munsell's Sons, 1886.

Hurtado, Albert L. "Frontiers, Filibusters, and Pioneers: The Transitional World of John Sutter." In *Pacific Historical Review* 77:1 (Feburary 2008): 19–47.

Hutchinson, Elizabeth Quay, Thomas Miller Klubock, Nara B. Milanich, and Peter Winn, editors. *The Chilé Reader: History, Culture, Politics*. Durham, NC: Duke University Press, 2014. Kindle Edition.

Hyde, Lewis. *Trickster Makes This World: Mischief, Myth, and Art*. New York: Farrar, Straus, and Giroux, 2010. Kindle Edition.

Igler, David. "Diseased Gods: Global Exchanges in the Eastern Pacific Basin, 1770–1850." In *American Historical Review* 109 (2004): 693–719.

"Exploring the Concept of Empire in Pacific History: Individuals, Nations, and Ocean Space Prior to 1850." In *History Compass* 12:11 (2014): 879–887.

The Great Ocean: Pacific Worlds from Captain Cook to the Gold Rush. New York: Oxford University Press, 2013.

"On Coral Reefs, Volcanoes, Gods, and Patriotic Geology; or, James Dwight Dana Assembles the Pacific Basin." In *Pacific Historical Review* 79:1 (2010): 23–49.

James, C. L. R. *Mariners, Renegades, and Castaways: The Story of Herman Melville and the World We Live In*. Donald E. Pease, editor. Hanover, NH: University Press of New England, 2001.

Jasanoff, Maya. *Liberty's Exiles: American Loyalists in the Revolutionary World*. New York: Knopf, 2011.

Jensz, Felicity. "Missionaries and Indigenous Education in the Nineteenth-Century British Empire – Part I: Church-State Relations and Indigenous Actions and Reactions." In *History Compass* 10:4 (2012): 294–305.

Johnston, Anna. "Antipodean Heathens: The London Missionary Society in Polynesia and Australia, 1800–50." In *Colonial Frontiers: Indigenous Encounters in Settler Societies*. Lynetter Russell, editor. Manchester: Manchester University Press, 2001: 68–81.

Missionary Writing and Empire, 1800–1860. New York: Cambridge University Press, 2003.

Jones, Ryan Tucker. *Empires of Extinction: Russians and the North Pacific's Strange Beasts of the Sea, 1741–1867*. New York: Oxford University Press, 2014.

"Running into Whales: The History of the North Pacific from Below the Waves." In *The American Historical Review* 118:2 (April 2013): 349–377.

Kennedy, Dane, *The Last Blank Spaces: Exploring Africa and Australia*. Cambridge, MA: Harvard University Press, 2013. Kindle Edition.

Kennedy, Gavin. *Bligh*. London: Duckworth & Co., 1978.

Kennedy, Tom. *An Ocean of Islands: A Pacific Memoir*. Ngakuta Bay, New Zealand: Nandina Press, 2004.

Kirch, Patrick Vinton. *A Shark Going Inland Is My Chief: The Island Civilization of Ancient Hawai'i*. Los Angeles: University of California Press, 2012. Kindle Edition.

Unearthing the Polynesian Past: Explorations and Adventures of an Island Archaeologist. Honolulu: University of Hawai'i Press, 2015.

Kirch, Patrick Vinton, and Jean-Louis Rallu. "Long-Term Demographic Evolution in the Pacific Islands: Issues, Debates, and Challenges." In *The Growth and Collapse of Pacific Island Societies: Archaeological and Demographic Perspectives*. Patrick V. Kirch and Jean-Louis Rallu, editors. Honolulu: University of Hawai'i Press, 2007: 1–14.

Kirk, Robert. *History of the South Pacific since 1513: Chronicle of Australia, New Zealand, New Guinea, Polynesia, Melanesia, and Robinson Crusoe Island*. Denver, CO: Outskirts Press, Inc., 2011. Kindle Edition.

Paradise Past: The Transformation of the South Pacific, 1520–1920. Jefferson, NC: McFarland & Co., 2012.

Pitcairn Island, the Bounty *Mutineers, and Their Descendants*. Jefferson, NC: McFarland & Co., 2008.

Klein, Bernhard and Gesa Mackenthun. "Introduction: The Sea Is History." In *Sea Changes: Historicizing the Ocean*. Bernhard Klein and Gesa Mackenthun, editors. New York: Routledge, 2004: 1–12.

Kreeft, Peter. *The Sea Within: Waves and the Meanings of All Things*. South Bend, IN: St. Augustine's Press, 2006.

Klieger, P. Christiaan, *Kamehameha III: He Mo'olelo no ka Mō'ī Lokomaika'I – King of the Hawai'ian Islands, 1824–1854*. San Francisco: Green Arrow Press, 2015.

Knight, David. *Voyaging in Strange Seas: The Great Revolution in Science*. New Haven, CT: Yale University Press, 2014. Kindle Edition.

Kritsiotis, Dino and A. W. B. Simpson. "The Pitcairn Prosecutions: An Assessment of Their Historical Contexts." In *Justice, Legality, and the Rule of Law: Lessons from the Pitcairn Prosecutions*. Dawn Oliver, editor. New York: Oxford University Press, 2009: 93–129.

L., J. K. "John Adams." In *The Dictionary of National Biography – Volume I*. London: Oxford University Press, 1921–1922: 98–99.

Lal, Brij V., and Kate Fortune, editors. *The Pacific Islands: An Encyclopedia*. Honolulu: University of Hawai'i Press, 2000.

Lamb, Jonathan. *Preserving the Self in the South Seas, 1680–1840*. Chicago: University of Chicago Press, 2001.

Scurvy: The Disease of Discovery. Princeton, NJ: Princeton University Press, 2017. Kindle Edition.

Lamb, Jonathan, Vanessa Smith, and Nicholas Thomas, editors. *Exploration and Exchanges: A South Seas Anthology, 1680–1900*. Chicago: University of Chicago Press, 2000.

Lambert, David and Alan Lester. "Introduction: Imperial Spaces, Imperial Subjects." In *Colonial Lives across the British Empire: Imperial Careering in the Long Nineteenth Century*. David Lambert and Alan Lester, editors. New York: Cambridge University Press, 2006: 1–31.

Landon, Robert. "'Dusky Damsels': Pitcairn Island's Neglected Matriarchs of the '*Bounty*' Saga." In *The Journal of Pacific History* 35: 1 (June 2000): 29–47.

Landsdown, Richard, editor. *Strangers in the South Seas: The Idea of the Pacific in Western Thought*. Honolulu: University of Hawai'i Press, 2006.

Lester, Alan. *Imperial Networks: Creating Identities in Nineteenth-Century South Africa and Britain*. New York: Routledge, 2001.

Letsas, George. "Rights and Duties on Pitcairn Island." In *Justice, Legality, and the Rule of Law: Lessons from the Pitcairn Prosecutions*. Dawn Oliver, editor. New York: Oxford University Press, 2009: 157–182.

Lewis, Andrew. "Pitcairn's Tortured Past: A Legal History." In *Justice, Legality, and the Rule of Law: Lessons from the Pitcairn Prosecutions*. Dawn Oliver, editor. New York: Oxford University Press, 2009: 39–61.

Lewis, David. *We, the Navigators: The Ancient Art of Landfinding in the Pacific*. Honolulu: University of Hawai'i Press, 1994.

Liebersohn, Harry. *The Travelers' World: Europe to the Pacific*. Cambridge, MA: Harvard University Press, 2006.

Lindstrom, Lamont. "Social Relations." In *The Pacific Islands: Environment and Society*. Moshe Rapaport, editor. Honolulu: University of Hawai'i Press, 2013. Kindle Edition: Locations 7538–8053 of 21398.

Linnebaugh, Peter, and Marcus Rediker. *The Many-Headed Hydra: Sailors, Slaves, Commoners, and the Hidden History of the Revolutionary Atlantic*. Boston: Beacon, 2000.

Linnekin, Jocelyn. "New Political Orders." In *The Cambridge History of the Pacific Islanders*. Donald Denoon, editor. New York: Cambridge University Press, 1997: 185–217.

Lummis, Trevor. *Life and Death in Eden: Pitcairn Island and the Bounty Mutineers*. London: Phoenix, 1999.

   Pacific Paradises: The Discovery of Tahiti and Hawai'i. Stroud, Gloucestershire: Sutton Publishing, 2005.

Lyons, Paul. *American Pacificism: Oceania in the U.S. Imagination*. New York: Routledge, 2006.

Mack, John. *The Sea: A Cultural History*. London: Reaktion Books, 2011.

Mackay, David. "Myth, Science, and Experience in the British Construction of the Pacific." In *Voyages and Beaches: Pacific Encounters, 1769–1840*. Alex Calder, Jonathan Lamb and Bridget Orr, editors. Honolulu: University of Hawai'i Press, 1999: 100–113.

Mackenthun, Gesa. "Chartless Voyages and Protean Geographies: Nineteenth-Century American Fictions of the Black Atlantic." In *Sea Changes: Historicizing the Ocean*. Bernhard Klein and Gesa Mackenthun, editors. New York: Routledge, 2004: 131–148.

MacLaren, I. S. "John Barrow's Darling Project." In *Arctic Exploration in the Nineteenth Century: Discovering the Northwest Passage*. Frédéric Regard, editor. Brookfield, VT: Pickering and Chatto, 2013: 19–36.

Macklin, Robert. *Dark Paradise: Norfolk Island – Isolation, Savagery, Mystery, and Murder*. Sydney: Hachette, 2013.

Matsuda, Matt K. "AHR Forum: The Pacific." In *The American Historical Review* (June 2006): 758–780.

   Empire of Love: Histories of France and the Pacific. New York: Oxford University Press, 2005.

   Pacific Worlds: A History of Seas, Peoples, and Cultures. New York: Cambridge University Press, 2012.

Matthews, Jodie, and Daniel Travers. "Introduction." In *Islands and Britishness: A Global Perspective*. Jodie Matthews and Daniel Travers, editors. Newcastle upon Tyne: Cambridge Scholars Publishing, 2012: 1–11.

Maude, H. E. "Beachcombers and Castaways." In *The Journal of the Polynesian Society* 73:3 (September 1964): 254–293.

"The History of Pitcairn." In *The Pitcairnese Language*. Alan S. C. Ross and A. W. Moverley, editor. New York: Oxford University Press, 1964: 45–101.

"History – Past, Present, and Future." In *The Journal of Pacific History* 6 (1971): 3–24.

"In Search of Home: from the Mutiny to Pitcairn Island (1789–1790)." In *The Journal of the Polynesian Society* 67:2 (June 1958): 104–131.

"The Migration of the Pitcairn Islanders to the Motherland in 1831." In *The Journal of the Polynesian Society* 48:2 (June 1959): 115–140.

Maxton, Donald A., *The Mutiny on HMS* Bounty: *A Guide to Nonfiction, Poetry, Films, Articles, and Music*. Jefferson, NC: McFarland and Company, Inc., 2008.

May, Robert E. *Manifest Destiny's Underworld: Filibustering in Antebellum America*. Chapel Hill: University of North Carolina Press, 2002.

McArthur, Norma. "Essays in Multiplication: European Seafarers in Polynesia." In *The Journal of Pacific History* 1 (1966): 91–105.

McCalman, Iain. *The Reef: A Passionate History – The Great Barrier Reef from Captain Cook to Climate Change*. New York: Farrar, Straus, and Giroux, 2013. Kindle Edition.

McCook, Stuart. "'Squares of Tropic Summer': The Wardian Case, Victorian Horticulture, and the Logistics of Global Plant Transfers, 1770–1910." In *Global Scientific Practice in an Age of Revolutions, 1750–1850*. Patrick Manning and Daniel Rood, editors. Pittsburgh, PA: University of Pittsburgh Press, 2016: 199–215.

McFlynn, Frank. *Captain Cook: Master of the Seas*. New Haven: Yale University Press, 2011.

McIntyre, W. David. *Winding Up the British Empire in the Pacific Islands – Oxford History of the British Empire, Companion Series*. New York: Oxford University Press, 2014.

McKenzie, Kirsten. *Imperial Underworld: An Escaped Convict and the Transformation of the British Colonial Order*. New York: Cambridge University Press, 2016. Kindle Edition.

Scandal in the Colonies: Sydney and Cape Town, 1820–1850. Melbourne: Melbourne University Press, 2004.

A Swindler's Progress: Nobles and Convicts in the Age of Liberty. Cambridge, MA: Harvard University Press, 2010.

McNeil, John R. "Islands in the Rim: Ecology and History in and around the Pacific, 1521–1996." In *Pacific Centuries: Pacific and Pacific Rim History Since the Sixteenth Century*. Dennis O. Flynn, Lionel Frost, and A. J. H. Latham, editors. New York: Routledge, 1999: 70–84.

"Of Rats and Men: A Synoptic Environmental History of the Island Pacific." In *Journal of World History* 5:2 (Fall 1994): 299–349.

McWilliams, Rohan. *The Tichborne Claimant: A Victorian Sensation*. London: Hambledon Continuum, 2007.

Mead, Hirini Moko, and Neil Grove. *Ngā Pēpeha a ngā Tīpuna: The Sayings of the Ancestors*. Wellington, New Zealand: Victoria University Press, 2007.

Meleisea, Malama. "The Postmodern Legacy of a Premodern Warrior Goddess in Modern Samoa." In *Voyages and Beaches: Pacific Encounters, 1769–1840*. Alex Calder, Jonathan Lamb and Bridget Orr, editors. Honolulu: University of Hawai'i Press, 1999: 55–60.

Miller, Peter N. "Introduction: The Sea Is the Land's Edge Also." In *The Sea: Thlassography and Historiography*. Peter N. Milled, editor. Ann Arbor, MI: The University of Michigan Press, 2013: 1–26.

Mitchell, Andrew. *The Fragile South Pacific: An Ecological Odyssey*. Austin: University of Texas Press, 1989.

Moon, Paul. *A Savage Country: The Untold Story of New Zealand in the 1820s*. New York. Penguin Books, 2012. Kindle Edition.

Moorehead, Alan. *The Fatal Impact: An Account of the Invasion of the South Pacific, 1767–1840*. New York: Harper & Row Publishers, 1966.

Morrell, W. P. *Britain in the Pacific Islands*. New York: Oxford University Press, 1960.

Morrison, Dane A. *True Yankees: The South Seas & The Discovery of American Identity*. Baltimore: Johns Hopkins University Press, 2014.

Neumann, Klaus. "Starting from Trash." In *Remembrance of Pacific Pasts: An Invitation to Remake History*. Robert Borofsky, editor. Honolulu: University of Hawai'i Press, 2000: 62–77.

Newell, Jennifer. *Trading Nature: Tahitians, Europeans, and Ecological Exchange*. Honolulu: University of Hawai'i Press, 2010.

Newbury, Colin. *Tahiti Nui: Change and Survival in French Polynesia, 1767–1945*. Honolulu: The University of Hawai'i Press, 1980.

Niau, Josephine Hyacinthe. *The Phantom Paradise: The Story of the Expedition of the Marquis de Rays*. Sydney: Angus & Robertson, Ltd., 1936.

Nicholls, Henry. *The Galápagos: A Natural History*. New York: Basic Books, 2014. Kindle Edition.

Nicholson, Robert. *The Pitcairners*. Honolulu: University of Hawai'i Press, 1997.

Nobbs, Raymond. *George Hunn Nobbs, 1799–1884: Chaplain on Pitcairn and Norfolk Island*. Norfolk Island: The Pitcairn Descendants Society, 1984.

Novick, Peter. *That Noble Dream: The "Objectivity Question" and the American Historical Profession*. New York: Cambridge University Press, 1988.

Obeyesekere, Gananath. *The Apotheosis of Captain Cook: European Mythmaking in the Pacific*. Princeton: Princeton University Press, 1992.

   Cannibal Talk: The Man-Eating Myth and Human Sacrifice in the South Seas. Los Angeles: University of California Press, 2005.

O'Brian, Patrick. *Joseph Banks: A Life*. Chicago: University of Chicago Press, 1987.

O'Brien, Patty. *The Pacific Muse: Exotic Femininity and the Colonial Pacific*. Seattle: University of Washington Press, 2006.

O'Cinneide, Colm. "'A Million Mutines Now': Why Claims of Cultural Uniqueness Cannot Be Used to Justify Violations of Basic Human Rights." In *Justice, Legality, and the Rule of Law: Lessons from the Pitcairn Prosecutions*. Dawn Oliver, editor. New York: Oxford University Press, 2009: 131–156.

Oliver, Dawn. "The Pitcairn Prosecutions, Paper Legal Systems, and the Rule of Law." In *Justice, Legality, and the Rule of Law: Lessons from the Pitcairn Prosecutions*. Dawn Oliver, editor. New York: Oxford University Press, 2009: 23–37.

   "Preface." In *Justice, Legality, and the Rule of Law: Lessons from the Pitcairn Prosecutions*. Dawn Oliver, editor. New York: Oxford University Press, 2009: ix-xii.

   "Problems on Pitcairn." In *Justice, Legality, and the Rule of Law: Lessons from the Pitcairn Prosecutions*. Dawn Oliver, editor. New York: Oxford University Press, 2009: 1–21.

Oliver, Douglas L. *The Pacific Islands*. Honolulu: University of Hawai'i Press, 1989.

Osorio, Jonathan Kay Kamakawiwo'ole. *Dismembering Lāhui: A History of the Hawai'ian Nation to 1887*. Honolulu: University of Hawai'i Press, 2002.

Pocock, J. G. A. "Nature and History, Self and Other: European Perceptions of World History in the Age of Encounter." In *Voyages and Beaches: Pacific Encounters, 1769–1840*. Alex Calder, Jonathan Lamb and Bridget Orr, editors. Honolulu: University of Hawai'i Press, 1999: 25–44.

Porter, Andrew. "An Overview." In *Missions and Empires – Oxford History of the British Empire, Companion Series*. Norman Eitherington, editor. New York: Oxford University Press, 2005: 40–63.

Religion Versus Empire?: British Protestant Missionaries and Overseas Expansion, 1700–1914. Manchester: Manchester University Press, 2004.

Price, A. Grenfell. *The Western Invasions of the Pacific and Its Continents: A Study of Moving Frontiers and Changing Landscapes, 1513–1958.* New York: Oxford University Press, 1963.

Price, Henry R. *Hawkins County Tennessee: A Pictorial History.* Virginia Beach, VA: Donning Company Publishers, 1996.

Quilley, Geoff. *Empire to Nation: Art, History, and the Visualization of Maritime Britain, 1768–1829.* New Haven: Yale University Press, 2011.

Raeside, J. D. *Sovereign Chief: A Biography of Baron de Thierry.* Christchurch, New Zealand: Caxton Press, 1977.

Ralston, Caroline. *Grass Huts and Warehouses: Pacific Beach Communities of the Nineteenth Century.* St. Lucia, Queensland: University of Queensland Press, 2014. Kindle Edition.

Rasmussen, Vaine. "Our Pacific." In *Remembrance of Pacific Pasts: An Invitation to Remake History.* Robert Borofsky, editor. Honolulu: University of Hawai'i Press, 2000: 399–400.

Rector, John. *The History of Chilé.* New York: Palgrave MacMillan, 2003.

Reidy, Michael S., *Tides of History: Ocean Science and Her Majesty's Navy.* Chicago: University of Chicago Press, 2008.

Richards, John F. *The World Hunt: An Environmental History of the Commodification of Animals.* Los Angeles: University of California Press, 2014. Kindle Edition.

Roberts, Cokie, *Founding Mothers: The Women Who Raised Our Nation.* New York: Harper Perennial, 2005.

Rodger, N. A. M., *The Command of the Ocean: A Naval History of Britain, 1649–1815.* New York: W.W. Norton and Company, 2004.

Rodriguez O., and Jaime E. *The Independence of Spanish America.* New York: Cambridge University Press, 1998.

Ross, Alan S. C., and A. W. Moverley. *The Pitcairnese Language.* New York: Oxford University Press, 1964.

Royle, Stephen A. *A Geography of Islands: Small Island Insularity.* New York: Routledge, 2001.

"Health and Health Care in Pitcairn Island in 1841: The Report of Surgeon William Gunn of HMS *Curaçoa.*" In *The Journal of Pacific History* 35:2 (September 2000): 213–218.

"Identity and the Other British Isles: Bermuda and St. Helena." In *Islands and Britishness: A Global Perspective.* Jodie Matthews and Daniel Travers, editors. Newcastle upon Tyne: Cambridge Scholars Publishing, 2012: 12–23.

Sabine, Lorenzo. *The American Loyalists; or, Biographical Sketches of Adherents to the British Crown in the War of the Revolution; Alphabetically Arranged, with a Preliminary Historical Essay.* Boston: Little Brown, 1847.

Biographical Sketches of Loyalists of the American Revolution, with an Historical Essay. Boston: Little Brown, 1865.

Sahlins, Marshall. *How "Natives" Think: About Captain Cook, For Example.* Chicago: University of Chicago Press, 1995.

Islands of History. Chicago: University of Chicago Press, 1985.

Salesa, Damon Ieremia. "The Pacific in Indigenous Time." In *Pacific Histories: Ocean, Land, People.* David Armitage and Alison Bashford, editors. New York: Palgrave, 2014: 31–52.

Racial Crossings: Race, Intermarriage, and the Victorian British Empire. New York: Oxford University Press, 2011.

Salmond, Anne. *Bligh: William Bligh in the South Seas*. Los Angeles: University of California Press, 2011.

The Trial of the Cannibal Dog: The Remarkable Story of Captain Cook's Encounters in the South Seas. New Haven, CT: Yale University Press, 2003.

Samson, Jane. *Imperial Benevolence: Making British Authority in the Pacific Islands*. Honolulu: University of Hawai'i Press, 1998.

Scarr, Deryck. *Fragments of Empire: A History of the Western Pacific High Commission, 1877–1914*. Honolulu: University of Hawai'i Press, 1968.

A History of the Pacific Islands: Passages through Tropical Time. Richmond, Surrey: Curzon Press, 2001.

Viceroy of the Pacific: The Majesty of Colour – A Life of Sir John Bates Thurston. Canberra: The Australian National University, 1980.

Schalansky, Judith. *Pocket Atlas of Remote Islands – Fifty Islands I Have Not Visited and Never Will*. Christine Lo, translator. New York: Penguin Books, 2009.

Schubert, E. "Pitcairn Island Today." In *The Pitcairnese Language*. Alan S. C. Ross and A. W. Moverley. New York: Oxford University Press, 1964: 26–36.

Schwartz, Bill. *Memories of Empire: The White Man's World*. New York: Oxford University Press, 2011.

Scott, Jonathan. *When the Waves Ruled Britannia: Geography and Political Identities, 1500–1800*. New York: Cambridge University Press, 2011.

Shapiro, Harry L. *The Pitcairn Islanders (Formerly The Heritage of the Bounty)*. New York: Clarion Books, 1962.

Shelden, Michael. *Melville in Love: The Secret Life of Herman Melville and the Muse of Moby-Dick*. New York: Harper Collins, 2016. Kindle Edition.

Sherry, Frank. *Pacific Passions: The European Struggle for Power in the Great Ocean in the Age of Exploration*. New York: William Morrow and Company, 1994.

Shineberg, Dorothy. *They Came for Sandalwood: A Study of the Sandalwood Trade in the South-West Pacific, 1830–1865*. New York: Melbourne University Press, 1967.

Shoemaker, Nancy, editor. *Living with Whales: Documents and Oral Histories of Native New England Whaling History*. Boston: University of Massachusetts Press, 2014.

Native American Whalemen and the World: Indigenous Encounters and the Contingency of Race. Chapel Hill, NC: The University of North Carolina Press, 2015.

Silverman, David. *Pitcairn Island*. New York: The World Publishing Company, 1967.

Sivasundaram, Sujit. *Islanded: Britain, Sri Lanka, and the Bounds of an Indian Ocean Colony*. Chicago: University of Chicago Press, 2013.

Nature and the Godly Empire: Science and Evangelical Mission in the Pacific, 1795–1850. New York: Cambridge University Press, 2005.

Smith, Bernard. *European Vision and the South Pacific, 1768–1850*. New York: Oxford University Press, 1960.

Smith, Vanessa. *Intimate Strangers: Friendship, Exchange, and Pacific Encounters*. New York: Cambridge University Press, 2010.

Literary Culture and the Pacific: Nineteenth-Century Textual Encounters. New York: Cambridge University Press, 1998.

Snow, Philip, editor. *Best Stories of the South Seas*. London: Faber and Faber, 1967.

Souhami, Diana. *Coconut Chaos: Pitcairn, Mutiny, and a Seduction at Sea*. London: Phoenix Press, 2008.

Spate, O. K. H. *Monopolists and Freebooters*. Minneapolis: University of Minnesota Press, 1983.

Paradise Found and Lost. Minneapolis: University of Minnesota Press, 1988.

The Spanish Lake. Canberra: The Australian National University Press, 2004.

Spruson, J. J. *Norfolk Island: Outline of Its History, from 1788–1884*. Sydney: Thomas Richards, 1885.

St. Julian, Charles. "Alternative Diplomacy in Polynesia." In *More Pacific Island Portraits*. Deryck Scarr, editor. Norwalk, CT: Australian National University Press, 1978: 19–33.

Stanley, Brian. *The Bible and the Flag: Protestant Missions and British Imperialism in the Nineteenth and Twentieth Centuries*. Leicester: Inter-Varsity Press, 1990.

Stewart, Marie Avellino. "Britain in Aspic: Tourists Visits to Malta." In *Islands and Britishness: A Global Perspective*. Jodie Matthews and Daniel Travers, editors. Newcastle upon Tyne: Cambridge Scholars Publishing, 2012: 53–64.

Sturma, Michael. *South Sea Maidens: Western Fantasy and Sexual Politics in the South Pacific*. Westpoint, CT: Greenwood Press, 2002.

Tansley, Rebecca. *Big Pacific*. Princeton, NY: Princeton University Press, 2017.

Tattersall, Robert. *Diabetes: The Biography*. New York: Oxford University Press, 2009.

Taylor, Miles. "Introduction." In *The Victorian Empire and Britain's Maritime World, 1837–1901 – The Sea and Global History*. Miles Taylor, editor. New York: Palgrave, 2013: 1–18.

Teaiwa, Katerina Martina. *Consuming Ocean Island: Stories of People and Phosphate from Banaba*. Bloomington, IN: Indiana University Press, 2015.

Theroux, Paul. *The Happy Isles of Oceania: Paddling the Pacific*. New York: Houghton Mifflin Company, 2006.

Thigpen, Jennifer, *Island Queens and Mission Wives: How Gender and Empire Remade Hawai'i's Pacific World*. Chapel Hill, NC: The University of North Carolina Press, 2014.

Thomas, Nicholas. "The Age of Empire in the Pacific." In *Pacific Histories: Ocean, Land, People*. David Armitage and Alison Bashford, editors. New York: Palgrave, 2014: 75–96.

Colonialism's Culture: Anthropology, Travel, and Government. Princeton, NJ: Princeton University Press, 1994.

Cook: The Extraordinary Voyages of Captain James Cook. New York: Walker and Company, 2003.

Entangled Objects: Exchange, Material Culture, and Colonialism in the Pacific. Cambridge, MA: Harvard University Press, 1991.

Islanders: The Pacific in the Age of Empire. New Haven: Yale University Press, 2010.

Thomas, Nicholas, and Richard Eves. *Bad Colonists: The South Seas Letters of Vernon Lee Walker and Louis Becke*. Durham, NC: Duke University Press, 1999.

Thomas Jr., William L. "The Variety of Physical Environments among Pacific Islands." In *Man's Place in the Island Ecosystem: A Symposium*. F. R. Fosberg, editor. Honolulu: Bishop Museum Press, 1965: 7–37.

Thompson, Christina. *Come on Shore and We Will Kill and Eat You All: A New Zealand Story*. New York: Bloomsbury, 2008.

Tobin, Beth Fawkes. *Colonizing Nature: The Tropics in British Arts and Letters, 1760–1820*. Philadelphia: University of Pennsylvania Press, 2005.

Toohey, John. *Captain Bligh's Portable Nightmare: From the Bounty to Safety – 4,162 Miles across the Pacific in a Rowing Boat*. New York: Harper Collins Publishers, 1998.

Tuljapurkar, Shripad, Charlotte Lee, and Michelle Figgs. "Demography and Food in Early Polynesia." In *The Growth and Collapse of Pacific Island Societies: Archaeological and Demographic Perspectives*. Patrick V. Kirch and Jean-Louis Rallu, editors. Honolulu: University of Hawai'i Press, 2007: 35–51.

Turnbull, Paul. "Enlightenment Anthropology and the Ancestral Remains of Australian Aboriginal People." In *Voyages and Beaches: Pacific Encounters, 1769–1840*. Alex Calder, Jonathan Lamb and Bridget Orr, editors. Honolulu: University of Hawai'i Press, 1999: 202–225.

Wahlroos, Sven. *Mutiny and Romance in the South Seas: A Companion to the Bounty Adventure*. Topsfield, MA: Salem House Publishers, 1989.

Ward, John. *British Policy in the South Pacific, 1786–1893*. London: Australasian Publishing Co., 1948.

Watt, James. "Medical Aspects and Consequences of Cook's Voyages." In *Captain James Cook and His Times*. Robin Fisher and Hugh Johnson, editors. Seattle: University of Washington Press, 1979: 129–157.

Williams, Glyndwr. *Buccaneers, Explorers, and Settlers: British Enterprise and Encounters in the Pacific, 1670–1800*. Aldershot, NH: Ashgate Publishing, 2005.

Naturalists at Sea: From Dampier to Darwin. New Haven: Yale University Press, 2013.

Wilson, Kathleen. *The Island Race: Englishness, Empire, and Gender in the Eighteenth Century*. New York: Routledge, 2003.

Wiltgen, Ralph M. *The Founding of the Roman Catholic Church in Oceania, 1825–1850*. Norwalk, CT: Australian National University Press, 1981.

Winchester, Simon. *Pacific: Silicon Chips and Surfboards, Coral Reefs and Atom Bombs, Brutal Dictatorships, Fading Empires, and the Coming Collision of the World's Superpowers*. New York: Harper Collins Publishers, 2015. Kindle Edition.

Withey, Lynne. *Voyages of Discovery: Captain Cook and the Exploration of the Pacific*. New York: William Morrow and Company, Inc., 1987.

Wollacott, Angela. "Gender and Sexuality." In *Australia's Empire – The Oxford History of the British Empire, Companion Series*. Deryck M. Schreuder and Stuart Ward, editors. New York: Oxford University Press, 2008: 312–335.

Woodman, Gordon. "Pitcairn Island Law: A Peculiar Case of Diffusion of the Common Law." In *Justice, Legality, and the Rule of Law: Lessons from the Pitcairn Prosecutions*. Dawn Oliver, editor. New York: Oxford University Press, 2009: 63–91.

Woodward, Bob, and Carl Bernstein. *The Final Days: The Classic, Behind-the-Scenes Account of Richard Nixon's Dramatic Last Days in the White House*. New York: Simon & Schuster, 1976.

W-T., F. "Sir George Elliot." In *The Dictionary of National Biography – Volume VI*. London: Oxford University Press, 1921: 669–671.

Young, Adrian. *Mutiny's Bounty: Pitcairn Islanders and the Making of a Natural Laboratory on the Edge of Britain's Pacific Empire*. Princeton: A Dissertation Presented to the Faculty of Princeton University in Candidacy for the Degree of Doctor of Philosophy, 2016.

Zimmerman, Elwood C. "Nature of the Land Biota." In *Man's Place in the Island Ecosystem: A Symposium*. F. R. Fosberg, editor. Honolulu: Bishop Museum Press, 1965: 57–63.

Zoellner, Robert. *The Salt-Sea Mastodon: A Reading of Moby-Dick*. Los Angeles: University of California Press, 1973.

Index